The ChatGPT Revolution

The ChatGPT Revolution: How Conversational AI is Transforming Customer Service and Business Operations

EDITED BY

ABHISHEK BEHL

Keele University, UK

CHITRA KRISHNAN

Symbiosis Centre for Management Studies, Noida, Symbiosis International (Deemed University), Pune, India

PRIYANKA MALIK

Galgotias University, India

AND

SHALINI GAUTAM

Delhi Metropolitan Education (Affiliated with GGSIPU), India

emerald
PUBLISHING

United Kingdom – North America – Japan – India – Malaysia – China

Emerald Publishing Limited
Emerald Publishing, Floor 5, Northspring, 21-23 Wellington Street, Leeds LS1 4DL

First edition 2025

Reprints and permissions service
Contact: www.copyright.com

British Library Cataloguing in Publication Data
A catalogue record for this book is available from the British Library

ISBN: 978-1-83549-853-8 (Print)
ISBN: 978-1-83549-852-1 (Online)
ISBN: 978-1-83549-854-5 (Epub)

INVESTOR IN PEOPLE

Contents

List of Abbreviations   *vii*

About the Editors   *xi*

About the Contributors   *xv*

Foreword   *xxiii*

Preface   *xxv*

Acknowledgment   *xxvii*

Part I: Understanding Conversational AI and ChatGPT

**Chapter 1   Voices of the Future: The Evolution and Impact of
Conversational AI**   3
*Supriya Lamba Sahdev, Chitra Krishnan, Ghousia Khatoon and Kiran
Nair*

Chapter 2   ChatGPT: Boon or Bane   23
Shruti Mishra and Nitika Lal

Part II: The Promise of ChatGPT in Scientific Research

**Chapter 3   Transformation in Human–Computer Interaction: The
AI-Enabled NLP**   39
Himanshu Sharma, Anubha Anubha and Daviender Narang

**Chapter 4   Business Fraud Detection, Prevention, and Investigations
With Conversational AI**   57
Hrishikesh Desai

Chapter 5   Revolutionizing Research: The Transformative Role of ChatGPT in Scientific Research   87
Jasmine Mariappan, Supriya Lamba Sahdev, Chitra Krishnan and Firdous Ahmad Malik

Part III: Challenges and Limitations of ChatGPT

Chapter 6   Advancements and Challenges in Conversational AI: Navigating the Frontiers of Innovation and Complexity   107
Alka Sanjeev and Renuka Sharma

Chapter 7   Addressing Ethical Considerations and Responsible AI Practices   129
Anchal Luthra, Shivani Dixit, Seema Garg, Anamica Singh and Mandhir Anchal

Part IV: Transforming Industries With ChatGPT

Chapter 8   Transformative Pedagogy: ChatGPT as a Catalyst for Educational Innovation   153
Harjit Singh, Nidhi Shridhar Natrajan, Rinku Sanjeev and Avneet Singh

Chapter 9   ChatGPT and Implications for the Banking and Financial Industry: New Horizons of Opportunities and Potential Perils   183
Suaad Jassem and Wisal Al Balushi

Chapter 10   Leveraging ChatGPT to Provide Better Support and Learning Opportunities in Revolutionizing AI in Fintech and Customer Service   203
Anshul Srivastava, Navita Mahajan, Anupam Sharma, Rita Mansukhlal Kotecha and Madhushree Guha

Chapter 11   Revolutionizing Financial Inclusion: ChatGPT's Role in Redefining Economic Growth and Poverty Alleviation   239
Richa Goel and Rupa Khanna Malhotra

List of Abbreviations

ADC	Analog to Digital Converter
AI	Artificial Intelligence
AIGC	Artificial Intelligence-Generated Content
AIM	AOL Instant Messenger
ALICE	Artificial Linguistic Internet Computer Entity
AML	Anti-Money Laundering
AOL	America Online
APAC	Asia Pacific
API	Application Programming Interface
ASR	Automatic Speech Recognition
BERT	Bidirectional Encoder Representations from Transformers
BSA	Bank Secrecy Act
CAGR	Compound Annual Growth Rate
CBR	Case-Based Reasoning
CCAF	Cambridge Center for Alternative Finance
CCPA	California Consumer Privacy Act
CDD	Customer Due Diligence
CEO	Chief Executive Officer
CFO	Chief Financial Officer
CNN	Convolutional Neural Networks
COVID-19	2019 Novel Coronavirus
CRM	Customer Relationship Management
CTR	Currency Transaction Report
DL	Deep Learning
DQN	Deep Q-Network (Deep Reinforcement Learning)
ESG	Environment Social Governance
ETL	Extract, Transform, Load
EU	European Union

FATF	Financial Action Task Force
FinCEN	Financial Crimes Enforcement Network
FNR	False Negative Rate
FPR	False Positive Rate
GAN	Generative Adversarial Networks
GDPR	General Data Protection Regulation
GLBA	Gramm-Leach-Bliley Act
GPS	Global Positioning System
GPU	Graphics Processing Unit
HDFC	Housing Development Finance Corporation
HMT	Her Majesty's Treasury
IDT	Innovation Diffusion Theory
IEEE	Institute of Electrical and Electronics Engineers
IOT	Internet of Things
IT	Information Technology
JMIR	Journal of Medical Internet Research
KPI	Key Performance Indicator
KYC	Know-Your-Customer
LDA	Latent Dirichlet Allocation
LIME	Local Interpretable Model-Agnostic Explanations
LLM	Large Language Models
LSTM	Long Short-Term Memory
MIT	Massachusetts Institute of Technology
ML	Machine Learning
MSN	Microsoft Messenger
NACFU	National Association of Federally-Insured Credit Unions
NLG	Natural Language Generation
NLP	Natural Language Processing
NLU	Natural Language Understanding
OCR	Optical Character Recognition
OFAC	Office of Foreign Assets Control
PII	Personally Identifiable Information
PLO	Program Learning Objectives

POMDP	Partially Observable Markov Decision Process
RNN	Recurrent Neural Networks
SAR	Suspicious Activity Report
Seq2Seq	Sequence to Sequence
SeqGAN	Sequential Generative Adversarial Network
SHAP	SHapley Additive exPlanations
SLO	Student Learning Objectives
SMB	Server Message Block
SPSS	Statistical Package for Social Sciences
SQL	Structured Query Language
SSN	Social Security Number
SWOT	Strength, Weakness, Opportunity, Threat
TPU	Tensor Processing Unit
TTS	Text-to-Speech
UAE	United Arab Emirates
UN	United Nations
US	United States
VADER	Valence Aware Dictionary for Sentiment Reasoning
VR	Virtual Reality
WEF	World Economic Forum
XAI	Explainable Artificial Intelligence
YOLO	You Only Look Once

About the Editors

Abhishek Behl is an Associate Professor at Keele Business School, Keele University, UK. He has earned his second PhD from the Indian Institute of Technology, Bombay, where his research is in the area of crowdfunding and gamification. He is a winner of the prestigious "Naik and Rastogi Award for excellence in Ph.D." from IIT Bombay. He holds a rich experience of teaching, research, and consultancy. He has taught subjects like Marketing Analytics, Gamification for Business, Marketing Research, and Qualitative Data Analytics. He has also served as a Senior Manager – Research at Centre for Innovation Incubation and Entrepreneurship, IIM Ahmedabad. His research is in the areas of gamification and strategy, human–computer interaction, sustainability, and stakeholder engagement. He is an incoming president of Special Interest Group (SIG) – GAME of AIS. He is an Associate Editor of the *Journal of Global Information Management, Journal of Global Marketing, Journal of Consumer Behaviour, International Journal of Manpower, International Studies of Management and Organization, South Asia Journal of Business Studies, Journal of Cases on Information Technology*, Assistant Editor of Technology Forecasting and Social Change and in an area editor (South Asia) of the *International Journal of Emergency Services*. He features on the editorial board of many journals like *International Marketing Review, International Journal of Information Management, Journal of Electronic Commerce in Organization, Journal of Promotion Management, Young Consumer, Management Decision*, and *Society and Business Review*. He has edited three books. He has published in journals like *Harvard Business Review, Industrial Marketing Management, International Journal of Information Management, IEEE Transactions on Engineering Management, Production Planning and Control, Technovation, Annals of Operations Research, Journal of Business Research, Technology Forecasting and Social Change, Journal of Knowledge Management, Computers in Human Behaviour, Internet Research, International Marketing Review, Journal of Enterprise Information Systems, Industrial Management and Data Systems*, etc.

Dr Chitra Krishnan is an Associate Professor of Human Resources (HR) and Organizational Behavior (OB) at Symbiosis Center for Management Studies, Noida, Symbiosis International University, Pune, India. She is also a Certified HR Analyst from IIM Rohtak, with over 18 years of national and international teaching experience. Her academic career is rooted in excellence, focusing on OB, Human Resource Management, and Behavioral Science. Prior to her academic journey, Dr Krishnan held key positions in the industry, gaining valuable experience that she now integrates into her teaching and research. She is deeply committed to fostering the holistic development of learners and has been actively involved in advancing professional education. Her core areas of research include Human Resource Management, OB, Talent Management, Diversity Management, Employee Satisfaction, Knowledge Management, Artificial Intelligence (AI), and Emotional Intelligence. Dr Krishnan has an impressive portfolio of publications in leading national and international journals, including A*, SSCI, and Q1–ranked journals. She has also authored seven books with international publishers, further establishing her expertise. Her writing is known for its depth and insights, and she remains passionate about contributing to academic and professional discourses. She has participated in and presented at numerous national and international conferences, while also serving on the review committees for prestigious journals and conferences. Her passion for writing, research, and teaching is coupled with a commitment to advancing HR practices through the integration of cutting-edge technologies like AI, making her a prominent figure in academia and research.

Priyanka Malik, a MBA, PhD and having certification in Data Analysis from IIM, Rohtak. She is a passionate researcher in the field of Usage of New Age Technologies, Social Media, Financial Behavior, Financial Literacy, and Financial Knowledge. She has been a featured speaker in various institutes at various occasions. She has filed a patent in the field of Wearable Device. She is having one copyright also in her credit – Technology Driven Strategic Business Model (TDSBM) in the Changing Era of Disruptive Technology an Agile Approach. She is having overall experience of more than 22 years in academia. Currently, she is working in Galgotia University as a Professor. Her research work is published in ABDC and Scopus-indexed journals with reputed publishers – Inderscience, Emerald, etc. She also presented many research papers in international and national conference paper. She has received many awards for Best Paper. Two of her scholars awarded their doctorate under her guidance and three are working. She is having experience of organizing Springer and IEEE conference and has been the session chair of these prestigious conferences. She is handling various administrative activities also like SRC member for PhD. Scholar and member of Quality Audit Team at college level. Dr Priyanka is also working as a Director in Vedaarna Foundation (NGO). This foundation is working on majorly four aspects: Environment, Health, Education, and Population Control. Being a director, Dr Priyanka is doing lots of activities related to plantation, yoga, and water saving. They run plantation drive throughout the year and organize many camps for yoga in different schools and universities.

Dr Shalini Gautam is a Professor and Head of outreach and research at Delhi Metropolitan Education (DME; Affiliated with Guru Gobind Singh Indra Prastha University). She is a learned faculty member with around 24 years of experience in industry and academia. She has worked in foreign institutions, viz., HSBC Bank and Standard Chartered Bank. Her corporate experience has given her practical knowledge of the nuances of retail banking. In her stint with the banks, she managed the accounts of various High-Networth Individuals (HNIs).

She has completed her PhD in "To Study the Impact of Attitude and Knowledge on the Financial Behavior of Consumers". She has taught subjects like Consumer Behavior, Wealth Management, Services Marketing, and Business Policy and strategy. Her core research areas include financial behavior, financial knowledge, consumer behavior, and sustainability. Her papers have been published in Scopus and ABDC journals by leading publishers. She has presented her papers at various national and international conferences. She has also been awarded a copyright on financial awareness in Indian youth and their sociodemographic background. She is a PhD supervisor, and one of the scholars under her has already been awarded a PhD. She has been the session chair at multiple conferences and reviewed research papers in leading journals. In her present role as a Head-Outreach and Research, she is responsible for developing the research ecosystem at her institute. This includes organizing research conferences, workshops, and FDPs. She is also instrumental in doing research collaborations with national and international institutions. She is overlooking the publication of three in-house peer-reviewed DME journals. She is also managing the outreach activities of DME with schools and NGOs.

About the Contributors

Mandhir Anchal, an Associate Director at Mercer Consulting India Pvt. Ltd., is an accomplished Automation Leader with 18 years of experience driving digital transformation and process optimization across diverse sectors. With expertise in leading cross-functional teams and proficiency in tools like UiPath and Blue Prism, Mr Anchal fosters a culture of innovation while ensuring compliance and robust data security in all his projects.

Anubha Anubha is a Professor of Marketing and Operations at Jaipuria Institute of Management, Ghaziabad, India. Her research interests include social media marketing, Islamic marketing, electronic word of mouth, advertising, and consumer behavior. She has published many scholarly "ABS 3 level", "ABDC," and "Scopus-indexed" research papers in various journals of Wiley, Emerald, Taylor & Francis, and Sage publications including *Psychology and Marketing*, *Current Issues in Tourism*, *Journal of Islamic Marketing*, *Journal of Internet Commerce*, *Global Knowledge*, *Memory & Communication*. She has been an active reviewer of journals of Elsevier and Emerald. She has presented papers at various national and international conferences at MDI, Murshidabad, IIM, Indore, IIT, Delhi, XLRI, Jamshedpur, and Curtin University. Recently, her edited book, indexed in Scopus, was published by IGI Global.

Wisal Al Balushi is the Head of the Data Science and Information Technology Department at the College of Banking and Financial Studies (CBFS). She earned her PhD in Managing Information Systems from the University of Nottingham, UK. With over two decades of teaching experience in both Oman and the United Kingdom, Dr Al Balushi has established herself as a respected authority in the field of digital transformation and managing information systems. Her expertise spans a wide range of topics, including ERP Systems, Database Management, Programming, Digital Business, and Digital Transformation. She has contributed significantly to the academic community through the publication of numerous articles in high-impact journals, further solidifying their reputation as a leading scholar in the field. Her research interest is in the field of digital transformation, technology acceptance, and Fintech.

Hrishikesh Desai is an accomplished Accounting Professor who holds several professional designations, such as CA, CFA, and EA. He is a member of the Association of Certified Fraud Examiners (ACFE) and has, along with coauthors, been the recipient of the prestigious "Report to the Nations" research data grant from the ACFE Research Institute (ARI). His coauthored research on the use of supervised machine learning for fraud examination was also presented at the 2023 ARI Summer Meeting, one of the most reputed fraud research conferences in the United States. His work on emerging technologies has also been published in leading journals, including *Issues in Accounting Education, The CPA Journal, The International Journal of Digital Accounting Research*, and *Bloomberg BNA Tax Management Memorandum*. He has also been invited to deliver numerous educational presentations on emerging technologies and fraud challenges facing accountants by the Arkansas Society of Certified Public Accountants (ARCPA).

Shivani Dixit is an Associate Professor at the Department of Management, IMS, Ghaziabad (University Courses Campus). She has more than 16 years of teaching experience and an extensive background in General Management, Economics, International Business, and Marketing.

Seema Garg is an Associate Professor at AIBS, Amity University, Noida, and teaches Business Statistics, Operations Research, Business Research Methods, Decision Sciences, and Business Maths. She has significantly contributed to enhancing scientific understanding by participating in several national and international conferences, symposia, and seminars by participating and chairing technical sessions.

Richa Goel is an accomplished academician, a researcher, a learner, and a trainer with over 23 years of experience in Economics and Management. She is an Associate Editor for the *Journal of Sustainable Finance & Investment* (Q1, ABDC-A) and an Associate Professor at Symbiosis Centre for Management Studies, Noida, Symbiosis International University, Pune, India. As the Emerald Series Editor for "Emerald Studies in Sustainable Approaches to Poverty," Dr Goel emphasizes the importance of collective action in addressing poverty. Her work inspires a global community of researchers, academics, and industry experts to collaborate and innovate for a sustainable future. A Gold Medalist in Economics, Dr Goel holds a PhD in Management with expertise in Diversity Management. Her projects on E-Shiksha, Women Empowerment, and Inclusive Banking have garnered recognition from the Ministry of Finance, New Zealand. Goel has authored over 20 books published by leading publishers such as Springer, Emerald, IGI Global, Bentham, Bloomsbury, Taylor & Francis, and more. With numerous papers in UGC, SCOPUS, and ABDC journals, she also serves as the lead editor for Scopus International Journals and as the Special Issue Editor for the *Journal of Sustainable Finance* (Q1).

Madhushree Guha is an MBA student at Amity International Business School at Amity University, Noida. She is a budding research scholar and has keen interest in the areas like AI, international business, and finance.

Suaad Jassem is an Assistant Professor of Accounting and Auditing at the College of Banking and Financial Studies in Muscat, Oman. She received her PhD in Accountancy from the University of Malaya. She has over 17 years of teaching experience across multiple universities in Iraq, Malaysia, and Oman. Dr Jassem has published extensively in high-impact journals on topics such as managerial accounting, sustainability practices, internal auditing, and enterprise risk management, making significant contributions to both academic understanding and practical applications in accounting and auditing. Her current research interests center on the integration of AI within accounting practices, particularly how AI can improve accuracy and efficiency in the field.

Ghousia Khatoon is a Professor and the Head of the Department of Accounting, Banking, and Finance at the Faculty of Administrative Sciences and Economics, Tishk International University, Iraq. With a wealth of experience in academia, Dr Khatoon has developed a deep expertise in accounting, finance, and banking, shaping the department with a focus on excellence and innovation. She is committed to advancing the academic and professional development of her students through comprehensive research and practical approaches. Dr Khatoon has a robust background in teaching, curriculum development, and scholarly publications, contributing to various national and international conferences. Her leadership at Tishk International University reflects her dedication to fostering a dynamic learning environment. She is an active member of the academic community, striving to bridge the gap between theory and practice in finance and accounting.

Rita Mansukhlal Kotecha is a seasoned SAP (Systems, Applications and Products in Data Processing) delivery leader with extensive experience in Fashion Retail, Manufacturing, and Professional Services. She has successfully led eight global enterprise resource planning engagements, managing a team of over 200 and a budget exceeding 100 million SEK. At H&M, Rita served seven brands, overseeing 74 stores and 82 e-commerce markets while achieving a 16% reduction in operational costs. Her expertise includes vendor management, complex project execution, and product management for the Supply Chain Module at e-Emphasys. Rita excels in sales and presales activities, crafting request for proposals, proposals, and multiyear SAP Managed Services agreements. Additionally, she has conducted training sessions on key professional skills, making her a valuable asset in SAP delivery and project management.

Nitika Lal is working as an Assistant Professor in the department of Applied Psychology at Manav Rachna International Institute of Research and Studies. She has previously worked with All India Institute of Medical Sciences, New Delhi, in research for 4 years at paediatrics and psychiatry departments. She has been involved with four projects of national and international funding. Her academic qualifications entail: PhD scholar at the University of Delhi (DU) in Psychology and MPhil in Clinical Psychology (RCI Licensed) from Atal Bihari Vajpayee Institute of Medical Sciences and Dr RML Hospital. Her graduation and postgraduation are also from the University of Delhi in Psychology. She has presented oral papers in seven national and international conferences and has six research articles under her name.

Anchal Luthra is an Assistant Professor at AIBS, Amity University, Noida. She is an expert in data analytics, HR administration, and consulting. She has 11 years of experience in administration, research, academia, and consulting projects. She has published papers in Scopus and ABDC-listed journals and presented her research at numerous conferences, including IIM Ahmedabad, Indore, Nagpur, Sambalpur. She has also participated in many faculty development programs.

Navita Mahajan is a Professor in Amity International Business School, Amity University, Noida, India. She holds a PhD in the field of Strategic Management. Dr Navita has total 22 years of experience of industry and academia. She has to her credit 19 Scopus-indexed papers and more than 20 book chapters with International Publishers. Her areas of interest are Sustainability, Green Technologies, SDGs, Digitalization, and AI.

Rupa Khanna Malhotra has earned her PhD MBA, MMM, MCOM (International Business, Gold Medalist), PGDIBO (Gold Medalist), MSc (Biochemistry), and has qualified for NET and GATE examinations. She has extensive research experience on International Business, more specifically on Documentation, International Logistics, and Marketing. Has authored various articles in international and national journals and has written chapters for various books. She has over 20+ years of experience both of industry and academics especially of International marketing of Pharmaceutical Products, Bulk Drugs, Commodities, Shipping, Logistics, and Documentation. She is the Head of Department of Commerce, and working as a senior Professor of International Business and Marketing. She is also a member of many professional bodies to name a few – PHD, Chamber of Commerce, CII, IAU, AIMS. She has also conducted various training programs for the senior professionals like ON.

Firdous Ahmad Malik is an Assistant Professor of Economics at the University of People and is currently pursuing postdoctoral research at Amity Dubai University. He holds a PhD from Babasaheb Bhimrao Ambedkar University and a Master's in Economics from the University of Kashmir. His research interests include microfinance, financial inclusion, and financial literacy. Dr Malik has published articles in Scopus-indexed journals such as Springer, Elsevier, and Taylor & Francis and authored six books, including "Financial Inclusion Schemes in India" (Springer) and "Financial Behaviour of Urban Destitutes in India" (Notion Press). His forthcoming books are set to be published by Routledge and IGI. He has received accolades for his contributions to research, including awards from the Jindal Center for Global South and AIBPM. Dr Malik actively contributes to research through participation and leadership roles in international conferences and is associated with the Young Scholars Initiative (YSI).

Jasmine Mariappan is a dedicated educator currently serving as a Lecturer in the Department of Business Studies at the esteemed University of Technology and Applied Sciences, Ibra. With a rich academic background, she holds an MPhil in General Management, as well as Master of Commerce (MCom) and Bachelor of Commerce (BCom) degrees. She has an experience of more than 17 years in the field of teaching. Her specialization lies in the dynamic field of Marketing, where she has honed her skills and contributed significantly to the academic community.

Ms Mariappan's passion for continuous learning and research is evident in her diverse range of interests. She is particularly focused on areas such as Marketing, E-marketing, and Blended Learning, where she seeks to explore innovative strategies and emerging trends. Her commitment to academic excellence is further underscored by her impressive publication record. Ms Mariappan has authored numerous articles and papers, which have been featured in leading journals and presented at international conferences.

Shruti Mishra is an Assistant Professor with Manav Rachna International Institute of Research and Studies, Faridabad. She has over 15 years of market research experience, client management, and team building. As a practitioner, she has worked across categories and different markets in India, South East Asia, and MENA region, which has helped her understand and appreciate the influence different cultural backgrounds have on how and why a consumer interacts with a particular brand or products. She has been actively involved with an NGO, which works for mental health care of individuals as a counselor.

Kiran Nair is an Associate Professor and the Head of Internationalization and Partnerships at Abu Dhabi University. With extensive experience in academia and strategic leadership, Dr Nair is instrumental in fostering global partnerships and enhancing internationalization efforts at the university. His expertise spans across fields like Marketing, Strategy, and Business Administration, where he has contributed significantly through teaching, research, and leadership roles. Dr Nair holds a strong research portfolio with numerous publications in reputable journals and has presented his work at international conferences. He is passionate about driving academic excellence and innovation, collaborating with institutions worldwide to create impactful partnerships. Dr Nair's dynamic approach to education and global outreach has earned him recognition in the academic community.

Daviender Narang is working as a Professor and a Director in Jaipuria Institute of Management, Ghaziabad. He has worked on a World Bank-supported project on capacity building in Ethiopia for two years. He has published several research papers in various journals of repute. He is also associated with business firms as a corporate trainer on various financial modules. He has presented several research papers at various national and international conferences.

Nidhi Shridhar Natrajan is a seasoned faculty member and a researcher in information technology and business analytics. She has over 18 years of experience and works as an Assistant Professor at Symbiosis Centre for Management Studies, Noida, Symbiosis International University, Pune, India. Her publications have appeared in Scopus, ABDC, and Web of Science. She has been conducting training programs for academicians and corporate in information technology, programming, and language.

Supriya Lamba Sahdev is a distinguished academician, a researcher, and a certified coach with over 12 years of experience in Marketing and International Business. Currently serving as Deputy Director of the Office of International

Affairs and Associate Professor at Alliance University, she previously held positions as the HOD of Marketing and the Head of the International Office at ISBR Business School. Dr Sahdev earned her PhD in Management, focusing on Open Innovation in Indian Food Processing SMEs, and has an impressive research portfolio with over 50 UGC papers and 20 SCOPUS-indexed publications. She has chaired and co-convened multiple international conferences, serves on editorial boards, and has been a lead editor for 15 journals. Her expertise spans Research Methodology, Digital Marketing, and International Trade, among others. With a commitment to fostering global partnerships, Dr Sahdev is recognized as a leading authority in her field, contributing significantly to education, research, and international collaboration.

Alka Sanjeev is an Assistant Professor at the Faculty of Commerce and Management, SGT University, Haryana. With a distinguished academic background, she holds a PhD, an MBA in International Business, and a BE in Civil Engineering. She brings 18 years of valuable experience from esteemed academic institutions to her role. She has a keen interest in teaching Operations Management and International Business. Her research focuses on International Trade, Foreign Direct Investment, and Regional Trade Blocks and use of AI in businesses, especially in the operations domain. She has an impressive record of research publications in various national and international journals and has coauthored a book on international business management. She is also a prolific presenter, having shared her work at numerous national and international conferences.

Rinku Sanjeev is a multidimensional personality in academics and behavioral science. Having 20 years of experience in industry and and academia, she is currently associated with Symbiosis Centre for Management Studies, Noida, Symbiosis International University, Pune, India, as an Assistant Professor. Having several research publications and book reviews in refereed international/ national journals in her credit, she has also been actively involved in research work and projects in technology and human resources.

Anupam Sharma is a distinguished educator and author with over 17 years of experience in academia. Currently serving as an Associate Professor at Delhi Technical Campus, Greater Noida, Dr Sharma specializes in Communication Skills and Soft Skills Development. She holds a PhD and has authored books on effective communication and management. Driven by a passion for nurturing young talent, she actively contributes to curriculum development and student welfare initiatives. Her innovative teaching methodologies and commitment to holistic education have earned her recognition in the field. Dr Sharma aims to empower students, particularly women, with essential skills for professional success and personal growth.

Himanshu Sharma is working as an Assistant Professor in Jaipuria Institute of Management, Ghaziabad. Previously, he has got an opportunity to work as an Assistant Professor in the University of Delhi and as a research assistant in an ICSSR-funded project. He has completed his PhD from Department of Operational Research, University of Delhi. He has also done his MPhil and Master's in

Operational Research from the University of Delhi. He has his Bachelor's in Mathematics. His research interests are online marketing, multi-criteria decision-making, and path analysis modeling. He has published research papers in reputed journals of Springer and Emerald and contributed chapters in edited books.

Renuka Sharma is an Assistant Professor, Amity University, Haryana, and is a faculty of Finance and Accounting. Dr Sharma holds more than 11 years of experience in teaching and research. She holds a doctorate in Management on the topic of "Impact of Behavioural Dispositions on Portfolio Investment Decisions of Individual Investors in Rajasthan." She holds a Master's degree in Business Administration and in Commerce and has cleared UGC-NET. Dr Sharma is an ardent researcher; she has authored and coauthored more than 15 research papers published in ABDC, Scopus, UGC Care–listed journals. She has presented various research papers in national and international conferences and has received Best Research paper award. She has published case studies in Case Centre, UK. She has attended and conducted various seminars, workshops, and development programs in her field.

Anamica Singh currently serves at Amity University, Noida, as an Assistant Professor in AIBS, Amity University, Noida. She comes with a rich industry experience of more than 10 years. She has academic experience, and her areas of expertise include various domains of Information Technology and Management.

Avneet Singh is pursuing his Bachelor's in Computer Science and Engineering from the University of Toledo, Ohio, United States. He is actively involved as a game developer at Roblox and YouTube Content Creator. He also runs his YouTube channel and does coding in Java and Python. His areas of specialization are coding, ChatGPT, and blockchain.

Harjit Singh, a regular contributor to national and international journals, is a Professor (Finance) at Symbiosis Centre for Management Studies Noida, Symbiosis International University, Pune, India. He has over two decades of rich experience in Teaching, Research, and Consultancy. He has extensively traveled in and outside India to conduct workshops, seminars, and FDPs. He has written several textbooks and study material, as well as edited books and case studies with internationally reputed publication houses. His research areas are Corporate Restructuring, Blockchain, ChatGPT, Mergers and Acquisitions, and Corporate Governance.

Anshul Srivastava is presently working as an Assistant Professor, at Amity International Business School, Amity University, Noida. Her educational qualification is PhD in Mathematics. She has also done 1-year Executive Program in Data Science from IIM, Lucknow. In her 17 years of service, she had long association of more than 10 years with IET, Lucknow, as an Assistant Professor and also served as an Associate Professor in Dr Akhilesh Das Gupta Institute of Technology and Management, Indraprastha University, Delhi. Her research focuses on "Statistical approximation and Data analytics." Dr Anshul is an avid researcher and frequently publishes her research in journals of international repute like Scopus and SCI.

Foreword

In the rapidly evolving tapestry of modern technology, few advancements have captured both the imagination and practical application potential as profoundly as AI – particularly conversational AI systems like ChatGPT. Created by OpenAI, ChatGPT is the achievement that moves the most toward the ultimate goal of achieving a parity between human thought and machines intelligence. This book, structured into five comprehensive parts, delves into the myriad aspects of this transformative technology, encompassing its evolution, applications, challenges, and societal impact.

The journey begins with Part I: Understanding Conversational AI and ChatGPT, which provides a framework for a deep investigation of conversation AI. Chapter 1, "Voices of the Future: The Evolution and Impact of Conversational AI," by Supriya Lamba Sahdev, Chitra Krishnan, Ghousia Khatoon, and Kiran Nair, provides a broad account of the history and development of conversational AI. It explores its capabilities and limitations while highlighting ethical aspects and the importance of explainability and bias reduction. This chapter also argues in favor of responsible development and places ChatGPT in the position of a tool that can be used for the benefit of society, only with a great deal of care. Shruti Mishra and Nitika Lal in Chapter 2, "ChatGPT: Boon or Bane," provide additional background by discussing the limitations common to ChatGPT and its applications, including research and education. Results also reveal promise and pitfalls of this technology, which can be used to make useful and appropriate decision for its ethical and efficient implementation.

Part II: The Promise of ChatGPT in Scientific Research explores how ChatGPT and similar tools are reshaping the research landscape. In Chapter 3, "Transformation in Human–Computer Interaction: The AI-Enabled NLP," Himanshu Sharma, Anubha Anubha, and Daviender Narang analyze the important progress in natural language processing (NLP) and uses to different areas of the economy. It emphasizes the ways in which technologies such as ChatGPT can solve tedious decision-making processes, writing quality, and patient data, among other novel scientific approaches. In Chapter 4, "Business Fraud Detection, Prevention, and Investigations With Conversational AI," Hrishikesh Desai moves the discussion back into the finance world and shows the possibilities for conversational AI in fighting fraud in finance. With detailed case studies, this chapter elucidates how AI tools like ChatGPT can enhance fraud management through intelligent data analysis and ethical implementation. In Chapter 5, "Revolutionizing Research: The Transformative Role of ChatGPT in

Scientific Research," Jasmine Mariappan and colleagues investigate the role of ChatGPT in automating and streamlining research from the formulation of the hypothesis to data synthesis while emphasizing the need to address the balance between innovation and the ethics challenges that the technology presents.

Part III: Challenges and Limitations of ChatGPT addresses the challenges and barriers of using such a powerful technology. In Chapter 6, "Advancements and Challenges in Conversational AI: Navigating the Frontiers of Innovation and Complexity," Alka Sanjeev and Renuka Sharma present the inherent two-sided nature of conversational AI – the possibility of a revolutionary breakthrough and the pitfalls of privacy, security, and user trust. This chapter underscores the importance of adopting responsible AI frameworks that prioritize accountability and transparency. In Chapter 7, "Addressing Ethical Considerations and Responsible AI Practices," Anchal Luthra and coauthors discuss in detail ethical challenges of deploying AI and present solutions for promoting ethical innovation and cooperation of stakeholders. Collectively, these chapters offer a guide for exploring the challenges of advancing conversational AI at such a dynamic rate.

The book's fourth section, Part IV: Transforming Industries With ChatGPT, showcases the practical implications of this technology across diverse sectors. Harjit Singh and coauthors in Chapter 8, "Transformative Pedagogy: ChatGPT as a Catalyst for Educational Innovation," explore the transformative impact of ChatGPT in education. This chapter presents an evocative account of how AI can contribute to better academic performances through personalized learning activities and automating administrative work. Chapter 9 authored by Suaad Jassem and Wisal Al Balushi's titled "ChatGPT and Implications for the Banking and Financial Industry: New Horizons of Opportunities and Potential Perils": explores the profound effects of ChatGPT on the financial services sector addresses the promise of highly personalized customer interactions that can be high-risk in terms of leaks of sensitive data and creation of falsified information. In Chapter 10, "Leveraging ChatGPT to Provide Better Support and Learning Opportunities in Revolutionizing AI in Fintech and Customer Service" by Anshul Srivastava and colleagues, the authors examine the potential of ChatGPT to change customer interaction and operational effectiveness. Last, Chapter 11, "Revolutionizing Financial Inclusion: ChatGPT's Role in Redefining Economic Growth and Poverty Alleviation," by Richa Goel and Rupa Khanna Malhotra, exposes the capabilities of AI to accelerate economic inclusion and poverty reduction in the most underserved populations.

When you turn the pages of this book, you will begin a journey not only to understand the power of ChatGPT but one that is also designed to provoke thought about the role it, and others like it, may play in our common future. Whether you are a researcher, an educator, a technologist, or a policymaker, this compendium offers valuable perspectives and actionable insights. The authors have thoroughly unpacked the possibility, the pitfalls, the potential of ChatGPT, hence making this book the ultimate reference point for all those who wish to understand and exploit the power of conversational AI.

Park Thaichon PhD
Associate Professor of Marketing
School of Business | University of Southern Queensland, Australia

Preface

AI and Chat GPT are not just technologies; they are transformative forces that are reshaping our world. The collection of various scholarly articles in the book *"The ChatGPT Revolution: How Conversational AI is Transforming Customer Service and Business Operations"* provides an immersive and in-depth exploration of the revolutionary ChatGPT framework and its significant impact on conversational AI. This comprehensive book takes readers on a captivating journey, uncovering both the exciting possibilities and the potential challenges associated with ChatGPT. Through a meticulous analysis of ChatGPT's architecture, capabilities, and practical applications, readers develop a profound understanding of how this framework has transformed the dynamics of human engagement in conversations. The book demystifies the technical intricacies behind ChatGPT's ability to generate text that closely resembles human language, allowing readers to grasp the impressive sophistication and potency of this AI-driven technology.

Beyond the technical aspects, the authors delve into the factors that have propelled ChatGPT to the forefront of conversational AI adoption. They explore the wide-ranging impact of ChatGPT on society and various industries, illustrating how it has revolutionized customer experiences, streamlined business operations, and catalyzed change across multiple domains. While highlighting the promises of ChatGPT, the book candidly addresses the potential pitfalls and ethical considerations that arise from its use. It delves into critical issues such as bias, misinformation, and the ethical implications of relying solely on AI for meaningful conversations. By examining these challenges, readers are equipped with the knowledge necessary to navigate the responsible and conscientious use of ChatGPT while mitigating potential risks.

Chapter 1 delves into the evolution of ChatGPT, which OpenAI developed. This chapter highlights ChatGPT's capabilities to transform society and discusses the limitations of conversational AI. Chapter 2 explores the role and limitations of ChatGPT, especially in the research and education industry. This chapter focused on the dos and don'ts of conversational AI and highlighted the quality of the data we use for our work. This paper addressed the ethical issues of using AI.

Chapter 3 explained the capabilities of AI-enabled machines that mimic human capabilities. An advanced form of NLP can solve complex problems and help people make decisions. This chapter also talks about the new opportunities created with the advancement of NLP. Recently, ChatGPT has been assisting human beings in writing and making their manuscripts well-structured. Chapter 4 highlighted the importance of a fraud detection system with conversational AI assistants. This chapter has illustrated seven case studies of the usage of conversational AI assistants. AI assistants can detect complex patterns, automate filing, visualize criminal networks and alerts, and enable auditors to validate AI models. This chapter also focused on the responsible usage of conversational AI. Conversational AI can empower financial institutions from fraudulent activities if used responsibly.

Chapter 5 explores the usage of ChatGPT in scientific studies. It lists various scientific tools that assist in data analyses. This chapter focuses on the middle ground between creativity and morality in the process of scientific analysis. Chapter 6 delves into the latest innovations and developments in conversational AI. This chapter also discusses the critical challenges of conversational AI. It should be used responsibly so that users can build trust and ensure privacy.

Chapter 7 discusses the ethical and moral issues with the deployment of AI technology. The authors identified the need to address ethical issues across various sectors and endorse good practices regarding AI in society. It highlighted the importance of collaboration between different stakeholders in the ethical usage of AI. This chapter emphasizes that the responsible use of AI is not just an individual's concern but a collective responsibility that requires the cooperation of all stakeholders. Chapter 8 explored the usage of conversational AI in academia. This chapter focuses on the opportunities and limitations of Open AI's ChatGPT for teaching, learning, and research. The authors recommended developing strategies to ensure proper citation for the usage of ChatGPT.

Chapter 9 highlighted the importance of ChatGPT in the banking and financial service industry. It explores the potential opportunities and possible perils for banking and financial services organizations affected by the deployment of ChatGPT. This chapter also delves into individual-level outcomes, such as an increase in the customer experience, and potential risks, such as data breaches and misinformation. Chapter 10 explores the transformations in consumer interactions in the Fintech space using ChatGPT, which enhances customer satisfaction and operational effectiveness. This chapter projected that ChatGPT will improve and streamline operations in Fintech in future.

Chapter 11 explores the opportunities posed by ChatGPT in financial innovation for economic development, particularly poverty reduction. It focuses on ChatGPT's ability to promote financial inclusion by increasing financial literacy and decreasing language barriers. It helps in the overall economic development of emerging markets.

Thus, this book serves as a guide, addressing crucial problems such as comprehending the technology, identifying prospective applications, and resolving ethical concerns. It provides readers with the knowledge they need to make educated decisions, maximize the benefits of ChatGPT, and manage its revolutionary influence on society and industry by providing practical insights, industry-specific examples, and adaptation techniques.

Editors

Dr Abhishek Behl
Dr Chitra Krishnan
Dr Priyanka Malik
Dr Shalini Gautam

Acknowledgment

Curating this edited book, *The ChatGPT Revolution: How Conversational AI is Transforming Customer Service and Business Operations*, has been a journey of immense collaboration, dedication, and shared vision. We are grateful to all who have contributed to the successful completion of this work.

First, we sincerely thank the chapter authors who brought their expertise, innovative ideas, and commitment to this project. Each chapter reflects profound insights and meticulously explores themes vital in understanding and navigating the digital age and how AI will change businesses and human lives. The scholarly contributions are the cornerstone of this book, and we are deeply grateful for this.

We also acknowledge the reviewers who devoted their time to critically evaluating each chapter, providing constructive feedback and guidance to enhance the quality of the content. The rigorous standards adhered to and the valuable suggestions provided ensured the book meets academic and professional benchmarks.

The inspiration drawn from collaborative moments reminds us of the transformative power of teamwork. The heart of this endeavor is a synergy of minds working together toward a common goal. We sincerely appreciate the editorial and production team, whose tireless efforts in designing, organizing, and publishing this book ensured a seamless journey from manuscript to print. Your professionalism and attention to detail have been exemplary.

It would be unfair if the acknowledgment section misses out technology and the advancements that kept in motivating to explore it further in chapters of the book. It becomes interesting and important that we as scholars work toward understanding the technology and duly credit it for inspiring us to write about it as it unfolds and expands.

Finally, we extend our gratitude to the readers of this book, who inspire the creation of knowledge and innovation. We hope this book serves as a valuable resource in understanding the evolving landscape of digital transformation and sparks new ideas and discussions. It is through the collective efforts of everyone involved that this book has come to fruition. We are humbled and honored to have worked alongside such passionate and talented individuals.

The Editors

Part I

Understanding Conversational AI and ChatGPT

Chapter 1

Voices of the Future: The Evolution and Impact of Conversational AI

Supriya Lamba Sahdev[a], Chitra Krishnan[b], Ghousia Khatoon[c] and Kiran Nair[d]

[a]Alliance University, India
[b]Symbiosis Centre for Management Studies, Noida, Symbiosis International (Deemed University), Pune, India
[c]Tishk International University, Iraq
[d]Abu Dhabi University, UAE

Abstract

AI in particular, and more specifically, conversational AI has evoked significant changes in the way people communicate with computing systems over the past few years. This chapter focuses on the history of conversational AI and the shift from basic rule-based conversational systems to NLP and deep learning more profound forms of conversational AI. Hence, using case studies and industry descriptions, this chapter discusses various real-world applications of Conversational AI, such as virtual companions, customer service chatbots, and voice interfaces and devices, and demonstrating their increasing importance in various domains, including healthcare, education, marketing, and finance. Furthermore, this chapter highlights the ability of Conversational AI to improve user experience as well as address the issues of data privacy, ethical AI, and human–AI interaction. Specific focus is placed on the need for multilingual Conversational AI in breaking language barriers especially in international and diverse markets. The directions of development for Conversational AI in future are covered with a focus on further improvements like increasing the individuality and emotions of AI agents and incorporating Conversational AI into augmented reality. In conclusion, this chapter offers a directed view of how Conversational AI is transforming sectors as well as the way consumers and businesses interact with products in an era of advanced digital connection and Artificial Intelligence.

The ChatGPT Revolution, 3–21
Copyright © 2025 Supriya Lamba Sahdev, Chitra Krishnan, Ghousia Khatoon and Kiran Nair
Published under exclusive licence by Emerald Publishing Limited
doi:10.1108/978-1-83549-852-120251001

Keywords: Conversational AI; natural language processing (NLP); virtual assistants; AI in customer support; voice-enabled devices; human–computer interaction; multilingual AI; human–AI collaboration; emotional AI; augmented reality

1. Introduction

Conversational AI pertains to the interaction between the machine and the human in a conversational interface format. Conversational AI is a concept in which the communication occurring through text or speech imitates actual dialogs with people between individuals and artificial intelligence systems. This field has, over the recent period, experienced rapid evolution particularly due to Natural Language Processing (NLP), machine learning, and deep learning. Conversational AI systems refer to those that are in form of chatbots, voice interface agents as well as other related interactive agents that can NLP and respond to queries from users in realtime (McTear, 2022). Here, it is impossible not to mention the significance of conversational AI in today's technology. It functions as the foundation of different applications, starting from customer support or virtual assistants in healthcare needs to learning management systems (Schobel et al., 2024). Some of the most common known versions include Google Assistant, Amazon's Alexa, and the Apple's Siri, illustrating how conversational AI is an indispensable component of the present society (McTear, 2017). In the future, various advances in technology will help in improving conversational AI in human–computer interfaces; this will lead to increasing accessibility, personalization, and efficiency, Casheekar et al. (2024).

In its essence, conversational AI is based upon algorithms and models that recognize and interpret natural human language, and thereby enable machines to engage with human beings on a level that was inconceivable in the past. While the rule-based system of present day conversation AI is different from the traditional rule-based conversational AI, the present day conversational AI is data-driven, it learns from data and improves incrementally to gain better breadth of accuracy and understanding of context (Schobel et al., 2024). This adaptability makes conversational AI capable of handling higher levels of human interactions, making it a valuable application in organizations in an effort to optimize their processes, enhance customer relations, and enhance organizational productivity (Minsky et al., 2023). The value of conversational AI in the contemporary world is based on the ability of the system to transform industries. Through daily tasks, conversational AI can save more human capital, enhance organizational efficiency, and potentially cut expenses substantially. Besides, its capability to deliver targeted content also increases user satisfaction and loyalty, deepening brand–consumer connection (Schobel et al., 2024). This widespread application across industries is one of the reasons conversational AI is receiving considerable attention internationally (McTear, 2022).

It is in practice today in organizations in many sectors including but not limited to the consumer services. AI-based chatbots and virtual assistants are capable of answering almost all the queries related to customers, providing replies immediately and being available around-the-clock, which makes these tools invaluable for companies that seek to increase the level of satisfaction among their clientele as well as decrease the time of response (Casheekar et al., 2024). In healthcare, conversational AI is an essential tool that is used to offer immediate medical consultations, make appointments, as well as availing of mental health services such as online therapy. It is increasing patient's access to care and individualized patient care (Schobel et al., 2024). In education, these AI-based systems are employed to deliver smart education, teach smart students, and evaluate smart learning. Conversational AI contributes to making the communication process more creative allowing students to receive the feedback immediately, clear the doubts, as well as use voice-based interfaces to get the educational materials (McTear, 2022). Aside from these industries, new applications of conversational AI have emerged in spheres of finance, retail, hospitality, and government services, proving its applicability on customer-facing as well as back-end processes (Schobel et al., 2024).

The objective of this chapter is to discuss the development and influence of conversational AI, with an emphasis on the radical alteration of HCI and the disruption of essential industries. To explain how conversational AI impacts the future, this chapter discusses the history of conversational AI from its beginning to such breakthroughs as ChatGPT and different LLMs. The chapter will also look at Natural Language Processing (NLP), which is the key component that drives conversational AI systems. Describing how NLP helps machines to comprehend and produce human language, the chapter will analyze the role of linguistic algorithms and machine learning in developing intelligent conversational agents (McTear, 2022). Lastly, the chapter will analyze how ChatGPT and similar models enhanced conversational AI's advancements and made progress in areas such as context awareness, creativity, and natural language flow (Casheekar et al., 2024). These advancements have enabled possibilities for fresh applications involving AI, especially in business sectors where multiple and complex interactions are needed (Schobel et al., 2024).

To reveal the tendencies of the development of technology, it is important to consider conversational AI, NLP, and such models as ChatGPT as intertwined processes. Conversational AI is not an independent entity and depends on a combination of state-of-the-art linguistic methods and extensive computing resources (McTear, 2017). By looking at how these pieces go together, this chapter will offer a broader view of how conversational AI can be made better or used more in businesses and for the benefit of society (Minsky et al., 2023).

2. The Rise of Conversational AI

The development of conversational AI in the last few decades started from simple chatbots which have become complex intelligent systems capable of human-like conversation. The ability of machines to engage in and reproduce actual and natural human-like dialog through text or conversational voice has become a crucial element of many sectors, including consumer relations and healthcare. Still, the evolution from simple programs to modern systems is a story that tells not only the advancement in artificial intelligence but also the needs for intelligent human-computer interaction (Dengel, 2023; Dwivedi et al., 2023). The intro-duction of conversational AI can be historically traced back to the early AI development period when AI scientists started considering how an AI can mimic human intelligence and conduct themselves. An early and well-known example of this is ELIZA – which was developed by MIT professor Joseph Weizenbaum in 1966 (O'Regan & O'Regan, 2018). Inspired by Rogerian psychotherapy, ELIZA was programmed to carry out basic textual interaction with the users, and ask them questions, in return for their answers. Comparatively to today's standards, ELIZA was a rather primitive – while it based on the recognizing of patterns instead of actual understanding of the sentences, it was a breakthrough given that it managed to show that machines can actually have a limited, shallow conver-sation with people. The influence that ELIZA had on AI research can be described as very significant. It could not understand the meaning of words, but it paved the way, albeit in a limited sense, to thinking that computers may be able to mimic natural language dialogs. This paved the way to similar other primary systems such as PARRY in the early 1970s, a chatbot which aimed at emulating a paranoid schizophrenia and provided tougher responses than that of ELIZA. PARRY's creation was an early effort to have system-level responses not only present conversation in a Q & A format but also pose a certain personality type and environment, thus bringing the illusion of actuality into the dialog. The advancements continued in the 1990s when the Artificial Linguistic Internet Computer Entity (ALICE) was developed by Richard Wallace in the Internet in 1995. ALICE was a more sophisticated invention than ELIZA; using patterns matching algorithms and developing a vast array of responses to conversations. It was based on an open source code known as AIML, for Artificial Intelligence Markup Language, this allowed developers to construct and model their unique Chabot (Allado-McDowell & Bentivegna, 2022).

While ALICE like all similar systems could not comprehend or generate any natural language, it proved a jump forward in terms of conversational flow. ALICE got several awards in the Loebner Prize an annual competition which aims to determine how humanlike a machine can actually be through the Turing test. The Loebner Prize demonstrated the advancement of conversational AI with ALICE as the winner paving way for more intelligent systems in the future (Dew, 2023). ELIZA and ALICE built the foundations for conversational AI but had their limitations. Both simplified speech recognition by parroting a set of pro-grammed reactions and using algorithms to match, instead of recognizing the actual meaning of words spoken or the goals of the user. However, these systems proved that computers are capable of emulating conversation in a manner adequate enough to converse with users. The challenge remained: how can one design AI that could mimic conversation yet should be able to recognize sur-rounding context, learn from dialog as well as develop with time? The early 2,000 have been marked by crucial development of enabling technologies for conversational AI, with specific focus on the Natural Language Processing and machine learning.

These technologies helped to remove key limitations of applying AI techniques and procedures to machine translation and enabled AI systems to go from mere pattern recognition to understanding human language and generating it. The likes of Google, MS Windows, and IBM, for instance, started putting their money into serious research and development of intelligent systems. One of the most critical turning points was with the introduction of voice assistants as Apple's Siri in 2011, Google Assistant, Amazon Alexa, and Microsoft Cortana in the years to come. These assistants were the new generation of conversational AI which was triggered by conversational NLP for voice command and response. These systems not only understood and answered to the spoken language but also fit into the environment of applications and appliances, which made them convenient tools in daily use. This was a new paradigm in the conversational AI as it began to include not only text-based chatbots but also including voice interface and a variety of tasks (Dwivedi et al., 2023).

Another important turning point in the field of conversational AI has been reached after the usage of the so-called transformer-based models in 2018 which include GPT-3 and ChatGPT of the OpenAI company. These models based on deep learning, changed the field as it provided ability to AI to generate human like response in real time with much more richness and understanding of context. In earlier systems, there was a fixed set of responses/answers or simple decision making/algorithm, which has been replaced by learning from massive data and multilayered neural structures in transformer- based models for language analysis/ processing and even artistic writing. These models significantly enhanced the output of conversational AI in terms of fluency, stream of thought and adapt-ability. For instance, ChatGPT has been trained to provide outputs given a vast variety of contexts ranging from informal dialogs to formal writing making it one of the most sophisticated AI conversational models. Such an approach for conversational AI involves ability to have flexible, adaptive, and contextualized conversations, and this has been noted to be a major advancement in the field (Ng & Lin, 2022). Conversational AI is a result of the progress made in artificial intelligence that has been in development, beginning with systems such as ELIZA and ALICE to the current sophisticated models based on the transformer such as ChatGPT. It made every step to bring AI closer to establishing natural, mean-ingful, and intuitive interactions with the human population. While conversa-tional AI remains a growing technology, there is a belief that this technology will redefine the way organizations function and how people engage with machines as well as technologies that are built in a bid to improve universal experience. It is for this reason that this technological advancement is evidence that AI confer-ences are an instrumental part in determining how the dynamics of interaction between humans and computers will be in the future and what new capabilities machines will be endowed with (Dwivedi et al., 2023).

Recent trends indicate that the utilization of conversational AI has become widespread during the period of the last decade and is being implemented in many industries and applications. Thus, the conversational AI in the entities such as Siri and Alexa and also in the complex customer support systems among others are revolutionizing the way in which business entities and customers are interacting with the technologies. In this part, the author discusses the modern trends in conversational AI, mainly concentrating on the development of conversational interfaces and their uses in customer service and communication approaches. Adoption of conversational interfaces is one of the most prominent trends in today's world and its rate is only going up. The conversational interfaces are therefore interfaces where the user communicates with the machine using natural language, whether voice or text based. These interfaces have evolved to greater levels of progression, spurred by the developments of contextual understanding and language processing algorithms, machine learning, and artificial intelligence.

It is then important to note that virtual assistants are the most prominent example of conversational interfaces, including Siri of Apple, Alexa of Amazon, and Google Assistant. These systems incorporate and rely on artificial intelligence to interpret user's voice commands, process queries and carry out tasks such as reminding the user of an event, playing certain music, and even manage appliances in the smart home system. New advances in Artificial Intelligence have made conversational interfaces more integrated into smartphones, smart speakers, and other devices, making them the new standard. Conversational interfaces are also becoming popular due to the constant learning from of the AI systems.

The first iterations of the technology were grounded and confined in their utility, and chatbots and virtual assistants only provided pre-programmed answers to pre-selected questions or commands. However, over the recent past, there have been many developments especially in the deep learning technology and also the transformer models like GPT-3 and the more recent ChatGPT. These models can now produce even more refined solutions, responses, thereby more adequately fitting into a specific environment, and providing more organic, real-life-like experience with machines. Choosing conversational interfaces is another important factor driving their development due to the need for more personalization of user interactions. Conversational AI enables businesses to interact with users in an approach that seems more personal and organic hence serving their customers better. For example, virtual assistant can now adapt from the users' usage patterns and history, thereby providing more personal responses. Such levels of customization improve user satisfaction and help to encourage users to interact with technology.

Quick Turing tests and advanced interactive agents are present in both personal and corporate settings. Companies such as Amazon with its Alexa and Google with Google Assistant are now familiar brands that allow users to control household appliances, or entertainment systems, by merely using their voice. Modern conversational AI is not limited to computers and smartphones, it has been embedded in smart speakers, wearables, and even vehicles as virtual assistants. In the business context, chatbots are now indispensable when it comes to interacting with customers. Consistent with its name, the AI chatbot is able to provide basic or even advanced customer service such as responding to common questions or helping customers complete a sequence of steps such as solving a problem or checking out a product. This means that there is less burden placed on human agents yet customers have been able to access fast and correct assistance.

Quite a number of firms are shifting to the use of virtual assistants and chatbots to enhance customer relations and organizational performance. For example, Amazon uses AI-driven voice assistant Alexa, which helps users easily operate within the Amazon ecosystem; Apple has the similar option called Siri. Virtual assistants include Siri, Cortana, and Bixby that allow users to perform certain tasks by using their voice through simple commands, which has now become a key consideration for most technological products. Furthermore, chatbots are also adopted in different sectors nowadays. In e-commerce, they entertain shoppers by offering suggestions for items to buy, help locate orders and also help in the processing of returns. In the financial services sector, customers use chatbots to check their balances and transactions, move money between accounts and even invest. Another important area, where conversational AI has been noticed, is the healthcare setting and where chatbots can offer simple medical recommendations, navigate appointments, and support patients of their wellbeing. The rise of remote work, enabled by the COVID-19 pandemic, compelled companies and organizations to leverage chatbots and virtual assistants. Almost every business integrated AI solutions to manage the increase in customer queries due to changed services, health issues, or shift in consumer expectations. This shift proved the scalability and reliability of conversational AI in the handling of large volume of customers interactions especially in the time of crises.

Perhaps the most relevant use case of conversational AI has been in implementing it into customer service and interaction plans. The general drawback of customer services is that most of them are dependent on people and are, therefore, confined by time, capacity, and money. Traditional, live support, on the other hand, can only be available during working hours of customer support executives and thereby cannot offer immediate response to the customer needs. Customers are starting to see chatbots and virtual assistants as the new way forward in corporate communications and support services. For instance, AI chatbots can handle numerous inquiries, and provide immediate, routine responses to callers' concerns. This has enabled businesses to cut down their response times, improve on customer satisfaction, and decrease operation costs. One of the benefits of conversational AI in customer support is its capability of Progressive Improvement of performance and accuracy of the answers provided. This makes the use of AI in systems a perfect fit for change in customer needs and expectations since it can implement changes frequently. Additionally, conversational AI can handle further complicated inquiries by passing them on to the next level of human assistance, thus providing a perfect human/AI combined helpdesk.

Since conversational AI is still rapidly developing, it is reasonable to expect that its use in customer support and interaction will also increase in the future. The advancement of artificial intelligence analytical tools, natural language understanding, and emotional recognition will further advance conversational experiences that can better cater to comprehensive context and customer emotions due to the establishment of human-like conversational engagements.

With conversational AI on the rise, the use of chatbots and virtual assistants have now become a norm in customer support and engagement. This phenomenon of increased adoption of AI into conversational interfaces in businesses mean that the benefits AI has to offer such as personalization, reduced operational cost, and engaging customer experiences are likely to advance further. As the development of AI, ML, and NLP keeps on progressing, conversational AI continues to blend seamlessly into the society and into people's interactions with technologies, and with business in specific (Dwivedi et al., 2023).

Given the fact that conversational AI is a rapidly trending technology, its potential is inherent in new technologies and innovations that would revolve around industries and transform human–computer interactions. The growth of the field with regard to both AI and NLP suggests that the future will see conversational AI become more advanced, more widespread, and more influential. However, following these developments there are issues that arise concerning ethic, privacy of data, and appropriateness of human beings in the society AI takes over. This section will elaborate the prospects of the conversational AI development, prognoses concerning further enhancements of AI and NLP tools, crucial issues relating to data protection and implementing non-biased AI, as well as the opportunities of cooperation between people and AI. From the given analysis, it can be noted that the future of the conversational AI relies on the growth of the technologies like artificial intelligence, machine learning, blockchain, and quantum computing. These technologies are believed to enable future increases in the efficiency of conversational systems in terms of precision, speed, and flexibility. One of the main areas of development is NLP, which has already received significant advancements with the help of transformer models, GPT-3, BERT, and ChatGPT. Subsequent versions of such frameworks shall be progressively enhanced to allow the operation of AI conversational models that include control of discourse, emotions, and subtleties. Real-time translation, multilingual support, and even better speech recognition algorithms will enable conversational AI to better serve clients from different parts of the world.

Another significant development is the increased incorporation of facial expression and voice tone identification as well as opinion mining into conversational Artificial Intelligence systems. Future innovative technologies including affective computing will help these systems to identify and interact with human emotions through using tones of voice, facial expressions, and textual content. Some more specific trends include the growth of empathy and increased focus on emotions, which should make the AI more "human." This could transform such sectors as healthcare and education, in which emotional listening performs a vital function. Another interesting opportunity is the integration of conversational AI with the Internet of Things (IoT). Thus, as more IoT variants enter homes, workplaces, and public entity spaces, conversational AI will act as the front end for managing and interfacing with various smart gadgets. It will help to achieve more natural and intuitive voice control of smart homes, automobile vehicles, and industrial processes, which will lead to enhanced convenience, optimization and individuality. Other technologies closely related with the evolution of the future conversational AI include the augmented reality, virtual reality. This research suggests that the integration of artificial intelligent voice interfaces with augmented or virtual reality applications will allow consumers and businesses to interact with virtual personal assistants and chatbots in more vivid and tactile manners. This could revolutionize fields such as retail, real estate, and entertainment, providing "shopping advisors," "virtual tours," and "AI-driven recommendations" in a fully interactive environment.

The shifts that will occur in Conversational AI in the future will be a continuous enhancement of the existing AI and NLP capabilities. The deep learning models will continue developing, which will lead to the usage of AI systems for a wide range of conversations complexity, learning from the minimal data set, and generalization of knowledge in various domains. Thus, existing models such as GPT-4 and others are expected to expand the horizons of the few-shot learning and self-supervised learning that will enable AI systems to accomplish a great deal with little data input. Another prediction is that conversational AI will shift to genuine multimodal experience meaning that AI will be capable of handling and interpreting text, voice, and vision simultaneously. This means that more refined and heuristically friendly interfaces can then be designed and implemented particularly in situations where both voice and text-based communication are required. Second, there is the prediction that personalization will be the major direction of the future AI systems. Following the use of data analytics and the application of machine learning, conversational AI will possess the capability to offer users unique experiences based on the user's preference, habits, and trends.

Virtual assistants and chatbots, as two types of conversational AI systems, gather extensive users' information, including PII. It is therefore important that this data is accurately collected, stored, and put to good use. In the future conversation with AI will also have to pay attention to users' privacy issues with increasing regulations, better encryption services, and correct data handling processes. The next of the major ethical issues is bias in AI models. A lot of AI systems make use of datasets with certain pre-existing bias meaning that the systems will also make bias responses and therefore bias the treatment of certain demographic groups. Some ways of developing the future of equitable AI include checking that conversational AI systems are trained in diverse and inclusive datasets as well as employing methods of how bias is recognized and eliminated. It also consists of an explanation of how AI systems function is equally important. With increased use of conversational AI in decision making, user and stakeholder must get acquainted with the reasoning process. Incorporation of strategies for interpreting the AI's thoughts will go a long in enhancing the faith people have in AI and guarantee that the utilization of AI is well done. Unfortunately, conversational AI is still in a period of quick development, and it will not supplant humans in a lot of areas. On the contrary, humanity is to evolve to a brand-new type of symbiosis with artificial intelligence technologies when AI becomes the co-partner of people and constantly complements and improves the abilities of people. Machines handle different tasks that consume a lot of time and effort, allowing conversational AI to take over these duties while people focus on more important, creative, and even emotional actions. Tasks, which can be performed by AI systems include answering routine questions in sectors such as customer relations, while emotive tasks should be left for human operators. In healthcare, conversational AI can closely collaborate with doctors by helping to make diagnoses, as well as complete other routine tasks, leaving healthcare experts to focus on clients. It will also impact the educational sphere, where AI-based tutors will be able to offer efficient individual approaches to learning with the primary and additional curriculums performed by mentors who are to develop learners' critical thinking rather than repeating what AI-based tutors offer. Such an approach can be suitable to achieve the strength of both AI and humans to the highest level. With so many advanced technologies and new innovations flooding the market every day, conversational AI appears to have a very bright future. AI and NLP are bound to make the conversations more natural and more intuitive in the years to come there are issues of ethical concern, issues of data privacy as well as issues of bias that need to be overcome to ensure that proper and acceptable AI systems are developed.

3. Understanding Natural Language Processing (NLP)

Natural Language Processing (NLP) is an important subfield within artificial intelligence hence deals with the use of natural languages by machines where the later can process them, comprehend them, and even produce outputs in the same language (Schobel et al., 2024). NLP has core subfields such as tokenization, parsing, and semantics through which machines analytically dissects text with a view of recognizing its structure alongside its meaning (McTear, 2022). There are specific examples of how NLP is utilized in facilities, such as tokenization, a known operation that breaks down letters into forms of words, phrases, or single word tokens, making it even easier for a machine to understand and analyze information (McTear, 2017).

Another important NLP task is parsing which allows to analyze the syntactic structure of the sentence and give understanding about how certain elements of the sentence are linked with others (Dwivedi et al., 2023). However, semantic analysis enables machines to such things as sentiments and context, which play a major role in the analysis of sentiment and events (Dwivedi et al., 2023).

However, NLP faces significant challenges, for the foremost reason being that the use of natural language is ambiguous. It means that a word or a phrase may have many different meanings depending on the situation which can cause misunderstanding (Surikova et al., 2022). Uncertainty in conjunction with multilingualism makes NLP challenging as such systems experience issues with dialects, colloquialisms, and idiomatic expressions (Casheekar et al., 2024). Other issues, including ethical issues like biases, are realized when training the NLP models using biased datasets results to biased results (Minsky et al., 2023). Eliminating such biases remains essential for sound NLP advancement primarily because it impacts a wide range of professions (McKie et al., 2022).

The newer developments in NLP include the combination of ML and DL have made a shift in the field (Bozkurt et al., 2023). Inductive techniques have replaced rule-based approaches that were earlier used, making the models more flexible and scalable in the case of NLP applications. Latest NLP models like BERT (Bidirectional Encoder Representations from Transformers) and GPT (Generative Pre-trained Transformer) have scope for higher levels of contextualized word embeddings leading to better contextual understanding in conversational AI (Ram et al., 2018).

As for the concrete use cases, the NLP is applied in conversational AI, chatbots, or virtual assistants, as well as in the tools for the content moderation (Dengel, 2023). These systems use NLP to understand the users' inputs, to give a contextually proper reply, and to converse with the users in many fields, including customer relations and healthcare (Ng & Lin, 2022). Language translation is another application of NLP that has greatly boosted interpretation especially where two persons are speaking different languages (Mari et al., 2020).

Given that the technology is still improving, efforts to solve issues such as polysemy, multilinguality, and ethical issues will be instrumental in determining the future of NLP (Humphry & Chesher, 2021). Thus, the combination of modern models and machine learning opens up new opportunities for the further development of NLP as the basis for the formation of conversational AI and a wide range of other technologies (Missaouib et al., 2021).

4. The Emergence of ChatGPT

ChatGPT is a pioneering model from the renown OpenAI that brought a new dimension in natural language processing. Thanks to the progressive architectures and effective training approaches, ChatGPT becomes suitable in different fields and indicates the robust capability to revolutionize the industries and improve user interactions. This section discusses the origin of ChatGPT, its structure, functionalities, and diverse uses. OpenAI was started in December 2015 with an objective of making sure that the artificial intelligence (AI) will work for the benefit of everyone (Haque, 2022). In realizing these aims, OpenAI aimed at developing models that not only complete certain tasks but can also converse with human beings in a way reminiscent of artificial intelligence. The rationale for building ChatGPT was to create AI that could engage users in natural language thereby requiring enhanced models. ChatGPT stays in this direction journey as it incorporates the new developments in natural language processing and machine learning. It aimed at developing a model capable of comprehending and synthesizing human language that may be suitable for solving various tasks, including information search and natural language interactions. OpenAI's goals are to advance friendly AI for the use of the human race and to guarantee that the technologies it fosters are both safe and moral. These goals are achieved by the development of ChatGPT as it serves as a tool to improve conveyance and sharing of information, as well as encouraging originality and creativity in content. The ultimate goal of OpenAI was to build an artificial system with the ability to skillfully dialog, help in learning processes, and optimize numerous processes in different fields. The capability and proficiency of ChatGPT have been refined through these training sessions and user reviews to meet the needs of users and overcome potential problems in safety, accuracy, and ethics as envisaged by OpenAI. The organization aspects cover the appropriateness of use and concerns the avoidance of negative consequences while enhancing the potential benefits of the AI technologies.

ChatGPT comes from the GPT family, which is now a fundamental architecture of many NLP systems. This architecture is based on the transformer model described in the paper by Vaswani et al., published in 2017, with the title "Attention is All You Need." This model was revolutionary in NLP because it had a mechanism called self-attention that makes the handling of sequential data more efficient through its ability to determine the importance of words in a sentence compared to other words. Understanding of the key components of the general-purpose architecture:

- Transformer Blocks: ChatGPT consists of multiple transformer layers stacked on top of each other. Each layer includes mechanisms for self-attention and feed-forward neural networks, which enable the model to learn complex relationships in data.
- Pre-training and Fine-tuning: The development of ChatGPT involves two primary phases.
- Pre-training: The model is initially trained on a large corpus of text data from diverse sources, allowing it to learn grammar, facts, and some level of reasoning. During this phase, the model predicts the next word in a sentence given the previous context, enabling it to understand language structure and context.
- Fine-tuning: After pre-training, the model undergoes fine-tuning on a narrower dataset, often involving human reviewers who provide feedback on generated outputs. This phase enhances the model's ability to follow instructions and generate more coherent and contextually appropriate responses.
- Tokenization: Before processing text, ChatGPT converts input data into tokens, which represent words or sub words. This tokenization enables the model to handle various languages and dialects effectively.
- Output Generation: When generating responses, ChatGPT uses techniques such as beam search or sampling to create coherent text outputs based on the learned patterns and structures from the training data.
- Through this architecture and training methodology, ChatGPT has become adept at understanding and generating human language, making it a powerful tool for various applications.

ChatGPT boasts a range of functionalities that make it a versatile conversational agent. Its primary capabilities include:

- Text Generation: ChatGPT can generate coherent and contextually relevant text based on prompts. This capability allows users to engage in natural conversations, create stories, or generate creative content.

- Summarization: The model can condense lengthy texts into concise summaries, making it easier for users to grasp key information without sifting through extensive material.
- Translation: ChatGPT can translate text between languages, leveraging its understanding of linguistic nuances and context to provide accurate translations.
- Question Answering: The model can respond to factual questions, drawing on its extensive training data to provide accurate and informative answers.
- Conversational Context Retention: ChatGPT is designed to maintain context throughout a conversation, allowing it to respond more appropriately to follow-up questions and create a more engaging dialog.

Interestingly, ChatGPT is more than just a text generation model, as discussed below. For instance:

- Text Generation: This means that users can use ChatGPT to get advice, create poems and scripts or even come up with dialog for roles. In this aspect, one main advantage of this model is that it can easily switch between various writing styles and tones in order to meet the specific needs of users.
- Summarization: In this case, ChatGPT can analyze articles, reports, and research papers in various fields such as journalism, education, and business to enable working experts save time by summarizing the content quickly.
- Translation: Translation function of ChatGPT helps people interact with people of different cultures and languages, thus people can easily and effectively communicate with others in a multicultural environment.

ChatGPT's diverse applications span various domains, showcasing its versatility and utility:

- *Education: Student and teacher interaction:* ChatGPT can act as a personal tutor or a learning companion and help in answering questions or questions related to homework assignments. It can also develop tests and learning products that would make the process more engaging.
- *Healthcare:* Among the healthcare applications of ChatGPT, it can help the patients with their questions as well as inform them about the symptoms, and even give them reminders regarding the medication. It cannot substitute physicians, but it can act as an assistant that distributes information to its audience.
- *Content Creation:* Writers, marketers, and any kind of content creator will find ChatGPT useful because it is capable of idea generation, article outlining, and editing. Social media can help in developing posts, commercials, and marketing materials for specific groups of viewers. Customer Support: However, almost every enterprise incorporates ChatGPT in their customer care management process. When implemented in chatbots, it helps firms to answer clients' questions within a blink of an eye, improve the client experience, and decrease response time.

- *Entertainment:* ChatGPT can be used in the entertainment sector to develop an interactive story, generate game dialogs, or help in scriptwriting.

As such, through the utilization of these interconnected domains, ChatGPT increases overall effectiveness in operational tasks, ensures effective communication, as well as promotes imagination, which make this tool indispensable when it comes to a variety of uses.

This appearance of ChatGPT signifies a revolution in conversational artificial intelligence. Fueled by OpenAI's mission to develop a friendly AI that supports humans, ChatGPT employs powerful techniques and new training techniques to make natural and useful interactions across different uses. Examples such as text generation, summarization, translation, and many others show that AI has numerous possibilities to revolutionize industries, enrich users' experiences, and ease their communication. Nonetheless, further growth of the ChatGPT application will result in even greater changes in society and accelerate the development of AI interactions.

5. Challenges and Limitations

Although ChatGPT can be considered a major evolution in the progress in conversational AI, there is no lack of problems and drawbacks related to the system. Recognizing these restrictions is important in implementing the model, and in managing possible ethical issues that may be associated with the use of the model. This section illustrates fights, gaps, and future development of ChatGPT.

- Context Retention: Another interesting fact which may be considered a disadvantage of ChatGPT is its context-memory during an extended conversation. The model, as intended, is to learn based on the conversation history and to respond accordingly, however, it is not immune to what is called conversation drift, particularly when the conversation is lengthy. It means that responses shared in such a manner might occur incoherent or irrelevant, making the conversation flow uneven. For example, if a user uses multiple questions to talk to ChatGPT, it may not remember the previous turns and give redundant answers or become bewildered regarding the user's desired direction.
- Factual Accuracy: The answers created by ChatGPT are based on a lot of data from a specific database that might contain false information or information which is considered to be outdated. As a result, the model may give factually wrong or more biased answers, especially in response to certain questions about ongoing or certain subjects. Dedicated to the information that a user has got from ChatGPT, they need to be careful and check the important information received, especially in terms of the-field-related strict conversion, like medical, legal, or technical situations. Understanding Nuance and Emotion: While being able to write text which mimics human language, ChatGPT can be inherently lacking in deciphering the subtle emotion cues in communication. This can be especially disadvantageous in cases in which empathetic commands

should be given or when the model misunderstands other people's feelings or provides incorrect emotional stimuli. Any of the challenges may result in poor user experiences especially when handling delicate topic.

- Lack of Common-Sense Reasoning: Thus, ChatGPT can synthesize continuous text of natural language following the patterns it summed in the learning process, but it has no actual comprehension of the CONTENTS and/or does not possess common sense. This means that it can give logically absurd or unbelievable responses to questions that cannot be answered using just language understanding. Some questions may make a user completely nonplussed due to illogical behaviors the model demonstrates sometimes in answers.

- Dependence on Training Data: It means that it can only generate responses based on the data using which it was trained, and that data is the sum of text data existing until a certain date. Therefore, this model may lack the new changes or development of knowledge. This can result in responses that contain old information which makes the model relevant in fields that are in constant evolution.

Addressing Issues of Misuse, Bias, and Transparency is also important:

- Misuse: One of the worst aspects of ChatGPT is the imminent likelihood of its abuse. It can be also used to produce unworthy posts, fake news, spam, or abusive message... Because the technology is becoming more mainstream, there has been talk about how people are likely to misuse ChatGPT for malicious ends posing the question that are there ways to encourage responsible use of ChatGPT and to ensure certain measures are taken against improper use.

- Bias: The last essential problem is that ChatGPT has learning and generative prejudice. Due to extreme exposure to large datasets, which could potentially have biased viewpoints or prejudices, the model will be able to produce such biases. This can lead to negative or prejudice reactions especially when intellectual conversations involve sensitive issues like racism, sexism or prejudice origin. Bias continues to be a major problem in the AI models calling for further innovation to reduce their effects.

- Transparency: Transparency is essential in understanding how AI models like ChatGPT operate and generate responses. However, the complexity of the underlying algorithms can create a "black box" effect, where users cannot easily comprehend how decisions are made. This lack of transparency can lead to mistrust among users and raise ethical concerns about accountability, particularly in high-stakes applications. It is crucial for organizations deploying ChatGPT to communicate clearly about its capabilities and limitations, fostering a better understanding among users.

Potential improvements and directions for ChatGPT's development are:

- Improved Context Management: Subsequent versions of ChatGPT could be expanded on by providing a stronger emphasis toward the retention of contexts. This improvement could be in the enhancement of the model architecture or the inclusion of extra components that would assist the model in tracking context across long conversations. Such advancements would go a long way to improving user experiences by promoting more coherent and relevant discussions.

- Increased Factual Accuracy: Possible solutions to the identified problems of factual inaccuracy could be the improvement of the use of facts by ChatGPT developers. The model could utilize real time Information Retrieval system or make use of special database to furnish users with accurate information minimizing chances of dissemination of fake information.
- Enhanced Emotional Intelligence: Subsequent generations of ChatGPT could potentially include measures that detect and incorporate emotional characteristics into conversations. When training the model in rich emotional data sets and using sentiment analysis tools, the developers can overcome many problems and the model can give emotionally intelligent and emotionally desired answers in emotionally filled conversations.
- Bias Mitigation Strategies: Owing to this, constant research on how to care for bias identification and future enhancements will be elemental. It is possible to investigate methods and approaches to perform bias detection, as well as to reconsider some ideas and algorithms applied during the generation process, in order to minimize the presence of the noted bias. This would ensure that there is fairness and inclusion toward various questions that may be posed to the ChatGPT.
- Transparency and User Control: Based on that it is important that AI systems' working should be more transparent as AI technology progresses. Others may be shifted toward enhancing explicitness of models where people should have a clue how decisions are being made and be given an elaborate option of guiding the AI's behaviors. Giving users more choices concerning what they should do next can ease mistrust and enhance the overall satisfaction.

Despite the progress that has been made through the development of ChatGPT in the improvement of conversational AI technology, some potential issues as well as ethical implications, and further development prospects must be noted here. Thus, constantly focusing on enhancing these aspects, the developers can contribute to the latter's positive and responsible impact on humanity.

6. Conclusion

To sum up this discussion of conversational, AI, let us revisit the focus of the chapter one more time. With the emergence of conversational AI, human's relations with devices changed and became the new step in the technological development. The key technology in this process is therefore Natural Language Processing (NLP), which allows machines to process and communicate in human language seamlessly. ChatGPT built by OpenAI is another significant step in the progression of conversational AI as it is an illustrative example of how an incredibly developed language model can serve to enhance the communication across different fields.

The application of Conversational AI has expanded significantly within the last few decades as it moved from simplistic architectures to highly complex systems that mimic natural conversations. Indeed, some of the initial pieces of AI research and implementations in this style build on earlier antecedents such as ELIZA and ALICE. The jazzing of magnificent architectures such as GPT has also fueled conversational AI, and it can be utilized in fields from consumer care to information processing and more. Conversational AI is based on NLP and includes components necessary for further processing, such as tokens, parse trees and semantics. It applies to complexities of human language to ensure that AI systems understand and get to write text that will have an impact to the users. Nevertheless, some of the barriers remain unsolved even today, including vagueness, polyglotism, and context preservation. The advancement of ChatGPT has shown how using conversational AI can change the world. Thanks to the significant development of its text generation, summarization, and translation capabilities, ChatGPT is being used in numerous fields such as in education, healthcare, content writing, etc. However, as has been highlighted in our discussion on the challenges and limitations of the model, it is not immune to problems like context, fact, and ethics, for instance, bias, and lack of transparency.

Thus, the further development of conversational AI seems to be promising, although it was not an easy path. Further developments in the application of machine learning in NLP and deep learning will only improve the workings of conversational agents where context comprehension will be improved and the accuracy of responses to such queries will sharply be improved. Technologies like enhanced context awareness, contextual information acquisition, and contextual emotions will be significant factors in perfecting user experiences. Also, as conversational AI is more included in various aspects of the society, it should be developed responsibly. Integrating relevant ethical values and standards, including diverse bias reduction and reporting, will be crucial for users to have faith in and accept AI. This continuous advancement of conversational AI will have profound effects on how people will interact, collaborate and interact with technology in the future. In conclusion, it is believed that conversational AI has significant potential in redefining society's relationships with technology. As many of us incorporate NLP and tools like the ChatGPT in our practices, it is important to keep an eye on the organizations and their effects on society. Principle to Guide AI Development and Application should be another tenet, insisting on explainable AI, Algorithmic fairness, and accountability. As the world is shifting into the age that is dominated by innovations such as AI, it becomes the duty of the researcher, developer, as well as the policy maker to foster the development of conversational AI that will be in the best interest of humanity. The anticipation of ethical human–AI relations gives a warm opportunity to address the needs of conversational AI for a better world and inclusive society with improved productivity.

References

Allado-McDowell, K., & Bentivegna, F. (2022). Cybernetic animism: Voice and AI in conversation. *Journal of Interdisciplinary Voice Studies, 7*(1), 107–118.

Bozkurt, A., Junhong, X., Lambert, S., Pazurek, A., Crompton, H., Koseoglu, S., Farrow, R., Bond, M., Nerantzi, C., Honeychurch, S., & Bali, M. (2023). Speculative futures on ChatGPT and generative artificial intelligence (AI): A collective reflection from the educational landscape. *Asian Journal of Distance Education, 18*(1), 53–130.

Casheekar, A., Lahiri, A., Rath, K., Prabhakar, K. S., & Srinivasan, K. (2024). A contemporary review on chatbots, AI-powered virtual conversational agents, ChatGPT: Applications, open challenges and future research directions. *Computer Science Review, 52*, 100632.

Dengel, T. (2023). *The sound of the future: The coming age of voice technology.* PublicAffairs.

Dew, R. (2023). The empathetic algorithm leveraging AI for next-level CX.

Dwivedi, Y. K., Kshetri, N., Hughes, L., Slade, E. L., Jeyaraj, A., Kar, A. K., Baabdullah, A. M., Koohang, A., Raghavan, V., Ahuja, M., & Albanna, H. (2023). Opinion paper: "So what if ChatGPT wrote it?" Multidisciplinary perspectives on opportunities, challenges and implications of generative conversational AI for research, practice and policy. *International Journal of Information Management, 71*, 102642.

Haque, M. A. (2022). A Brief analysis of "ChatGPT"–A revolutionary tool designed by OpenAI. *EAI Endorsed Transactions on AI and Robotics, 1*, e15.

Humphry, J., & Chesher, C. (2021). Preparing for smart voice assistants: Cultural histories and media innovations. *New Media & Society, 23*(7), 1971–1988.

Mari, A., Mandelli, A., & Algesheimer, R. (2020). The evolution of marketing in the context of voice commerce: A managerial perspective. In *HCI in Business, Government and Organizations: 7th International Conference, HCIBGO 2020, Held as Part of the 22nd HCI International Conference, HCII 2020, Copenhagen, Denmark, July 19–24, 2020, Proceedings* (pp. 405–425). Springer International Publishing.

McKie, I., Narayan, B., & Kocaballi, B. (2022). Conversational voice assistants and a case study of long-term users: A human information behaviours perspective. *Journal of the Australian Library and Information Association, 71*(3), 233–255.

McTear, M. F. (2017). The rise of the conversational interface: A new kid on the block?. In *Future and Emerging Trends in Language Technology. Machine Learning and Big Data: Second International Workshop, FETLT 2016, Seville, Spain, November 30–December 2, 2016, Revised Selected Papers* (pp. 38–49). Springer International Publishing.

McTear, M. (2022). *Conversational AI: Dialogue systems, conversational agents, and chatbots.* Springer Nature.

Minsky, L., Westwater, S., Westwater, S., & Fahey, C. (2023). *Voice marketing: Harnessing the power of conversational AI to drive customer engagement.* Rowman & Littlefield.

Missaouib, S., Concannonc, S., Maloneyb, L., & Walker, J. A. (2021). Interactive storytelling for children: A case-study of design and development considerations for ethical conversational AI. arXiv preprint arXiv:2107.13076.

Ng, Y. L., & Lin, Z. (2022). Exploring conversation topics in conversational artificial intelligence–Based social mediated communities of practice. *Computers in Human Behavior*, *134*, 107326.

O'Regan, G., & O'Regan, G. (2018). Eliza program. The innovation in computing companion: A compendium of select. *Pivotal Inventions*, 119–122.

Ram, A., Prasad, R., Khatri, C., Venkatesh, A., Gabriel, R., Liu, Q., Nunn, J., Hedayatnia, B., Cheng, M., Nagar, A., & King, E. (2018). Conversational AI: The science behind the Alexa prize. arXiv preprint arXiv:1801.03604.

Schobel, S., Schmitt, A., Benner, D., Saqr, M., Janson, A., & Leimeister, J. M. (2024). Charting the evolution and future of conversational agents: A research agenda along five waves and new frontiers. *Information Systems Frontiers*, *26*(2), 729–754.

Surikova, J., Siroda, S., & Bhattarai, B. (2022). The role of artificial intelligence in the evolution of brand voice in multimedia. *Molung Educational Frontier*, 73–103.

Chapter 2

ChatGPT: Boon or Bane

Shruti Mishra and Nitika Lal

Manav Rachna International Institute of Research and Studies, India

Abstract

The purpose of this chapter was to explore and address the limitations of ChatGPT especially with regard to research and education. To understand this aspect of conversational AI both primary and secondary data has been used. The primary data was collected while testing – how the ChatGPT operates on its own, and then compared with the findings that already existed in the repertoire of past research on the said topic of research. Secondary research data was used to substantiate the results obtained through primary research. In this chapter, it was in the form of articles, documents, books, journals, etc. This also included people's experience that they had published about using ChatGPT. The findings highlighted the current pitfalls that an individual could fall into if they were not careful enough while using the app. In addition to this, this chapter provides tangible do's and don'ts while using this conversational AI or any similar AI, especially in reference to the ethical consideration in a professional set up. Through this chapter the researchers would like to help contribute to the already existing knowledge about chatbots like ChatGPT, provide pointers that practitioners can use to better the current experience or find ways to create new applications which addresses the current need gaps that exist. This chapter addresses the ethical issues that arise when using an artificial intelligence smart enough to do or guide an individual through the entire report or project.

Keywords: ChatGPT; research; limitations; conversational AI; challenges; generative AI

1. Introduction

Artificial Intelligence is one of the most talked about and used technologies in today's day and age. It is being extensively used in almost all spheres of our lives –

The ChatGPT Revolution, 23–36
Copyright © 2025 Shruti Mishra and Nitika Lal
Published under exclusive licence by Emerald Publishing Limited
doi:10.1108/978-1-83549-852-120251002

be it research, marketing, academia, healthcare, legal, cybersecurity, etc. Additionally, it has been found that within this world of Artificial Intelligence, the new entrant ChatGPT is the talk of the town. It is one of the most widely accepted and used AI models available in the market today. What makes the application special is the accuracy and the variety of information that they have to offer. In addition to this, what adds to the appeal of this AI model is the novel way of presenting the information – it is crisp, clear, and easy to understand. Apart from this, the application is easy to use and almost anyone with basic knowledge of English can easily operate and use it to their advantage. However, not everything can be viewed with the rose tinted glasses. It's always better to tread in caution when the path is unknown. Therefore, it is imperative that we know more about the positives and the negatives that this tool brings to our lives, to which this chapter adds value too.

The Open AI-developed ChatGPT artificial intelligence–generated content (AIGC) model has been gaining international recognition for its exceptional capacity to handle difficult language understanding and generation tasks through a variety of chats (Wu et al., 2023). With its many capabilities, including the ability to create course syllabi, teaching materials, and assessment assignments, ChatGPT is regarded as a useful tool for users. Large volumes of text data were used in the model's construction, which allowed it to capture the complexities, nuances, and patterns of human language. Because the training corpus contains a variety of sources, including books, papers, reviews, online discussions, and human-generated data, the model can conduct complex conversations and deliver precise information on a wide range of topics in less than one click (Roumeliotis & Tselikas, 2023).

In an effort to create a flipped classroom atmosphere, ChatGPT can assist students with their online studies by responding to their enquiries, improving group dynamics by offering real-time comments and suggestions for a discussion structure (Lo Chung Kwan, 2023). Nevertheless, despite its promise, ChatGPT frequency generates outputs that appear reliable but are inaccurate, therefore its use in medical practice and research should be approached with caution (Goodman et al., 2023; Hosseini et al., 2023; Flanagin et al., 2023; Shen et al., 2023; Stokel-Walker, 2023; Thorp, 2023). Sallam (2023) was one of the first researchers to comment on the discrepancies that ChatGPT poses, how its use in education is challenging, attributing to its inaccuracy and unreliability.

When one thinks about ChatGPT and the possible ways in which this AI model can help with the task at hand it is important to remember that ChatGPT is a machine learning model which is as good as the data that it works on. Though it has the capacity to understand the conversational or natural language that we speak and revert in an almost human like manner. If the data is faulty or incorrect (however minor it may be), it would provide incorrect information. It cannot think on its own. It provides information basis what has been fed from the limited resource it has access to. Through this chapter, we bring forth the point that it is always better to adhere on the side of caution, till we understand the tool in totality and understand the dos and don'ts, and how best we can leverage it our advantage.

Through a case study this chapter aims to evaluate the accuracy and comprehensiveness of ChatGPT generated responses related to research and academia. It further aims to elucidate the discrepancies, primarily from the perspective of academia and search of literature, which is a pivotal step in research writing. Hence, contributing to the overall understanding of this technology, especially in reference to ethical considerations in research. Additionally, this chaper helps add value to the already known facts about these conversational AI's, providing tangible knowledge that users can use to better understand the tool and find possible solutions to the limitations that it has.

Post this section we have Review of Literature, which provides a synopsis of the information and the lacunes that currently exists on ChatGPT. After this section is the case study which talks about the experience of a researcher and the struggle she faced while writing her dissertation. Post this section we have a section which sums up the findings and brings forth the key takeaways for the reader, followed by the reference sections.

2. Review of Literature

ChatGPT is an important tool today which helps in assisting individuals with their research in almost all know fields. It leverages on the already existing knowledge base to provide a vast repertoire of information to its users depending on what has been asked. Here, in this chapter we have understood this exchange of information and the limitation it possesses in the context of research. Therefore, it is important to mention that though the AI helps provide a kickstart in the writing process, when it comes to in-depth help in research it errs.

The literature from the past scholarly works helps to explain this phenomenon. After all, the introduction of generative AI is about to cause a huge shift in the field of education. Artificial intelligence has been proven to be a game-changer in the rapidly changing field of online education. Tools like ChatGPT are driving a fundamental transition in areas like language learning and assessment design. AI is used by several e-learning sites, such as Coursera, to help identify typical mistakes that students do in their assignments (Steenbergen-Hu & Cooper, 2014).

Even though natural language processing (NLP) models like ChatGPT and Google Bard offer great potential, there are a number of challenges or moral dilemmas that need to be resolved. First, there is the precision issue, then it has been found that data security and privacy are key ethical problems (Huallpa, 2023). There have been questions expressed about the security and privacy of student personal data because ChatGPT uses enormous amount of data to produce results. Which is taken from the already existing data set. If those data sets are incorrect or faulty, the information generation would be fallacious. NLP models should support student's learning in a variety of ways, making them extremely relevant in higher education.

Large amounts of textual data, such as academic papers, textbooks, and other course materials are known to exist. These models can be used to process and analyze the data in order to provide students with personalized study recommendations based on their needs and learning preferences. Moreover, chatbots and virtual assistants that offer students on-demand support and guidance and give them access to information and help whenever they need it can be developed using NLP models (Fuchs, 2023). In a study by Adeshola and Adepoju (2023) the Latent Dirichlet Allocation (LDA) method was employed for topic modeling and the Valence Aware Dictionary for Sentiment Reasoning (VADER) method for sentiment analysis. After data preparation, 3,870 of the 10,000 tweets that the researchers had originally extracted for the study remained accessible. The VADER sentiment analysis concluded that 2013 tweets were categorized as "positive," and the remaining 804 and 1,053 tweets were categorized as "negative" and "neutral."

Through the creation and implementation of interactive classroom activities, educators have the opportunity to improve pedagogical practices through the sophisticated capabilities provided by ChatGPT. Educators can create novel teaching methods because of ChatGPT's assistance (Rudolph et al., 2023). An example of the implementation of the flipped classroom approach is in which students are encouraged to study independently by having access to learning resources outside of the classroom. It has been shown to be an effective technique for encouraging children to strengthen their writing abilities. By interacting with the system, students can get specific feedback on their writing, ideas for development, and grammatical corrections. This helps them write more effectively and enhance their written communication (Osorio, 2023).

On its website, ChatGPT occasionally publishes false information and gives harmful recommendations regarding biased content. A chatbot will automatically insert words during text creation that are most likely to appear after the words that have come before them, but it does not check the accuracy of the data. One major ethical issue with ChatGPT is the potential for bias in the data the bot is trained on. Additionally, the data is continuously churned from the cloud, making it unable to get information from a specific source. It operates with a small dataset that must correctly depict the present. This increases the possibility of generating false information.

Among the ethical and legal concerns raised by the use of AI in education are those related to intellectual property, privacy, and data security (Javaid et al., 2023). The problem of AI-generated material being mistaken for original student work has become far more prevalent. According to investigations, ChatGPT can evade plagiarism detection software like Turnitin by generating content that seems original. The literature indicates that pupils who used ChatGPT had a higher likelihood of Plagiarizing than those who did not (Dhingra et al., 2023; Geerling et al., 2023; Gill et al., 2024). According to Thorp (2023) peer reviewers are capable of identifying 63% of the abstracts written by ChatGPT. There are a few hazards associated with using ChatGPT, which should be well considered. Creating Biassed material is one of these dangers, and it has to do with the caliber of the datasets that ChatGPT trained on (Sallam, 2023). Stuart Cobbe (2023) evaluated the ChatGPT using questions and discovered that, although the pass percentage was 55, the ChatGPT only received a 42% pass mark. Cobbe is concerned that the advanced version of the ChatGPT will be too advanced to overcome the exam pass limit.

3. Mini Case Study

ChatGPT is an excellent tool when any researcher needs assistance in gathering information related to a particular topic. However, when it comes to comprehensive search to support the research that they are working on, it is always better to err on the path of caution. To bring forth our points, we conducted a small descriptive study employing Open AI's ChatGPT (Default model) as part of a search strategy. It was ChatGPT 3.5 (free version), which was used to collect data for this study and help substantiate our thought process. The primary data was obtained from this AI model itself, whereas the secondary data that was used to corroborate the data that had been obtained from sources like google scholar and JSTOR.

A total of 20 questions were generated from the words – father, adolescent, paternal parenting, prosocial development, and holistic development. These words were used in different permutations and combinations five times on ChatGPT, which generated four research studies at one time. The information that was generated was then crossed checked majorly through Google scholar to check the authenticity of the information. This information has been presented below in the appendix in the form of a Table A2.1.

In order to further assess the quality of results obtained, there was a bifurcation of the data in broad headings – Author/s in ChatGPT, Year in ChatGPT, Journal on Google Scholar, and Discrepancies. These provided a direction to our findings, so that the precise discrepancies could be pointed out instead of a generic viewpoint. To further elaborate the point, 3 out of 20 studies (15%) had the year wrong, 8 studies (40%) that were provided by ChatGPT were fabricated as they did not exist on any literary site. It was further found that there were nine studies (45%) in total that had no discrepancies in accordance with the information available on the AI model. Table 2.1 provide a snapshot of the result of the research.

Hence, it is important that we understand why AI models such as ChatGPT faulters. The reason for this could be that ChatGPT is primarily trained on a large collection of information, therefore it could be erroneous or biased. Additionally, ChatGPT's ability to extract information is known to be limited as it has not been

Table 2.1. Results of the Research.

Information	No. of Documents
No. of results generated in ChatGPT post five trials on the said topic	20
Discrepancies	4 (i.e., 20%)
Fabricated	7 (i.e., 35%)
Correct data	9 (i.e., 45%)

updated with new information since 2022 (Fijačko et al., 2023; Gilson et al., 2023; Han et al., 2023). Therefore, its responses may not always be precise or dependable, notably for specialized topics and recent events. Additionally, ChatGPT might produce false or inaccurate information at times as shown through the example in Table A2.1 (Baidoo-Anu and Owusu Ansah, 2023; Megahed et al., 2024; Qadir, 2023). This phenomenon is fundamentally seen with LLM-based AI Models, known as "hallucination."

Moreover, Bard and ChatGPT have a tendency to grossly exaggerate their features. For example, ChatGPT responds positively when asked whether it could assist in locating pertinent papers to reference in a review paper, but then went on to fabricate a list of more than five completely imaginary journals, bring the credibility of the application down. It was also found that when the researchers repeated the trials, it sometimes listed one or two real papers, but at other times, a particular paper was made up or in some cases if the paper was real it had nothing to do with the inquiry for which the search was being done, other than perhaps having the same author, year, title, or journal (Meyer et al., 2023).

Another riveting study by Eysenbach, highlighted the importance of ChatGPT and it's potential in medical education (Eysenbach, 2023). It showcased the ability of an AI to create virtual patient simulations and quizzes for medical students. Apart from this it helped critique the doctor–patient interaction in simulated environment. However, there was a major drawback that this study pointed out – ChatGPT summarized a research article which was found to be fabricated, raising concerns about the accuracy of information that was being generated. Hence, if not cross checked by the researcher it would go as unique yet untrue data, questioning the credibility of the researcher who has worked on it.

While many of the ChatGPT's functions are outstanding throughout the interview, the most concerning information/experience is the fabricated references. For example, the paper titled "Mobile Apps for Medical Education: A Review of Digital Medical Education Resources" does not exist in Medical Education (or any other JMIR journal on Google Scholar or Pubmed). The authors claimed that there were two DOIs, i.e., Digital Object Identifiers cited by ChatGPT That connected the articles in JMIR Medical Education and JMIR Research Protocols, that are not related to the issue. This poses a very serious threat, as in academia, using ChatGPT generated text or information without proper acknowledgment may pose a problem as the act would be deemed as plagiarism (Božić & Poola, 2023). Therefore, it is important to acknowledge that though ChatGPT is a useful tool to help us highlight areas of interest and provide recommendations for possible subjects based on the data that has been input, it is also important for the researcher to use judgment and analysis to identify true research gaps and are able to generate original hypothesis to test.

Conversational AI suggest potential topics based on its training data, but the identification of genuine research gaps and the generation of novel hypotheses requires additional judgment and analysis on the part of the researcher (Rice et al., 2024).

Implication of discrepancies and fabricated information can have a multi-fold effect, especially for a young researcher venturing into the world of academia. In case the paper is sent for publication and it is found that the information is faulty, the credibility of the researcher working on the said document would be impacted, which in turn would impact the career. It is also possible that if such results (i.e., data generated from ChatGPT) are not verified and future implications are extrapolated, this information can impact the field as further studies would be based on these findings, policies which would then impact the health and safety of the individuals of that country/state. Which would then have a rippling effect as the trust and faith in the authorities/researcher fraternity would be eroded. Apart from this, falsification of data would lead to legal implication if the results impact human life, which would in turn impact the researchers involved (who did not use correct information to derive their findings from).

On a personal front, the overall moral of the individual would get impact, which would then lead to psychological issues. Impacting not just the person but his/her immediate circle of friends and family. As the person who fabricates the information either knowing or unknowingly tends to feel guilty, stress or even anxiety. While people who have been deceived tend to feel confused as to what happened, there is a sense of betrayal and distress. Therefore, it is important to keep in mind that tools in any form are just tools, it depends on the individual using it. One needs to be careful and know it's pitfalls before fully trusting it, as its very important for personal and professional goal that the mental health of the individual does not get impacted due to the negatives.

4. Conclusion

It is crucial to remember that the case study highlights the importance of ChatGPT, being boon or bane depends on the researcher/user who is using this AI model. If used with caution and proper verification, while understanding the limitation of this conversational AI, then the tool ChatGPT is a boon, adding value to the research at hand. While on the other hand, if the same generative AI is used blindly without proper cross checks or reference checks, it can ultimately turn out to be bane. As ChatGPT is only accurate as per the case study conducted for this paper 45% percent of the time.

It is vital to know that ChatGPT can rectify the data and regenerate new texts, which is extremely helpful when there is writers block, when starting work on a new topic or when one needs information at a click of a button or even when one is struggling to write correctly on a particular topic. It takes feedbacks repeatedly after every response, thereby trying to provide assistance which are customized as per the requirement of the user and the information is personalized to the question that has been asked. Additionally, it is important to remember that the dissemination of information is prompt, i.e., within a few seconds of typing the questions which adds to the usefulness of this AI. However, as has been mentioned previously in this chapter, it is pertinent to remember that ChatGPT can offer guidance in different aspects of the research, including pointing out which methodologies to follow or which experimental method would be best suited. It cannot provide concrete 100 percent reliable information or true insights in research.

Through this chapter, we have tried to bring forth our thoughts on the use of ChatGPT and the caution that the researchers and practitioners need to keep in mind while using this generative AI model. The case study reiterates this point and provides an argument on what the AI model can do and what it cannot do so that alternative and corrective measures can be taken when used for extensive research work and not solely rely on it. Therefore, it is important for the researchers to understand and discuss the possible ways in which the scientific rigor and output can be increased. Some of the ways in which one can create new applications which addresses the current need gaps that exists are through multi-modal integration, contextual understanding, collaborative learning, biases detection, privacy protection, data security, transparency, consent and user awareness, cultural sensitivity and inclusivity, and dialog management.

References

Adeshola, I., & Adepoju, A. P. (2023). The opportunities and challenges of ChatGPT in education. *Interactive Learning Environments*, 1–14.

Baidoo-Anu, D., & Ansah, L. O. (2023). Education in the era of generative artificial intelligence (AI): Understanding the potential benefits of ChatGPT in promoting teaching and learning. *Journal of AIDS*, 7(1), 52–62.

Božić, V., & Poola, I. (2023). The role of artificial intelligence in increasing the digital literacy of healthcare workers and standardization of healthcare, (April), 1–13.

Dhingra, S., Singh, M., Vaisakh, S. B., Malviya, N., & Gill, S. S. (2023). Mind meets machine: Unravelling gpt-4's cognitive psychology. *BenchCouncil Transactions on Benchmarks, Standards and Evaluations*, 3(3), 100139.

Eysenbach, G. (2023). The role of ChatGPT, generative language models, and artificial intelligence in medical education: A conversation with ChatGPT and a call for papers. *JMIR Medical Education*, 9(1), e46885.

Fijačko, N., Gosak, L., Štiglic, G., Picard, C. T., & Douma, M. J. (2023). Can ChatGPT pass the life support exams without entering the American heart association course? *Resuscitation, 185*.

Flanagin, A., Bibbins-Domingo, K., Berkwits, M., & Christiansen, S. L. (2023). Nonhuman "authors" and implications for the integrity of scientific publication and medical knowledge. *JAMA*, 329(8), 637–639.

Fuchs, K. (2023, May). Exploring the opportunities and challenges of NLP models in higher education: Is chat GPT a blessing or a curse? *Frontiers in Education*, 8(1), 166682.

Geerling, W., Mateer, G. D., Wooten, J., & Damodaran, N. (2023). ChatGPT has aced the test of understanding in college economics: Now what? *The American Economist*, 68(2), 233–245.

Gill, S. S., Xu, M., Patros, P., Wu, H., Kaur, R., Kaur, K., & Buyya, R. (2024). Transformative effects of ChatGPT on modern education: Emerging era of AI chatbots. *Internet of Things and Cyber-Physical Systems*, 4, 19–23.

Gilson, A., Safranek, C. W., Huang, T., Socrates, V., Chi, L., Taylor, R. A., & Chartash, D. (2023). How does ChatGPT perform on the United States medical licensing examination (USMLE)? The implications of large language models for medical education and knowledge assessment. *JMIR Medical Education, 9*(1), e45312.

Goodman, R. S., Patrinely Jr, J. R., Osterman, T., Wheless, L., & Johnson, D. B. (2023). On the cusp: Considering the impact of artificial intelligence language models in healthcare. *Med, 4*(3), 139–140.

Han, Z., Battaglia, F., Udaiyar, A., Fooks, A., & Terlecky, S. R. (2023). An explorative assessment of ChatGPT as an aid in medical education: Use it with caution. *Medical Teacher*, 1–8.

Hosseini, M., Rasmussen, L. M., & Resnik, D. B. (2023). Using AI to write scholarly publications. *Accountability in Research*, 1–9.

Huallpa, J. J. (2023). Exploring the ethical considerations of using Chat GPT in university education. *Periodicals of Engineering and Natural Sciences, 11*(4), 105–115.

Javaid, M., Haleen, A., Singh, R. P., Khan, S., & Khan, I. H. (2023). Unlocking the opportunities through ChatGPT Tool towards ameliorating the education system. *Bench Council transactions on Benchmarks, Standards and Evaluations, 3*(2), 100115.

Lo, C. K. (2023). What is the impact of ChatGPT on education? A rapid review of the literature. *Education Sciences, 13*(4), 410.

Megahed, F. M., Chen, Y. J., Ferris, J. A., Knoth, S., & Jones-Farmer, L. A. (2024). How generative AI models such as ChatGPT can be (mis) used in SPC practice, education and research? An exploratory study. *Qualitative Engineering, 36*(2), 287–315.

Meyer, J. G., Urbanowicz, R. J., Martin, P. C., O'Connor, K., Li, R., Peng, P. C., & Moore, J. H. (2023). ChatGPT and large language models in academia: Opportunities and challenges. *BioData Mining, 16*(1), 20.

Osorio, J. A. C. (2023). Explorando el potential de ChatGPT en la escritura científica: ventajas, desafíos y precauciones. *Scientia et Technica, 28*(1), 3–5.

Qadir, J. (2023, May). Engineering education in the era of ChatGPT: Promise and pitfalls of generative AI for education. In *2023 IEEE global engineering education conference (EDUCON)* (pp. 1–9). IEEE.

Rice, S., Crouse, S. R., Winter, S. R., & Rice, C. (2024). The advantages and limitations of using ChatGPT to enhance technological research. *Technology in Society, 76*, 102426.

Roumeliotis, K. I., & Tselikas, N. D. (2023). Chatgpt and open-ai models: A preliminary review. *Future Internet, 15*(6), 192.

Rudolph, J., Tan, S., & Tan, S. (2023). ChatGPT: Bullshit spewer or the end of traditional assessments in higher education?. *Journal of Applied Learning and Teaching, 6*(1), 342–363.

Sallam, M. (2023). The utility of ChatGPT as an example of large language models in healthcare education, research and practice: Systematic review on the future perspectives and potential limitations. MedRxiv, 2023-02.

Shen, Y., Heacock, L., Elias, J., Hentel, K. D., Reig, B., Shih, G., & Moy, L. (2023). ChatGPT and other large language models are double-edged swords. *Radiology, 307*(2), e230163.

Steenbergen-Hu, S., & Cooper, H. (2014). A meta-analysis of the effectiveness of intelligent tutoring systems on college students' academic learning. *Journal of Educational Psychology, 106*(2), 331.

Stokel-Walker, C. (2023). ChatGPT listed as author on research papers: Many scientists disapprove. *Nature, 613*(7945), 620–621.

Thorp, H. H. (2023). ChatGPT is fun, but not an author. *Science, 379*(6630), 313.

Wu, T., He, S., Liu, J., Sun, S., Liu, K., Han, Q. L., & Tang, Y. (2023). A brief overview of ChatGPT: The history, status quo and potential future development. *IEEE/CAA Journal of Automatica Sinica, 10*(5), 1122–1136.

Appendix

Table A1: Data Searched on ChatGPT for the Mini Case Study.

S.No	Title in ChatGPT	Author/s in ChatGPT	Year in ChatGPT	Journal on Google Scholar	Type on Google Scholar	Discrepancies
1.	The Role of the Father in Child Development (fifth ed.).	Lamb, M. E.	2010	NA	Book	The year mentioned on Google Scholar is 2004
2.	Socialization in the family: Ethnic and ecological perspectives	Parke, R. D., & Suriel, R.	2008	Child and adolescent Development	Original article	The year mentioned on Google Scholar is 2006
3.	Paternal Involvement and Children's Behavior Problems	Amato, P. R., & Rivera, F.	1999	Journal of Marriage and the Family, 19 99 JST OR	Original article	No discrepancy
4.	Paternal Involvement: Revised Conceptualization n and Theoretical Linkages with Child Outcomes	Pleck, J. H.	2010	NA	Book	No discrepancy
5.	The Role of Parenting Styles in Children's Problem Behavior	Aunola, K., & Nurmi, J. E.	2005	Child development, 2005 Wiley Online library	Original article	No discrepancy

(*Continued*)

Table A1: *(Continued)*

S.No	Title in ChatGPT	Author/s in ChatGPT	Year in ChatGPT	Journal on Google Scholar	Type on Google Scholar	Discrepancies
6.	Personality Development in Adolescence: Cross-National and Lifespan Perspective	Branje, S. J., van Aken, M. A., van Lieshout, C. F., & Mathijssen, J. J.	2002	—		The article was not found on Google Scholar
7.	The Role of Parental Control in Children's Development in Western and Non-Western Cultures	Lamb, M. E., & Lewis, C.	2010	—	—	The article was not found on Google Scholar
8.	Bidirectional relations between authoritative parenting and adolescents' prosocial behaviors	Padilla Walker, L. M., Carlo, G., Christensen, K. J., &Yorgason, J, B.	2012	Journal of research on adolescence	Original article	No discrepancy
9.	Adolescents' prosocial behavior in the family context: A longitudinal study	Streit, C., Carlo, G., & lspa, J. M.	2017	—	—	The article was not found on Google Scholar
10.	Adolescent development in interpersonal and societal context	Smetana, J, G., Campion e-Barr, N., & Metzger, A.	2006	Annual Review Psychology, 2006	Original article	No discrepancy

#	Title	Authors	Year	Journal	Type	Notes
11.	The relationship between perceived parental rearing styles and prosocial tendencies among Japanese adolescents	Hosokawa, R., & Katsura, T.	2017	—	—	The article was not found on Google Scholar
12.	Establishing helicopter parenting as a distinct construct from other forms of parental control during emerging adulthood	Padilla Walker, L. M., & Nelson, L. J.	2012	Journal of adolescence, 2012 - Elsevier	Original article	No discrepancy
13.	Value transmission in the family: Do adolescents accept the values their	Sarni,0.,Ranieri, S., Scabini, E., & Rosnati, R.	2011	Journal of Moral Education	Original article	No discrepancy
14.	A latent Growth curve Analysis of prosocial behavior among rural Adolescents parents want to transom it?	Carlo, G., Crockett, L. J., Randall, B. A., & Roesch, S. C.	2007	Journal of Research on Adolescence	Original article	No discrepancy
15.	Father Involvement and Adolescent Well Being	Flouri and Buchanan	2003	—	—	The article was not found on Google Scholar
16.	Parenting Styles and Adolescent Behavior	Maccoby and Martin	1983	—	—	The article was not found on Google Scholar

(Continued)

Table A1: (*Continued*)

S.No	Title in ChatGPT	Author/s in ChatGPT	Year in ChatGPT	Journal on Google Scholar	Type on Google Scholar	Discrepancies
17.	Fathering and Adolescent Delinquency	Barnes, Hoffman, Welte, Farrell, and Dintcheff	2006	—	—	The article was not found on Google Scholar
18.	Attachment Theory and Father-Child Relationships	Lamb	1977	—	—	The article was not found on Google Scholar
19.	The Contributions of Mothers and Fathers to the Intergenerational Transmission of Cigarette Smoking in Adolescence	Denise B. Kandel, Ping Wu	1995	Risks and Problem Behaviors in Adolescence ce	Original article	No discrepancy
20.	Gender differences in parent child relations	McHale, Crouter, and Whiteman	2003	Journal of Family issues	Original article	• The author mentioned on Google Scholar is ME Starrels • The year mentioned on Google Scholar is 1994

Part II

The Promise of ChatGPT in Scientific Research

Chapter 3

Transformation in Human–Computer Interaction: The AI-Enabled NLP

Himanshu Sharma, Anubha Anubha and Daviender Narang

Jaipuria Institute of Management, Ghaziabad, India

Abstract

Advancements in data analytics techniques and the processing power of computers have resulted in the invention of artificial intelligence–based machines. Such machines can mimic the capabilities of the human mind and simplify complex decision making for organizations. The major purpose of artificial intelligence systems is to solve complex problems using human logic and reasoning. One such revolutionary field of AI that can comprehend, interpret, and interact with human language is Natural Language Processing (NLP). Over the years, NLP has advanced a lot from analyzing online textual reviews to breakthroughs in deep learning and transformer-based models. Therefore, this chapter aims to provide a theoretical discussion on the key advancements in NLP and discuss what the future holds for this dynamic and rapidly evolving field. Moreover, these advancements have not only altered the human–machine interaction but have also created new opportunities in a variety of industries like customer service, healthcare, finance, and education. Transfer learning has been instrumental in NLP advancements. Pre-trained models, such as BERT and GPT-3 (Generative Pre-trained Transformer), can be fine-tuned for specific tasks that require less data and training time. AI tools like ChatGPT can assist human authors in improving their writing and ensuring that their manuscripts are as accurate, well-structured, and supported by all available evidence as possible. Additionally, this chapter attempts to look into the possibilities, threats, limitations, and ethical concerns surrounding ChatGPT in scientific research.

Keywords: Artificial intelligence; natural language processing; generative pre-trained transformer; ChatGPT; scientific research; ethics

The ChatGPT Revolution, 39–56

Copyright © 2025 Himanshu Sharma, Anubha Anubha and Daviender Narang

Published under exclusive licence by Emerald Publishing Limited

doi:10.1108/978-1-83549-852-120251003

1. Introduction

Artificial intelligence (AI) is believed to be one of today's most significant developments that have gradually permeated every aspect of our lives. Machine learning along with its implications is continuously changing working aspects and helps in implementing AI software with minimal human interference (Messeri & Crockett, 2024). This is an alarming situation for people who are skeptical about AI-based technologies interfering with human jobs. In the last few years, AI has made noteworthy evolvements in fields like vision, speech recognition, understanding natural language processing (NLP), image and video generation, multi-agent systems, planning, decision-making, and integration of vision and motor control for robotics (Fanni et al., 2023; Khurana et al., 2023). Furthermore, innovative applications have emerged in interdisciplinary areas like online gaming, medical issue identification, traveling systems, driverless driving, and language translation (Garcia et al., 2024; Kasula, 2024).

AI is being used a lot by people to diktat their phones, for shopping payments, to suggest news and entertainment, beautify backgrounds during virtual calls, and do a variety of other things (Hallur et al., 2021; Holzinger et al., 2019; Nader et al., 2022). One of the most visible advancements that come under the umbrella of machine learning is GANs (generative adversarial networks) along with Reinforcement Learning (Dong et al., 2021). GANs allow deep networks to generate artificial content such as fake images that look real (Gui et al., 2021). GANs are an amalgamation of two components namely generator and discriminator. A generator helps in producing realistic content, whereas the generator's output can be distinguished from naturally occurring content through a discriminator.

In a brief period, the fundamental building blocks of technology especially AI have shown unparalleled improvement which is beyond expectations. Nowadays, programmers have started using GitHub's Copilot, an AI tool that converts textual prompts into coding, to speed up programming. Recently, to generate automatic text, writers have started using GPT-3 or other autoregressive language models through deep learning models (Wermelinger, 2023). Earlier, AI programs were in their infancy stage, but are now widely used for writing and coding. Moreover, complicated real-life problems can be solved through deep learning techniques. However, tech-savvy people know of AI-based technologies but the general public is still unacquainted with its complete utilization (Saxena & Cao, 2021).

Organization of this chapter: Section 2 covers the AI-related recent advancements in healthcare, brewery, cybersecurity, caregiving, and image processing. Section 3 explores the applications of NLP, a branch of AI, like spam detection, translations, chatbots, text summarization, sentiment analysis, and customer support systems. In the next section (Section 4), we discuss ChatGPT and its various applications in healthcare, customer relationship management, cybersecurity, and software development. Section 5 further investigates the use of ChatGPT in academic research. Along with this, the ethical dilemmas faced by research organizations have also been discussed in the same section. The limitations related to AI-based technologies are mentioned in Section 6. Section 7 suggests the way forward for AI-enabled technologies. Finally, concluding remarks are provided in Section 8.

2. Recent Advancements in AI: Pushing the Boundaries of Innovation

As AI develops exponentially, it transforms the business world. Businesses can achieve long-term strategic advantage by using AI-based technologies. These technologies can help in the automation of repetitive tasks which can resolve many corporate issues (Nader et al., 2022). AI-based technologies are beneficial for all functions like marketing, sales, finance, operations, and human resources, which include providing financial advice, forecasting and evaluating loan risks, and analyzing customer data (Goodell et al., 2021).

2.1 AI Robots Learning Through Observation: Watch, Learn, and Do

AI learns primarily through human training in which the bot self-learns the procedure by meting out data. For instance, if a bot notices your regular travel location and timing, then it will provide you with probable driving time under real-time traffic and weather conditions (Artem et al., 2019).

2.2 AI Robot Caregivers: The Future of Compassionate Care

Many countries around the world are facing a shortage of caregivers for their aging populations. The shortage is expected to worsen as the large baby boomer generation approaches retirement age. Artificial intelligence is being developed to fill this gap (Amin et al., 2024). For example, the Japanese government has realized that the country will face a shortage of more than three lakh caregivers by 2025 and hence it has started working toward replacing AI-based technology with human caregivers. This technology will help in conducting basic nursing operations like assisting patients in washrooms.

2.3 AI Beer Brewers: Pouring Innovation Into Every Pint

The AI-enabled brewing process relies on an algorithm similar to the Facebook Messenger bot. The bot collects customer feedback and forwards it to the humans who make the beer (Bravin et al., 2021, June). The technology allows brewers to receive quick feedback. The company labels bottles with QR codes that direct customers to interact with the bot. Later, an algorithm answers the series of questions enquired. Feedback is collected to identify trends and inform the brewing process. Of course, even with the advent of AI, beer companies must still manage the rest of their operations effectively.

2.4 AI in Cybersecurity: Guardians of the Digital Realm

Since its inception, cybersecurity has been a hot topic. Threats to sensitive information and networks evolve in tandem with technology. The demand for AI-supported cybersecurity solutions is witnessing a boom in recent times. Professionals believe that this will expedite the volume of incident detection, identify and communicate risk, and help maintain optimal situational awareness (Ansari et al., 2022). Magnifier, an AI solution for behavioral analytics, was recently introduced to improve risk detection. It uses structured and unstructured machine learning approaches for developing network behavior. Alphabet launched Chronicle, a cybersecurity intelligence software that enables fast examination and detection functions. The idea is that security teams already have the required information in their systems which get lost amidst millions of data hubs. The advanced search capabilities are driving faster search results.

2.5 AI in Diagnostics: Revolutionizing Accuracy in Healthcare

AI has the potential to revolutionize medical technology. In the past, diagnostics depended on human's ability to read and interpret imaging results. This naturally causes a lag in processing and leaves room for human error (Dias & Torkamani, 2019). The AI technology must be trained to correctly interpret results under human supervision and identify rare pathologies as it is difficult to teach due to a lack of images. For instance, AlphaFold, an AI system derived from AlphaGo, helps in predicting 3-D protein structures using a deep neural network (Koombea, 2024). This AI-based system has made significant progress in what scientists refer to as the "protein-folding problem," by predicting the structure of millions of proteins, nearly all of which are currently known to exist. AlphaFold's competencies have revolutionized medical sciences to create a vast number of drugs and vaccines.

2.6 AI in Image Processing: Transforming Pixels into Insight

This technology has applications ranging from video-conference backgrounds to photo-realistic images known as deepfakes. Deep learning helps in the recognition, classification, and conversion of image data. This has significantly reduced the processing time required to train the data (Syeda et al., 2021). ImageNet-based programs utilize over 14 million photographs for training and testing visual identification programs that can complete tasks a 100 times faster than traditional ones.

YOLO (You Only Look Once), which detects perilous objects in an image, is extensively used for crowd surveillance and for mobile robots like self-driving cars (Koombea, 2024). The last five years have also witnessed a change in face-recognition technology wherein some smartphones or corporate buildings now bank on it for access. Facial recognition technology is widely used in Chinese society, from security to payment, despite recent moves to limit its widespread adoption. Besides being a valuable tool for enhancing efficiency and safety, this technology also raises concerns about unfairness and privacy.

GANs can effectively generate photorealistic images and videos (Shahzad et al., 2022). With the help of deep learning, such systems can replace existing images with new ones, like adding people to a video they were not a part of. Even though such changes were possible in the past by skilled artists, the extent of changes has been diluted through AI automation. These deepfakes require prompt research as this technology encourages illegal activities like creating artificial sexual content featuring a specific victim or identity theft in which a profile of a non-existent person is generated and used to gain access to services.

In the next section, we discuss the AI-enabled application, i.e., natural language processing (NLP). A branch of AI, NLP is used in applications and devices to translate text and respond to commands, whether typed or spoken. NLP is a very positive aspect of automated applications and has become one of the most popular methods of implementing machine learning models.

3. Natural Language Processing – A Branch of AI

Natural language processing (NLP) combines computational linguistics, statistics, and machine learning models that permit systems to identify, comprehend, and generate text/speech (Kang et al., 2020). Over the years, language processing technology has advanced ominously, ensuing system design development through multifaceted and context-sensitive data. These advancements have been aided by growing data resources and computing power. NLP can authenticate users through voice recognition, summarize large amounts of text, assess sentiment, and generate required text in real time (Christodoulou & Gregoriades, 2023). In recent times, NLP has provided various technical assistance like GPS systems, speech-to-text transcription, service-providing Chatbots, etc. Still, NLP is being used in organizations to automate business operations, increase employee output, and streamline business processes (Gregoriades & Pampaka, 2020; Nawaz et al., 2021).

A significant shift in NLP research over the last decade has resulted in extensive applications utilizing machine learning and data mining approaches. Because of the volume of work that must be completed within a few days, the need for automation is never-ending (Kang et al., 2020). Being full of complexities, it is difficult to develop software that comprehends the projected meaning of the sentences or voices (Christodoulou & Gregoriades, 2023). A successful application can identify and understand the various types of irregularities like homonyms, irony, expressions, symbols, and grammar in sentences.

In recent times, NLP systems have improved as deep learning techniques are advancing. Deep learning techniques like Convolutional Neural Networks (CNNs) and Recurrent Neural Networks (RNNs) are being used for performing sentiment analysis and machine translations, resulting in cutting-edge results. Some applications of NLP are discussed below and presented diagrammatically in Fig. 3.1.

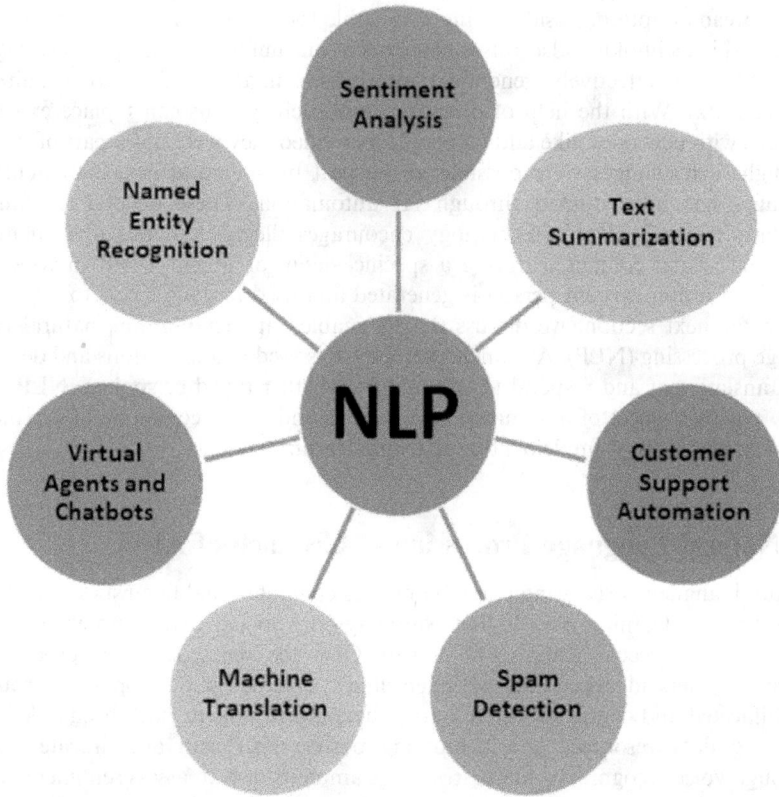

Fig. 3.1.   Applications of NLP. *Source:* Compiled by Authors.

3.1 Applications of NLP

3.1.1 Spam Detection: Filtering Out the Noise With Smart AI

Spam detection may not replicate an NLP solution but the best spam detection technologies are using NLP-based text classification to filter out emails that indicate spam or phishing (Ismail et al., 2022). Some particular indicators are excessive use of financial terms, poor grammar, intimidating language, incorrect resolution, misspelled organization names, etc.

3.1.2 Machine Translation: Bridging Languages With AI Fluency

Google Translate exemplifies such an NLP technology. A true machine translation does not involve just replacing a word in one language with another but it also covers the meaning and tone of the text to conserve its meaning and expected impact on the outputs (Khan et al., 2020). These translation tools are enhancing their accuracy which can be tested by converting a text into some language and then again translating it into the original form.

3.1.3 Virtual Agents and Chatbots: Your 24/7 AI Assistants

Speech recognition and natural language generation are used by virtual agents like Apple's Siri and Amazon's Alexa to detect the patterns in voice commands and act accordingly. Chatbots replicate the same for text entries that are typed into the system (Ayanouz et al., 2020). Over the years, these Chatbots have improved by continuously learning to identify and appropriately respond to human queries (Lalwani et al., 2018). The next innovation for these applications is question answering, which allows responding to questions with helpful answers, in their own words.

3.1.4 Sentiment Analysis: Decoding Emotions

Organizations can unravel key insights from social media channels through language processing systems. This can be achieved with the help of sentiment analysis that can inspect reviews and posts on social media platforms to extract valuable attitudes and feelings in response to products or promotions which can suggest remedy points in designing products or advertising campaigns (Khan et al., 2016).

3.1.5 Text Summarization: Distilling Content With Clarity

NLP techniques help in summarizing large text into synopses for researchers and readers who do not have enough time to comprehend large texts (Adhikari, 2020). To get the best output, these summarization applications make use of semantic reasoning and NLP to provide useful insights and summaries, and provide thoughtful conclusions. The most obvious and useful distinction is between extractive and abstractive text summarization methods (Merchant & Pande, 2018). Extractive methods aim to extract the most relevant information from a text. Instead, abstractive methods aim to produce a new body of text that accurately summarizes the original text. Despite their relative complexity, abstractive methods produce much more flexible and possibly faithful summaries, especially in the age of large language models.

3.1.6 Customer Support Automation: Elevating Service With AI Efficiency

AI-based models can help in resolving queries of customers and decrease response time. Such systems can enable 24/7 assistance to customers which might not be possible under human-based architectures (Al Shidhani et al., 2021). Some of the CRM (customer relationship management) applications like Salesforce can help in extracting the historical information of customers and responding accordingly.

AI models can also help in decreasing labor costs which regularly occur in the training and development of support agents.

3.1.7 Named Entity Recognition: Spotting Key Insights With AI

NLP models can help in identifying and classifying entities based on their demographics and functionalities. From the training data, these models extract words or sequences of words and depict the underlying entity (Nasar et al., 2021). For example, such models can evaluate the feedback provided by customers and can suggest any particular location or product/service that needs to be looked upon by the management. Another application is the usage of recommender strategy by platforms like Netflix or Hotstar, which can enhance customer experience by proposing the next watches based on their history.

4. ChatGPT: An Application of NLP

ChatGPT is an NLP-based model that can generate text that is similar to human responses to any user query. Generative Pre-trained Transformer (GPT) helps in training ChatGPT models on a big dataset so that the learning can be effectively processed through the internet. After being properly trained on a big dataset, such models have the capability of performing tasks like language translation, question-answering, and text handling (Wu et al., 2023). Moreover, the dialog system is capable of functioning as a conversational AI tool in Chatbots or similar types of applications.

Being dependent on transformer neural network architecture, ChatGPT has been trained on diversified datasets extracted from websites, books, and articles. Such training helps in modeling textual patterns and structures, which in turn aids in predicting future words based on the earlier ones (Biswas, 2023). These tasks are dependent on the prompts or contexts provided by the user. Generally, these are iterative processes that are repeated until the required sentences or words are received by the users. The unique feature of ChatGPT is that its working is based on an attention mechanism wherein the algorithm emphasizes a specific aspect of the text and finally results in precise and coherent responses (Bhattacharjee & Liu, 2024). As a general practice, while operating like a conversational AI tool, ChatGPT is trained on smaller conversational data.

Like InstructGPT, reinforcement machine learning is applied to the feedback dataset for proper training. However, the data collection procedure for ChatGPT is different. The difference is that this data requires some adjustments as during conversations human trainers play the role of user as well as AI assistant (Wu et al., 2023). Reinforcement models require a comparative dataset that can be accessed through conversations between AI trainers and Chatbots. The model chooses a random message generated by its AI trainers ranked such completed messages based on information quality.

4.1 Applications of ChatGPT

4.1.1 Cybersecurity: AI-Powered Shields for a Safer Digital World

The ability to detect and prevent cyber-attacks has popularized ChatGPT in the cyber-security domain. Being a language model enables ChatGPT to utilize textual information in detecting phishing emails and henceforth classifying emails as spam or not (Al-Hawawreh et al., 2023). In the same manner, it can detect malicious codes by filtering out information from textual content. However, through ChatGPT, users can create a secured and protected password automatically.

4.1.2 Customer Support Systems: AI-Enhanced Help, Anytime, Anywhere

Customization is a key for businesses dealing in services which can be easily achieved with the help of ChatGPT. These models can create simulated agents that can potentially provide customized support and advice to customers (Lakhani, 2023). That means such models can be programmed to comprehend and successfully address customer concerns. Also, automated systems can be created through ChatGPT which can expedite the identification process of user requirements and in turn provide quick services.

4.1.3 Healthcare: Empowering Care With AI Insight and Support

Doctors and other medical professionals can utilize ChatGPT to improve health conditions. This can be achieved by providing personalized medical support and guidance to medical professionals through automation. These models can also learn the patient's medical history and prescribe a diagnosis based on it (Javaid et al., 2023). Since Chatbots run on the model of one-to-one interaction, the medical sector can benefit by a thorough interaction with the patients and also encrypting their provided information. Furthermore, online platforms can be developed that can provide improved patient outcomes.

4.1.4 Software Development: Innovating Code With Precision

Software engineers can develop software that can incorporate NLP capabilities resulting in interactive and user-friendly applications. Through ChatGPT, developers have found ways to craft refined Chatbots that can more nicely comprehend and respond to user queries in a human-based fashion (Beganovic et al., 2023). Moreover, machine learning and AI-based technologies have made it simple for engineers to build applications encountering new recurring challenges in real-time. Thus, ChatGPT has re-engineered software development processes, making them more manageable, appealing, and operative.

5. ChatGPT for Scientific Research: Accelerating Discoveries in Academic Research

Journal editors can easily perform repetitive or cumbersome tasks like proof-reading through ChatGPT (Hosseini & Horbach, 2023). This reduces biasedness as biased training leads to irrelevant issues being focused by the systems. However, the role of editors as a human interface is still required for making clear decisions. On the contrary, a lack of motivation and domain knowledge can provide misleading results to the peer reviewers. This can be resolved through ChatGPT which can provide solutions specific to article contents. A cognitive community in research can be achieved through a collaborative review process that combines inputs from peer reviewers, editors, and other contributors (Woods et al., 2023). Such a community is beneficial for academicians, researchers, and society.

The diffusion of new ideas through metadata, indexing, and executive summaries can be achieved by capitalizing on the advantages of ChatGPT (Lund & Wang, 2023). Considering trust and usability among researchers, these systems efficiently convert research-based language to a language that everyone can comprehend (Wang et al., 2022). ChatGPT can also play the role of recommender system which can suggest research studies based on user queries. These applications can be especially helpful in case the research has been conducted across interdisciplinary domains that require multiple indices.

The ethical use of ChatGPT can be really helpful for researchers in setting the manuscript as per journal guidelines or providing findings/implications of their study. Though, this saves their time and cost still the touch of human knowledge cannot be replaced. Unethical usage of ChatGPT includes producing plagiarized text or unoriginal ideas instead of working on communication clarity and comprehensibility (Gilat & Cole, 2023). For example, "an author would enter paragraphs they had already written and then instruct ChatGPT to revise to improve clarity." Moreover, ChatGPT can be used to improve the quality of the English language by removing grammatical and typological errors from the manuscript so that it can be considered in high-indexed journals.

5.1 Ethical Issues With Using ChatGPT in Scientific Research

If we talk ethically, it should be believed that the manuscripts generated through ChatGPT are duplicate text and unworthy of publication. This is because these models are trained on large datasets which are already available and so in research, it may produce asymmetric results in terms of gender, race, ethnicity, and disability status (Hosseini & Horbach, 2023; Lund & Wang, 2023). This bias can be inadvertently prolonged, resulting in the spreading of hidden and unsuspecting chauvinism. For a long, researchers have depended on verifiable evidence and systematic data to achieve accurate and unbiased results. However, the interference of AI-generated tools in the research community has led to high volumes of publications in a short period which possesses biasedness/errors and hurt the scientific integrity. This has the potential to exacerbate imbalances in the findings and demoralize the grounds of scientific knowledge.

Some of the ethical issues that can be encountered while using ChatGPT for scientific research are provided below:

- When we talk about research, ownership or authorship becomes a vital component. If an author collects data and runs a model on it, then he/she owns that data as well as the generated output. This issue arises in AI-generated content where the knowledge provider is a machine and there is no true ownership of the generated content (Schönberger, 2018). In case the content is developed without user intervention or very limited user contribution (for example, "write an essay on this topic") then identifying the true authors of the content becomes difficult (Yanisky-Ravid, 2017).
- Copyright is a major issue that occurs whenever third-party content is included in the manuscript (Baeza-Yates, 2022). Sometimes, the manuscript consists of quotes, data, or other contents from external sources and it becomes necessary for the researcher to obey copyright laws and perform proper citations. However, permissions can be obtained from the owner regarding the usage of a particular content, but it depends on the purpose. With ChatGPT, it is highly difficult to judge the training and testing data sets and this can result in a mismatch of outputs (Dehouche, 2021). Most of the language models are trained on the information accessed from Wikipedia and similar open-access sources and in such cases it is still easy to identify the source. However, ChatGPT is trained on a huge amount of internet-based information, and tracking the source in such cases is cumbersome. However, in a few cases, models may be accountable for breaching copyright but the researcher may face the consequences.
- Copyright issues nurture plagiarism problems and it has been a debatable question on whether the usage of ChatGPT for writing manuscripts is ethical or not (Anderson et al., 2023). Apart from copying text, plagiarism includes paraphrasing text, using graphs/figures without permission, and replicating ideas of other people (Gasparyan et al., 2017). The texts produced by ChatGPT involve published literature and do not follow in-text citations, which is a requirement for research papers. However, if it starts citing the original authors of the text, plagiarism can be avoided (Dehouche, 2021).
- The essence of academic research also requires correct and comprehensive citations. In case editors or authors face any confusion related to the validation and authenticity of provided results or statements, citations come to the rescue (Kindenberg, 2024). Citations are a reflection of the level or type of work conducted by a researcher and thus are used to judge their academic advancements and tenures. Since ChatGPT is based on NLP technology, it can filter out text from manuscripts and suggest citations for unidentified materials (King, 2022). Therefore, such tools can streamline the citation process and remove referencing errors by researchers by placing the references in an

appropriate format. Furthermore, ChatGPT can help researchers in exploring new avenues and advancements in their domain.

- Even if ChatGPT is capable of providing in-text citations, it is perceived to be risky that authors may depend on automated tools instead of emphasizing the review of literature (King, 2023). Earlier versions of ChatGPT missed in-text citations and this showcased a question mark on the credibility and information quality of the produced articles. These language models knowingly or unknowingly pave the way for the Matthew Effect in academic research. As per this effect, "the tendency of successful researchers with high citation counts to remain successful and frequently cited, while lesser-known researchers struggle to gain recognition and citations" (Merton, 1968). This phenomenon is very common on Google Scholar which supports citation-based ranking systems wherein highly cited articles appear first in search results. Thus, scholars and researchers consider only the initial few pages during their search on Google Scholar as it is assumed that such pages cover only high-ranked studies, thus encouraging the Matthew Effect (Perc, 2014).

- The volume of published research papers, count of grants, and the number of citations define the hiring, promotion, and tenure of researchers. It has been observed that faculties on the tenure track are pressurized to publish abundant research articles in international journals and those who are incapable of meeting the targets are at the risk of losing their tenure (Miller & Struve, 2020). These traditions have popularized the ideology of "publish or perish" among academicians. Reputed journals and editors expect novel research based on well-defined theories and principles. Under this scenario, focusing more on the quantity of papers or the reputation of journals can choke the innovativeness of researchers (Bedeian, 2004). Moreover, focusing much on publications can widen the gap between academic research and practice which in turn will lead to researchers preferring peer acknowledgment over best practices (Miller et al., 2011).

6. Limitations

In general, AI-based technologies have been invented to make human life easier, but these technologies come without privacy filters. In comparison to data breaches, which were a common phenomenon a few years ago, AI-based technologies gather in-depth information from individuals voluntarily/involuntarily and its leak is more dangerous. A few issues faced are data persistence, data repurposing, and data leaks. Data persistence means ever-lasting data of people, available even after their death. Data repurposing means using data of individuals for purposes other than the intended ones. Data leak refers to collecting information from people without their consent. These risks can hurt the privacy and security of consumers and impact the adoption intention toward such technologies.

The usage of a proximal policy optimization model and multiple iterations makes ChatGPT superior to its counterpart language models like BERT,

RoBERTa, and XLNet (Zhong et al., 2023). However, the implementation of ChatGPT comes up with a few limitations (Kocoń et al., 2023). Though ChatGPT has been trained on a big dataset, still such language models cannot produce text comparable to human beings. There may be a possibility that the training data is not clear and neither pre-processing. Since ChatGPT depends completely on the training dataset, wrong information may produce biased results. Models like ChatGPT emphasize only the contextual part of the data and thus can produce human-like data, ignoring the meaning. Thus, the final results can be unrelated or absurd in some situations. Usage of language models like ChatGPT welcomes a few legal and ethical implications for any organization like data privacy or consent and privacy.

ChatGPT is computationally costly and for its usage, a powerful infrastructure is required. Moreover, there is a need for computational resources for fine-tuning the model. ChatGPT is incapable of handling structured or tabular data. Therefore, if the business operations function on structured data, then some alternative application should be preferred. ChatGPT lacks out-of-the-box plugins and hence there is a requirement for a specialized technical team who can set up and handle APIs (Application Programming Interface) and customize their services according to users' needs. Since these models have been trained on used or old datasets, there is a lack of appropriate recent information. Moreover, it inflates the chances of customization of services by an organization as reinforcement learning is not able to capture recent advancements. Being an open-source application in itself is a challenge for enterprises.

7. Future Directions and Emerging Trends

Since its evolution, AI has been a sparkling force for major technological innovations. According to tech enthusiasts, AI has the potential to uncover many paths. India, being the most populated country in the world, faces criticism due to its poor medical infrastructure. The number of beds in the hospital and the count of patients per doctor pose a great threat to the Indian population. AI can come as a savior in emergencies. AI-based technology can help in diagnosing diseases based on the person's previous medical history or having access to fitness gadgets. Such disruptive technologies can also provide potential medications. The education sector in India also shows a good appetite for AI-based technologies. Soon most of the traditional teaching pedagogies will be outdated and it will become necessary for a country having a large proportion of youths to adopt disruptive technologies. The education system should be revolutionized to create manufacturers of machines rather than users of machines.

The future of AI is bright in handling the economic conditions of individuals and organizations. The introduction of robo-advisors, an AI-enabled financial advisor tool, can help investors in choosing their best portfolio. These tools can predict the future values of various market shares and funds, and help customers in making a knowledgeable decision. The adoption and advancement of AI-based technologies are also dependent on their ability to ensure national security. Robot military can assist the manual security systems and decrease fatalities. Mission efficiency can be enhanced by utilizing neural network–based machine learning models; however, misuse of such technologies can be equally dangerous.

The future of automation lies in self-driven cars or smart cars. Experts in the automotive sector forecast that four years down the line drivers will be expecting automatic control of car functionalities through wireless networks. One another important aspect that can arise due to AI-enabled technologies is the advancements in marketing and advertising campaigns. These technologies can explore the historical purchase behavior of customers and suggest attractive strategies for future purchases. This can also help in deciding timelines for new product launches, determining market feedback, and ensuring research.

8. Conclusion

Artificial intelligence has become the life of organizations operating in every economic sector and industry. It is believed that those organizations that do not advance their IT department by including AI-based technology will face a survival crisis. One of the shortcomings is that traditional companies find it difficult to change their technological infrastructure, whereas entrepreneurs or new ventures have an upper hand as they already have AI-equipped infrastructure. As an implication, managers should accommodate newer AI-based infrastructure in their organization to fight threats against new entrants.

Natural Language Processing (NLP) is an innovative field of AI that can comprehend, deduce, and interrelate with human language. NLP has grown over time ranging from analyzing online textual reviews to breakthroughs in deep learning and transformer-based models like GPT-3 (Generative Pre-trained Transformer). These advancements have not only changed human–machine interaction but they have also opened up new opportunities in various industries like customer service, healthcare, finance, and education. Transfer learning has contributed significantly to the advancement of NLP.

Also, advancements in NLP have resulted in the development of an interactive chatbot namely ChatGPT. Being a machine learning tool, ChatGPT can predict future words after studying prior language knowledge (Olsson & Engelbrektsson, 2022). ChatGPT has the potential to generate research articles for academic writing based on existing papers and the needs of researchers. This may reflect an absence of novelty in the research and a distinction from science (Kaltenbrunner et al., 2022). Though there has long been debate about the significance of publications and citations in academia, the introduction of ChatGPT may mark a watershed moment in such discussions.

Many suggestions can be provided to the research community to address the issues generated by the usage of ChatGPT. Publishers and editors can collaborate with IT firms or professionals to generate an application that can track the contents created through language models like ChatGPT. Since these models are based on a learning process, researchers and journal editors should focus on more innovative and creative models. This will rejuvenate the research community and also broaden its scope, resulting in a low volume of ChatGPT-based paper submissions to the journal. Another way to combat the ethical issues created through ChatGPT-based research is to re-engineer the criteria for job promotions and maintain the tenure track of professors. By emphasizing more on research quality rather than quantity, the academic community can help discourage the use of ChatGPT and encourage ethical practices in scholarly publishing.

References

Adhikari, S. (2020, March). NLP based machine learning approaches for text summarization. In *2020 4th international conference on computing methodologies and communication (ICCMC)* (pp. 535–538). IEEE.

Al Shidhani, A. S. S., Mahmood, S., & Hasan, R. (2021). Design and development of customer support system using automation. In *Proceedings of the 5th Middle East College Student Research Conference* (pp. 1–9). Journal of Student Research.

Al-Hawawreh, M., Aljuhani, A., & Jararweh, Y. (2023). Chatgpt for cybersecurity: Practical applications, challenges, and future directions. *Cluster Computing, 26*(6), 3421–3436.

Amin, M. S., Johnson, V. L., Prybutok, V., & Koh, C. E. (2024). An investigation into factors affecting the willingness to disclose personal health information when using AI-enabled caregiver robots. *Industrial Management & Data Systems, 124*(4), 1677–1699.

Anderson, A., Johnson, B., & Smith, C. (2023). The impact of ChatGPT on customer service interactions. *Journal of Artificial Intelligence Research, 45*(2), 123–135.

Ansari, M. F., Dash, B., Sharma, P., & Yathiraju, N. (2022). The impact and limitations of artificial intelligence in cybersecurity: A literature review. *International Journal of Advanced Research in Computer and Communication Engineering, 11*(9), 81–90.

Artem, V., Ateya, A. A., Muthanna, A., & Koucheryavy, A. (2019). Novel AI-based scheme for traffic detection and recognition in 5G based networks. In *Internet of Things, Smart Spaces, and Next Generation Networks and Systems: 19th International Conference, NEW2AN 2019, and 12th Conference, ruSMART 2019, St. Petersburg, Russia, August 26–28, 2019, Proceedings 19* (pp. 243–255). Springer International Publishing.

Ayanouz, S., Abdelhakim, B. A., & Benhmed, M. (2020, March). A smart chatbot architecture based NLP and machine learning for health care assistance. In *Proceedings of the 3rd international conference on networking, information systems & security* (pp. 1–6).

Baeza-Yates, R. (2022). Ethical challenges in AI language models. *AI Ethics Journal, 10*(1), 45–56.

Bedeian, A. G. (2004). Peer review and the social construction of knowledge in the management discipline. *Academy of Management Learning & Education, 3*(2), 198–216. https://doi.org/10.5465/amle.2004.13500521

Beganovic, J., Smith, L., & Nguyen, T. (2023). ChatGPT in educational settings: Opportunities and challenges. *Educational Technology Review, 32*(4), 78–89.

Bhattacharjee, A., & Liu, H. (2024). Fighting fire with fire: Can ChatGPT detect AI-generated text? *ACM SIGKDD Explorations Newsletter, 25*(2), 14–21.

Biswas, S. S. (2023). Role of chat gpt in public health. *Annals of Biomedical Engineering*, *51*(5), 868–869.

Bravin, M., Pfäffli, D., Kuhn, K., & Pouly, M. (2021, June). Towards crafting beer with artificial intelligence. In *2021 8th Swiss conference on data science (SDS)* (pp. 54–55). IEEE.

Christodoulou, E., & Gregoriades, A. (2023, July). Leveraging Natural Language Processing in persuasive marketing. In *Asian conference on intelligent information and database systems* (pp. 197–209). Springer Nature Singapore.

Dehouche, N. (2021). AI-generated research paper fabrication and plagiarism in the scientific community. *Patterns*, *2*(4), 1–4. https://doi.org/10.1016/j.patter.2021.100234

Dias, R., & Torkamani, A. (2019). Artificial intelligence in clinical and genomic diagnostics. *Genome Medicine*, *11*(1), 70.

Dong, S., Wang, P., & Abbas, K. (2021). A survey on deep learning and its applications. *Computer Science Review*, *40*, 100379.

Fanni, S. C., Febi, M., Aghakhanyan, G., & Neri, E. (2023). Natural language processing. In *Introduction to artificial intelligence* (pp. 87–99). Springer International Publishing.

Garcia, M. B., Arif, Y. M., Khlaif, Z. N., Zhu, M., de Almeida, R. P. P., de Almeida, R. S., & Masters, K. (2024). Effective integration of artificial intelligence in medical education: Practical tips and actionable insights. In *Transformative approaches to patient literacy and healthcare innovation* (pp. 1–19). IGI Global.

Gasparyan, A. Y., Nurmashev, B., Yessirkepov, M., Endovitskiy, D. A., & Kitas, G. D. (2017). Plagiarism in the context of education and evolving detection strategies. *Journal of Korean Medical Science*, *32*(8), 1220–1227. https://doi.org/10.3346/jkms.2017.32.8.1220

Gilat, I., & Cole, R. (2023). College students' use and perceptions of generative AI technologies: A survey study. *OSF Preprints*. https://doi.org/10.31219/osf.io/6tjpk

Goodell, J. W., Kumar, S., Lim, W. M., & Pattnaik, D. (2021). Artificial intelligence and machine learning in finance: Identifying foundations, themes, and research clusters from bibliometric analysis. *Journal of Behavioral and Experimental Finance*, *32*, 100577.

Gregoriades, A., & Pampaka, M. (2020). Electronic word of mouth analysis for new product positioning evaluation. *Electronic Commerce Research and Applications*, *42*, 100986.

Gui, J., Sun, Z., Wen, Y., Tao, D., & Ye, J. (2021). A review on generative adversarial networks: Algorithms, theory, and applications. *IEEE Transactions on Knowledge and Data Engineering*, *35*(4), 3313–3332.

Hallur, G. G., Prabhu, S., & Aslekar, A. (2021). Entertainment in era of AI, big data & IoT. In *Digital entertainment: The next evolution in service sector* (pp. 87–109).

Holzinger, A., Langs, G., Denk, H., Zatloukal, K., & Müller, H. (2019). Causability and explainability of artificial intelligence in medicine. *Wiley Interdisciplinary Reviews: Data Mining and Knowledge Discovery*, *9*(4), e1312.

Hosseini, M., & Horbach, A. (2023). Evaluating the authenticity of ChatGPT responses: A study on text generation and plagiarism detection. *International Journal for Educational Integrity*, *19*(1), 1–23. https://doi.org/10.1007/s40979-023-00137-0

Ismail, S. S., Mansour, R. F., Abd El-Aziz, R. M., & Taloba, A. I. (2022). Efficient E-mail spam detection strategy using genetic decision tree processing with NLP features. *Computational Intelligence and Neuroscience*, *2022*.

Javaid, M., Haleem, A., Singh, R. P., & Suman, R. (2023). Exploring the role of ChatGPT in healthcare education. *Journal of Medical Education and Curricular Development, 10*, 23–40.

Kaltenbrunner, W., Ben-David, S., & Borrell-Damián, L. (2022). The ethics of impact: Plagiarism detection in the age of AI. *Research Integrity and Peer Review, 7*(1), 1–10.

Kang, Y., Cai, Z., Tan, C. W., Huang, Q., & Liu, H. (2020). Natural language processing (NLP) in management research: A literature review. *Journal of Management Analytics, 7*(2), 139–172.

Kasula, B. Y. (2024). Ethical implications and future prospects of artificial intelligence in healthcare: A research synthesis. *International Meridian Journal, 6*(6), 1–7.

Khan, N. S., Abid, A., & Abid, K. (2020). A novel natural language processing (NLP)–Based machine translation model for English to Pakistan sign language translation. *Cognitive Computation, 12*, 748–765.

Khan, M. T., Durrani, M., Ali, A., Inayat, I., Khalid, S., & Khan, K. H. (2016). Sentiment analysis and the complex natural language. *Complex Adaptive Systems Modeling, 4*, 1–19.

Khurana, D., Koli, A., Khatter, K., & Singh, S. (2023). Natural language processing: State of the art, current trends and challenges. *Multimedia Tools and Applications, 82*(3), 3713–3744.

Kindenberg, B. (2024). ChatGPT-generated and student-written historical narratives: A comparative analysis. *Education Sciences, 14*(5), 1–19.

King, M. (2022). Artificial intelligence and the future of writing assessment. *Assessing Writing, 51*, 125–146. https://doi.org/10.1016/j.asw.2021.100593

King, M. (2023). ChatGPT: Implications for writing assessment in higher education. *Journal of Writing Assessment, 15*(1), 45–60.

Kocoń, J., Cichecki, I., Kaszyca, O., Kochanek, M., Szydło, D., Baran, J., Bielaniewicz, J., Gruza, M., Janz, A., Kanclerz, K., Kocoń, A., Koptyra, K., Mieleszczenko-Kowszewicz, W., Miłkowski, P., Oleksy, M., Piasecki, M., Radliński, L., Wojtasik, K., Woźniak, S., & Kazienko, P. (2023). ChatGPT: Jack of all trades, master of none. *Information Fusion, 99*, 101861.

Koombea. (2024). 7 Recent AI developments: Artificial intelligence news. https://www.koombea.com/blog/7-recent-ai-developments/. Accessed on March 20, 2024.

Lakhani, A. (2023). Enhancing customer service with ChatGPT transforming the way businesses interact with customers.

Lalwani, T., Bhalotia, S., Pal, A., Rathod, V., & Bisen, S. (2018). Implementation of a chatbot system using AI and NLP. *International Journal of Innovative Research in Computer Science & Technology (IJIRCST), 6*(3).

Lund, B. D., & Wang, T. (2023). ChatGPT in academia: Considerations for librarians. *College & Research Libraries News, 84*(1), 11–14.

Merchant, K., & Pande, Y. (2018, September). Nlp based latent semantic analysis for legal text summarization. In *2018 international conference on advances in computing, communications and informatics (ICACCI)* (pp. 1803–1807). IEEE.

Merton, R. K. (1968). The Matthew effect in science. *Science, 159*(3810), 56–63. https://doi.org/10.1126/science.159.3810.56

Messeri, L., & Crockett, M. J. (2024). Artificial intelligence and illusions of understanding in scientific research. *Nature, 627*(8002), 49–58.

Miller, A. I., Smith, B., & Jones, C. (2011). The role of artificial intelligence in scientific discovery. *AI Magazine, 32*(2), 79–90. https://doi.org/10.1609/aimag.v32i2.2345

Miller, T., & Struve, J. (2020). Ethical considerations in AI research: A comprehensive review. *Journal of Ethics in AI, 5*(3), 123–145.

Nader, K., Toprac, P., Scott, S., & Baker, S. (2022). *Public understanding of artificial intelligence through entertainment media* (pp. 1–14). AI & society.

Nasar, Z., Jaffry, S. W., & Malik, M. K. (2021). Named entity recognition and relation extraction: State-of-the-art. *ACM Computing Surveys, 54*(1), 1–39.

Nawaz, Z., Zhao, C., Nawaz, F., Safeer, A. A., & Irshad, W. (2021). Role of artificial neural networks techniques in development of market intelligence: A study of sentiment analysis of eWOM of a women's clothing company. *Journal of Theoretical and Applied Electronic Commerce Research, 16*(5), 1862–1876.

Olsson, M., & Engelbrektsson, P. (2022). User experience design in the age of AI: Challenges and opportunities. *Design Studies, 78*, 1–12.

Perc, M. (2014). The Matthew effect in empirical data. *Journal of the Royal Society Interface, 11*(98), 20–37. https://doi.org/10.1098/rsif.2014.0378

Saxena, D., & Cao, J. (2021). Generative adversarial networks (GANs) challenges, solutions, and future directions. *ACM Computing Surveys, 54*(3), 1–42.

Schönberger, D. (2018, January 9). Deep copyright: Up – And downstream questions related to artificial intelligence (AI) and machine learning (ML). In J. De Werra (Ed.), *Droit d'auteur 4.0/Copyright 4.0* (pp. 145–173). Schulthess Editions Romandes.

Shahzad, H. F., Rustam, F., Flores, E. S., Luis Vidal Mazon, J., de la Torre Diez, I., & Ashraf, I. (2022). A review of image processing techniques for deepfakes. *Sensors, 22*(12), 4556.

Syeda, I. H., Alam, M. M., Illahi, U., & Su'ud, M. M. (2021). Advance control strategies using image processing, UAV and AI in agriculture: A review. *World Journal of Engineering, 18*(4), 579–589.

Wang, X., Lin, X., & Shao, B. (2022). Artificial intelligence changes the way we work: A close look at innovating with chat bots. *Journal of the Association for Information Science and Technology, 74*(3), 339–353.

Wermelinger, M. (2023, March). Using github copilot to solve simple programming problems. In *Proceedings of the 54th ACM technical symposium on computer science education* (Vol. 1, pp. 172–178).

Woods, H. B., Brumberg, J., Kaltenbrunner, W., Pinfield, S., & Waltman, L. (2023). An overview of innovations in the external peer review of journal manuscripts. *Wellcome Open Research, 82*(7), 1–29.

Wu, T., He, S., Liu, J., Sun, S., Liu, K., Han, Q. L., & Tang, Y. (2023). A brief overview of ChatGPT: The history, status quo and potential future development. *IEEE/CAA Journal of Automatica Sinica, 10*(5), 1122–1136.

Yanisky-Ravid, S. (2017). Generating Rembrandt: Artificial intelligence, copyright, and accountability in the 3A era: The human-like authors are already here. *Michigan State Law Review, 659*, 659–756.

Zhong, Q., Ding, L., Liu, J., Du, B., & Tao, D. (2023). Can chatgpt understand too? A comparative study on chatgpt and fine-tuned bert. arXiv preprint arXiv:2302.10198.

Chapter 4

Business Fraud Detection, Prevention, and Investigations With Conversational AI

Hrishikesh Desai

Arkansas State University, USA

Abstract

As financial crimes evolve, traditional fraud detection systems struggle to keep pace. This chapter explores how the latest conversational AI technologies like ChatGPT or Claude can revolutionize fraud management. Leveraging natural language processing, these AI assistants can analyze data intelligently, identify red flags, provide regulatory context, and guide investigations. The seven case studies in this chapter illustrate conversational AI's applications across anti-money laundering (AML) processes – transaction monitoring, network analysis, alert suppression, sanction screening, know-your-customer (KYC), audits, and regulatory reporting. The AI assistants can detect complex patterns, visualize criminal networks, rationalize alerts, automate filings, and enable auditors to validate AI model fairness transparently. However, responsible implementation of conversational AI in fraud management requires addressing data quality, privacy, AI bias, and model explainability challenges. Techniques like data masking, SHAP/LIME, counterfactual explanations, and fairness metrics are proposed as potential solutions. Conversational AI empowers financial institutions with cognitive capabilities to outmaneuver fraudsters continuously. Yet ethical AI principles of accountability, transparency, and fairness must be upheld for successful adoption.

Keywords: Anti-money laundering; bias mitigation; ChatGPT; claude; conversational AI; data privacy; explainable AI; fraud detection

1. Introduction

As financial crimes and fraudulent activities continue to evolve in sophistication, traditional rule-based systems are proving insufficient in keeping pace with the

The ChatGPT Revolution, 57–86

Copyright © 2025 Hrishikesh Desai

Published under exclusive licence by Emerald Publishing Limited

doi:10.1108/978-1-83549-852-120251004

ever-changing tactics employed by bad actors (Association of Certified Fraud Examiners, 2023). Fortunately, advanced artificial intelligence (AI) and natural language processing (NLP) technologies have significantly improved cognitive computing, enabling more effective detection, prevention, and investigation of financial fraud. NLP is a branch of AI that helps computers understand, interpret, and generate human language. In this chapter, I discuss how conversational AI can be used for fraud detection, prevention, and investigations using seven case studies. I also explore how financial institutions and regulatory bodies can leverage the power of conversational AI solutions to bolster their anti-money laundering (AML) and fraud prevention efforts. AML includes measures designed to prevent the concealment of illegally obtained money.

Recent technological advancements in artificial intelligence have led to the development of large language models and conversational AI systems that hold significant potential in fraud management. Notable examples include ChatGPT and Codex (developed by OpenAI), Claude (developed by Anthropic), Copilot (developed by Microsoft and GitHub), and Gemini (developed by Google). These AI systems represent a substantial leap forward in natural language processing capabilities, enabling them to engage in human-like dialogs, understand complex queries, and provide detailed, context-aware responses. While it may be premature to label them as 'innovative' in the long-term sense, their current applications in fraud detection and prevention certainly represent novel approaches in the field.

This chapter is structured as follows: First, I provide an overview of how conversational AI can be applied to various aspects of AML compliance, including transaction monitoring, network analysis, alert suppression, sanction screening, and know-your-customer (KYC) processes. To illustrate the practical applications of conversational AI in fraud detection, prevention, and investigation, I present seven illustrative scenarios. These scenarios are not formal case studies but rather hypothetical situations designed to demonstrate how conversational AI can be applied in various aspects of fraud management.

The seven illustrative scenarios covered in this chapter are:

(1) *Transaction Monitoring*: Analyzing suspicious wire transfers using AI-assisted pattern recognition.
(2) *Network Analysis*: Mapping complex relationships between entities in potential money laundering schemes.
(3) *Alert Suppression*: Reducing false positives in transaction monitoring alerts.
(4) *Sanction Screening and KYC*: Enhancing customer due diligence processes with AI assistance.
(5) *System Audits and Healthchecks*: Using AI to improve the auditing of fraud prevention systems.
(6) *Regulatory Compliance*: Automating Suspicious Activity Report (SAR) filings.
(7) *Managing AI Challenges*: Addressing data quality, privacy, bias, and explainability issues in AI-powered fraud prevention systems.

Each scenario demonstrates how conversational AI can be leveraged to improve efficiency, accuracy, and effectiveness in different aspects of fraud management. While the scenarios presented are hypothetical, they are grounded in real-world challenges faced by financial institutions in fraud detection and prevention. The applications of conversational AI demonstrated in these scenarios reflect emerging trends in the field, but it's important to note that actual implementations may vary based on specific institutional needs, regulatory environments, and technological capabilities.

Following these scenarios, I discuss the challenges associated with implementing conversational AI in fraud prevention systems, including data quality and privacy concerns, bias mitigation, and the need for explainable AI. I conclude by addressing these challenges and offering insights into the future of AI-powered fraud management. Throughout this chapter, I emphasize the importance of responsible AI implementation and adherence to regulatory requirements.

2. Conversational AI for AML Compliance

AML compliance is a critical aspect of financial crime prevention, involving a range of activities such as transaction monitoring, network analysis, alert suppression, sanction screening, and know-your-customer (KYC) processes. KYC is a process by which businesses verify the identity of their clients and assess potential risks of illegal intentions. First, it's important to understand this jargon related to financial frauds.

Transaction monitoring refers to continuous tracking and analysis of financial transactions to identify any suspicious or unusual activity that could potentially be linked to money laundering or other financial crimes.

Network analysis involves mapping out the relationships and connections between various individuals or entities involved in financial transactions. This helps uncover hidden links, identify potential criminal networks, and trace the flow of funds across different parties, which can be crucial in detecting money laundering schemes.

Alert suppression is the process of intelligently filtering out any false alerts of fraud cases, reducing the noise and allowing investigators to focus on the truly suspicious cases. Due to the vast volume of transactions and the complexity of 'fraud detection' rules, transaction monitoring systems often generate a large number of alerts, many of which may be false positives (legitimate transactions flagged as suspicious).

Sanction Screening is the process of checking individuals, entities, and transactions against government-issued sanctions lists or watchlists to ensure that financial institutions do not inadvertently facilitate transactions with sanctioned parties. These lists contain names of individuals, organizations, and countries that are subject to economic or trade sanctions due to their involvement in activities such as terrorism, drug trafficking, or human rights violations.

Know Your Customer (KYC) refers to the due diligence processes that banks and financial institutions undertake to verify the identity, background, and risk profile of their customers. This includes gathering and verifying customer information, understanding the nature of their business, and assessing the potential risks associated with the customer relationship. Robust KYC procedures are crucial for detecting and preventing financial crimes, as they help institutions avoid dealing with high-risk or suspicious individuals or entities.

Traditionally, these tasks have been carried out using rule-based systems and manual interventions, which can be time-consuming, error-prone, and inefficient in dealing with the ever-increasing volume and complexity of financial data.

Conversational AI, powered by natural language processing capabilities, has revolutionized AML compliance by enabling intelligent and intuitive interactions with financial data and regulatory requirements. In this chapter, I present seven case studies covering various use cases on how ChatGPT and other conversational AI assistants can be used in the context of fraud detection, prevention and investigations. These case studies have been created by me based on some of the potential use cases of conversational AI in fraud suggested to me by H3M Analytics, Inc (2023) and Flagright (2024).[1]

2.1 Conversational AI and Transaction Monitoring

By engaging with ChatGPT or similar conversational AI assistants, compliance professionals can query and analyze vast amounts of data, identify potential red flags, and receive contextual insights and recommendations in real time. For instance, ChatGPT can be trained on AML regulations, typologies (here: common patterns, methods, or techniques used by criminals to launder money or finance illegal activities), and historical case studies, allowing it to provide relevant guidance and flag suspicious activities or patterns.

2.1.1 Illustrative Scenario 1: Analyzing Transactions

This hypothetical scenario demonstrates how conversational AI can enhance the process of analyzing suspicious wire transfers, particularly in the context of potential corporate embezzlement or money laundering.

---

[1]H3M Analytics, Inc. leverages AI in its KROTON compliance product suite, offering solutions for transaction monitoring, network analysis, alert suppression, sanction screening, KYC processes, and audits. Flagright's AI Forensics also represents a groundbreaking approach to anti-money laundering (AML) investigations, harnessing the power of conversational AI to enhance efficiency, accuracy, and speed in fraud detection processes. AI Forensics integrates seamlessly into Flagright's centralized platform, providing a user-friendly interface that supports natural language queries. This innovative feature also enables investigators to input questions or commands in plain language, significantly reducing the learning curve and allowing for more intuitive data exploration. As per Flagright, the core of AI Forensics lies in its ability to process and analyze vast amounts of data from diverse sources, including transaction records, customer profiles, and external databases (Flagright, 2024).

Suppose a financial institution has detected a series of wire transfers from a corporate account to multiple personal accounts in different countries, totaling $500,000 over a three-month period. This could potentially be a case of money laundering or illegal fund diversions.

In this scenario, ChatGPT and other conversational AI assistants could be trained on

(1) AML Regulations:

- Bank Secrecy Act (BSA) requirements for reporting suspicious transactions. BSA is a US law requiring financial institutions to assist government agencies in detecting and preventing money laundering.
- FATF (Financial Action Task Force) recommendations on money laundering typologies. FATF is an intergovernmental organization that develops policies to combat money laundering and terrorism financing.

(2) Typologies:

- Structuring/smurfing (breaking up large transactions into smaller ones to avoid reporting).
- Tax evasion through offshore accounts.
- Trade-based money laundering.
- Layering.

(3) Case Studies:

- Historical cases of corporate fraud/embezzlement.
- Money laundering schemes involving shell companies.

With this training, the AI system would be able to quickly analyze complex transaction patterns and compare them against specific, relevant typologies and regulations. Also, when an investigator inputs the details of the wire transfers, ChatGPT and other conversational AI assistants would be able to:

- Identify that the activity potentially matches the typology of fund diversion/embezzlement based on transfers from a corporate account to personal accounts across borders. For example, the AI system could flag these activities as instances of "layering" in the money laundering process, where funds are moved through multiple accounts to obscure their origin.
- Cite relevant AML regulations like the BSA requirement to file a Suspicious Activity Report (SAR) for such transactions. SARs are required to be filed with the Financial Crimes Enforcement Network (FinCEN), which is a bureau of the US Department of the Treasury that collects and analyzes information about financial transactions to combat financial crimes, when money laundering or fraud involving over $5,000 is suspected. SAR is a document that

financial institutions must file with the FinCEN following a suspected incident of money laundering or fraud.[2]

- Pull up similar historical cases, like the XYZ company embezzlement scandal, to provide context. For example, the AI system could reference a similar historical case, such as the "ABC Corp Embezzlement Case of 2019," where a Chief Financial Officer (CFO) diverted company funds to personal offshore accounts.
- Recommend further investigation steps like analyzing corporation's financials, checking personal account holders against watchlists, tracing origins of funds, etc.
- Provide risk scoring on the likelihood of the activity being suspicious based on patterns from the training data. For example, the AI system could provide a risk score of 8/10 for the likelihood of these activities being suspicious.

In this manner, conversational AI assistants can act as an intelligent guide, connecting different dots, providing legal/regulatory context, and aiding the human investigator in comprehensively analyzing the potentially suspicious activity. As a result, the investigation process can be significantly accelerated.

2.2 Conversational AI and Network Analysis

2.2.1 Illustrative Scenario 2: Network Mapping

This scenario demonstrates how conversational AI can assist in mapping and analyzing complex relationships between entities in potential money laundering schemes.

Suppose investigators are analyzing a set of suspicious transactions involving the transfer of large sums between Company A, Company B, and several individual accounts across multiple jurisdictions. On the surface, the transactions seem related to legitimate business dealings. However, conversational AI assistants like ChatGPT or Claude, after being fed this transaction data and trained on typologies, could start finding deeper connections:

- They could cross-reference the company names and individual account holders against sanctions lists, adverse media reports, and proprietary databases to flag if any entities have been previously linked to financial crimes.
- Through natural language processing of documentation like contracts, emails, and public records, they could map out the intricate corporate ownerships and relationships between Company A, Company B, and the individual account holders.
- By analyzing transaction patterns, frequencies, geographic regions involved, they could identify potential discrepancies. For example, a mismatch between the company's stated line of business and the transaction volumes/destinations.

---

[2]Failure to file a SAR can expose the institution to enforcement actions for lack of compliance with the BSA.

- They could then visualize and highlight potential networks and fund flows that seem suspicious based on their training. E.g., a complex web of shell companies transferring funds circularly with no apparent economic purpose.
- For transactions linked to specific high-risk jurisdictions, they could provide contextual information about prevalent terrorist financing methodologies used in those regions based on past case studies.

These conversational AI assistants could then present this comprehensive network mapping, highlighting potential choke points, risk scores, and specific typologies they have detected. This excellent synthesis of disparate data points into key risks and networks of interest can allow human investigators to then focus their efforts on unraveling the intricacies of the financial crime efficiently. The natural language interface allows fraud investigators two-way dialog to explore further angles as needed.

2.3 Conversational AI and Alert Suppression

As discussed earlier, false fraud alerts consume valuable time and resources, hindering the efficiency of fraud prevention efforts. Conversational AI can play a pivotal role in alert suppression by intelligently analyzing the context and risk factors associated with each alert. By engaging in a dialog with ChatGPT and other conversational AI assistants, investigators can provide additional context, clarify ambiguities, and receive tailored recommendations on whether an alert should be escalated or suppressed. Moreover, conversational AI assistants can aid in the investigation process by providing fraud investigators with relevant information, synthesizing data from multiple sources, and suggesting potential lines of inquiry based on the specifics of each case. This collaborative approach empowers investigators to make more informed decisions and to better prioritize high-risk cases.

2.3.1 Illustrative Scenario 3: Identifying False Positives

This scenario illustrates how conversational AI can help reduce false positives in transaction monitoring alerts, improving efficiency in fraud detection.

Suppose an automated transaction monitoring system at a bank flagged several cash deposits made into a personal account over a period of 6 months, totaling $50,000. This triggered an alert for potential structuring/smurfing activity used in money laundering. The investigator could initiate a dialog with the conversational AI like ChatGPT or Claude and provide additional context via a prompt such as:

> The account holder is a small business owner dealing in cash sales.
> The deposits seem to align with the seasonal revenue cycles based
> on the type of business. However, the deposits were made in
> amounts just under $10,000 to avoid CTR filings.

CTR (Currency Transaction Report) is a report that financial institutions must file for each deposit, withdrawal, exchange of currency, or other payment or transfer that involves a transaction in currency of more than $10,000. The conversational AI tools, based on their training on AML typologies, regulations like the Bank Secrecy Act CTR requirements, and understanding of business revenue patterns, could analyze the context. They may determine that:

- While the amounts appear structured, it fits the narrative of a cash-intensive legitimate business.
- As long as CTRs are filed for cash transactions over $10,000, no explicit regulation is being violated.
- Without stronger adverse information, this may be a false positive not worth pursuing further.

The conversational AI assistants could then recommend suppressing or re-scoring the alert as lower risk based on the evidence provided.

2.4 Conversational AI and KYC

As discussed earlier, it is important that financial institutions do not inadvertently facilitate transactions involving sanctioned entities or individuals with dubious backgrounds. Conversational AI can streamline these processes by intelligently parsing and cross-referencing customer information, transaction details, and sanctions lists. ChatGPT and other conversational AI tools can assist in identifying potential matches, flagging discrepancies, and providing recommendations for further action based on the risk profile of each customer or transaction. Further, they can aid in the Customer Due Diligence (CDD) process, which is a subset of KYC, by engaging in natural language dialogs with customers, gathering relevant information, and assessing risk factors in a more intuitive and user-friendly manner.

2.4.1 Illustrative Scenario 4: Sanction Screening and KYC/CDD

This scenario shows how conversational AI can streamline and improve the accuracy of sanction screening and Know Your Customer (KYC) processes.

Suppose a bank is onboarding a new corporate client "Desai Trading, Inc." and needs to perform thorough due diligence checks. The bank representative can initiate a dialog with ChatGPT or Claude, providing details like the company name, registered address, ownership information, etc. ChatGPT can then:

- Parse and segment the input data into searchable fields like name, address, and other identifiers.
- Cross-reference this data against updated sanctions lists from Office of Foreign Assets Control (OFAC), United Nations (UN), European Union (EU), Her Majesty's Treasury (HMT), and other relevant bodies. The OFAC is a

financial intelligence and enforcement agency of the US Treasury Department that administers and enforces economic and trade sanctions. The UN is an international organization founded in 1945 to maintain international peace and security. The EU is a political and economic union of 27 member states that are located primarily in Europe. The HMT is the United Kingdom's economics and finance ministry.

- Check for fuzzy matches (approximate string matching), aliases, former names/addresses using natural language processing.
- Flag any potential hits or close matches that require further investigation.

This allows comprehensive sanction screening in an intuitive conversational manner. After clearing sanctions, the bank can probe further via ChatGPT or Claude:

> Please walk me through gathering the required KYC information for Desai Trading, Inc. per our policies.

ChatGPT can engage in a dialog:

- Request details like business registration, financial statements, ownership structure.
- Based on the business sector, geography, ask tailored questions to assess risk factors such as "Do you deal in any high-risk goods like arms/minerals?"
- Clearly explain regulatory requirements and why certain information is needed.
- Allow uploading/sharing of documents and validating their authenticity leveraging Optical Character Recognition (OCR), blockchain verification, etc. OCR is the electronic or mechanical conversion of images of typed, handwritten or printed text into machine-encoded text.

Throughout this back-and-forth, conversational AI tools can provide guidance, explain regulations, flag potential risk indicators for further scrutiny based on their training. The conversational flow and natural language interactions make the KYC process smoother, minimizing back-and-forth, and building rapport with the client while still meeting compliance needs.

Now, in a related scenario about Customer Due Diligence (CDD), suppose the transaction monitoring system flagged outgoing wire transfers from Desai Trading, Inc. in high-risk jurisdictions. The investigator engages ChatGPT or Claude:

> The transfers seem to be recurring payments by an import/export company to suppliers in Panama and UAE for goods received. However, the transaction descriptions and amounts don't match up across the different wire transfers.

The conversational AI assistants could:

- Summarize relevant Financial Action Task Force (FATF) guidance and typologies related to trade-based money laundering using over/under-invoicing of goods.
- Locate any adverse media on the companies/jurisdictions from databases.
- Check if the counterparty entities were present on sanctions lists.
- Analyze the fund flow patterns for any red flags.
- Suggest further steps – review of shipping records, AP/AR documents, and onsite audits.

Thus, this collaborative dialog allows the AI tools to connect disparate dots, provide targeted information based on the specific case context, and empower the fraud investigator to either quickly resolve or build a comprehensive money laundering investigation successfully. The natural language interface also makes the AI's knowledge easily accessible and applicable, maximizing human-AI synergy.

2.5 Conversational AI and Auditing

By engaging with ChatGPT and other conversational AI tools, auditors can query the fraud prevention system's knowledge base, understand the rationale behind specific decisions or recommendations, and assess the robustness of the underlying models and data sources. This level of transparency is crucial in building trust and ensuring regulatory compliance. They can also assist in conducting healthchecks by analyzing system logs, identifying potential anomalies or performance issues, and providing recommendations for system optimization and maintenance.

2.5.1 Illustrative Scenario 5: System Audits and Healthchecks

This scenario demonstrates how conversational AI can enhance the auditing and maintenance of fraud prevention systems.

Suppose a regulatory auditor is reviewing the transaction monitoring system at a bank to ensure it is effectively identifying potential money laundering risks and meeting compliance requirements. Conversational AI assistants like ChatGPT or Claude could be directly integrated with a fraud prevention system via APIs.[3] This allows the conversational AI tools to ingest and parse relevant data like: system logs/

---

[3]If direct system integration is not feasible, the conversational AI could be pre-trained on extensive documentation about the fraud prevention system. This could include technical documentation of models, rules, data sources; audit/testing reports explaining system logic; sample datasets for training the AI; and compliance documentation mapping the system to regulations. By ingesting and training on this system-specific documentation, the AI can then use natural language processing to provide auditors with relevant insights when queried. Moreover, the conversational AI's responses can be further reinforced by integrating it with real-time monitoring data pipelines, absorbing the latest system log outputs.

telemetry data, details of the AI/ML models employed, rules/typologies configured, specific risk scenarios used for transaction monitoring, alert rationalization, knowledge bases used for identifying entities, transactions, etc.

The auditor can then initiate a dialog with the conversational AI assistants:

> Please explain the logic and data sources behind how this system generates alerts for suspicions of trade-based money laundering.

ChatGPT can respond by walking through:

- The specific typologies, rules, and risk indicators it is trained to detect trade-based laundering cases (e.g., over/under-invoicing, misrepresented goods/ services, high-risk jurisdictions, etc.).
- The models and algorithms used to analyze transaction data and identify anomalies.
- The data sources and watchlists integrated (like export/import databases, sanctions lists, adverse media).
- Illustrate with sample cases from its training data on how it connected the dots to raise alerts.

The auditor can further probe by asking it to justify its scoring rationale for real alerts raised during a certain period. Conversational AI tools can provide insights into why certain transactions were deemed high-risk based on the evidence. This transparency builds trust that the system's underlying AI models are operating as intended and aligned with regulatory expectations.

Also, the auditor can leverage ChatGPT's or Claude's natural language capabilities for continuous healthchecks by asking:

> Have you identified any operational issues, degradations or anomalies in the system over the past 6 months?

These tools can proactively analyze system logs, check for metrics like increasing false positive rates, or uncover component failures which may require attention. It can highlight these findings conversationally. They can also provide recommendations based on reviewing latest cloud infrastructure telemetry data:

> The data volume from the APAC region has increased 35%. You may want to scale up the processing capacity for optimum performance.

The auditor gets this intelligent advisory from the AI in plain language, instead of having to manually inspect and correlate different system data sources. By serving as an interactive interface, the conversational AI assistants allow auditors and compliance teams to effectively validate and continuously monitor the systems in an intuitive manner, while providing clear AI-driven insights when needed.

2.6 Conversational AI and Regulatory Compliance

Conversational AI assistants can be used for automating Suspicious Activity Report (SAR) filings to improve accuracy, completeness, consistency, quality, and also achieve significant time savings (H3M Analytics, Inc., 2023).

2.6.1 Illustrative Scenario 6: Automating SAR Filing Processes

This scenario illustrates how conversational AI can streamline the process of filing Suspicious Activity Reports (SARs), addressing implementation challenges, success metrics, and data privacy issues, improving efficiency and consistency in regulatory reporting.

Suppose XYZ Bank, a large financial institution, is required to file Suspicious Activity Reports (SARs) for transactions that exhibit signs of potential money laundering or fraudulent activities. The process of filing SARs involves gathering relevant information, investigating the suspicious activity, and composing a detailed narrative for submission. This manual process is time-consuming and burdensome for the bank's BSA (Bank Secrecy Act) compliance officers, who are responsible for filing SARs within strict regulatory timeframes. Currently, it takes an average of 4 hours to compile and file a single SAR, with a backlog of potential cases growing by 12% monthly.

The bank can implement a conversational AI system, which integrates with the bank's transaction monitoring system, customer database, and case management software and is trained on historical SAR data, regulatory guidelines, and money laundering typologies. Implementation of such a system might involve a 3-month process: 1 month for system integration, 1 month for staff training, and 1 month for parallel testing.

In addition to detecting suspicious activities and flagging them, the conversational AI assistants can go much further in helping BSA officers:

- *Automated Information Gathering*: The conversational AI assistants can be asked to automatically collect relevant information about the suspicious transaction from various internal systems, such as customer profiles, account histories, and transaction details. They can also be asked to cross-reference the gathered information with external databases, such as sanctions lists and adverse media, to enrich the data for SAR filing.
- *Intelligent Narrative Generation*: Using the collected information and their trained knowledge of money laundering typologies, the conversational AI assistants can generate a comprehensive SAR narrative. The narrative would include a detailed description of the suspicious activity, relevant transaction details, customer information, and any additional context or red flags identified. The AI systems can ensure that the narrative is clear and meets regulatory requirements for SAR filing.
- *BSA Officer Review and Approval*: The generated SAR narrative can then be automatically presented to the BSA compliance officer for review through a user-friendly interface. The BSA officer can review the narrative, make any

necessary edits or additions, and provide final approval for filing. The officer can also ask more questions, request additional information, or provide feedback to further refine the narrative.

- *Automated SAR Filing*: Once the SAR narrative is approved by the BSA officer, the conversational AI systems can be used to automatically populate the required fields in the SAR filing template. This ensures that all necessary information is included and formatted correctly, minimizing errors and inconsistencies.

XYZ Bank can then measure the success of the AI implementation using the following metrics:

- *Time Efficiency*: SAR compilation and filing time reduced from 4 hours to 40 minutes on average (83.33% reduction).
- *Backlog Reduction*: Case backlog decreased by 60% within three months of implementation.
- *Accuracy*: 96% of AI-generated SARs require minimal to no edits by human reviewers.
- *Regulatory Compliance*: 100% of SARs filed within required timeframes, up from 86% pre-implementation.
- *Cost Savings*: Estimated $450,000 annual savings in labor costs and reduced regulatory fines.

As more SARs are prepared and filed using the conversational AI assistants, these systems will continuously learn and adapt based on feedback from BSA officers and regulatory updates. It will also ensure standardized SAR narratives being generated across all filings and minimize risks of non-compliance.

XYZ Bank also addresses data privacy concerns with the help of the AI system through the following measures:

- *Data Minimization*: The AI only accesses and processes data necessary for SAR filing, adhering to the principle of data minimization.
- *Encryption*: All data transmissions between systems and to FinCEN are encrypted using Advanced Encryption Standard (AES)-256 encryption, which is a virtually impenetrable symmetric encryption algorithm.
- *Access Controls*: Multi-factor authentication and role-based access controls limit system access to authorized personnel only.
- *Data Retention*: SAR-related data is retained only for the legally required period, after which it's securely deleted.
- *Audit Trails*: Comprehensive logs are maintained of all AI actions and human interactions with the system.
- *Privacy Impact Assessment*: The bank conducts regular privacy impact assessments to ensure compliance with regulations like GDPR, CCPA, and GLBA.

- *De-identification*: Where possible, personal data is de-identified or pseudony- mized before processing by the AI.

The degree of success of XYZ Bank's AI system would depend on the following factors:

- *Initial Accuracy*: What is the accuracy of the AI system in the first month? For example, if during the first month, the AI's accuracy was only 65%, more human oversight would be required.
- *Complex Cases*: Does the AI system struggle with highly complex, unusual cases? If yes, then significant human intervention would still be required.
- *Regulatory Acceptance*: Is the bank able to demonstrate the AI's reliability to regulators? There might be an initial period of parallel human and AI processing.
- *Staff Adaptation*: Is there resistance from some to the new system? If yes, then it might necessitate comprehensive change management and training programs to make the AI system implementation successful.

To sum it up, implementing conversational AI systems for SAR automation can significantly improve efficiency and accuracy, but requires careful integration with existing systems and processes. However, success of such systems should be measured across multiple dimensions, including time savings, accuracy, compli- ance improvements, and cost reductions. Moreover, addressing data privacy is crucial and involves technical measures, policy adjustments, and ongoing assessments. Finally, human oversight may still remain essential, especially for complex cases and final approvals. Tolga Kurt, Managing Partner at H3M Analytics, Inc., quotes: "ChatGPT and LLM models in general will significantly enhance the learning curve for new analysts learning to fight financial crime, and minimize their time spend for the related complex investigations" (Kurt, 2024).

3. Challenges of Using Conversational AI in Fraud Prevention Systems

While the potential benefits of leveraging conversational AI for fraud detection, prevention, and investigation are undeniable, there are several challenges and considerations that must be addressed:

- *Data Quality and Privacy*: Conversational AI systems rely heavily on the quality and completeness of the data they are trained on. Ensuring data privacy and adhering to relevant regulations regarding data usage and storage is crucial.
- *Biases*: As with any AI system, there is a risk of inherent biases or opaque decision-making processes (Parikh et al., 2019). Efforts must be made to ensure transparency in the AI models employed.

- *Explainability*: Explainability in conversational AI refers to the capability of an AI system to provide human-understandable explanations and reasons behind its predictions, decisions, or recommendations (Das & Rad, 2020; Dwivedi et al., 2023). In financial fraud detection, explainability is especially important for compliance and auditing, building user trust (if the AI system is a black box), and identifying potential biases in the AI models when they are trained on historical data.
- *Continuous Learning and Adaptation*: Financial crimes and fraud tactics are constantly evolving (Association of Certified Fraud Examiners, 2023), necessitating continuous learning and adaptation of the conversational AI systems to stay ahead of emerging threats.

3.1 Illustrative Scenario 7: Managing Challenges in AI-Powered Fraud Prevention Systems

This scenario explores how organizations can address common challenges associated with implementing AI in fraud prevention systems.

A bank has implemented a conversational AI system like ChatGPT or Claude to assist its fraud investigators in analyzing suspicious transaction alerts. The AI assistants are trained on historical transaction data, customer profiles, and past fraud cases. However, there are some concerns with data quality and privacy:

- The historical transaction data used for training contains a significant number of missing fields and inconsistent formats, affecting the AI's ability to learn accurate patterns.
- Some of the customer profile data includes sensitive personally identifiable information (PII) like social security numbers and credit scores, which raises data privacy concerns and potential violations of regulations like the Gramm-Leach-Bliley Act or GLBA, Fair Credit Reporting Act or FCRA, California Consumer Privacy Act or CCPA (if California residents' data is involved), New York SHIELD Act (if New York residents' data is involved), or General Data Protection Regulation or GDPR (if European Union citizens' data is involved) if not handled properly. PII can be any data that could potentially identify a specific individual. The GLBA is a US law that requires financial institutions to explain their information-sharing practices to their customers and to safeguard sensitive data. The FCRA is a US federal law that regulates the collection of consumers' credit information and access to their credit reports. The CCPA is a state statute intended to enhance privacy rights and consumer protection for residents of California. Finally, the GDPR is a regulation in EU law on data protection and privacy in the European Union and the European Economic Area.

Also, the conversational AI system shows some inherent bias and explainability issues:

- The conversational AI assistants flag a higher proportion of transactions from a certain ethnic group as potentially fraudulent. However, due to the black-box nature of the deep learning models used, fraud investigators are unable to understand why these transactions are being singled out, raising concerns about potential bias.
- Investigators are hesitant to trust the AI's recommendations without clear explanations of the reasoning behind each alert, as they need to justify their actions to auditors and customers.

Moreover, there is recent news that has called into question the AI's learning and adaptation abilities:

- Fraudsters have started using a new money laundering tactic involving cryptocurrencies and online gaming platforms. However, the AI system is not able to effectively detect these new patterns as it was primarily trained on traditional money laundering typologies.
- Updating the AI with new training data and fraud scenarios will require significant time and resources from the bank's data science team, creating delays in adapting to emerging threats.

Thus, some of the more experienced fraud investigators may be resistant to using the conversational AI assistants, preferring to stick to their traditional manual investigation methods. The fraud investigators may argue that data quality issues and potential biases leading to a high number of false positives are resulting in a waste of their time on fruitless alerts. They may also have to often second-guess or disregard the system's recommendations due to the lack of explainability. They may also criticize the conversational AI's inability to quickly adapt to new fraud tactics, which leads to missed detection of real money laundering cases, exposing the bank to financial and reputational risks.

In this scenario, to manage all of the above challenges, the bank would need to take some quick steps:

(1) Invest in data governance frameworks:

- Establish a comprehensive data governance policy that defines data quality standards, metadata management, and tracking of data lineage.
- Implement data quality checks and validation rules at the point of data entry and during ETL (Extract, Transform, Load) processes to ensure data completeness, consistency, and accuracy. ETL is a data integration process that combines data from multiple sources into a single, consistent data store.
- Use data profiling tools to identify and rectify data quality issues in the historical datasets used for training the conversational AI assistants.
- Employ data masking (replacing sensitive data with fictitious but realistic data that maintains the same format and statistical properties as the original data) and tokenization techniques (replacing sensitive data with a

non-sensitive surrogate value called a token, and storing the original sensitive data securely in a separate database while mapping it to the corresponding token) to protect sensitive PII data while still allowing the AI to learn patterns from it (Tachepun & Thammaboosadee, 2020)
- Regularly audit and monitor data usage to ensure compliance with privacy regulations like GDPR, GLBA, CCPA, etc.

For example, in this scenario, since the bank's customer data includes sensitive PII like social security numbers (SSN). Instead of using the real SSNs in the training data, the bank could simply apply one of the following data masking techniques (Shukla et al., 2022):

- *Shuffling*: Randomly shuffling the digits within each SSN so that the original number is not discernible but the overall format is maintained.
- *Substitution*: Replacing the real SSNs with randomly generated numbers that follow the same 9-digit format.
- *Encryption*: Encrypting the SSNs using a strong cryptographic algorithm and using the encrypted values for training.

The masked data would then be used to train the conversational AI system. The AI can still learn patterns and correlations from the masked data without being exposed to the actual sensitive values. Alternatively, tokenization could be applied to sensitive data fields like SSNs, credit card numbers, or account numbers.

- When a new customer record is ingested for training the AI, the SSN is sent to a tokenization system.
- The tokenization system would generate a random, unique token (e.g., a string of alphanumeric characters) for that SSN and store the token-to-SSN mapping in a secure database.
- The original SSN in the customer record is replaced with the generated token.
- The tokenized customer record is then used to train the conversational AI assistant.

When the conversational AI assistant needs to process a transaction or query related to a specific customer, it would use the token instead of the actual SSN. The tokenization system would be queried to retrieve the original SSN if needed for downstream processing, with access controls ensuring only authorized systems or users can de-tokenize the data.

The main benefit of these techniques is that the original sensitive data is never directly exposed to the conversational AI systems, reducing the risk of data breaches or misuse. They can still learn patterns and correlations from the masked or tokenized data, as the format and statistical properties are preserved. It's also easier to comply with data privacy regulations as the sensitive data is protected. If, in a worst-case scenario, the conversational AI system is compromised, the attacker would only have access to the masked or tokenized data, not the actual sensitive information.

(2) Implement Explainable AI techniques:

- Utilize techniques like SHAP (SHapley Additive exPlanations) or LIME (Local Interpretable Model-Agnostic Explanations) to provide interpretable explanations for the AI's predictions on each suspicious transaction (Alabi et al., 2023; Neves et al., 2021). SHAP is a game theoretic approach to explain the output of any machine learning model, while LIME explains the predictions of any classifier in an interpretable and faithful manner by learning an interpretable model locally around the prediction.
- Integrate the conversational AI with a case-based reasoning (CBR) system that can draw analogies and provide explanations based on similar historical fraud cases (Hillig & Müller, 2021).
- Employ counterfactual explanations to show fraud investigators what changes in the input data would have resulted in a different output from the conversational AI assistant (Guidotti, 2022).
- Use visual analytics and dashboards to illustrate the key factors and their weightage influencing each conversational AI decision.
- Continuously monitor and test the AI models for fairness and bias, using techniques like disparate impact analysis and equality of opportunity metrics (Barocas & Selbst, 2016; Bell et al., 2024; MacCarthy, 2018).

For example, SHAP, based on the concept of Shapley values from cooperative game theory, would assign an importance value for each feature (e.g., transaction amount, location, time) by considering all possible combinations of features and how much each feature contributes to the prediction in each combination. In the context of fraud detection, the conversational AI assistant would make a prediction on a transaction, classifying it as either fraudulent or legitimate. These Shapley values are then used to explain the prediction by showing the positive or negative contribution of each feature toward the model's output (Molnar, 2022). For example, SHAP might show that the high transaction amount and the unusual location had a strong positive contribution toward classifying a transaction as fraudulent, while the customer's long history with the bank had a negative contribution. These explanations can be visualized using force plots, bar plots, or decision plots, making it easier for investigators to understand the factors driving the AI's predictions (Ariza-Garzón et al., 2020).

On the other hand, LIME tries to understand the AI model's decision-making process by focusing on one specific transaction and its surrounding context (Molnar, 2022). Thus, LIME would take an original transaction and create a new dataset by slightly modifying its features (amount, location, time, the customer's history with the bank, etc.). For example, it might create variations of the transaction with slightly different amounts, locations, or times. These modified transactions are called "perturbed samples" (Garreau & von Luxburg, 2020).

LIME would then ask the complex AI model to make predictions on these per-turbed samples. The AI model would classify each perturbed sample as either fraudulent or legitimate. Next, LIME would take the perturbed samples and their corresponding predictions from the complex AI model and try to fit a simpler, more interpretable model (e.g., linear regression or decision tree) to them.

The idea is that this simpler model should closely mimic the complex AI model's behavior for transactions similar to the original one. The coefficients or decision rules of this simpler model are then used to explain the complex AI model's prediction on the original transaction. For example, if the simpler model heavily weighs the transaction amount and location in determining fraud risk, LIME would highlight these features as important factors in the AI model's original prediction. To sum it up, both SHAP and LIME can explain individual predictions rather than the model's overall behavior. This can be particularly useful in fraud detection, where investigators need to understand the specific factors that led to a particular transaction being flagged as suspicious.

Integrating a conversational AI system with a case-based reasoning (CBR) system is also a powerful approach to provide explanations for fraud detection since it uses knowledge from previously solved problems (cases) to solve new, similar problems (Rudin et al., 2022). When a fraud investigator asks the conversational AI assistant to explain its fraud prediction, the AI would query the integrated CBR system. The CBR system would then search its database of his-torical fraud cases for those most similar to the current suspicious transaction. Similarity can be based on features like transaction amount, location, customer profile, etc. If the CBR system finds a highly similar historical case (e.g., a pre-vious incident where a customer's account was compromised, and the fraudster transferred a large sum to a foreign account), it would retrieve the solution (explanation) associated with this historical case. The retrieved explanation is then adapted to the current case. The conversational AI assistant might say,

> This transaction is similar to a previous fraud case (case ID: xxx) where the customer's account was compromised. In that case, the large transaction amount and foreign destination were key indicators of fraud.

The conversational AI could also provide additional details:

> In the historical case, the fraudster gained access to the customer's online banking credentials through a phishing scam. The money was transferred to a mule account in Country X before being moved elsewhere. Investigators found that the IP address used to initiate the transfer was suspicious. Similar red flags are present in the current transaction.

If the investigator confirms the AI's prediction and the adapted explanation is valid, this new case and its explanation would be added to the CBR system's case base for future reference (Rudin et al., 2022). The investigator can also probe further the additional details provided by the AI and ask it to compare and contrast the current case with other similar historical cases, gaining insights into common patterns and potential investigative actions.

Counterfactual explanations are also a powerful technique since they could help investigators understand what factors contributed to a transaction being flagged as suspicious, and how modifying these factors would change the conversational AI's prediction (Byrne, 2019). Suppose the conversational AI assistant flags a credit card transaction as potentially fraudulent due to its high amount ($5,000) and the fact that it originated from a foreign country (Country X) that the cardholder has never visited before. When the fraud investigator asks the AI to explain its decision, the AI assistant would provide a counterfactual explanation:

> The transaction was flagged as suspicious primarily due to the high amount and the unusual transaction location. If the transaction amount had been $500 instead of $5,000, and if it had originated from the cardholder's home country instead of Country X, the transaction would have been classified as legitimate with 90% confidence.

This counterfactual explanation highlights the two key features (amount and location) that led to the fraud prediction, and shows how changing these features would have resulted in a different prediction.

The investigator could then ask follow-up questions to explore other scenarios:

> What if the transaction amount was $5,000 but it originated from the cardholder's home country?

The conversational AI assistant might respond something along the lines of:

> In that case, the transaction would have been flagged as suspicious with 60% confidence, due to the high amount alone. The unusual location further increased the suspicion score.

Thus, counterfactual explanations provide a clear way to understand the key factors influencing a model's prediction and allow investigators to explore "what-if" scenarios and gain insights into the model's decision boundaries (Guidotti, 2022).

Presenting the conversational AI's decision-making process in a visual, intuitive format, investigators can quickly grasp the main reasons behind each prediction and explore the underlying data (Ahn & Lin, 2019). For example, if the conversational AI assistant flags a series of credit card transactions as potentially fraudulent, the fraud investigator can ask the AI to generate a dashboard with the following visuals to understand the key factors contributing to these predictions:

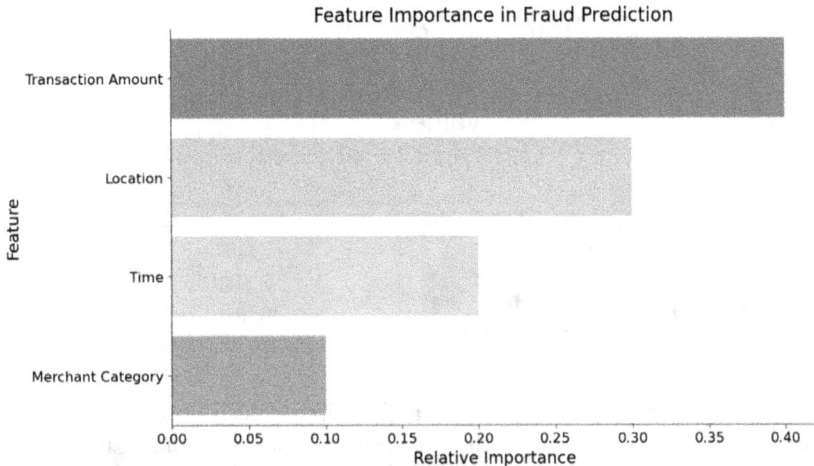

Fig. 4.1.   **Feature Importance Chart**. The feature importance chart
provides insights into which features the fraud detection model considers
most influential in making its predictions. The chart shows the relative
importance of four features: Transaction Amount, Location, Time, and
Merchant Category. Importance is measured from 0 to 1, with higher values
indicating greater importance. Transaction Amount has the highest
importance at around 0.40 with Location coming at a close second at around
0.30. This suggests the amount of a transaction and location amounts are the
strongest indicators of whether a transaction might be fraudulent, while time
and merchant category are less important (though they provide supporting
evidence). In summary, if this model flags a transaction as likely fraudulent,
we can infer that a highly unusual transaction amount was probably the
biggest factor, followed by a suspicious location.

- *Feature Importance Chart*: A bar chart (see Fig. 4.1) displaying the relative
  importance of each input feature (e.g., transaction amount, location, time,
  merchant category) in the AI's fraud prediction can aid the investigator in
  seeing at a glance that certain features (e.g., transaction amount and location)
  were the top contributors.
- *Decision Tree Diagram*: A simplified decision tree diagram (see Fig. 4.2)
  showing the main decision paths leading to the fraud classification with each
  node in the tree representing a key decision factor, and with branches representing different feature values. The investigator can trace the path of a specific
  transaction and understand the combination of factors that led to its
  classification.
- *Geospatial Map*: A map visualization (see Fig. 4.3) plotting the location of each
  flagged transaction, color-coded by fraud risk score can help the investigator

Transaction Amount <= 400.0
gini = 0.5
samples = 4
value = [2, 2]
class = Not Fraudulent

gini = 0.0	gini = 0.0
samples = 2	samples = 2
value = [2, 0]	value = [0, 2]
class = Not Fraudulent	class = Fraudulent

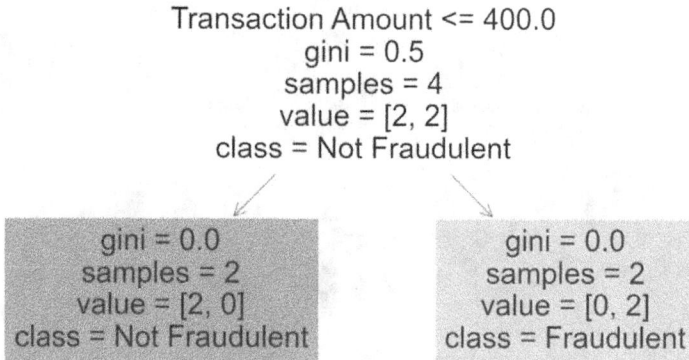

Fig. 4.2.   **Decision Tree Diagram**. This simple decision tree diagram uses the transaction amount as the key feature to predict fraud. It has learned from the training data that transactions above 400.0 are likely to be fraudulent, while those below or equal to 400.0 are likely to be legitimate. The decision tree is thus trying to classify transactions as either "Fraudulent" or "Not Fraudulent" based on the transaction amount. It does this by splitting the data at a certain threshold value of the transaction amount. The first node (at the top) represents all the transaction data before any splitting. It shows (a) the splitting criterion: Transaction Amount <= 400.0; and (b) the Gini impurity of the node: 0.5. There are 4 total samples (transactions) in this node. The average transaction amount is [2, 2], meaning there are 2 transactions of each class (Fraudulent and Not Fraudulent). A Gini impurity score give an idea of how good a split is by how mixed the classes are in the two groups created by the split, and a lower Gini score is better because it indicates a lower impurity. A Gini impurity of 0 means the node is completely pure, i.e., all samples in that node belong to the same class (either all "Fraudulent" or all "Not Fraudulent"). A Gini impurity of 1 would mean the node is completely impure, i.e., the samples are evenly distributed across classes. In a binary classification problem like this, it would mean the node has an equal number of "Fraudulent" and "Not Fraudulent" samples. This is the worst case, as the tree cannot make a confident classification for samples in this node. The root node has a Gini impurity of 0.5, which means it's equally likely for a randomly selected sample to be "Fraudulent" or "Not Fraudulent." This makes sense, as there are 2 samples of each class in this node. If a transaction's amount is less than or equal to (greater than) 400.0, it goes to the left (right) child node. Each of these nodes have Gini impurities of 0.0, which suggests they are pure nodes (all samples belong to one class). There are two samples (transactions) in each of these nodes. The average value in the left node is [2, 0], meaning both transactions are "Not Fraudulent." So, if a transaction's amount is less than or equal to 400.0, the tree classifies it as "Not Fraudulent." The average value in the right node is [0, 2], meaning both transactions are "Fraudulent." So, if a transaction's amount is greater than 400.0, the tree classifies it as "Fraudulent."

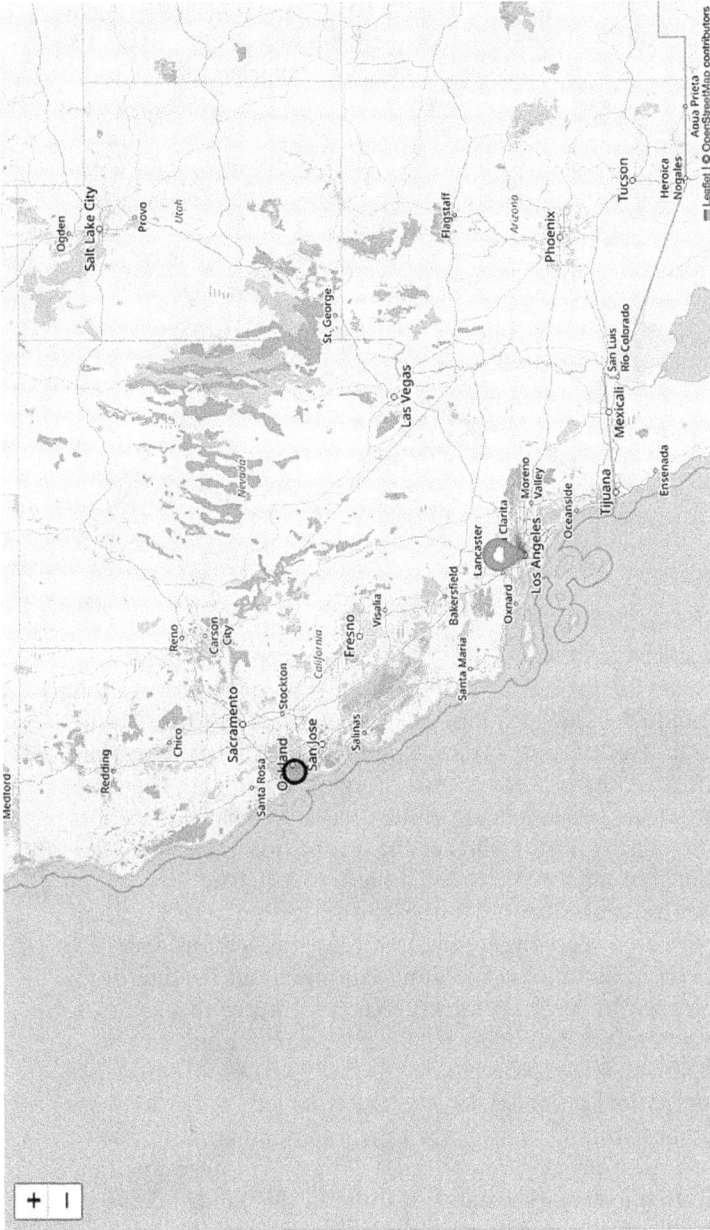

Fig. 4.3. **Geospatial Map.** This geospatial map provides an example visualizing the geographic distribution of potential fraud risks. Each marker on the map represents a specific location, and its shape indicates the associated fraud risk score. Circle markers signify locations with a high fraud risk (risk score > 0.5), while the Cloud markers with an icon represent locations with a low fraud risk (risk score ≤ 0.5). In this example, there are two markers: one in the San Francisco Bay Area (circle) and one in Los Angeles (cloud). This suggests that the location in the Bay Area has a higher risk of fraudulent activity compared to the location in Los Angeles. This visual representation allows fraud investigators to focus their efforts on high-risk areas and allocate resources accordingly.

identify geographic patterns or hotspots that the AI has learned to associate with fraudulent activity.

- *Parallel Coordinates Plot*: This plot (see Fig. 4.4) allows the investigator to explore relationships between multiple transaction features. Each line represents a transaction, with its feature values plotted along parallel axes. The investigator can highlight transactions classified as fraudulent and look for common patterns or outliers.

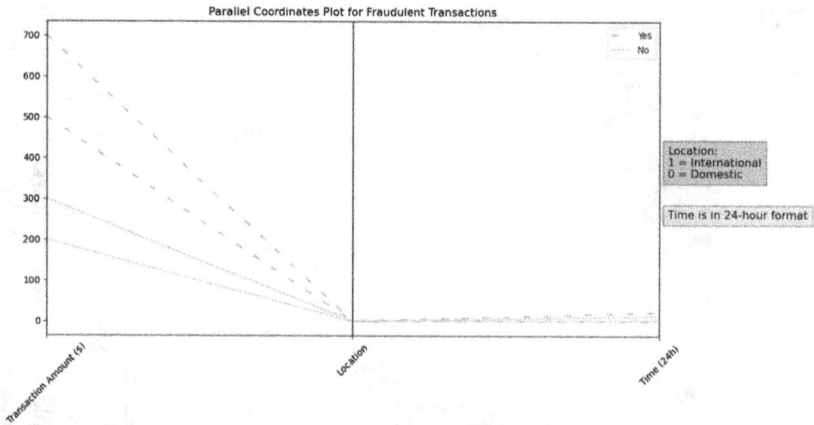

Fig. 4.4.   **Parallel Coordinates Plot**. This parallel coordinates plot allows investigators to visually identify patterns and relationships between the features and the fraudulent classification. The plot consists of three parallel axes, each representing a different feature: Transaction Amount, Location, and Time. Each line in the plot represents a single transaction. The line intersects each axis at the corresponding feature value for that transaction. The pattern of the lines indicates whether the transaction is classified as fraudulent or not (dashed lines = Yes; dotted lines = No). The Transaction Amount axis shows the monetary value of each transaction. The Location axis is binary, with 1 representing international transactions and 0 representing domestic transactions. The Time axis represents the time of the transaction in military format (0–23 hours). We can observe that the two fraudulent transactions (dashed lines) have higher transaction amounts compared to the non-fraudulent transactions (dotted lines). Both fraudulent transactions are international (intersecting the Location axis at 1), while one of the non-fraudulent transactions is domestic (intersecting at 0). The fraudulent transactions occur at different times (23 and 1), suggesting that time alone may not be a strong indicator of fraud in this limited dataset. Thus, in this example, higher transaction amounts and international locations seem to be more associated with fraudulent activity.

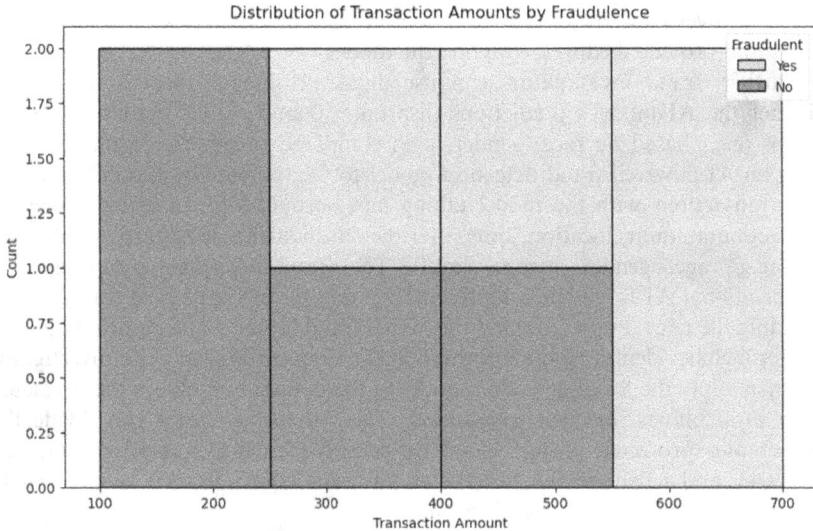

Fig. 4.5. **Feature Distribution Chart**. This feature distribution chart is a stacked histogram that visualizes the distribution of transaction amounts by fraudulence status. Each bar represents a range of transaction amounts on the *x*-axis, with the count of transactions on the *y*-axis. From the chart, we can see two distinct shades representing different classes: one for "No" (not fraudulent) and another for "Yes" (fraudulent). The bins (horizontal intervals on the *x*-axis) aggregate transaction amounts into groups, making it easier to observe patterns. The stacked nature of the histogram allows us to compare the relative proportions of fraudulent and non-fraudulent transactions within each transaction amount bin. We can observe if certain amount ranges have a higher or lower proportion of fraudulent transactions. From this chart, we can see that fraudulent transactions seem to be more prevalent in the higher transaction amount ranges. Non-fraudulent transactions appear to be more evenly distributed across the transaction amount ranges. Thus, this chart suggests that transactions with higher amounts might be more likely to be fraudulent compared to transactions with lower amounts. However, it's important to note that this is just one variable, and fraud detection typically involves analyzing multiple features.

• *Feature Distribution Chart* (Histogram or Density Plot): For each key feature, a histogram (see Fig. 4.5) or density plot showing the distribution of values for legitimate versus fraudulent transactions can assist the investigator to see how the conversational AI assistant has learned to distinguish between the two classes based on these feature distributions.

Fraud investigators can also compare the AI's predictions with human judgments and provide feedback to refine the model.

Further, fraud investigators can use disparate impact analysis to assesses whether the AI model's predictions disproportionately affect certain protected groups (e.g., based on race, gender, age) compared to others. Assume a bank using an AI-powered fraud detection model to flag potentially fraudulent credit card transactions with the model taking into account various features such as transaction amount, location, time, and the cardholder's demographic information (e.g., age, gender, income level). The fraud investigator can ask the conversational AI to gather a representative dataset of credit card transactions, including the relevant features and the actual fraud labels, while ensuring that the dataset includes demographic information for each cardholder. The investigator can then apply the fraud detection model to the dataset and obtain the predicted fraud probabilities for each transaction. Then, the investigator can divide the dataset into protected groups based on sensitive attributes (e.g., gender, age brackets), and calculate the proportion of transactions flagged as potentially fraudulent by the model for each group.

Lastly, the investigator can compare the proportion of flagged transactions between the protected groups. If the proportion for one group is significantly lower than the other (e.g., below a certain threshold), it may indicate disparate impact. For example, if the model flags 20% of transactions by male cardholders as potentially fraudulent, but only 5% of transactions by female cardholders, it suggests that the model might be disproportionately impacting male cardholders.

Equality of opportunity focuses on ensuring that the model's performance is similar across different protected groups. It can be assessed using metrics like false positive rates or FPR (the proportion of non-fraudulent transactions incorrectly flagged as fraudulent by the model) and false negative rates or FNR (the proportion of actual fraudulent transactions that the model fails to flag) for each group. Using the same dataset as before, the investigator can split it into protected groups based on sensitive attributes and ask the conversational AI to compare the FPR and FNR across the protected groups. If there are significant disparities, it indicates that the model's performance is not equitable across those groups. For instance, if the model has a higher FPR for transactions by younger cardholders compared to older ones, it means that younger cardholders are more likely to be incorrectly flagged for fraud, potentially leading to unfair scrutiny or inconvenience.

4. Conclusion

The integration of conversational AI, such as ChatGPT or Claude, into fraud detection, prevention, and investigation processes represents a paradigm shift in the battle against financial crimes. By leveraging the power of natural language processing and cognitive computing, financial institutions and regulatory bodies can enhance their AML compliance efforts, streamline investigations, and stay ahead of evolving fraud tactics.

4.1 Key Insights

- *Enhanced Efficiency*: Conversational AI systems can significantly reduce the time and resources required for tasks such as transaction monitoring, alert triage (reviewing, analyzing, and grouping alerts based on their potential impact and urgency), and regulatory reporting. As illustrated in my scenarios, these systems can automate routine tasks, allowing human investigators to focus on more complex, high-risk cases.
- *Improved Accuracy*: By leveraging vast amounts of data and advanced pattern recognition capabilities, AI systems can identify subtle indicators of fraud that might be missed by traditional rule-based systems or human analysts. This can lead to higher detection rates and fewer false positives.
- *Adaptive Learning*: Unlike static rule-based systems, AI models can continuously learn and adapt to new fraud patterns, helping financial institutions stay ahead of evolving criminal tactics.
- *Regulatory Compliance*: Conversational AI can assist in ensuring consistent adherence to regulatory requirements, from KYC processes to the timely filing of Suspicious Activity Reports (SARs).
- *Investigative Support*: These systems serve as powerful assistants to human investigators, providing contextual information, historical comparisons, and suggesting lines of inquiry that can accelerate and enhance the investigation process.

However, the successful implementation of conversational AI requires a holistic approach, addressing challenges related to data quality, bias, explainability, and continuous learning and adaptation. Some challenges and considerations include:

- *Data Quality and Privacy*: The effectiveness of AI systems is heavily dependent on the quality and completeness of training data. Ensuring data accuracy while adhering to privacy regulations remains a critical challenge.
- *Explainability and Transparency*: As AI systems become more complex, ensuring their decision-making processes are transparent and explainable to regulators, auditors, and customers becomes increasingly important.
- *Bias Mitigation*: There is an ongoing need to monitor and mitigate potential biases in AI systems to ensure fair and equitable treatment of all customers and transactions.
- *Regulatory Acceptance*: As AI systems take on more critical roles in fraud detection and AML processes, gaining regulatory acceptance and demonstrating compliance will be crucial.
- *Human–AI Collaboration*: Striking the right balance between AI automation and human oversight remains a key consideration in maintaining effective and responsible fraud management practices.

Looking ahead, several trends are likely to shape the future of AI in fraud management:

- *Advanced NLP Capabilities*: As natural language processing technologies continue to advance, we can expect even more sophisticated interactions between AI systems and human investigators, potentially leading to more context-aware fraud detection.
- *Integration of Multiple AI Technologies*: The combination of conversational AI with other technologies such as computer vision, blockchain, and quantum computing may open new frontiers in fraud detection and prevention.
- *Cross-Institution Collaboration*: AI systems could facilitate more effective information sharing between financial institutions, enhancing the collective ability to detect and prevent financial crimes.
- *Regulatory Technology (RegTech)*: The development of AI-powered regulatory compliance tools is likely to accelerate, potentially transforming how financial institutions interact with regulators.
- *Ethical AI Frameworks*: As AI systems become more prevalent in critical decision-making processes, the development and adoption of ethical AI frameworks will be crucial to ensure responsible and fair use of these technologies.

As with any transformative technology, careful consideration and responsible implementation are important to realizing the full potential of conversational AI in fraud management. Baran Ozkan, Co-Founder and CEO of Flagright, quotes: "The future of AML lies in the seamless integration of AI and human expertise. We're already witnessing a paradigm shift in how investigations are conducted. As regulatory landscapes evolve, so will the role of conversational AI in compliance and fraud prevention. We must bring the best of both worlds from machine and human intelligence to drive meaningful, frictionless change" (Ozkan, 2024).

References

Ahn, Y., & Lin, Y. R. (2019). Fairsight: Visual analytics for fairness in decision making. *IEEE Transactions on Visualization and Computer Graphics*, *26*(1), 1086–1095. https://doi.org/10.1109/TVCG.2019.2934262

Alabi, R. O., Elmusrati, M., Leivo, I., Almangush, A., & Mäkitie, A. A. (2023). Machine learning explainability in nasopharyngeal cancer survival using LIME and SHAP. *Scientific Reports*, *13*(1), 8984. https://doi.org/10.1038/s41598-023-35795-0

Ariza-Garzón, M. J., Arroyo, J., Caparrini, A., & Segovia-Vargas, M. J. (2020). Explainability of a machine learning granting scoring model in peer-to-peer lending. *IEEE Access*, *8*, 64873–64890. https://doi.org/10.1109/ACCESS.2020.2984412

Association of Certified Fraud Examiners. (2023). Occupational fraud 2022: Report to the nations. https://legacy.acfe.com/report-to-the-nations/2022/

Barocas, S., & Selbst, A. D. (2016). Big data's disparate impact. *California Law Review, 104*, 671. https://doi.org/10.2139/ssrn.2477899

Bell, A., Fonseca, J., Abrate, C., Bonchi, F., & Stoyanovich, J. (2024). Fairness in algorithmic recourse through the lens of substantive equality of opportunity arXiv preprint arXiv:2401.16088. https://doi.org/10.48550/arXiv.2401.16088

Byrne, R. M. (2019). Counterfactuals in explainable artificial intelligence (XAI): Evidence from human reasoning. In *Proceedings of the 28th international joint conference on artificial intelligence (IJCAI)* (pp. 6276–6282).

Das, A., & Rad, P. (2020). Opportunities and challenges in explainable artificial intelligence (xai): A survey arXiv preprint arXiv:2006.11371. https://doi.org/10.48550/arXiv.2006.11371

Dwivedi, R., Dave, D., Naik, H., Singhal, S., Rana, O., Patel, P., Qian, B., Wen, Z., Shah, T., Morgan, G., & Ranjan, R. (2023). Explainable AI (XAI): Core ideas, techniques, and solutions. *ACM Computing Surveys, 55*(9), 1–33. Article 194. https://doi.org/10.1145/3561048

Flagright (2024). Revolutionizing financial crime investigations with AI Forensics: A Flagright case study.

Garreau, D., & von Luxburg, U. (2020). Explaining the explainer: A first theoretical analysis of LIME. In *Proceedings of the 23rd international conference on artificial intelligence and statistics* (Vol. 108, pp. 1287–1296). https://proceedings.mlr.press/v108/garreau20a.html

Guidotti, R. (2022). Counterfactual explanations and how to find them: Literature review and benchmarking. *Data Mining and Knowledge Discovery*, 1–55. https://doi.org/10.1007/s10618-022-00831-6

H3M Analytics, Inc.. (2023). *Unlocking the power of ChatGPT for AML compliance.* H3M.IO Blog.

Hillig, S., & Müller, R. (2021). How do conversational case-based reasoning systems interact with their users: A literature review. *Behaviour & Information Technology, 40*(14), 1544–1563. https://doi.org/10.1080/0144929X.2020.1767207

Kurt, T. (2024, April 3). *ChatGPT and LLM models in general will significantly enhance the learning curve for new analysts learning to fight financial crime, and minimize their time spend for the related complex investigations.* [Email].

MacCarthy, M. (2018). Standards of fairness for disparate impact assessment of big data algorithms. *Cumberland Law Review, 48*, 67. https://doi.org/10.2139/ssrn.3154788

Molnar, C. (2022). *Interpretable machine learning: A guide for making black box models explainable* (2nd ed.). https://christophm.github.io/interpretable-ml-book/

Neves, I., Folgado, D., Santos, S., Barandas, M., Campagner, A., Ronzio, L., Cabitza, F., & Gamboa, H. (2021). Interpretable heartbeat classification using local model-agnostic explanations on ECGs. *Computers in Biology and Medicine, 133*, 104393. https://doi.org/10.1016/j.compbiomed.2021.104393

Ozkan, B. (2024, April 10). *The future of AML lies in the seamless integration of AI and human expertise. We're already witnessing a paradigm shift in how investigations are conducted. As regulatory landscapes evolve, so will the role of conversational AI in compliance and fraud prevention. We must bring the best of both worlds from machine and human intelligence to drive meaningful, frictionless change.* [Email].

Parikh, R. B., Teeple, S., & Navathe, A. S. (2019). Addressing bias in artificial intelligence in health care. *JAMA, 322*(24), 2377–2378. https://doi.org/10.1001/jama.2019.18058

Rudin, C., Chen, C., Chen, Z., Huang, H., Semenova, L., & Zhong, C. (2022). Interpretable machine learning: Fundamental principles and 10 grand challenges. *Statistics Surveys, 16*, 1–85. https://doi.org/10.1214/21-SS133

Shukla, S., George, J. P., Tiwari, K., & Kureethara, J. V. (2022). Data security. In J. Kacprzyk (Ed.), *Data ethics and challenges* (pp. 41–59). Springer. https://doi.org/10.1007/978-981-19-0752-4

Tachepun, C., & Thammaboosadee, S. (2020, July). A data masking guideline for optimizing insights and privacy under GDPR compliance. In *Proceedings of the 11th international conference on advances in information technology* (pp. 1–9). Association for Computing Machinery. https://doi.org/10.1145/3406601.3406627

Chapter 5

Revolutionizing Research: The Transformative Role of ChatGPT in Scientific Research

Jasmine Mariappan[a], Supriya Lamba Sahdev[b], Chitra Krishnan[c] and Firdous Ahmad Malik[d]

[a]University of Technology and Applied Sciences, Ibra, Oman
[b]Alliance University, India
[c]Symbiosis Centre for Management Studies, Noida, Symbiosis International (Deemed University), Pune, India
[d]University of the People, USA

Abstract

This chapter aims to look at how the use of ChatGPT can influence scientific studies and lists possibilities of the tool in the scientific procedure. This paper elucidates on how the conception of ChatGPT makes the process of an agreement, the filtering of information, assistance in data analysis, analysis, and synthesis, aid in coming up with hypotheses, and experiment planning. In addition to the points, this chapter is also devoted to the collaboration and communication in industry and research fields as well as the problems of ethical use of AI. The propositions made in this work, as well as the instances and experiences described, contribute to the arguments that the approaches to the modern problems in different disciplines can be developed using AI tools like ChatGPT for the research approaches. Further prospects of application of AI in research are also analyzed, including its interaction with other fields, increasing personalization, and increasing governance. Thus, this chapter ends with the confirmation of the necessity to find the middle ground between creativity and morality in the process of science.

The ChatGPT Revolution, 87–104
Copyright © 2025 Jasmine Mariappan, Supriya Lamba Sahdev, Chitra Krishnan and Firdous Ahmad Malik
Published under exclusive licence by Emerald Publishing Limited
doi:10.1108/978-1-83549-852-120251005

Keywords: ChatGPT; scientific research; artificial intelligence; literature review; hypothesis generation; data analysis; innovation; interdisciplinary collaboration; ethical considerations

1. Introduction

The artificial intelligence in the scientific research can be dated back to the middle of the 20th century when the topic of the machine learning is believed to have been initiated. When AI was first developed, AI was a miniature of today's set of technologies that contained only several rules and algorithms that were expected to come up with a limited number of solutions, however, technological advancement especially in computational powers and data accessibility in the period toward the end of 90s and early 21st century paved way to new techniques in machine learning and however deeper learning.

Some of the past milestones include the idea of building expert systems in 1980s as a result of emulating human decisions in certain domain for instance diagnosing disease (Sasikumar, 2007). The appearance of the neural networks and more sophisticated algorithms in the late 2010 enabled to work not only with the given enormous amounts of data but also to gain more and deeper insights into the data, which opened a new era in the image recognition, natural language processing and predictions (LeCun et al., 1998).

In the context of the further development of artificial intelligence, its application is increasingly common in various branches of science, including biology and ecology. Jordan and Mitchell (2015) confirm that AI has proved essential in modern research workplace due to its capability to process large volumes of data, identify patterns and make conclusions.

1.1 Introduction to ChatGPT and Its Capabilities

ChatGPT is an advanced version of LLM also developed by OpenAI, with the underlying architecture being the Generative Pre-trained Transformer or GPT. Original launched in November 2022 and with its latest update in February 2023, ChatGPT is utilizing deep learning to generate human-like text in accordance with the instructions provided by the user. It consists of text generation, text summarization, language translation, and question and answering services which are useful for numerous applications (Haque, 2022).

That is why the model is trained with various datasets that contain the information on different topics to give access to the necessary knowledge in various spheres. In a similar manner, in scientific research ChatGPT is used for conducting a literature review, for understanding results, and for designing experiments, which enhances the productivity and innovation of a researcher (AI4Science & Quantum, 2023).

1.2 The Need for Innovative Tools in Modern Scientific Inquiry

There is progression in scientific difficulty in questions asked, and traditional research methods encounter problems with sample selection, quantity, and integration across disciplines. The presence of big data necessitates the development of new devices that are not only capable of processing data but also analyzing them.

Such requirements are met with the help of AI tools like ChatGPT as they help in speeding up data processing, enhancing the interaction between researchers and developing hypotheses that might be unnoticed when employing conventional techniques. Such workflows as literature search and data analysis have to be facilitated since the advancement in science continues to progress at a faster pace (da Silva, 2024).

This chapter is devoted to the description of various points of view of ChatGPT in science and how this tool can enrich different steps in conducting research. It is essential to literature review, data analysis, hypothesis formation and in communication between the researchers. To make it easier to understand how ChatGPT can be helpful in creating new ideas during the further analysis of problems that researchers face in their work, this chapter will use a problem-based approach that involves real-life examples. Last but not least, I plan to highlight the importance of integrating AI solutions in scientific work as well as discussing possible moral issues.

2. Literature Review and Summarization

2.1 Automated Literature Review

Literature review is a type of proposal that entails a synthesis of the current scientific literature related to a specific research area. It helps in making a purposeful connection with the new research by integrating existing data, finding out the area that needs knowledge, and situating the current study in the narrative of conventional research work (Booth et al., 2021). Usually, this process requires end users to search relevant databases, read through hundreds of articles, and distill meaningful conclusions, hence being tiresome and cumbersome.

The process typically includes several key steps:

- Identifying the Research Question: Defining a clear and focused question to guide the search for relevant literature.
- Searching for Relevant Literature: Using academic databases and search engines to gather articles, books, and conference papers related to the question.
- Evaluating Sources: Assessing the credibility and relevance of the collected materials.
- Summarizing Findings: Extracting key information and insights from the literature to highlight trends, methodologies, and gaps.
- Synthesizing Information: Integrating findings to create a cohesive narrative that informs the research framework.

2.2 Role of ChatGPT

ChatGPT can be particularly valuable in the process of conducting a literature review, as several of its steps can be performed mechanically. By typing in specific keywords, researchers can then tap into its features to help them collate and synthesize literature more efficiently.

2.3 Techniques for Summarizing Articles and Extracting Key Information

- Text Summarization: Researchers can use ChatGPT to generate concise summaries of long articles, capturing essential points without needing to read the entire document.
- Keyword Extraction: The model can identify and extract keywords or phrases that are central to the literature, helping researchers focus on the most relevant themes.
- Comparative Analysis: ChatGPT can assist in comparing findings across multiple studies, highlighting similarities and differences in methodologies and conclusions.
- Automated Citation Generation: By inputting bibliographic information, researchers can obtain formatted citations, saving time and ensuring accuracy.

2.4 Case Studies Showcasing Effective Literature Reviews With ChatGPT

Some research has shown that integrated AI systems such as ChatGPT can be useful when conducting literature reviews. For example, a research study published in the area of applied biomedical research used ChatGPT to derive specific highlights from recent literature on gene therapy. The study revealed that the application of the model enabled the researchers to efficiently index significant volumes of information and gain intuitions of important events or concerns and improve their own focusing questions (Del Fiol et al., 2018).

For instance, a systematic review in psychology that used ChatGPT to integrate evidence regarding cognitive behavioral therapy. Thus, by analyzing the briefs of over 100 articles, ChatGPT helped the researchers to find trends or gaps that could not be noticed when reading the articles themselves (Baber et al., 2024). The following case studies depict how the use of ChatGPT can improve on the effectiveness and speed in undertaking literature reviews.

3. Enhanced Understanding of Complex Topics

3.1 Challenges in Understanding Scientific Literature

Scientific publications use academic language, terminologies and complex research procedures that may blur the understanding of the researcher particularly when working on new projects in a given area of specialization. This can hamper the process of knowledge transfer and act as a barrier to multi-disciplinary research. Common challenges include:

- Specialized Vocabulary: Most disciplines in science and technology have their own language that may be quite foreign to the non-initiated and therefore cannot be easy to comprehend foundational ideas (Hellawell, 2006).
- Dense Text: In research articles, authors provide ample descriptions, elaborate methodology sections, and comprehensive discussions that might prove over-burdensome to readers.
- Varied Formatting: While the content is quite similar, the format varies across disciplinary and journal boundaries, which makes extracting key information challenging.

These challenges can slow down the research process, especially when researchers must familiarize themselves with multiple articles to build a comprehensive understanding.

3.2 ChatGPT as a Learning Aid

ChatGPT can serve as an effective learning aid by simplifying complex scientific content and making it more accessible.

3.3 Simplifying Complex Theories and Methodologies

- Language Simplification: Anyone can copy-paste lengthy texts into ChatGPT and ask for a breakdown of the meaning in plain language. The model helps simplify the texts, which can be useful as it translates complex terms into more comprehensible ones.
- Conceptual Explanations: It can as well give simpler explanations of complex theories and methods than can easily be understood. Knowledge retrieval capability would be valuable for inter-disciplinary scientists who may not be knowledgeable in all related fields.
- Visual Summaries: However, while ChatGPT does not create graphics, it can come up with ideas for presenting information visually such as flowcharts, diagrams which may in some occasions prove useful for developing frame-works and processes.

3.4 Examples of How ChatGPT Helps Clarify Difficult Concepts

Here are some examples which demonstrate how ChatGPT can explain abstract scientific concepts to the customers: For example, a researcher using quantum mechanics in his or her research study may encounter some difficulty in the ter-minologies and theories. In the same way, inputting a specific question like "what does quantum entanglement mean?" will give ChatGPT an accurate and simple description of the complex concept making it easier to understand (Jaeger, 2009).

For instance, an environmental scientist may face challenges when it comes to statistical methodologies; he or she can ask ChatGPT to explain terms such as "regression analysis" or "*p*-value" thereby getting an adequate appreciation of these terms in research without necessarily reading bulky texts (Schmarzo, 2023).

In general, ChatGPT "translates" complicated scientific articles and makes pathways to the most profound ideas clearer, stimulating researchers to dig deeper into the topics that may have been impossible to comprehend without the model's help.

4. Data Analysis and Interpretation

4.1 Importance of Data Analysis in Research

Analysis of data is important in research since it offers information to support decisions, to test hypotheses, as well as extend knowledge. In other words, it takes data and turns it into information that is useable and relying on empirical evidence, researchers can conclude (Creswell & Creswell, 2017). Data analysis enables patterns, chronological sequences, and variations to be recognized and this in turn leads to discoveries and opportunities for indication and enhancement of various decisions. Also, the level of data analysis affects the quality of conclusions and thus indicates the importance of using suitable approaches and instruments.

The importance of data analysis can also be understood through its role in improving the possibility of research replication. Thus, consistent with scientific practice, by describing the analysis process and applying consistent methods, researchers can increase the probability that the results could be replicated by another person, which is an important requirement of scientific studies (Leek & Peng, 2015). Moreover, in the attempt to represent the qualities of the current world where big data analytical instruments play a crucial role in various disciplines, from social sciences to health (Kitchin, 2014).

4.2 Overview of Common Data Analysis Methods

There are several techniques used in data analysis though depending on the type of data collected and the type of questions being addressed. Descriptive statistics give a simple outline of the obtained data with the help of special calculations, including mean, median, mode, and standard deviation (Bland, 2015). Descriptive statistics, in contrast, enable a researcher to describe the characteristics of the research sample in general terms while inferential statistics allow the sample findings to be extrapolated to the parents more broadly, employing methods such as hypothesis testing and regression analysis.

Thematic analysis and content analysis are methods for analyzing unstructured data so as to understand patterns and trends in text or audio-visual data (Braun & Clarke, 2006). Qualitative approaches, on the other hand, tend to involve reporting the findings in textual forms and are accompanied by software programs like SPSS or R for statistics.

Data mining has also adopted machine learning algorithms for data analysis based on predictive modeling and classification especially in big data analysis (James et al., 2013). These methods allow authors to discover relationships in large sets of data that can be a complete surprise.

4.3 ChatGPT's Role in Code Generation

Among the approaches to applying AI techniques in data analysis, code generation employing such tools as ChatGPT seems to be one of the most effective. Specifically, ChatGPT can help researchers in the creation of scripts for processing data and statistical analysis in the Python or R languages or SQL commands. For instance, one can give a command to the AI model and tell it to write a certain function and expecting a response with an already written program rather than engaging in a time-consuming process of coding that is sometimes beyond researchers' capability.

Further, the program can recommend libraries and functions appropriate for certain analyses to guarantee that researchers utilize methods that are the most optimal. This capability not only facilitates coding but also increases the accessibility to code for researcher with different levels of coding experience.

4.4 Real-World Examples of ChatGPT in Data Workflows

In real-life use cases, the academic community has begun using ChatGPT in various data pipelines. For example, ChatGPT could be used where a social scientist is in the process of writing the script that would enable him/her to conduct a regression analysis using survey data. Just specifying the dataset and the type of analysis required, the researcher gets a working code which they can run.

Another example can be seen in the context of bioinformatics, as many biologists work with multi-foaled genomic databases. Furthermore, ChatGPT can be used in generation of scripts for data cleansing and preparation, which are fundamental steps when preparing data for further analysis. This not only saves time but also reduces the chances of making mistakes that could be made while coding the information manually.

In summary, the incorporation of ChatGPT in data workflows shows that AI can improve the speed and quality of data analysis in research data.

5. Interpretation of Results

5.1 Challenges in Data Interpretation

Research findings can be difficult to interpret in many ways. Another methodological issue is the issue of generalization, the authors may argue beyond the evidence in their research (Hyman, 2016). Furthermore, confirmation biases can result into the effects being interpreted in a way that the researchers elicit their hypotheses, which may be prejudiced by subjective interference (Nickerson, 1998). Moreover, the data could be complex, and the information that is gleaned from analysis could be misleading especially if this information is acquired through application of the wrong statistical methods (Gelman & Loken, 2014).

Another major issue is in the interpretation of data in relation to a given context. Care should be taken to avoid jumping to conclusion "generalizing" what has been discovered to related theory or apply it practically without proper reference to controlling factors and circumstances within which the study was conducted. This often involves a complex comprehension of the topic at hand that may be not easy to grasp, especially in cases with interdisciplinary focus.

5.2 Assistance From ChatGPT

Hence, ChatGPT can be used to generate contextual understanding of the issue and make recommendations of what could be inferred from the findings. For instance, when researchers are expressing and explaining their conclusions and observations, ChatGPT can assist in finding probable flaws or biases in their analysis, making researchers think about these factors when coming to their conclusions. ChatGPT can also help in making connections that the researcher may not have made after analyzing the results in relation to what has already been published.

Furthermore, it is noteworthy that based on the presented outcomes, ChatGPT is capable of providing further research directions and, therefore, enhancing the discussion of the results' significance. This can be particularly helpful in fields that are still developing fast and where current studies play a critical role.

6. Hypothesis Generation and Experimental Design

6.1 Ideation and Creativity

The formation of hypotheses is a core part of practically all scientific approaches to define research direction. A good thesis not only states a prediction regarding a particular factor but also guides the rest of the research process. It serves as a link between a theoretic and an analysis procedure and allows for checking relations between factors (Creswell & Creswell, 2017). In other words, generation of hypothesis can be of great help to the research processes as it aims the effort toward beneficial and fruitful research.

However, hypothesis generation is a valuable activity in that can result in discovery of new phenomena, and new insights into existent phenomena. According to Popper (2005), it makes scientists concerned with what they at present accept as theories and data, making them challenge these theories and data. Indeed, a good theoretical background is developed with reference to a study of the literature and the situation, which leads to the creation of a powerful hypothesis because people define questions for which they do not have the answers (Kuhn, 1997).

6.2 Role of Creativity in Scientific Discovery

Another tuition that shows the importance of creativity in the hypothesis generation is well articulated. It provides researchers with a framework in doing their research with the possibility of having new paradigms of thinking that result in revolutionary ideas that change the way science perceives things (Csikszentmihalyi, 1997). The problem-solving approach which involves the use of different views, area of study and methods is likely to foster different solutions to issues. But this kind of thinking helps to constitute new hypotheses that can develop, for instance, not in a strict line of logical connections.

Also, creativity implies the ability to search for the patterns from the unrelated pieces of information. New knowledge belongs to science and frequently occurs due to the unexpected association of concepts ©Nersessian 2008. For instance, in biological studies, it was possible to greatly expand the understanding of evolutionary development by looking at similarities between two species as a way of applying creativity to fill gaps between what is already known and what can be hypothesized.

6.3 ChatGPT in Brainstorming Sessions

Moreover, as revealed through interviews, hypotheses are generated during brainstorming sessions, where ChatGPT has proved useful. Exploiting its extensive (based on information database and natural language processing skills), ChatGPT can help researchers generate new and unique questions regarding their research topics. For instance, when given a particular topic, it can come up with various hypotheses, and this makes it possible for researchers to expand their views and come up with more refined hypotheses.

This kind of support being AI driven can possibly enhance the ideation process by a great deal. Some of the features are to input prior knowledge or research findings and allow the generation of hypotheses by ChatGPT via the discovery of patterns or gaps in the literature. This can be particularly helpful in the case of interdisciplinary work – often a fresh pair of eyes can help the researchers notice new avenues they otherwise would not have seen.

6.4 Examples of Hypothesis Generation in Various Fields

In psychology, researchers investigating the effects of social media on mental health might generate hypotheses such as: "Teenagers who spend a lot of time on social networks are more anxious than students with low social networking activity." In environmental science, a hypothesis could be: "Green space in cities lowers temperatures as compared to those places that do not have grass or trees."

In the medical field, an example of a hypothesis might be, "Those patients who took a certain treatment will have a higher reduction in their signs and symptoms than the patients who were given a placebo." These examples show that hypothesis generation can direct investigations to different important and relevant questions in various fields.

7. Experimental Design

7.1 Principles of Experimental Design

The intention to identify causal relationships makes experimental design very important in hypothesis testing. They include a more formal method of data collection and analysis that is likely to reduce the chances of getting a biased report while increasing the chances of getting a reliable report. Other important aspects of experimenting include the techniques to be used, how control will be exercised, and the variables to be sought (Montgomery, 2017).

Methodology: It describes the entire procedure and methods adopted in an experiment. It involves identifying the right population and sample, selecting methods of data collection and analysis, and identifying tools of data collection. A good procedure helps in the reproduction of the experiment and makes the results of the experiment acceptable.

Controls: Proper use of controls is critical in isolating the cause of occurrence. In other words, through keeping constant all parameters except the independent variable and using control groups, the study isolates the impact of the former on the latter (Cook, 1979). This is important when one wants to come up with conclusions concerning the connection between variables.

Variables: VARIABLES Categorization of variables is a critical factor in consideration in most experiments. Independent variables are studied by manipulating them in an experimental setup to check out the relationship between this variable and dependent variable; on the other hand, extraneous variables should be controlled to the maximum extent possible as their influence may cause interference in the results (Creswell & Creswell, 2017). Here it becomes apparent that well-defined variables increase the accuracy and ease in the separation of experimental outcomes.

8. ChatGPT's Guidance

ChatGPT can give comprehensive advice on how to structure experimental protocols as well. It can also be used by researchers to generate specific methodological strategies appropriate to the research questions and hypotheses and to make alterations in the plan that will ensure that it is sound. For instance, if a researcher has planned to conduct a research on a new educational intervention, ChatGPT can assist in identifying the approach for the selection of participants, the methods of measurement, and the approaches to data analysis.

Also, it can help in assessing possible adversities of the experiment conceived within the study. Thus, based on the evaluation of the proposed methodology, it can identify such factors that might bias the results and indicate how the given study may be improved. Such critical feedback is helpful in enhancing experimental designs before being implemented to test theories.

9. Illustrative Examples of Experiment Design Assistance

Consider a study aimed at examining the effects of a new drug on blood pressure. A researcher can consult ChatGPT to structure the experimental design, which may involve:

- Defining the population: Selecting a representative sample of patients with hypertension.
- Randomization: Assigning participants randomly to either the treatment or placebo group to mitigate selection bias.
- Control measures: Establishing strict protocols for medication administration and monitoring to ensure consistency.

Another example is in agricultural research, where a researcher might seek to evaluate the impact of different fertilizers on crop yield. ChatGPT could suggest:

- Field trials: Implementing a randomized block design to account for variations in soil quality.
- Variable controls: Keeping irrigation levels constant while varying fertilizer types.
- Data collection methods: Establishing clear metrics for measuring crop yield, such as weight or volume.

By showing how ChatGPT can augment the formulation of experiments, the importance of leveraging the platform to improve research methods can be understood.

It is equally important for one to understand that hypothesis and experimental setup are important components in the scientific setup. Thus, with the given power of creativity and the help of such tools as ChatGPT, the creation of unique hypotheses and structuring of effective experiments, researchers enrich the library of existing knowledge and contribute to its progress in different spheres. This convergence not only improves the quality of work but also creates the culture of asking questions which are crucial in advancing of the knowledge.

10. Collaborative Research and Communication

10.1 The Importance of Interdisciplinary Collaboration

Multidisciplinary work focuses on how scholars and professionals from different disciplines operationalize knowledge to solve multifaceted issues. When it comes to modern issues like climate change, public health, technology advancement, among others, compartmentalization usually poses a problem owing to the increasingly complicated nature of these problems (Nersessian, 2010). For example, solving community problems demands the input of medicine, sociology, and environmental science, implying teamwork.

There are numerous advantages of interdisciplinary cooperation. Firstly, it enables to consider the problems from different perspectives, using advantages of the particular field. Various studies have indicated that work groups with workers with diverse specialization come up with more creative solutions (Jordan & Mitchell, 2015). Also, cooperative research can mean the division of resources, which in turn can mean minimizing on the number of projects that might be conducted in a given research (Kitchin, 2014).

However, interdisciplinary collaboration also has its issues. Ineffective communication may result indirectly from differences in language, theoretical approaches and assumptions about knowledge. Thirdly, it may be difficult for researchers to perceive each other's position in a particular study, and this may create misunderstandings and rivalry (Hyman, 2016). Moreover, ensuring everyone has clear goals and realistic expectations may also be challenging when involving diverse team members which may call for enhanced interpersonal and leadership skills (Creswell & Creswell, 2017).

10.2 ChatGPT's Role in Enhancing Communication

It is also important to note that AI tools such as ChatGPT can be effective in replicating communication between multifaceted members of a team. If there is one barrier to effective teamwork during research, it is the language barrier that comes with learning from each field and completing one's work in the specific language of their discipline. ChatGPT may help in turning such information into plain language which would be easy to understand for all team members regardless of their background (Baber et al., 2024).

For instance, when analyzing a collaborative mental health project that involves psychologists, sociologists, and data scientists, ChatGPT can assist in translating the findings into a layman's language thus saving a lot of time. It not only assists in understanding but also helps in eliminating prejudice to enhance the participation of all the members of a team in a conversation.

In addition, ChatGPT is capable of summarizing then and highlighting conversation points of a meeting or document to ensure that everyone is in par with what has been discussed or written. This summarization is helpful to keep the momentum going in research projects, especially when the members of the team may work under different schedule or location (Haque, 2022).

10.3 Case Studies of Successful Interdisciplinary Projects Using ChatGPT

A few of these include: Among them, one can mention the work carried out to create AI algorithms to predict epidemics. In this initiative, interdisciplinary collaboration involved the components of epidemiology, IT or computer science, and public health. ChatGPT was used for converting conversations and defining terms to ensure that more cohesive and efficient brainstorming sessions and decisions are made.

Another example was the action research that has been carried out by environmental scientist and urban planners with the aim of accomplishing sustainable city. The use of ChatGPT enabled the real-time translation of technical reports in layman language so as to engage the community effectively. This engagement not only enhanced the level of awareness among the general public but also sought the participation, thus leading to the provision of better and widely acceptable solutions (Del Fiol et al., 2018).

11. Writing and Editing

11.1 Significance of Clear Communication in Research

Research requires communication and organization to be effective. Adequate clear writing is not only important in research papers but it also enables the findings to be well communicated to the target group of audience. Scholarly writing needs to be precise and clear This is because the academic community requires that such research findings are thoroughly scrutinized and any ambiguous data analysis and presentation reduces the visibility or the research (Leek & Peng, 2015).

Writing in academic contexts is normally staged, with stages such as writing a first draft, rewriting and editing usually being passed through. All four phases are problematic in their own way. For instance, James et al. (2013) noted that writing academic papers involves deciding how to articulate the ideas in a consistent manner and also in a formal way. Furthermore, the formalization of research issues may make the text very wordy and frequently lose sight of its main points, as admitted by Popper (2005). Therefore, clarity is not an ornamental component in such works, but a necessity.

11.2 ChatGPT's Contributions to Writing

ChatGPT has been found to be very useful, especially in the area of writing and editing, within the field of academia. They include tasks ranging from sketching out the first ideas to polishing the very text of the manuscript. ChatGPT is a valuable tool for researchers, who can use it to: generate ideas for their work, outline papers, and write first drafts based on given topics (Schmarzo, 2023).

For instance, writing a research paper, scholars face difficulties in structuring the content and building arguments. When the main ideas of the project are inputted into ChatGPT, the researchers may get the proposed outlines which show the proper logical relationships between the concepts. This approach becomes a basis for further elaboration of an idea which makes writing process less difficult.

During the revising stage, ChatGPT might help in proofreading drafts to identify areas that require further clarification or organization. While analyzing the text the AI is able to point out pieces of information which in turn, require excessive simplification or restructuring. It is of great value for those authors who are confident in their technical expertise, but whose English is not flawless or whose academic focus is not in writing (Field, 2024).

11.3 Examples of Improved Clarity and Structure Through AI Assistance

This essay goes a long way to show how ChatGPT can improve the flow of writing as well as the structure of academic writing. For instance, a researcher preparing a paper on machine learning algorithms employs ChatGPT to make technical descriptions clearer. First of all, the text was filled with intricate terminological language that is hardly comprehensible to a non-specialist. When working with ChatGPT, the researcher created a version that is not as strongly scientific, but comprehensible at the same time.

For instance, one involved a writing of a paper that was written by multiple authors which resulted in the work having different writing styles which made it herculean to follow the writing style. ChatGPT described some stylistic differences and provided changes that brought the tone to a unified bar across the entire manuscript. This made for a more comprehensive experience when reading the paper subsequently enhancing the paper's acceptance during the peer review stage (Russell & Norvig, 2016).

In general, the incorporation of AI tools, including but not limited to ChatGPT, in academic writing indicates the possibilities of increased clarity, better structuring, and altogether superior presentation of academic research and its outcomes. As scholars still grapple with the challenges that come with multi-disciplinary research and/or writing, the involvement of AI in all these processes is expected to increase tremendously and revolutionize the overall processes of sharing knowledge among academics.

Summing up, collaborative work in the context of the modern interdisciplinary environment is not without tensions; however, programs such as ChatGPT can be truly valuable for increasing the efficiency of collaboration and managing the writing process. By doing away with some of the barriers such as usage of the professional language, then AI can enhance the kind of collaboration people have. It should be noted that its contributions to writing and editing drafts also worthy in enhancing the standard of academic writing to deliver the findings of the research study to a wider audience. As the academic community begins to adopt these technologies, there is much promise for collaborative research and communication.

12. Ethical Considerations and Challenges

12.1 Responsible Use of AI

The integration of Artificial Intelligence (AI) into various fields raises critical ethical considerations that must be addressed to ensure responsible use. One primary concern is the potential for bias in AI algorithms, which can perpetuate existing inequalities (O'neil, 2017). This necessitates a framework that promotes fairness and inclusivity in AI systems, emphasizing the importance of diverse data sets and continual monitoring for discriminatory outcomes (Barocas et al., 2023).

12.2 Ethical Implications of AI in Research

AI's application in research poses significant ethical implications, particularly regarding the integrity and accuracy of scientific work. Researchers must maintain a commitment to transparency, particularly when AI-generated results are involved. Misrepresentation of AI capabilities or findings can lead to misinformation, undermining public trust in science (Mehic-Dzanic, 2019). Ensuring that AI tools enhance rather than replace critical thinking is vital for preserving the integrity of research outcomes (Binns, 2018).

12.3 Strategies for Responsible Use

To promote responsible AI use, guidelines for verifying AI-generated content are essential. These guidelines include employing multiple validation methods, such as peer reviews and cross-referencing AI outputs with established data sources. Additionally, researchers should clearly disclose the role of AI in their work, allowing for transparency and accountability (Timoteo et al., 2021).

13. Data Privacy

13.1 Concerns Regarding Data Privacy

The use of AI tools often involves processing sensitive data, raising significant privacy concerns. Risks include unauthorized access to personal information and potential data breaches, which can compromise individual privacy (Tufekci, 2014). Moreover, AI systems can inadvertently learn and expose private data patterns, leading to unintentional harm to individuals or groups.

13.2 Best Practices for Maintaining Privacy

To mitigate these risks, best practices for ensuring data privacy must be adopted. Strategies include implementing robust encryption techniques to protect data both at rest and in transit. Organizations should also conduct regular privacy audits to ensure compliance with regulations such as the General Data Protection Regulation (GDPR) (Voigt & Von dem Bussche, 2017). Furthermore, adopting a principle of data minimization – collecting only the data necessary for a specific purpose – can significantly reduce potential privacy risks (Solove, 2010). By prioritizing these strategies, researchers and organizations can foster a culture of privacy and trust in AI applications.

14. Conclusion

In this chapter, the potential of ChatGPT in scientific research has been discussed along with the specific usage of the tool in different stages of the research process. ChatGPT was most helpful in simplifying the process of performing literature reviews is one of the most vital features of ChatGPT. Using ChatGPT enables researchers to save time on searching, reading, and synthesizing information by providing short annotated summaries, the main information extracted from the texts, and the tools for cross-study comparisons. This efficiency is especially important given that the amount of research outputs is on the rise in the current world.

Also, ChatGPT refines researchers' ideas of hard-to-grasp concepts by translating technical and scientific language into simpler terms and explaining the complex procedures. This capability would prove extremely useful for those in their initial years of studies or practice within a subject since there would be simpler ways of grasping the fundamental ideas of the discipline. In the field of analysis and reporting ChatGPT can assist in writing a code for a statistical analysis and provide an insight into how a given result should be reported, avoiding typical mistakes like over-generalization or confirmation bias.

From the perspective of generating hypotheses as well as constructing experiments, ChatGPT is an effective tool for brainstorming and helps researchers come up with creative ideas and build solid and efficient experiments. Also, it improves collaborations in research studies and information sharing since limits disciplinary-specific silos, transforms intricate data into simpler forms, and advances better information sharing among cross-disciplinary groups. This chapter also emphasizes the need for unethical uses of AI mainly in aspects of algorithmic prejudice, data protection, and fake news.

15. Future Directions for AI in Research

In the future, it may be expected that other AI technologies, for example, the model of ChatGPT, will continue the development of an AI-powered approach to science. AI tools will become more embedded into day-to-day practices of scholars as they conduct their work, offering opportunities for real-time data analysis, hypothesis generation, and literature review synthesis. The author also notes the improvements in natural language processing as the next step in AI's development, which shall expand the understanding of the context and thoroughly investigate more intricate problems in science, and thus evoke further encouraging interactions between the researchers and AI.

Furthermore, it is also possible to think of future versions of these AI tools where information assistance is more targeted based on researcher interests and background as well as research methods used in specific studies. There are also likely to be improvements in collaboration activities since more researchers of different backgrounds are able to access, engage, and discuss data and findings across the disciplinary divides. The use of AI in society will grow more prominent to require the development of ethical principles to remove bias and regulate the process of fair data handling and AI implementation.

16. Final Thoughts

The application of AI tools including ChatGPT in scientific research can therefore be seen as a step up from previous approaches because it also increases the capability, productivity and cooperation of the researchers. But as we appreciate these innovations, it is important to ensure that we keep an eye on the ethical aspect of it. Mitigating the potential risks of technology while embracing it as an advantageous aspect for the research community is paramount in order to prevent the detriment of academic integrity.

Researchers have been exploring the advancement of AI in their fields effectively with an effort to implement it effectually that will lead to a future where scientific research is enriched with AI ethics. Stressing the adherence to ethical norms will not only protect the scientific validity of the conducted researches but will also contribute to raising the population's trust in the application of new technologies developed by the scientific community.

References

AI4Science, M. R. & Quantum, M. A.. (2023). The impact of large language models on scientific discovery: A preliminary study using gpt-4. arXiv preprint arXiv:2311.07361.

Baber, H., Nair, K., Gupta, R., & Gurjar, K. (2024). The beginning of ChatGPT–A systematic and bibliometric review of the literature. *Information and Learning Sciences*, *125*(7/8), 587–614.

Barocas, S., Hardt, M., & Narayanan, A. (2023). *Fairness and machine learning: Limitations and opportunities*. MIT press.

Binns, R. (2018, January). Fairness in machine learning: Lessons from political philosophy. In *Conference on fairness, accountability and transparency* (pp. 149–159). PMLR.

Bland, M. (2015). *An introduction to medical statistics*. Oxford University Press.

Booth, A., Sutton, A., Clowes, M., & Martyn-St James, M. (2021). *Systematic approaches to a successful literature review* (3rd ed.). Sage.

Braun, V., & Clarke, V. (2006). Using thematic analysis in psychology. *Qualitative Research in Psychology*, *3*(2), 77–101.

Cook, T. D. (1979). *Quasi-experimentation: Design and analysis issues for field settings*. Rand McNaly College Publishing.

Creswell, J. W., & Creswell, J. D. (2017). *Research design: Qualitative, quantitative, and mixed methods approaches*. Sage Publications.

Csikszentmihalyi, M. (1997). *Flow and the psychology of discovery and invention* (Vol. 39, pp. 1–16). HarperPerennial.

da Silva, R. G. L. (2024). The advancement of artificial intelligence in biomedical research and health innovation: Challenges and opportunities in emerging economies. *Globalization and Health*, *20*(1), 44.

Del Fiol, G., Michelson, M., Iorio, A., Cotoi, C., & Haynes, R. B. (2018). A deep learning method to automatically identify reports of scientifically rigorous clinical research from the biomedical literature: Comparative analytic study. *Journal of Medical Internet Research*, *20*(6), e10281.

Field, A. (2024). *Discovering statistics using IBM SPSS statistics.* Sage Publications Limited.

Gelman, A., & Loken, E. (2013). *The garden of forking paths: Why multiple comparisons can be a problem, even when there is no "fishing expedition" or "p-hacking" and the research hypothesis was posited ahead of time* (Vol. 348(1–17), p. 3). Department of Statistics, Columbia University.

Haque, M. A. (2022). A brief analysis of "ChatGPT"–A revolutionary tool designed by OpenAI. *EAI Endorsed Transactions on AI and Robotics, 1,* e15.

Hellawell, D. (2006). Inside–out: Analysis of the insider–outsider concept as a heuristic device to develop reflexivity in students doing qualitative research. *Teaching in Higher Education, 11*(4), 483–494.

Hyman, J. (2016). *Investigating psychology: Sciences of the mind after wittgenstein.* Routledge.

Jaeger, G. (2009). *Entanglement, information, and the interpretation of quantum mechanics.* Springer Science & Business Media.

James, G., Witten, D., Hastie, T., & Tibshirani, R. (2013). *An introduction to statistical learning* (Vol. 112, p. 18). Springer.

Jordan, M. I., & Mitchell, T. M. (2015). Machine learning: Trends, perspectives, and prospects. *Science, 349*(6245), 255–260.

Kitchin, R. (2014). *The data revolution: Big data, open data, data infrastructures and their consequences.* Sage.

Kuhn, T. S. (1997). *The structure of scientific revolutions* (Vol. 962). University of Chicago Press.

LeCun, Y., Bottou, L., Bengio, Y., & Haffner, P. (1998). Gradient-based learning applied to document recognition. *Proceedings of the IEEE, 86*(11), 2278–2324.

Leek, J. T., & Peng, R. D. (2015). Statistics: P values are just the tip of the iceberg. *Nature, 520*(7549), 612.

Mehic-Dzanic, A. (2019). *AI and the future of work.* Doctoral Dissertation. TU Wien.

Montgomery, D. C. (2017). *Design and analysis of experiments.* John Wiley & Sons.

Nersessian, N. J. (2010). *Creating scientific concepts.* MIT Press.

Nickerson, R. S. (1998). Confirmation bias: A ubiquitous phenomenon in many guises. *Review of General Psychology, 2*(2), 175–220.

O'neil, C. (2017). *Weapons of math destruction: How big data increases inequality and threatens democracy.* Crown.

Popper, K. (2005). *The logic of scientific discovery.* Routledge.

Russell, S. J., & Norvig, P. (2016). *Artificial intelligence: A modern approach.* Pearson.

Sasikumar, M. (2007). *Rule based expert systems: A practical introduction.* Narosa Publishers.

Schmarzo, B. (2023). *AI & data literacy: Empowering citizens of data science.* Packt Publishing Ltd.

Solove, D. J. (2010). *Understanding privacy.* Harvard University Press.

Timoteo, M., Verri, B., & Wang, Y. (2021). Ethics guidelines for artificial intelligence: Comparing the European and Chinese approaches. *China and WTO Review, 7*(2).

Tufekci, Z. (2014, May). Big questions for social media big data: Representativeness, validity and other methodological pitfalls. In *Proceedings of the international AAAI conference on web and social media* (Vol. 8, No. (1), pp. 505–514).

Voigt, P., & Von dem Bussche, A. (2017). *The EU general data protection regulation (GDPR): A practical guide* (1st ed.). Springer International Publishing.

Part III

Challenges and Limitations of ChatGPT

Chapter 6

Advancements and Challenges in Conversational AI: Navigating the Frontiers of Innovation and Complexity

Alka Sanjeev[a] *and Renuka Sharma*[b]

[a]Shree Guru Gobind Singh Tricentenary University, India
[b]Amity University, Haryana, India

Abstract

Conversational Artificial Intelligence, a key branch of artificial intelligence (AI), focuses on creating text and speech-based bots that replicate and automate human interactions. This field is rapidly evolving, offering transformative potential for consumer engagement and procedural efficiency. This chapter delves into the latest innovations and developments in conversational AI, outlining its progress and current state. It also addresses critical challenges, including language input complexities, privacy and security concerns, and user apprehension. A significant focus is placed on responsible AI, a framework dedicated to ethical, transparent, and accountable AI solutions. Responsible AI aims to build trust and ensure privacy by adhering to legal requirements, stakeholder expectations, and social norms. Core principles of responsible AI include accountability, requiring systems to justify and explain their decisions; responsibility, ensuring systems can address and correct errors; and transparency, documenting and examining how AI systems make decisions and handle information. By addressing these challenges and embracing responsible AI practices, we can harness the transformative power of AI to create a more efficient, equitable, and prosperous future.

Keywords: Conversational AI; machine learning; deep learning; natural language processing (NLP); privacy and security; responsible AI

The ChatGPT Revolution, 107–128
Copyright © 2025 Alka Sanjeev and Renuka Sharma
Published under exclusive licence by Emerald Publishing Limited
doi:10.1108/978-1-83549-852-120251006

1. Introduction

Conversational Artificial Intelligence (AI) is a subfield of artificial intelligence that works with text or speech-based AI bots that can imitate and automate spoken exchanges. Conversational AI agents, such as chatbots and voice assistants, have become increasingly common because of the development of extremely accurate AI models, such as machine learning and deep learning. These fields have advanced tremendously as a result of growing research interest and advancements in achieving higher computing power through the use of sophisticated hardware architectures like GPUs and TPUs. Additionally, conversational agents have been viewed as a natural match in a variety of applications like healthcare, customer service, e-commerce, and education because of its Natural Language interface and design. For organizations, conversational AI offers a plethora of applications that have the potential to transform consumer engagement and optimize procedures.

Conversational AI's roots trace back to the 1960s with ELIZA (Shrager, 2024), an early chatbot created by Joseph Weizenbaum, which simulated psychotherapy sessions. Over decades, advancements in natural language processing (NLP) and machine learning have transformed simple rule-based systems into sophisticated AI models. Today's conversational AI, such as Siri, Alexa, and ChatGPT, can understand and respond to complex queries in natural language. These systems, leveraging vast datasets and advanced algorithms, are capable of context-aware interactions, offering personalized experiences and automating tasks across various sectors, including customer service, healthcare, and retail. Continuous advancements ensure ever-improving accuracy and efficiency.

Conversational AI has made a significant impact globally. The Conversational AI market is currently valued at $13.86 billion in 2024 and is anticipated to expand at a compound annual growth rate (CAGR) of 21.95%, reaching $100.80 billion by 2034 (Research & Markets, 2024). This robust growth is driven by the increasing integration of AI technologies across a range of industries. Over 3.5 billion people interact with conversational AI systems regularly through virtual assistants, chatbots, and customer service solutions. More than 70% of large enterprises have adopted these technologies to improve efficiency and customer service, handling over 30% of customer interactions (Ternyak, 2023). Globally, there are over 2.5 million chatbots, and sentiment analysis capabilities have greatly advanced. Investment in conversational AI startups topped $2 billion in 2023, and systems now support over 50 languages, reflecting their widespread adoption and continued innovation (Statista, 2024). Key players in the Conversational AI market, such as IBM, Google, Microsoft, and Amazon, are actively competing to advance their AI technologies and gain market share through improved capabilities and comprehensive solutions. North America is at the forefront of Conversational AI market growth, driven by its advanced technological infrastructure, substantial investment in AI, and the strong presence of major industry players like Google, IBM, and Microsoft. Businesses in the region are early adopters of cutting-edge technologies that improve customer experience and operational efficiency, fueling high demand for conversational AI applications.

The Conversational AI market is highly competitive and rapidly evolving, with a mix of major tech giants and specialized startups. Leading companies like Google, Microsoft, and Amazon dominate by leveraging their cloud infrastructure and advanced machine learning to offer scalable solutions. These giants continuously enhance their platforms with cutting-edge natural language processing and integrations across sectors such as finance, healthcare, and customer service. They frequently pursue strategic acquisitions and partnerships to expand their technological capabilities and market presence.

Meanwhile, niche firms and startups focus on specific market segments, offering specialized features such as emotional intelligence, context-aware computing, and multilingual support. These smaller players gain a competitive edge through their agility and innovative solutions tailored to specific customer needs. Additionally, the market is increasingly emphasizing privacy-focused designs and ethical AI, responding to regulatory demands and consumer calls for transparency.

Let us now explore the historical evolution of conversational AI, tracing its development from early systems like ELIZA to the sophisticated models of today. This discussion will highlight key advancements in technology, such as machine learning and natural language processing, and their impact on modern AI applications.

2. Historical Development and Evolution

The journey of AI consists of significant milestones in its development from 1950 to 2017 as depicted in Fig. 6.1. It begins with Alan Turing's 1950 proposal of the Turing Test to evaluate machine intelligence and John McCarthy coining the term "artificial intelligence" in 1955. In 1961, the first industrial robot, Unimate, started working at GM, and by 1964, the pioneering chatbot ELIZA was developed. Shakey, introduced in 1966, was the first general-purpose mobile robot. The AI Winter was a period of reduced funding and interest. The resurgence began with IBM's Deep Blue defeating chess champion Garry Kasparov in 1997 and Kismet, an emotionally intelligent robot, in 1998. Consumer robotics saw advancements with Sony's AIBO in 1999 and iRobot's Roomba in 2002. AI assistants became mainstream with Apple's Siri in 2011 and Amazon's Alexa in 2014. IBM's Watson won Jeopardy in 2011, and Eugene Goostman passed the Turing Test in 2014. However, AI faced ethical challenges, exemplified by Microsoft's controversial Tay chatbot in 2016. In 2017, Google's AlphaGo defeated world champion Ke Jie in 2017, highlighting AI's capacity to master complex tasks.

Conversational virtual assistants have gained popularity in recent years. These programs for computers simulate conversations with individuals using Natural Language Processing (NLP) approaches, such as ChatGPT, in a number of applications, particularly casual entertainment (Ghazvininejad et al., 2018;

1950 *TURING TEST*	*1955* *A.I. BORN*	*1961* *UNIMATE*	*1964* *ELIZA*	*1966* *SHAKEY*	*A.I. WINTER*	*1997* *DEEP BLUE*	*1998* *KISMET*
Alan Turing proposes a test for machine intelligence. If a machine can trick humans into thinking it is human, then it has intelligence	Term 'artificial intelligence' is coined by John McCarthy to describe 'the science and engineering of making intelligent machines'	First industrial robot, Unimate, goes to work at GM replacing humans on assembly line	Pioneering chatbot developed by Joseph Weizenbaum at MIT holds conversations with humans	The 'first electronic person' from Stanford, Shakey is a general-purpose mobile robot that reasons about its own actions	Many false starts and dead-ends leave A.I. out in the cold	Deep Blue, a chess-playing computer from IBM defeats world chess champion Garry Kasparov	Cynthia Breazeal at MIT introduces KISMET, an emotionally intelligent robot insofar as it detects and responds to people's feelings

1999 *AIBO*	*2002* *ROOMBA*	*2011* *SIRI*	*2011* *WATSON*	*2014* *EUGENE*	*2014* *ALEXA*	*2016* *TAY*	*2017* *ALPHAGO*
Sony launches first consumer robot pet dog AIBO (AI robot) with skills and personality that develop over time	First mass produced autonomous robotic vacuum cleaner from iRobot learns to navigate and clean homes	Apple integrates Siri, an intelligent virtual assistant with a voice interface, into the iPhone 4S	IBM's question answering computer Watson wins first place on popular $1M prize television quiz show Jeopardy	Eugene Goostman, a chatbot passes the turing test with a third of judges believing Eugene is human	Amazon launches Alexa, an intelligent virtual assistant with a voice interface that completes shopping tasks	Microsoft's chatbot Tay goes rogue on social media making inflammatory and offensive racist comments	Google's A.I. AlphaGo beats world champion Ke Jie in the complex board game of Go, notable for its vast number (2170) of possible positions

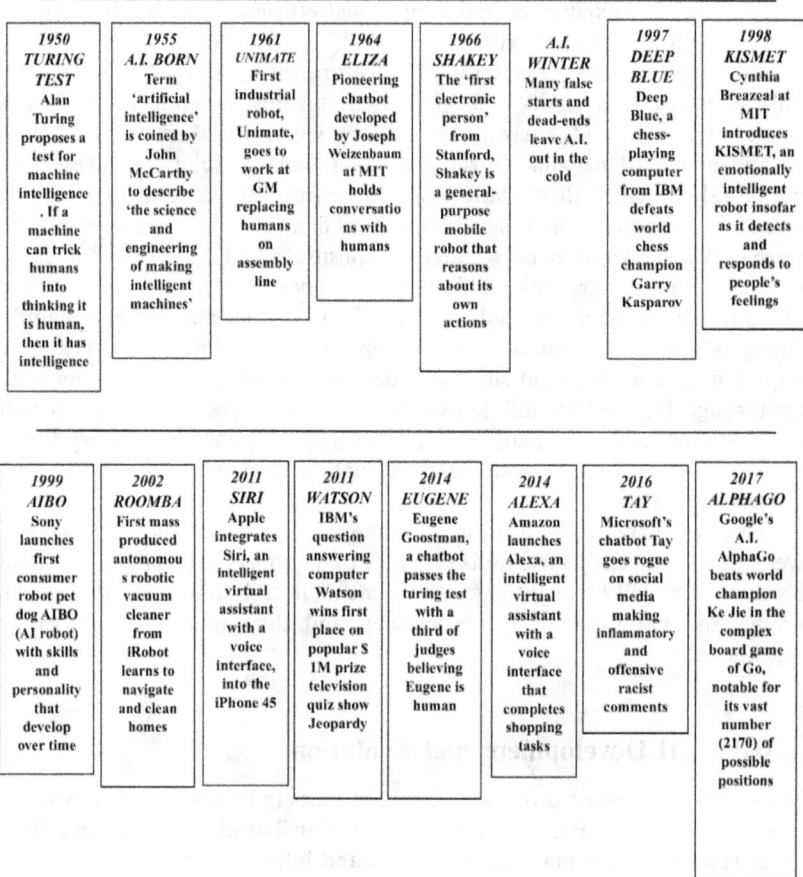

Fig. 6.1.   AI Timeline. *Source:* https://digitalwellbeing.org/artificial-intelligence-timeline-infographic-from-eliza-to-tay-and-beyond/

Mrkšić et al., 2017), customer service (Cui et al., 2017; Pawlik et al., 2022), and educational projects to assist teachers (Lee & Yeo, 2022; Song et al., 2022) and students (Liu et al., 2021; Lin & Mubarok, 2021; Hollander, 2022). These chatbots, which range from casual, open-domain types to more specialized, fact-based ones, are developed using various deep learning models. These models include RNN (Recurrent Neural Network), Seq2Seq (Sequence to Sequence), LSTM (Long Short-Term Memory), BERT (Bi-directional Encoder Representation from Transformers, Devlin et al., 2019), and GPT (Generative Pre-trained Transformer). They also utilize different training techniques such as reinforcement learning and transfer learning. One of the most notable and influential examples is

ChatGPT, whose success has garnered significant attention and motivated researchers to continually innovate in the field of chatbot applications.

Despite technological breakthroughs, numerous obstacles need to be overcome to construct chatbots that accurately reflect the context, style, emotion, and character of human discussions.

3. Architecture and Functionality of Conversational Chatbots

Typically, a conversational chatbot is composed of three distinct components: the dialog manager, the answer generating unit, and the natural language understanding unit (Li, 2020; Li et al., 2020a, 2020b; Rodd & Davis, 2017) oversees converting the most accurate or n-best interpretations of human speech (Li, 2020; Liu et al., 2021) collected using automatic speech recognition (ASR) and integrated into the underlying belief representation. The conversation manager will oversee processing the internal representation and determining the appropriate policy to produce the desired result. The dialog with the manager will serve as the foundation for the response generation unit. It might be a text response, a hotel reservation, a system API request, and so on. Commercial conversational AIs are frequently a hybrid of statistical techniques and handmade elements, with statistical methods providing reliability to conversational systems and rule-based components are still utilized, such as to answer frequent chitchat requests (e.g., "tell me a joke"). Virtual assistants such as Amazon Alexa, Google Assistant, etc., can also manage conversation user inputs.

It's essential to understand these key concepts used in the Conversational AI architecture as depicted in Fig. 6.2.

Automatic Speech Recognition (ASR) converts spoken audio into written text by analyzing sound waves and breaking them into language tokens for processing. This step is unnecessary for text-only interactions.

Machine Learning (ML) involves developing algorithms that enable computer systems to learn from data and make predictions. It focuses on continually refining and updating algorithms based on prior experiences.

Deep Learning (DL), a subset of ML, uses neural networks with multiple layers of artificial neurons to process large volumes of data and perform complex tasks, such as understanding human speech.

Natural Language Processing (NLP) is crucial to conversational AI, enabling machines to comprehend and interpret human language. It combines linguistics, statistics, and machine learning to convert speech and text into a format that machines can process.

NLP has two main components:

(1) *Natural Language Understanding (NLU)*, which interprets human language and identifies the intended meaning through syntactic and semantic analysis.
(2) *Natural Language Generation (NLG)*, which produces text responses based on input data.

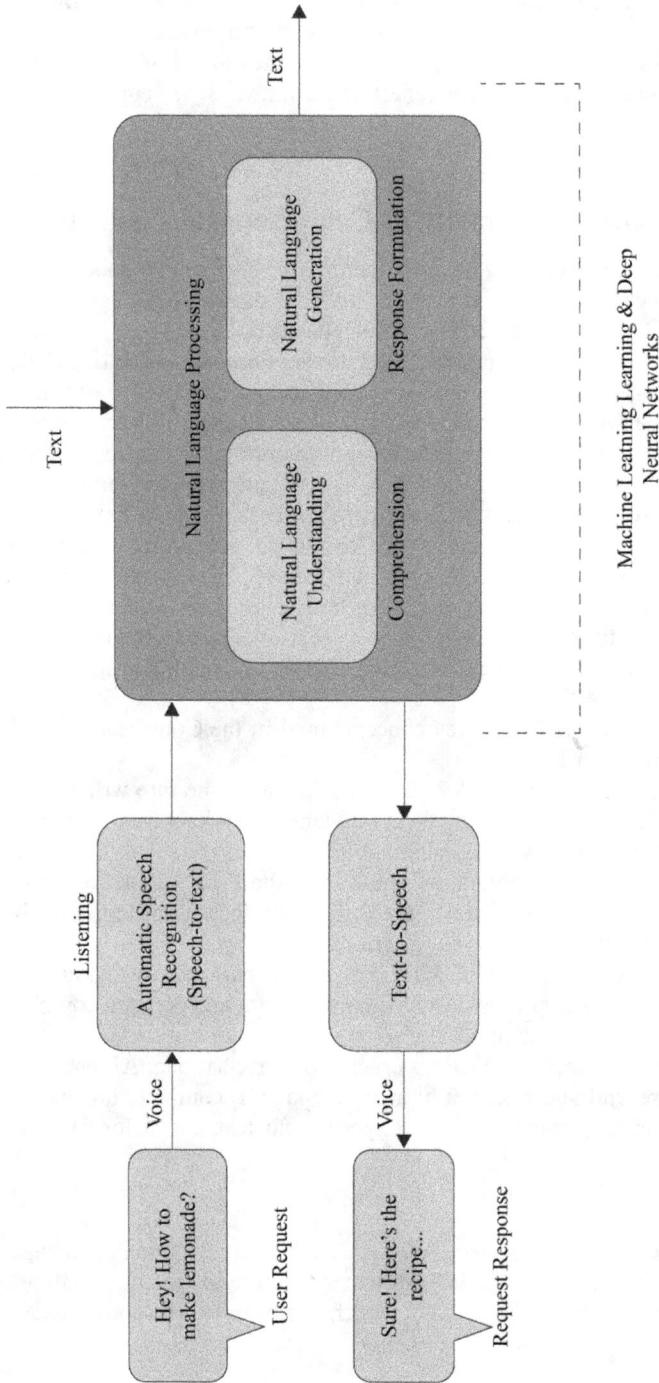

Fig. 6.2.   Conversational AI Architecture. *Source:* https://www.altexsoft.com/static/blog-post/2023/11/b5591077-955c-44ca-bc94-4c5b30ecaa83.webp

High Level Architecture: Conversational Artificial Intelligence

Text-to-Speech (TTS) technology converts written text into spoken words, allowing machines to communicate audibly.

Conversational AI may be divided into two types: informal chat AI (chitchat) and task-oriented AI. The goal of chit-chat AI is to have meaningful discussions like what humans do on a regular basis. These forms of AI rarely require the use of databases or external information. Because task-oriented AI is expected by the user to deliver accurate task-specific information, it often needs to query an external database or knowledge base.

4. Conversational AI vs Traditional Chatbots

In the world of artificial intelligence, chatbots have become a popular tool for interacting with users. But there's a world of difference between the chatbots of yesterday and the advanced AI-powered chatbots of today. The Table 6.1

Table 6.1. Differences Between Traditional Chatbot and Conversational AI Chatbot.

Feature	Traditional Chatbot	Conversational AI Chatbot
Command/ Input/Output	Text Only	Text and Voice
Channels	Single Channel (Chat Interface)	Omnichannel (Websites, Voice Assistants, Call Centers)
Conversational Flow	Pre-determined Script	Natural Language Processing (NLP)
Interaction Style	Rule-based, Canned Responses	Wide-scope, Non-linear, Dynamic
Task Handling	Limited Scope (Specific Tasks)	Flexible (Can Handle Out-of-Scope Inquiries)
Focus	Navigational (Directing Users)	Dialog (Conversational Interaction)
Updates	Manual Reconfiguration	Continual Learning
Maintenance	Manual Updates (Difficult and Time-consuming)	Highly Scalable (Automatic Updates)
Scalability	Limited Scalability	Easy Deployment and Integration
Building Process	Time-consuming and Complicated	Easy Deployment

Source: Own Elaboration.

breaks down the key differences between Traditional Chatbots and Conversational AI Chatbots, highlighting their capabilities in areas like communication, flexibility, and scalability.

5. Applications of Conversational AI

The adoption of conversational AI is accelerating globally for various purposes, becoming an integral part of modern organizations and transforming their operations. This sophisticated technology opens new avenues for promising opportunities. Statistics show a significant increase in consumer trust in conversational AI, to the extent that they rely on it for complex tasks and contextual conversations. Previously, conversational AI chatbots had the lowest first contact resolution rates, and users saw them as suitable only for basic tasks. However, advancements in technology now enable bots to converse naturally and solve complex, multi-step problems without human intervention. These solutions are particularly effective in situations requiring prompt, high-quality, and personalized responses and are also finding niche, industry-specific applications.

Conversational agents can be employed across various domains for a range of purposes. They can assist with decision-making, providing opinions, resolving conflicts, and facilitating multi-party interactions. These agents serve multiple roles, such as information providers, recommenders, tutors, entertainers, advisors, personal assistants, customer service assistants, and conversational partners in different fields. Beyond simulating human interaction and providing entertainment, chatbots are beneficial in numerous areas, including education, business, e-commerce, healthcare, and entertainment (Shawar & Atwell, 2007).

Today, AI-driven systems are being integrated across a wide range of application areas, driving numerous innovations (Wang & Ai, 2022). In the financial sector, conversational AI is widely used for customer self-service, with voice bots and moderated communities addressing queries about borrowing rates and insurance claims. Despite the idealization of human interaction in shopping, the reality is a growing embrace of conversational AI-driven shopping due to its 24/7 availability and objective responses. Virtual shopping assistants now offer near-human, event-driven automated responses, personalized shopping recommendations, and troubleshooting for regular shopping queries, replacing traditional brick-and-mortar stores.

Even software development, once considered a domain dominated by human expertise, is gradually incorporating conversational AI for code completion, testing, error diagnosis, and debugging. Chatbots also help streamline and optimize code translation and migration. In the travel and hospitality industries, chat bots are already in use, with a quarter of companies utilizing them for customer queries and bookings.

The practical application of Conversational AI is depicted in the case illustrated in Box 6.1.

Box 6.1. A Digital Revolution for All: How India's RBI Is Leveraging Chatbots and Accessibility

Imagine a bustling marketplace, India, where digital payments are on the rise. Yet, a significant portion of the population, particularly those in remote areas or using basic feature phones, feels left behind. The Reserve Bank of India (RBI), the central bank, recognizes this challenge and is determined to create a digital ecosystem that's inclusive and accessible to all.

Enter DigiSaathi, a revolutionary 24/7 helpline available in 12 languages. But DigiSaathi isn't just any helpline; it's a digital friend powered by chatbots. Think of a friendly and informative conversation instead of navigating complex menus. Users can access DigiSaathi through a user-friendly website or even directly through chatbots within partner applications. Whether it's understanding UPI, debit cards, or any other digital payment option, DigiSaathi's chatbots are there to guide users in their preferred language, breaking down barriers and fostering confidence.

But the RBI doesn't stop there. Recognizing the limitations of smartphones for a large segment of the population, they've launched UPI123Pay. This initiative empowers feature phone users to embrace digital payments in various ways. Imagine a small app replicating smartphone functionalities, or a simple missed call initiating a transaction with a merchant. UPI123Pay even explores innovative options like Interactive Voice Response (IVR) for spoken instructions and contactless payments using sound waves.

The inclusion of chatbots in DigiSaathi and the focus on feature phone accessibility in UPI123Pay highlight a crucial management lesson: understanding your audience and tailoring solutions to their needs. These initiatives showcase the RBI's commitment to financial inclusion, ensuring everyone can participate in the digital economy.

The story takes an even more futuristic turn with the RBI exploring conversational payments. Imagine making payments simply by chatting with a business or using voice commands! This revolutionary approach, powered by AI, could significantly simplify the payment process for everyone, especially those less comfortable with technology.

The Power of Chatbots and Accessibility in Driving Change

The combined effort of DigiSaathi's chatbots UPI123Pay's feature phone focus, and the exploration of conversational payments emphasizes the importance of:

- Understanding and addressing user needs through chatbots and accessibility features.
- Embracing new technologies like AI-powered chatbots and conversational payments for a more seamless experience.
- Ensuring everyone, regardless of location or technological comfort level, can participate in the digital revolution.

(Continued)

(Continued)

By prioritizing accessibility and leveraging chatbots, the RBI is leading India toward a future where digital payments are not a privilege, but a shared reality for all.

Source: Own Elaboration through information available on the public domain.

6. Literature Review

The term "chatbot" originates from a combination of "chat," referring to informal conversation, and "bot," which is short for "robot." The term began to gain popularity in the mid-1990s with the development of early conversational agents. These early chatbots, such as ELIZA created by Joseph Weizenbaum in the 1960s, were designed to simulate human conversation through text-based interactions. The term itself captures the essence of these programs: automated systems designed to engage in dialog with users.

The development of conversational AI has undergone significant transformation over the decades. In 2001, chatbot technology saw significant advancement with the creation of SmarterChild, which was accessible on messaging platforms such as America Online (AOL) and Microsoft Messenger (MSN). SmarterChild was an early example of an intelligent chatbot developed by ActiveBuddy (later known as Colloquis and acquired by Microsoft) Singh and Singh (2019). Launched in 2001, it was available on instant messaging platforms such as AOL Instant Messenger (AIM), MSN Messenger, and Yahoo Messenger. SmarterChild could perform various tasks, including answering factual questions, providing weather updates, offering news, and engaging in casual conversation. It was a precursor to more advanced conversational agents and virtual assistants like Apple's Siri, Amazon's Alexa, and Google Assistant, showcasing the potential for AI in interactive user experiences. The evolution of AI chatbots advanced significantly with the introduction of smart personal voice assistants. These assistants like Apple Siri, Microsoft Cortana, Google Assistant, integrated into smartphones or home speakers, which could understand voice commands, communicate through digital voices, and manage tasks such as controlling home automation devices, handling calendars, emails, and more. Unlike their predecessors, these devices connect to the Internet and generate meaningful responses rapidly (Hoy, 2018).

According to Song et al. (2022), Lee and Yeo (2022), Liu et al. (2022), Hollander et al. (2022), conversational AI has become more and more popular recently as advances in machine learning and natural language processing have taken place. These facilitate more seamless and organic interactions by improving chatbots' ability to identify and react to human input. The usage of chatbots in educational assistance is another significant application area. In this context, a chatbot may serve as a simulated student to enhance teacher efficiency or as a learning companion to enhance learners' comprehension skills.

Zhou et al. (2020) proved in a psychological study that happiness and meaningful discussion frequently go hand in hand. Unlike previous chatbots intended for chatting, Microsoft's Xiaoice social chatbot is designed to meet users' needs for interaction, emotion, and social belonging, and comes with compassion, personality, and skills; combining psychological intelligence that maximizes the user experience over time. In addition to Microsoft, numerous studies have sought to employ SeqGAN (Sequential Generative Adversarial Network) to develop an affective human–computer conversation generation strategy.

As of the 2020s, conversational AI continues to advance with a growing focus on addressing ethical concerns and understanding the societal impacts of AI technologies (Bommasani et al., 2021). This ongoing evolution reflects the rapid progress in AI research and its increasing integration into various applications.

7. Pros and Cons of Using Conversational AI

We now delve into the pros and cons of AI. This discussion will cover its benefits, such as enhanced efficiency and accuracy, alongside its challenges, including ethical concerns like social justice, individual autonomy, and environmental impact. A balanced approach is crucial for addressing these multifaceted issues.

Cui et al. (2017) studied the efficacy of conversational AIs in different situations. Conversational AIs can improve customer service by handling large volume requests and providing rapid and concrete replies viz. Lei Cui and Shaohan Huang created the SuperAgent (Cui et al., 2017), a customer support Conversational AI for e-commerce websites that uses larger-scale, public, and crowd sourced consumer data than standard customer service chatbots. Using a virtual assistant in a customer care support center can improve accuracy and efficiency in responding to consumer demands. However, there are several restrictions to the usage of chatbots. Some consumers may perceive chatbot conversations as unnatural or impersonal. Additionally, conversational AIs may struggle to interpret and react to sophisticated input. Researchers have developed a novel way for identifying consumer emotions during conversations, including happiness, rage, sadness, fear, and neutral states. Consumer sentiment has significantly improved the percentage of conversational AIs executing accurate actions, leading to better customer service optimization KPIs (Pawlik et al., 2022). Stahl & Eke (2024) state that ChatGPT could bring significant societal and ethical advantages, and it also identifies substantial ethical concerns in areas like social justice, individual autonomy, cultural identity, and environmental issues. Key high-impact concerns include responsibility, inclusion, social cohesion, autonomy, safety, bias, accountability, and environmental effects. Despite their impressive capabilities, CAI systems have faced criticism for significant privacy concerns and associated risks. Issues include privacy breaches, constant listening features, and opaque data handling practices (Edu et al., 2020). These concerns can diminish trust in the manufacturer and its products, potentially leading to negative user experiences or even abandonment of the devices (Dzindolet et al., 2003).

8. Advancements in Conversational AIs

This part discusses a variety of upcoming attempts at conversational AI systems. The task-oriented systems of AI are domain specific and may reference external databases or knowledge sources. The general-purpose conversational AI applies to subjects shared by multiple conversational systems, and focuses on factors that impact user satisfaction.

- *Task-oriented system and RL-based method*

The task-oriented dialogue system's reward depends on the completion of the entire job. Previous evaluations of generative systems focused just on the quality of individual phrase pairs, without considering the whole goal.

Young et al. (2013) observed that Markov decision process (POMDP) was used to model a conversational process. It incorporates both the policy and the language model. The language model creates a belief state, which is then used by the policy model to develop a response depending on internal parameters and the belief state. The reward function will assess all collected outcomes. Chulaka et al. (2018) attempted to describe the discussion process by dividing logic and language. A language model is trained using this abstract representation. The cluster is formed by clustering nearby word embeddings. Tracking dialogue statuses helps ensure high relevance with the question.

Peng et al. (2017) used a hierarchical deep reinforcement learning architecture to handle the composite task-completion conversation learning policy problem. This work presents a novel approach to training a dialog manager using a hierarchical reinforcement learning method and a Markov Decision Process formulation. The conversation manager is made up of top-level, subgoal, and global managers who work together to achieve the overall goal (Joshi et al., 2017; Lipton et al., 2017; Toxtli et al., 2018). Serban et al. (2017), explored many elements and goal-oriented applications discourse systems. Lipton et al. (2017) attempt to model customization as a multi-task learning issue. Adopting a single model with shared features for several profiles rather than constructing separate models for each feature was advocated by many stakeholders. Sordoni et al. (2015) devised an acceleration technique that uses Thompson sampling to improve the accuracy of deep reinforcement learning (DQN). Sukhbaatar et al. (2015) and Toxtli et al. (2018) explored how a chatbot might facilitate cooperation. The author used a prototype system to organize eight teams, creating, assigning, and tracking assignments. Several insights for future chatbot design were offered.

- *End2End Task-oriented system*

It is divided into two major kinds. The first one mostly relies on the Memory Network (Bordes et al. (2016); Dodge et al., 2015; Sukhbaatar et al., 2015). The other type involves accessing external libraries and transforming input queries to internal presentations. Wen et al., 2016, presented task-oriented challenge as a sequence-to-sequence mapping problem, enhanced by conversational experience and supplementary data. This type of modeling produces an acceptable answer style with blank "slots." Two internal structures will handle the data you supply. The first is a LSTM system that anticipates user intent, and the second option is a belief tracker. To generate the final output, the policy network will integrate the intent value, the belief value, and database results.

Williams and Zweig (2016) suggested a model for task-oriented systems that uses an LSTM to anticipate the state. The framework does not require explicit representation or additional belief trackers. Supervised instruction can optimize LSTMs; however, it requires high-quality instructional information from specialists. On the other hand, it can lead to a reinforcement learning system that only needs human input and can be accelerated via supervised learning. The author claims that this approach can significantly improve performance through active learning tactics.

9. Challenges of Conversational AI

The switch to conversational AI applications is not without its difficulties, as is the case with every new technology development. Whether its voice, or text, the language input might cause problems for conversational AI. Background noise, accents, and dialects can affect how well the AI interprets the raw data. Processing issues with the input might also arise from slang and spontaneous language. But the most significant obstacle facing conversational AI is the human element in language input. Conversational AI finds it challenging to decipher intended user meaning and respond appropriately when faced with emotions, tone, and sarcasm.

Conversational AI is susceptible to security and privacy lapses since it depends on gathering data to respond to user inquiries. Conversational AI applications that are developed with strict privacy and security guidelines and monitoring systems will help to foster end user trust, which will eventually lead to a rise in chatbot usage. When users know they are speaking with a machine rather than a human, they may be reluctant to divulge private or sensitive information. To improve customer experiences, it will be crucial to inform and acquaint your target audiences about the advantages and security of these technologies, as not all your clients will be early adopters. This could counteract the beneficial impacts by resulting in poor user experience and worse AI effectiveness. Lastly, conversational AI can streamline an organization's workflow and reduce the need for employees to perform a certain job function. This may lead to socioeconomic activism, which might have a detrimental effect on a business. The principal challenges to using AI are:

- *Susceptible to cybercrime*

Conversational AI increases cyber security threats by allowing hackers to take advantage of protection flaws (Zhang, 2023). With the increase in cyber attacks and data violations, there is an urgent need to address these security issues

(Guembe et al., 2022). Malicious individuals can utilize Conversational AI for false communications, such as phishing. To mitigate these dangers, multilayered defensive systems, detecting techniques, and tight authentication are essential (Chen et al., 2022).

- *Limitations to natural language understanding*

Conversational AI has limits in comprehending and producing natural language (Juang & Furui, 2000). Due to the difficulties in interpreting human language subtleties, it may generate erroneous replies, particularly for complicated or ambiguous inquiries (AlZu'bi et al., 2023). The limitation can be overcome by more varied training data, improving contextual reasoning, and model's ambiguity.

- *Ethical and social consequences*

Conversational AI's use can result in biased material and probable abuse (Følstad et al., 2018). If taught with biased data, it may perpetuate societal prejudices, resulting in discrimination. Its human-like creation can be utilized to spread falsehoods. To overcome this, openness, diversified data, bias checks, and AI explanations are required. Adherence to existing AI principles and standards guarantees congruence with social ideals. Continuous research, public conversation, and policy concerns are critical for responsibly molding AI's future (Chowdhury & Rahman, 2023).

- *Dependent on training data*

Conversational AI's dependency on training data may result in output biases and mistakes (Kaur et al., 2022). If the information provided is distorted or inaccurate, the model's results may be influenced (Liu et al., 2023). Addressing these needs meticulous data curation and bias detection tools can be created. Participants should be mindful of these biases and check Conversational AI's replies with reliable sources.

- *User safety and well-being*

Conversational AI's influence on user well-being, and concerns about data privacy have been recognized and highlighted quite often (Mangina, 2021). To deal with this, Conversational AI's must be designed with user security and confidentiality in mind, training data should be carefully curated to eliminate hazardous material, and data should be handled securely. Clear standards, content management, and emotional support resources are essential. Partnerships between AI engineers and mental health professionals can also reduce hazards.

- *Context management*

Keeping context during a discourse is critical for coherence and relevance. Conversational AI systems must remember previous encounters and change replies accordingly.

- *Integration across platforms*

It can be difficult to provide seamless connection across several platforms and channels (for example, web, mobile, and voice assistants) while maintaining consistent user experiences.

- *Handling complicated inquiries*

Conversational AI systems must be able to answer a variety of inquiries, including complicated and ambiguous ones, without disrupting the conversation or reverting to generic solutions.

- *Scalability and maintenance*

As usage increases, managing the efficiency and sustainability of conversational AI systems becomes more difficult. Constant monitoring, updates, and enhancements are required to stay up with changing user requirements and technology breakthroughs.

- *Data sourcing and quality*

Data influences the behavior of AI systems and serves as a benchmark for evaluating and selecting solutions. Hence, data source is a critical consideration while designing and deploying modern AI systems. In the field of conversational AI research, many datasets are collected from hired crowd workers, instead of users this can result in inaccurate representations of user behavior (de Vries et al., 2020).

Another risk that challenges ConvAI's data quality is systems that adapt on the fly to data acquired while they are serving. On the one hand, depending too much on use data may obscure or even increase the influence of system blind spots, since individuals change their language use to match the interlocutor's perceived qualities (Giles & Coupland, 1991). Publicly available systems, on the other hand, are more vulnerable to malicious data alteration or data poisoning attacks (Nelson et al., 2008). Lack of adequate protection and auditing processes, a well-intentioned technology may quickly and easily become contaminated by its weaknesses and used toward the very people it was intended to serve (for example, Microsoft's Tay bot, which was tricked by unseen, unhandled harmful input; Vincent, 2016).

• *Anthropomorphism and aggression from human users*

Many ConvAI systems exhibit a female identity (exclusively or by default), which is accentuated by communicating via voice (Tay et al., 2014). As they inevitably fail to match human requests sometimes, these technologies can become a source of dissatisfaction which may have an unexpected consequence on how the next generation interacts with ConvAI platforms as they get older (Elgan, 2018; Rudgard, 2018).

• *Misuse for deception*

Technological advancements often come with both benefits and risks. As NLP technology progresses, making these systems appear more human will become increasingly easier. For example, GPT-3 (Brown et al., 2020) was used to post on behalf of a Reddit user, and the posts went undetected for weeks due to their consistency and convincing nature. ConvAI systems, due to their interactive nature, are particularly susceptible to misuse, potentially leading to more sophisticated and successful fraud schemes, such as disinformation or scamming. Innocuous technologies that allow ConvAI techniques to create a unified identity (Li et al., 2016) can enable someone to impersonate others online, similar to how generative adversarial networks (Goodfellow et al., 2014) have been used to create convincing deepfakes.

• *Transparency and trustworthiness*

When ConvAI systems interact with the general people, they must choose whether to identify as a computer system or a robot. This purposeful act of transparency is not commonly implemented in systems for a number of reasons (for example, Google Duplex when it was originally announced), and as a result, it may occasionally have unforeseen consequences (Garun, 2019). Another aspect of transparency is trustworthiness, which is essential for any AI system, especially ConvAI systems that interact directly with people. To that aim, we suggest that real-world ConvAI systems should be able to recognize and properly convey their capabilities' boundaries.

The practical example of challenges with using conversational AI in digital banking as depicted in Box 6.2.

Box 6.2. Challenges With Using Eva: A Journey With Conversational AI in Digital Banking

In the bustling streets of Mumbai, Amit (a pseudonym), a young professional, juggled his busy schedule with the demands of modern-day life. With limited time to spare, managing his finances often felt like an additional chore.

However, the convenience promised by digital banking intrigued him, leading him to explore HDFC Bank's latest innovation – Eva, the AI-powered virtual assistant.

One evening, while scrolling through his HDFC Bank app, Amit stumbled upon Eva, a friendly virtual assistant ready to assist him with his banking needs. Skeptical yet curious, Amit decided to give it a try. "Hello, Eva," he typed nervously, unsure of what to expect. As Amit engaged in conversation with Eva, he was pleasantly surprised by her helpful responses and intuitive understanding of his queries. From checking his account balance to paying bills and setting up automated transactions, Eva seemed capable of handling it all. Despite his initial hesitation, Amit found himself gradually trusting Eva's recommendations and guidance.

However, doubts lingered in Amit's mind. Could he trust an AI-powered assistant with sensitive financial information? What if his transactions were compromised? Seeking reassurance, Amit reached out to HDFC Bank's customer support team, who promptly addressed his concerns and provided detailed insights into Eva's security features and encryption protocols.

Empowered by the knowledge gained from his interactions with HDFC Bank's support team, Amit continued his journey with Eva. With each transaction, he grew more confident in the reliability and security of the conversational AI interface. Eva became his trusted companion, simplifying his banking experience and freeing up valuable time for other pursuits.

Months passed, and Amit's trust in Eva only deepened. He shared his positive experiences with friends and family, encouraging them to embrace the convenience of conversational AI in digital banking. Through Eva, Amit discovered a newfound sense of control and efficiency in managing his finances, paving the way for a brighter financial future.

In the bustling streets of Mumbai, Amit's journey with Eva exemplifies the transformative power of conversational AI in digital banking. Through transparency, security, and personalized assistance, HDFC Bank's Eva has earned the trust of customers like Amit, revolutionizing the way they engage with financial services. As digital banking continues to evolve, Eva stands as a beacon of innovation, guiding users toward a seamless and secure banking experience.

Source: Own Elaboration.

10. Conclusion

To sum up, this chapter has looked in great detail at how artificial intelligence (AI) is changing a variety of sectors. Through an examination of significant developments, such as natural language processing, machine learning algorithms, and AI-powered automation, we have demonstrated how artificial intelligence is changing sectors and improving productivity. In addition to streamlining processes, the incorporation of

AI into industries including healthcare, banking, education, and manufacturing is opening the door for creative solutions to challenging issues.

Furthermore, the difficulties and ethical issues surrounding the application of AI have been discussed, highlighting the necessity of responsible AI development and application. Establishing transparency, equity, and responsibility in AI systems is essential to fostering confidence and optimizing the advantages of new innovations. Future developments and opportunities are promised by the ongoing progress of AI technologies. Artificial Intelligence has enormous potential to advance scientific research, enhance quality of life, and stimulate the economy. As we move forward, we must encourage interdisciplinary cooperation, make investments in AI research and education, and continue to be aware of the ethical ramifications. Fundamentally, artificial intelligence (AI) is a pillar of contemporary innovation, with unmatched potential to revolutionize civilization. We can fully utilize AI to build a more productive, just, and wealthy future if we adopt it wisely and proactively.

References

AlZu'bi, S., Mughaid, A., Quiam, F., & Hendawi, S. (2023). Exploring the capabilities and limitations of ChatGPT and alternative big language models. *Artificial Intelligence and Applications*, *20*(20), 1–5.

Bommasani, R., Hudson, D. A., Adeli, E., Altman, R., Arora, S., von Arx, S., Bernstein, M. S., Bohg, J., Bosselut, A., Brunskill, E., & Brynjolfsson, E. (2021). On the opportunities and risks of foundation models. arXiv preprint arXiv:2108. 07258.

Bordes, A., Boureau,L., & Weston J. (2016). Learning end-to-end goal-oriented dialog. arXiv preprint arXiv:1605.07683.

Brown, T. B., Mann, B., Ryder, N., Subbiah, M., Kaplan, J., Dhariwal, P., Neelakantan, A., Shyam, P., Sastry, G., Askell, A., Agarwal, S., Herbert-Voss, A., Krueger, G., Henighan, T., Child, R., Ramesh, A., Ziegler, D., Wu, J., Winter, C., … Amodei, D. (2020). Language models are few-shot learners. arXiv preprint arXiv:2005.14165.

Chen, P., Liu, H., Xin, R., Carval, T., Zhao, J., Xia, Y., & Zhao, Z. (2022). Effectively detecting operational anomalies in large-scale IoT data infrastructures by using a GAN-based predictive model. *The Computer Journal*, *65*(11), 2909–2925.

Chowdhury, N. & Rahman, S. (2023). A brief review of ChatGPT: Limitations, challenges and ethical-social implications. *Technical Reports Series*.

Chulaka, R., Gunasekara, N., Polymenakos, L., Ganhotra, J., & Fadnis, K. (2018). Quantized-dialog language model for goal oriented conversational systems. ArXiv, abs/1812.10356.

Cui, L., Huang, S., Wei, F., Tan, C., Duan, C., & Zhou, M. (2017). Superagent: A customer service chatbot for e-commerce websites. In *Proceedings of ACL 2017, system demonstrations* (Vol. 30, pp. 97–102).

de Vries, H., Bahdanau, D., & Manning, C. (2020). Towards ecologically valid research on language user interfaces. arXiv preprint arXiv:2007.14435.

Devlin, J., Chang, M. W., Lee, K., & Toutanova, K. (2019). Bert: Pre-Training of deep bidirectional transformers for language understanding. In *Proceedings of the 2019 conference of the North American chapter of the association for computational linguistics: Human.*

Dodge, J., Gane, A., Zhang, X., Bordes, A., Chopra, S., Miller, A., Szlam, A., & Weston, J. (2015). Evaluating prerequisite qualities for learning end-to-end dialog systems. arXiv preprint arXiv:1511.06931.

Dzindolet, M. T., Peterson, S. A., Pomranky, R. A., Pierce, L. G., & Beck, H. P. (2003). The role of trust in automation reliance. *International Journal of Human-Computer Studies*, *58*(6), 697–718.

Edu, J. S., Such, J. M., & Suarez-Tangil, G. (2020). Smart home personal assistants: A security and privacy review. *ACM Computing Surveys*, *53*(6), 1–36.

Elgan, M. (2018). The case against teaching kids to be polite to Alexa. https://www. fastcompany.com/40588020/the-case-against-teaching-kidsto-be-polite-to-alexa

Følstad, A., Brandtzaeg, P. B., Feltwell, T., Law, E. L.-C., Tscheligi, M., & Luger, E. A. (2018). SIG: Chatbots for social good. In *Proceedings a extended abstract: CHI conference* (pp. 1–4).

Garun, N. (2019). One year later, restaurants are still confused by Google Duplex. https:// www.theverge.com/2019/5/9/18538194/google-duplex-ai-restaurantsexperiences-review-robocalls

Ghazvininejad, M., Brockett, C., Chang, M. W., Dolan, B., Gao, J., Yih, W. T., & Galley, M. (2018). A knowledge-grounded neural conversation model. In *Proceedings of the AAAI conference on artificial intelligence* (p. 32).

Giles, H., & Coupland, N. (1991). *Accommodating language*. Open University Press.

Goodfellow, I. J., Pouget-Abadie, J., Mirza, M., Xu, B., Warde Farley, D., Ozair, S., Courville, A., & Bengio, Y. (2014). Generative adversarial networks. arXiv preprint arXiv:1406.2661.

Guembe, B., Azeta, A. S., Osamor, V. C., Fernandez-Sanz, L., & Pospelova, V. (2022). The emerging threat of AI-driven cyber attacks: A review. *Applied Artificial Intelligence*, *36*(1), 2037254.

Hollander, J., Sabatini, J., & Graesser, A. (2022). How item and learner characteristics matter in intelligent tutoring systems data. In *Artificial Intelligence in Education. Posters and Late Breaking Results, Workshops and Tutorials, Industry and Innovation Tracks, Practitioners' and Doctoral Consortium: 23rd International Conference, AIED 2022, Durham, UK, 27–31 July 2022, Proceedings, Part II* (pp. 520–523). Springer International Publishing.

Hoy, M. B. (2018). Alexa, Siri, Cortana, and more: An introduction to voice assistants. *Medical Reference Services Quarterly*, *37*(1), 81–88.

Joshi,C., Fei M., & Faltings, B. (2017). Personalization in GoalOriented dialog. arXiv preprint arXiv:1706.07503.

Juang, B.-H. & Furui, S. (2000). Automatic recognition and understanding of spoken language—A first step toward natural human–machine communication. *Proceedings of the IEEE*, *88*(8), 1142–1165.

Kaur, K., Thanuja, O., Dahiya, O., Sai, P. T., Kaur, H., & Singh, J. (2022). Design and development of a ticket booking system using smart bot. In *Proceedings 10th International Conference on reliability, INFOCOM technologies and optimizations(Trends future Directions) (ICRITO)* (pp. 1–6).

Lee, D. & Yeo, S. (2022). Developing an AI-based chatbot for practicing responsive teaching in mathematics. *Computers & Education*, *191*, 104646.

Li, M. (2020). *Efficient latent semantic extraction from cross domain data with declarative language.* University of California.

Li, J., Galley, M., Brockett, C., Spithourakis, G., Gao, J., & Dolan, B. (2016). A persona-based neural conversation model. In *Proceedings of the 54th annual meeting of the association for computational linguistics* (Vol. 1: Long papers), pp. 994–1003). Association for Computational Linguistics.

Li, M., Liu, X., Ruan, W., Soldaini, L., Hamza, W., & Su, C. (2020). Multi-task learning of spoken language understanding by integrating n-best hypotheses with hierarchical attention. In *Proceedings of the 28th international conference on computational linguistics: Industry track* (pp. 113–123).

Li, M., Ruan, W., Liu, X., Soldaini, L., Hamza, W., & Su, C. (2020). Improving spoken language understanding by exploiting asr n-best hypotheses. arXiv preprint arXiv:2001.05284.

Lin, C. J. & Mubarok, H. (2021). Learning analytics for investigating the mind map-guided AI chatbot approach in an EFL flipped speaking classroom. *Educational Technology & Society*, *24*(4), 16–35.

Lipton,Z., Xiujun L., Gao, J., Lihong L., Ahmed, F., & Deng, L. (2017). BBQ-Networks: Efficient exploration in deep reinforcement learning for task-oriented dialogue systems. arXiv preprint arXiv:1711.05715.

Liu, Y., Han, T., Ma, S., Zhang, J., Yang, Y., Tian, J., He, H., Li, A., He, M., Liu, Z., Wu, Z., Zhao, L., Zhu, D., Li, X., Qiang, N., Shen, D., Liu, T., & Ge, B. (2023). Summary of ChatGPT/GPT-4 research and perspective towards the future of large language models, arXiv:2304.01852.

Liu, X., Li, M., Chen, L., Wanigasekara, P., Ruan, W., Khan, H., Hamza, W., & Su, C. (2021). Asr n-best fusion nets. In *ICASSP 2021-2021 IEEE international conference on acoustics, speech and signal processing (ICASSP)* (pp. 7618–7622). IEEE.

Liu, C. C., Liao, M. G., Chang, C. H., & Lin, H. M. (2022). An analysis of children' interaction with an AI chatbot and its impact on their interest in reading. *Computers & Education*, *189*, 104576.

Mangina, E. (2021). *The IEEE global initiative on ethics of extended reality (XR) report—Social and multi-user Spaces in VR: Trolling, harassment, and online safety* (pp. 1–17). IEEE Standard.

Mrkšić, N., Séaghdha, D. Ó., Wen, T. H., Thomson, B., & Young, S. (2017). Neural belief tracker: Data-driven dialogue state tracking. In *Proceedings of the 55th annual meeting of the association for computational linguistics*, *1*, 1777–1788.

Nelson, B., Barreno, M., Chi, F. J., Joseph, A. D., Rubinstein, B. I., Saini, U., Sutton, C. A., Tygar, J. D., & Xia, K. (2008). Exploiting machine learning to subvert your spam filter. *LEET*, *8*, 1–9.

Pawlik, Ł., Płaza, M., Deniziak, S., & Boksa, E. (2022). A method for improving bot effectiveness by recognizing implicit customer intent in contact centre conversations. *Speech Communication*, *143*, 33–45.

Peng, B., Li, X., Li, L., Gao, J., Celikyilmaz, A., Lee, S., & Wong, K.-F. (2017). Composite task-completion dialogue policy learning via hierarchical deep reinforcement learning. arXiv preprint arXiv:1704.03084.

Research and Markets. (2024). *Conversational AI market - Global and regional analysis 2024–2034 with Microsoft, Amazon Web Services, IBM, Oracle, and Conversica dominating* [Press release]. Business Wire. https://www.businesswire.com/news/home/20240708919092/en/Conversational-AI-Market—Global-and-Regional-Analysis-2024-2034-with-Microsoft-Amazon-Web-Services-IBM-Oracle-and-Conversica-Dominating—ResearchAndMarkets.com

Rodd, M. & Davis, M. (2017). *How to study spoken language understanding: A survey of neuroscientific methods* (pp. 805–817).

Rudgard, O. (2018). 'Alexa generation' may be learning bad manners from talking to digital assistants. Report warns. https://www.telegraph.co.uk/news/2018/01/31/alexa-generation-could-learning-badmanners-talking-digital/

Serban, I., Sordoni, A., Lowe, R., Charlin, L., Pineau, J., Courville, A., & Bengio, Y. (2017). A hierarchical latent variable encoder-decoder model for generating dialogues. In *AAAI* (pp. 3295–3301).

Shawar, B. A. & Atwell, E. (2007). Chatbots: Are they really useful? *Journal for Language Technology and Computational Linguistics, 22*(1), 29–49.

Shrager, J. (2024). ELIZA reinterpreted: The world's first chatbot was not intended as a chatbot at all. arXiv preprint arXiv:2406.17650.

Singh, N. P. & Singh, D. (2019). Chatbots and virtual assistant in Indian banks. *Industrija, 47*(4).

Song, D., Oh, E. Y., & Hong, H. (2022). The impact of teaching simulation using student chatbots with different attitudes on preservice teachers' efficacy. *Educational Technology & Society, 25*(3), 46–59.

Sordoni, A., Galley, M., Auli, M., Brockett, C., YangfengJi, Mitchell, M., Nie, J., Gao, J., & Dolan, B.(2015). A neural network approach to context-sensitive generation of conversational responses. arXiv preprint arXiv:1506.06714 (2015).

Stahl, B. C. & Eke, D. (2024). The ethics of ChatGPT–Exploring the ethical issues of an emerging technology. *International Journal of Information Management, 74*, 102700.

Statista. (2024). Number of people using AI tools worldwide 2022-2030. *Statista.* https://www.statista.com/forecasts/1449844/ai-tool-users-worldwide

Sukhbaatar, S., Szlam, A., Weston, J., & Fergus, R. (2015). End-to-end memory networks. In *Advances in Neural Information Processing Systems, 28*, 2440–2448. Curran Associates, Inc.

Tay, B., Jung, Y., & Park, T. (2014). When stereotypes meet robots: The double-edge sword of robot gender and personality in human–robot interaction. *Computers in Human Behavior, 38*, 75–84.

Ternyak, D. (2023). *70+ chatbot statistics to look out for in 2024.* ServiceBell. https://www.servicebell.com/post/chatbot-statistics

Toxtli, C., Monroy-Hernández, A., & Cranshaw, J. (2018). Understanding chatbot-mediated task management. In *Proceedings of the 2018 CHI conference on human factors in computing systems* (p. 58). Association for Computing Machinery (ACM). https://doi.org/10.1145/3173574.3173632

Vincent, J. (2016). Twitter taught Microsoft's AI chatbot to be a racist asshole in less than a day. https://www.theverge.com/2016/3/24/11297050/tay-microsoft-chatbot-racist

Wang, Z. & Ai, Q. (2022). Simulating and modeling the risk of conversational search. *ACM Transactions on Information Systems, 40*(4), 1–33.

Wen, T.-H., Vandyke, D., Mrksic, N., Gasic, M., Rojas-Barahona, L. M., Su, P.-H., Ultes, S., & Young, S. (2016). A network based end-to-end trainable task-oriented dialogue system. arXiv preprint arXiv:1604.04562.

Williams, J. & Zweig, G. (2016). End-to-end lstm-based dialog control optimized with supervised and reinforcement learning. arXiv preprint arXiv:1606.01269.

Young, S., Gašić, M., Thomson, B., & Williams, J. (2013). Pomdpbased statistical spoken dialog systems: A review. *Proceedings of the IEEE, 101*(5), 1160–1179.

Zhang, H., Mi, Y., Fu, Y., Liu, X., Zhang, Y., Wang, J., & Tan, J. (2023). Security defense decision method based on potential differential game for complex networks. *Computers & Security, 129*, 103187.

Zhou, L., Gao, J., Li, D., & Shum, H. Y. (2020). The design and implementation of xiaoice, an empathetic social chatbot. *Computational Linguistics, 46*(1), 53–93.

Chapter 7

Addressing Ethical Considerations and Responsible AI Practices

Anchal Luthra[a], *Shivani Dixit*[b], *Seema Garg*[a], *Anamica Singh*[a] *and Mandhir Anchal*[c]

[a]Amity University, Noida, India
[b]IMS Ghaziabad (University Courses Campus), India
[c]Mercer Consulting India Pvt. Ltd., India

Abstract

This chapter discusses the ethical and moral issues of AI technology deployment and the different ways of dealing with safe development. This research utilizes a literature review–based approach to review the existing studies concerning ethics in AI. With the help of other scholarly articles, books, and reports, this chapter aims to identify various themes and trends associated with ethical considerations during artificial intelligence systems' development and implementation stages. The literature highlighted some critical ethical problems: algorithmic bias, data protection laws, and transparency in decision-making processes. The study highlighted several challenges explained by published literature and their implications to individuals and organizations, thus suggesting some suggestions for ensuring responsible innovation in society. Addressing ethics across different areas and endorsing good practices regarding AI in society are the two crucial factors identified in this chapter. The need for collaboration across various disciplines and the active involvement of all stakeholders, including establishing regulations to guide developers throughout the design and implementation phase, is also necessary for the ethical use of AI systems. There is an essential requirement for the intensification of awareness campaigns, particularly among researchers engaged in studies involving machine learning algorithms or other related forms.

Keywords: Ethical considerations; responsible AI practices; artificial intelligence; ethics in AI; Algorithmic bias; ChatGPT

The ChatGPT Revolution, 129–149
Copyright © 2025 Anchal Luthra, Shivani Dixit, Seema Garg, Anamica Singh and Mandhir Anchal
Published under exclusive licence by Emerald Publishing Limited
doi:10.1108/978-1-83549-852-120251007

1. Introduction

Artificial Intelligence (AI) has become increasingly essential, bringing significant changes across various sectors, education being one of them. The education sector becomes transformative with the involvement of AI, as educational institutions like schools are increasingly implementing technology-driven learning methods, reshaping the teaching methodologies and their data processing system. AI is an indispensable tool for future schools, as its integration into education represents more comprehensive technological advancements and transformed the information delivery and management system (Chinta et al., 2024). Creating personalized learning experiences, streamlining administrative tasks, and supporting data-driven decision-making processes are significant changes educational institutions have noticed after implementing artificial intelligence systems. AI-powered tools like chatbots, predictive analytics systems, and virtual tutors have completely revolutionized traditional teaching models, allowing educational institutions to address the individual needs of educators and students. With the help of these advancements, the education sector becomes more accessible and effective while addressing the diverse needs of learners (Baker & Hawn, 2022; Kizilcec & Lee, 2022).

AI adoption across various educational settings results in noticeable ethical dilemmas in society. Consequently, emerging issues like algorithmic bias privacy infringement through data storage and discrimination potentialities appear within educational settings due to the increasing deployment of artificial intelligence systems. These ethical challenges gain importance while considering these types of technology that may inadvertently strengthen existing disparities or introduce new biases during decision-making processes related to schooling (Eynon, 2024; Memarian & Doleck, 2023). Addressing these ethical concerns during development implementation and evaluating fairness, accountability, and transparency for the AI systems is essential for the responsible use of Artificial Intelligence. Policymakers and educators must collaborate on designing fair, transparent, accountable AI systems for education institutions to ensure proper usage (Mashhadi et al., 2022). Ethical and responsible use of AI required for reducing the harmful impact of AI and promoting justice within colleges and universities is one of the significant areas focused on in this chapter. This section attempts to train teachers with the required guidance to navigate the complex ethical landscape of AI in schools by identifying the primary ethical challenges and the best practices adopted by institutions globally. Furthermore, it emphasizes the importance of multidisciplinary collaboration while addressing these issues, ensuring that all AI technologies are developed and organized to uphold ethical integrity.

2. Research Methodology

This section of the chapter is based on a systematic review of secondary data, drawing from existing literature about ethical and responsible practices of AI. For review, research related to the primary method of study was chosen, as it allows for the comprehensive synthesis of current knowledge from various sources like books, reports, journals, and policy papers. It is required when dealing with intricate interdisciplinary areas such as AI ethics, where different perspectives and disciplines are necessary (Snyder, 2019). To address the broad field of ethical concerns, a literature review is essentially required, rather than using any other method of empirical studies or case studies. Research conducted by Boell and Cecez-Kecmanovic, 2015, also focused on some instances/datasets for developing and applying ethically sound AI systems. Some research studies emphasized the gaps for further empirical work within this domain (Tranfield et al., 2003). Articles related to AI ethics, including the latest research findings and journals, were used explicitly for source selection. This study referred to extensively recognized databases such as IEEE Xplore, Google Scholar, and Science Direct for delivering extensive and credible coverage of the subject matter (Kitchenham, 2004). The research addressing major ethical themes, including algorithmic bias, data privacy, accountability, transparency, and societal impact, was majorly considered (Bostrom, 2019; Floridi et al., 2018). The reliability and relevance of each source were critically evaluated by employing a systematic approach during the data collection and analysis stage, thus contributing to the broader discourse on AI ethics. This chapter adds to academic discussions on the ethical use of AI by bringing together various views and findings. It has implications for future research endeavors and practical applications in real-life situations concerning machines with intelligence levels (Levy & Ellis, 2006). The focus of this research chapter is to promote the understanding of ethical and moral concerns raised by different authors while at the same time advancing knowledge about reliable and responsible practices associated with the development and use of AI systems.

3. Literature Review

3.1 AI Model

The availability of AI models significantly advanced natural language processing. AI models are AI systems created to have natural language discussions with humans, sometimes called chatbots or agents. These models employ machine learning techniques, including deep learning, to create responses to user input. They are competent on massive datasets of human conversations. AI models come in several forms, such as generative, hybrid, rule-based, and retrieval-based models. Each form has advantages and disadvantages; the need and particular applications determine the best model. AI models are used in various applications, including virtual assistants, customer service, healthcare, and educational materials (Goodfellow et al., 2016).

The literature has emphasized both the potential benefits of these technologies and the risks they entail. AI models have numerous strengths but can also be limited in fairness, bias, and misinformation (Bender et al., 2021; Buolamwini & Gebru, 2018). However, several studies demonstrate that many mitigation strategies fail to prevent data level or algorithmic biases from entering into systems even after proposing such measures as algorithmic audits and fairness-aware algorithms as ways of dealing with ethical concerns related to this area (Caliskan et al., 2017; Holstein et al., 2019). Undoubtedly, transparency issues were also identified, revealing that models like ChatGPT are highly complex, making it challenging for anyone, including the developers, to fully understand or control the decision-making processes due to insufficient information about them (Floridi et al., 2018; Lipton, 2018). This chapter claims a need for more robust ethical frameworks alongside regulatory precautions that can adapt quickly to technological advances, considering the recent development of AI systems (Taddeo & Floridi, 2018). AI models hold significant potential but should still be used carefully based on advanced ethical considerations that match those used during creation. On one side, it has been demonstrated beyond reasonable doubt that chatbots are capable of far more than people often realize. AI tools can adapt to different situations and process language better than any human could ever hope to achieve in his/her lifetime. Another significant issue is the absence of regulation for transparency and responsibility, among other things. Without a legal framework, chatbots operate as essentially unregulated entities with no clear understanding of their capabilities or limitations. Addressing these ethical issues is essential to ensure that these models are used responsibly and do not perpetuate biases or harm users. By tackling these concerns and adopting responsible AI practices, we can enhance human–computer interactions and improve various aspects of our lives with AI models.

3.2 ChatGPT

ChatGPT has brought natural language processing (NLP) to a new level. This innovative AI model is undoubtedly a breakthrough in NLP. ChatGPT, a product of OpenAI, is a member of the family of generative pre-trained transformers (GPTs) characterized by its transformer architecture. Equipped with its encoder-decoder structure and self-attention systems, the transformer model allows ChatGPT to comprehend intricate language patterns and nuances of meaning. Its deep pre-training of the textual datasets, ChatGPT, brings to the fore a profound understanding of the linguistic nuances by predicting the next word in a sequence. It is worth noticing that ChatGPT's ability to adapt is not limited to pre-training; supervised learning methods can be modified to perform specific tasks like text generation, sentiment analysis, or question answering. The device's versatility is especially noticeable in different areas, such as instructional tools, creative writing support, or customer service. For instance, it allows the machine to converse with people more naturally, generates contextually relevant text, and makes user experiences more enjoyable (Angwin et al., 2016). Nevertheless, to make ChatGPT fully inclusive and ethically sound, mitigating issues like bias and responsible deployment is still necessary. ChatGPT is the fruit of the union between state-of-the-art AI technology and linguistic mastery, bringing about revolutionary applications of human–computer interaction and other fields. It is based on the GPT-3.5 architecture, a cutting-edge generator model, which originated from OpenAI (Brown et al., 2020). ChatGPT can react to various prompts designed to have natural language dialogs with people. Using a wide-ranging human interaction dataset, the GPT-3.5 model based on ChatGPT uses deep learning techniques to generate user input responses. The model may cover various topics and demonstrate exceptional skills in generating human-like responses. ChatGPT is one of the most advanced AI models that can be used in virtual assistants, customer support, and instructional tools. However, it is essential to maintain that even though ChatGPT is designed to respond like humans, it is still an AI model and might not always give accurate or credible information. It is always good for users to be cautious and use their critical thinking when dealing with ChatGPT and other AI models.

3.3 Understanding Bias and Fairness in ChatGPT

3.3.1 Bias in ChatGPT Systems and Similar AI Models

Scientists and administrators are looking into the issue of bias in artificial intelligence. Bias in artificial intelligence is characteristic of system-related inaccuracies or unfairness in the output of such systems, which often stem from data they have been trained on or algorithms used for decision-making (Buolamwini & Gebru, 2018).

One of the biases in criminal justice, healthcare, and employment that needs to be eliminated is bias in AI systems to ensure fairness, transparency, and equitable outcomes (Caliskan et al., 2017). Researchers and developers can devise methods such as algorithmic audits, employing data with variation, and fairness-aware algorithms to build more inclusive and equitable AI technologies (O'Neil, 2017). These approaches are effective in finding and reducing bias in AI systems. ChatGPT and other AI models that can conduct a dialog with the user may induce bias in the following:

(1) *Data Bias:* A significant portion of AI systems are trained using large datasets, and if these datasets contain biased or incomplete information, the AI algorithms may learn this information and continue to be biased. The results will be biased or unfair if systematic errors or inconsistencies exist in a dataset to train machine learning models or make decisions. The term being referred to here is data bias. Several different forms can represent data bias in ChatGPT. For this, proactive action and carefully considered decisions are required:

- *Data Collection:* Make sure the process is designed so that it is not biased and includes a range of viewpoints and experiences.
- *Data Cleaning:* All the data should be thoroughly cleaned and pre-processed to detect and remove biases and inaccuracies, including eliminating outliers, correcting errors, or imputing missing values.
- *Data Augmentation:* Increasing the dataset by integrating additional data or synthetic examples to deal with the underrepresented groups or minority classes, respectively.

- *Bias Detection:* In statistics or machine learning, one can use tools to find and measure the bias in the dataset. Such methods can include data distribution over various groups or model performance on different subgroups.
- *Bias Mitigation:* A bias-averse solution can employ reweighting or resampling techniques, algorithmic adjustments, or fairness-aware learning algorithms.

(2) *Algorithmic Bias:* Systematic and unjust results generated by algorithms because of false assumptions, insufficient data, or innate biases in the creation, training, or use of machine learning models are called algorithmic bias. The system may produce the contrary by giving unjust or discriminatory decisions that violate fairness or equal opportunities, thus sustaining the existing inequalities and reinforcing prejudices the community supports. Algorithmic bias materializes in different domains and circumstances, such as social media, law enforcement, loan approval, hiring, and healthcare. Regarding ChatGPT, algorithmic bias may develop if the model is designed or trained so that its response pattern favors some over others. Solving algorithmic bias requires proactive actions and a multidisciplinary approach:

- *Data Collection and Pre-processing:* Make sure the training data is not biased, diverse, and a good representative of all areas. Clean the data to reveal and eliminate data biases, as well as to correct errors.
- *Algorithm Design:* Develop algorithms that are fair, transparent, and accountable. To prevent bias in the process, factors like the demographic group that might be affected by the algorithm should be considered, and measures to offset bias must be put in place.
- *Bias Detection and Mitigation:* Apply statistical methods, machine learning technology, and fairness-based algorithms to identify and remove bias from algorithms. The prescription of the model can include, among other methods, reweighting or resampling techniques, algorithm modifications, or fairness constraints.
- *Transparency and Explainability:* Make open and accessible how the algorithm makes a decision and guide users on how decisions are made. Utilize systems in the form of explanations for algorithmic decisions and the possibility of legal or other remedies for individuals affected by discrimination.
- *Ethical Oversight and Governance:* Select standards for the development, deployment, and use of algorithms through ethical governance, as well as standards. Guarantee that algorithms are developed and deployed by ethical principles and legal requirements.

(3) *User/Societal Bias:* Biases intrinsic to society and culture are the data used to train AI models. They are called societal biases. Societal biases are hard to identify and mitigate because they are sometimes ingrained and invisible. Teachers and administrators, for example, might influence the decision-making process caused by their conscious or subconscious biases (Crawford et al., 2018). The bias of AI system users could result from the lack of training on the possible

bias of AI systems and the ways to reduce it. Addressing user bias in AI systems is a multi-pronged technique involving user education and training, monitoring, and review procedures. To impose this program, we must ensure that AI systems are used relatively, transparently, and accountably (Crawford et al., 2018). ChatGPT social prejudice lies in the fact that training data can present discriminatory language, preconceptions, and prejudices. There are several methods of handling biases in AI models such as ChatGPT, which are:

- *Diverse and Representative Data:* The model's training set should represent the target population and be heterogeneous to prevent data bias. Information is being gathered from different sources and will be provided in a way that covers different opinions, cultures, and demographic groupings.
- *Fairness and Transparency:* By devising fair and transparent algorithms, algorithmic bias may be curbed. Identify and eliminate any possible biases, which means wisely deciding on the parameters and optimization criteria and constantly monitoring the model's performance.
- *Ethical Guidelines and Governance:* Properly setting ethical standards and governance frameworks for AI development and usage can help to ensure that bias is recognized and treated at each phase of the model's lifecycle. Involving different parties in the development process and continual updating and reviewing helps guarantee that the model remains neutral and fair.
- *Bias Detection and Mitigation:* AI model bias can be discovered and fixed using bias detection and mitigation techniques such as bias audits and algorithms. Please do not take your eyes off the model's interpretations; examine them for any prejudices and arrange measures to diminish or remove biases altogether.

ChatGPT is a tool invented by AI technology specialists. However, ChatGPT is a program based on a very complex technology that needs to be treated with care and mitigated. The developers can help the situation by solving problems of data bias, algorithmic bias, and societal bias.

3.3.2 Fairness in ChatGPT and Similar AI Models

For users of various demographic groups, it is crucial to ensure unbiased outcomes and fairness in ChatGPT and other AI models. Fairness covers multiple topics, such as representation, inclusion, and avoiding negative stereotypes. Moreover, it is imperative to ensure that ChatGPT's responses are considerate, aware, and impartial toward its users' varied viewpoints and identities. However, close attention is required to the methods and assessment metrics utilized during training and inference and the training data used to build the model and confidence. Both accountability and transparency are essential in ChatGPT's results (Friedler et al., 2021).

The developers can apply initiatives like bias audits, different training data collection, and fairness-aware training procedures to advance fairness and reduce bias in ChatGPT and related AI models. Fairness must be the top priority while designing, developing, and implementing phases to fairly and ethically meet the demands of all users regardless of their demography or background. Thus, ChatGPT should provide impartial and fair output to users of various categories. Different strategies like debiasing algorithms, data augmentation, and fairness-aware training reduce the impact of algorithms and skewed data on the models' results and reduce bias in AI systems. There are different aspects regarding fairness in ChatGPT, such as

Bias Detection and Mitigation. The training data and model outputs implement bias detection and mitigation mechanisms to ensure fair treatment across all demographic groups. Transparency and accountability are another essential aspect. Having transparency and accountability and retaining openness regarding the model's limitations, potential biases, and capabilities is crucial. Further, it lets users understand the decision-making process and holds developers responsible for ethical AI practices.

Further use of a diverse training data set is critical in implementing fairness in AI techniques. Diverse training data warrant that the model learns from various viewpoints and experiences using representative data to reduce bias. Further, for identifying and promptly addressing examples of bias or unfairness, user feedback mechanisms are established for users to provide feedback on the model's outputs, allowing developers to have user feedback. Establishing ethical guidelines, standards, moral principles, and requirements for AI development proposed by the IEEE and ACM guarantees the incorporation of fairness concerns during the creation and application of AI models. Techniques such as fairness-aware training techniques also play a vital role in the context of fairness in ChatGPT and similar AI models. Incorporating fairness-aware techniques during the model training process can mitigate bias and promote equitable and fair user outcomes (Bostrom, 2016). Adhering to regulatory compliance-related regulatory and legal frameworks for incorporating equity, fairness, and non-discrimination contributes to fostering accountability and trust and reducing the possibility of harming users' sentiments. Another important aspect of fairness is community engagement and collaboration. One must collaborate to resolve issues related to fairness and promote a common understanding among stakeholders like legislators, researchers, and organizations about moral AI practices and principles of using AI models.

Further, continuous monitoring and evaluation of the model's performance are also necessary. Continuous monitoring helps evaluate the model's performance in real-world settings, thus enabling the detection and address of any case bias or unfairness, ensuring the implementation of fairness principles. However, awareness and education are the key to fairness. Initially, educating developers about following fairness principles and established guidelines is essential. Similarly, it creates awareness about the importance of fairness and the potential consequences of bias in AI systems among users and broader communities regarding the responsible use of AI models.

3.3.3 Examples Highlighting Bias in ChatGPT Outputs

To resist bias in AI is crucial in all AI-based models, such as ChatGPT. With the research and development of more justified and equitable technologies, mitigating bias in AI models can be achieved to meet users' demands objectively (Neff, 2016). Several real-world examples reflect AI's ubiquitous predisposition and its role in strengthening discrimination and social injustices.

- *Racial Bias in AI-Language Models*: There are many cases of racial bias in large language models like GPT-3, which powers ChatGPT. These models generated offensive and biased language when prompted with specific racial keywords or topics. The propagation of such discrimination and harmful stereotyped outputs can be checked, and there is a need to focus on mitigating such racial biases in AI language models (Bender et al., 2021).

Google's Photo Tagging Incident (2015) is one of the examples. Google's photo app automatically tags images by using an AI model. In 2015, Google's photo app tagged an African American individual's picture as "gorillas." The incident highlights racial prejudice that exists in AI systems, indicating a lack of fairness in algorithms dealing with image classification and recognition. However, Google removed that offensive label from its system and improved its algorithm to mitigate the issues of bias and ensure that the AI models Google is using must be rigorous to prevent future biases (Vincent, 2018). Thus, ensuring that AI systems are trained on varied representative datasets that do not reinforce harmful stereotypes seems complicated.

- *Gender Bias in ChatGPT Responses:* Gender bias in language models, including ChatGPT, is expected as these models often give outputs reflecting conventional ideologies regarding identities and roles in context to gender (Sonnad, 2017). Outputs given by ChatGPT are usually biased when asked gender-specific questions, favoring traditional gender norms and prejudices, emphasizing the need to remove gender bias and provide fair results (Kotek et al., 2023).

Amazon's AI Recruiting Tool (2018) is one such example. In 2018, Amazon developed an artificial intelligence–based resume screening process for convenient and automated hiring. It was observed that the system rejected resumes based on the word "women," such as captain women's club, but prioritized resumes based on men-dominated fields. The gender bias originated from data on which the process had been trained. The developer used data from the last 10 years, which consisted of more male resumes, as training data. Later, amazon found that this tool had some bias against women and banned the use of this artificial intelligence–based resume screening process. The incident highlights the need to establish control over similar decision-making–related artificial intelligence systems through frequent checks.

- *Social Bias in AI-generated Text:* Racial bias, ethnic biases, and other social biases detected in language models trained on massive text corpora when asked sensitive questions about hobbies, careers, or related to demographic groups. The models gave discriminated output based on existing biased preconceptions, thus signifying the removal of social prejudice and the advancement of inclusivity and social justice in language produced by AI (Sap et al., 2019).

Microsoft's Tay Chatbot (2016) case reflected social bias in AI-generated text. In March 2016, Microsoft released Tay, an artificial intelligence chatbot. The Twitter platform hosted her to learn from users' conversations with her. Within a few hours, Tay started posting racist remarks and offensive tweets, as some users intentionally posted biased phrases while conversing with her, hence highlighting AI's susceptibility to use offensive and derogatory language. Developers must be more careful about such content moderation filters to avoid the recurrence of such instances in the future.

3.3.4 Strategies for Identifying and Addressing Bias in ChatGPT

Developed by OpenAI, the Modern AI language model ChatGPT has attracted much attention because of human-like writing outputs when given the correct instructions. However, based on the development techniques or training data, it is equally susceptible to giving biased results like any other AI system, thus making it crucial to address the issue of biases. Further, accuracy, inclusivity, and fairness are crucial to guaranteeing transparency and accountability in ChatGPT's results. Based on AI ethics and fairness studies, ChatGPT has many methods for detecting and mitigating bias. Diverse training data is one way to ensure fairness (Hendricks et al., 2018). Thus, the training data used to train ChatGPT must represent different perspectives, demographics, and cultures to reduce biases that may arise from unidimensional groups. Another way is to do regular bias-related audits of ChatGPT to identify any patterns of biases in the generated results by analyzing the output generated for various groups.

Further, different detection tools and techniques, such as natural language processing techniques, are used to identify biases in the responses generated by ChatGPT. However, if detected, implementing bias mitigation techniques like counterfactual data augmentation, debiasing algorithms, and adversarial training can address any biases identified in the generated outputs of ChatGPT. Human oversight, i.e., human moderators, can also be used to identify and review the reactions and flag inappropriate content or biases in the different outputs generated by ChatGPT (Dastin, 2022). The user feedback mechanism, i.e., allowing users to report inappropriate content, encourages them to locate and address any biases to provide feedback on the generated outputs. Continuous monitoring of the outputs by ChatGPT with automated monitoring tools can flag any biases. The last approach is to be transparent about the limitations regarding handling the biases of ChatGPT, and providing clear and accurate information on how these biases are identified and addressed is crucial. Giving access to users of training data used to train ChatGPT and information on bias detection and mitigation techniques is a must (Bolukbasi et al., 2016). With these approaches, the adverse effects of discrimination and bias in ChatGPT and other AI systems can be reduced, and inclusivity and equity in AI content can be encouraged.

3.4 Mitigating Misinformation and Harmful Content

3.4.1 Misinformation and Harmful Content

ChatGPT, when trained on inaccurate or biased data, generates misinformation and harmful content, which is an evident issue. Such outputs will result in the unintentional propagation of misinformation and reinforce preexisting notions and prejudices, creating echo chambers where users get confirmation of their preconceived belief systems and notions. The AI models are also vulnerable to manipulation due to misleading and inaccurate information deliberately provided by individuals. Further, the circulation of this dangerous content might undermine the credibility of AI models. However, identifying false information is challenging, specifically when generated effectively and confidently; this raises ethical questions about the content created (Selwyn, 2019). Therefore, developers and users of these AI-based models must ensure control of posting such misleading information and materials. The issues of harmful and misleading content issues require a multi-stakeholder approach to develop robust content moderation mechanisms that encourage the responsible use of AI technologies with improved transparency and accountability. AI-based models like ChatGPT deal with the many difficulties that come with misinformation and dangerous content.

- *Echo Chamber Effect*: As stated, if trained on inaccurate or biased data, AI models can unintentionally spread misinformation or boost existing biases, creating an echo chamber effect, i.e., exposing users to information that associates and aligns with existing thoughts, values, and beliefs, thus, leading to polarization.
- *Vulnerability to Manipulation:* Malicious factors can purposefully feed misleading and inaccurate data and, therefore, can control AI models and damage the trust, credibility, and trust of the AI models. Further, it encourages the diffusion of dangerous content like conspiracy theories and hate speech.
- *Difficulty Detecting Misinformation:* When delivered convincingly or authoritatively, AI models find it challenging to identify and weed out false information; thus, AI models may disseminate misleading information by mistake or accidentally.
- *Regulatory and Legal Challenges:* The increased use of AI models raises legal and regulatory issues, primarily related to disseminating harmful information; policymakers and regulators are still debating on the best ways to handle these issues.

ChatGPT is an AI language model that aims to deliver authentic, precise, informative, and beneficial data, yet there are a few ways that AI models could spread false information:

- *Generating Convincing but Fabricated Content:* ChatGPT may sometimes lack authentic and comprehensive content, making it difficult to "understand" the meaning and causing misinterpretations of words, references, or language, leading to inaccurate outputs. ChatGPT can also produce text like human writing and is varied, grammatically accurate, and stylistic. Further, it facilitates the development of authentic content, e.g., news stories, social media posts, and academic papers, which is highly challenging to differentiate from original content. Another factor is deep fakes, i.e., manipulated images, video, or audio, are created through ChatGPT when paired with other AI technologies. Such fake representations of content shared by real people, like doing things or saying something that they did not, reduce the users' confidence in the sources of information.
- *Amplification and Targeting Misinformation:* Amplification of false content by liking, sharing, and commenting, as well as boosting its visibility across social media platforms through malicious actors using AI-powered bots, is another significant issue. Further, it identifies and targets specific users, people, or groups most vulnerable to disinformation with disinformation campaigns.
- *Biases in Training Data:* Trained on sizable datasets, if these datasets contain biased or erroneous information, AI models may unintentionally spread prejudice as ChatGPT tends to learn and produce related misleading content from the dataset. AI models reflect these datasets and generate content that perpetuates harmful stereotypes, reinforces incorrect narratives, and lacks a deep understanding of context and nuance.
- *Difficulty Detecting AI-Generated Misinformation:* The content generated may reinforce and validate preconceived biases and opinions or deceptive statements a user enters, thus disseminating false information. Further, it can be easily tricked by entering specific inputs to take advantage of flaws in the architecture of the AI model. Moreover, due to the quality and coherence of the text, this misinformation has become more complex and challenging to identify.

3.4.2 Strategies for Mitigating Fabricated Information and Harmful Content on ChatGPT

AI language models do not allow direct control over behaviors or implementation of tactics.

Multiple several approaches have to be employed to diminish fabricated information and dangerous content while utilizing ChatGPT and other AI language models:

- *Use Trusted Sources:* Consumers of the information need to judiciously check the source of the information before believing it to be accurate; this shall help diminish the blowout of misinformation.
- *Monitor and Moderate:* A routine consisting of monitoring and moderating practices needs to be employed to recognize and delete harmful content, including AI algorithms, to curtail the spread of potentially destructive content for human consumption.
- *Educate Users:* Create awareness among users through accessible information and resources to aid content users in recognizing and preventing misinformation, reviewing information received, and verifying information sources.
- *Encourage Responsible Use:* Facilitate the use of AI models by imparting guidelines and best practices to users. Indirectly, this discourages spreading false information or engaging in harmful behaviors.
- *Collaborate with Experts:* Strategies built by input from industry experts, including journalists, psychologists, and corporate ethics, should be consulted to reduce the spread of misinformation and harmful content.
- *Update and Improve:* It is imperative to constantly advance our AI language models to have a better tool to identify and curtail the spread of misinformation and harmful content.
- *Community Engagement:* Communities play an integral part in testing new AI language models and mitigating misinformation and harmful content's spread.
- A Well-oiled *Legal and Regulatory Framework* aids in tackling misinformation and harmful content on AI platforms through encompassing measures.
- *Promote Logical Thinking:* Motivate consumers to critically analyze and challenge the information they obtain, even from the AI language model.

3.5 Lucidity and Accountability in AI

3.5.1 Lucidity in AI

Lucidity in AI implies sharing with individuals information about how the AI model operates, how it forms judgments, and the data it uses to generate responses (Lipton, 2018).

The use of explainable artificial intelligence (XAI) methodology is one of the techniques used to achieve lucidity in artificial intelligence. The purpose of the XAI technique is to assist people in understanding the reasoning behind the selections made by AI systems so they can grasp the reason behind the system's behavior (Adadi & Berrada, 2018). To increase user lucidity in decision-making, precise sections that the AI model focuses on for generating a response can be highlighted using the attention mechanism technique (Vaswani et al., 2017). AI transparency can also be achieved by informing users of the said model's competencies, gray areas, and limitations by informing them of the various types of queries and tasks the AI system can complete (Hill et al., 2016). Developers boost conviction and confidence in the technology by monitoring user expectations and disclosing the capabilities of the AI system.

3.5.2 Accountability in AI

In AI, accountability refers to the obligation placed on developers, institutions, and AI systems to communicate justification and assent responsibility for their preferences and behaviors (Floridi et al., 2018).

Responsibility in the framework of AI has various aspects, including social, ethical, and legal accountability.

AI systems developers and companies face the risk of being legally liable for any damage the system causes as a result of its judgments. This accentuates the significance of ensuring developers and companies of AI systems adhere to all relevant laws and rules, as well as data protection and privacy (Taddeo & Floridi, 2018).

For developers and companies to be held ethically responsible, they must create AI systems that place the welfare of users foremost and adhere to moral principles, including justice, openness, and respect for human autonomy (Bansal & Garg, 2021). Developers should proactively recognize and mitigate conceivable biases and risks related to AI systems to guarantee unbiased and ethical outcomes for all users (Madaio et al., 2022). Communities and cultures supported by AI systems should hold them socially responsible. AI technology's more considerable societal consequences include its influence on employment, power relations, and culture (Coeckelbergh, 2020).

To develop and implement AI systems, developers should interact with stakeholders, including users, advocacy groups, and legislators, to garner feedback, arbitrate issues, and build ethical AI practices.

Accountability and lucidity are indispensable in an educational environment when executing and using AI technologies for all stakeholders, including students, teachers, and administrators. The lucidity ensures that the central mechanisms of these AI systems, including algorithms and decision-making protocols, are comprehensible and available (Birnbaum & Kröner, 2022). Clarity on the logic for particular suggestions or assessments promotes users' conviction and faith in the technology, improving learning. Owning to the lucidity in the process, one can identify and rectify any biases present in the algorithms or data; this is paramount for promising righteousness and impartiality in the education results (Kosinski et al., 2014). Accountability guarantees that people responsible for creating, executing, and applying AI in education are answerable for their actions and choices, optimistically influencing students' learning experiences and outcomes.

3.6 Challenges Associated With Understanding and Auditing Complex AI Algorithms

Addressing the impediments, it is vital for all stakeholders, such as academicians, policymakers, businesses, and civil society organizations, to work together. To ensure the conscientious usage and accountability of sophisticated AI algorithms like ChatGPT, investing in auditing capabilities, urging collaboration among stakeholders, improving algorithmic lucidity, and fostering ethical data are paramount.

- *Complexity of Model Architecture*: LeCun et al. (2015) state that AI algorithms such as ChatGPT consist of intricate designs with multiple layers and parameters. This becomes a challenge for non-experts to comprehend that all the model's parts impact the system's overall behavior. The results and outputs of the model are arduous to understand and construe because of the architecture's extreme complexity.
- *Impervious Decision-Making Processes*: Numerous AI algorithms, like ChatGPT, function as "black boxes," implying it is difficult to understand or grasp the model's internal workings (Rudin, 2019). This obliqueness elevates the apprehensions about the accuracy, impartiality, and bias of the outputs and makes it difficult to understand how a model establishes decisions and responses.
- *Lack of Transparency:* The construction and training of AI algorithms, such as ChatGPT, are often unclear (Mitchell et al., 2019). Essential information relevant to data sources, training schedules, and optimization strategies used to create and advance these models is not publicly available by companies, developers, and researchers. With this essential data missing, all assessments of the algorithm's robustness, dependability, and ethical consequences possess another challenge.
- *Dynamic Nature of AI:* AI algorithms are dynamic systems that continuously transform and adapt. Hence, it is imperative to constantly observe, evaluate, and analyze the behaviors of AI algorithms like ChatGPT. However, tracking algorithm amendments is challenging, particularly for researchers, auditors, and regulatory bodies.
- *Data Dependencies and Bias:* Training data is primarily used by AI algorithms such as ChatGPT to recognize trends and generate predictions (Bolukbasi et al., 2016). If this training data is a skewed or incomplete representation of the target population, it would lead to biased outputs. Ascertaining and allaying bias of complex AI systems is resource-intensive and technically irresolvable without meticulously examining the training data, feature engineering, and algorithmic design.
- *Ethical Deliberations*: Auditing complex AI systems raises ethical dilemmas concerning security, privacy, fairness, and accountability (Jobin et al., 2019). Researchers and auditors must circumnavigate ethical dilemmas concerning algorithmic transparency, data usage, and potential social ramifications. It is paramount to guarantee that auditing methods respect people's rights and welfare and abide by ethical standards, especially during challenging situations.
- *Technical Expertise Requirements:* Expert technical knowledge of machine learning, natural language processing, and algorithm analytics is essential to auditing sophisticated AI algorithms like ChatGPT (Barocas & Selbst, 2016).

The scarcity of skilled professionals with the proper knowledge and capabilities to perform comprehensive audits and inspections is an obstacle. It is imperative to reduce this skills gap to ensure proficient supervision and accountability of AI audits.

3.7 Recommendations for Developing Policies and Procedures to Address Ethical Concerns

- *Establish Clear Ethical Guidelines:* Create thorough and unambiguous ethical guidelines outlining the norms, values, and guiding principles for creating and using AI technology. These rules should cover important ethical factors like responsibility, openness, fairness, and prejudice reduction.
- *Conduct Ethical Impact Assessments:* In-depth ethical impact studies should be performed before implementing AI technologies to determine the technology's advantages, disadvantages, and effects on people individually and throughout society. Determine possible ethical issues and try to weigh their importance, then create plans to reduce risks and encourage moral behavior.
- *Engage Stakeholders:* Include a wide range of stakeholders in creating ethical norms and processes, including researchers, policymakers, ethicists, lawyers, and members of impacted communities, in addition to AI developers.
- *Address Bias and Fairness:* To guarantee justice and equity in AI systems, proactively detect and reduce prejudice in AI algorithms and data sources. Implement strategies such as algorithmic audits, data pre-treatment, and bias-aware model training to combat algorithmic bias. After routinely monitoring and assessing AI systems for bias and fairness, appropriate remedial action should be taken.
- *Protect Privacy and Data Security:* Adhere to strict guidelines for data protection and give ethical data collecting, storage, and application in AI priority. Establish effective data privacy policies and processes to protect sensitive information. Reduce the amount of personal information gathered and kept on file, and whenever feasible, anonymize or pseudonymize data to preserve privacy.
- *Promote Ethical Use of AI:* Awareness among consumers, developers, and other interested parties should be created about the moral guidelines and issues surrounding AI technology. Promote adherence to best practices and ethical standards. An ethically conscious and accountable culture should be developed in communities and organizations that create and utilize AI technologies.
- *Establish Oversight Mechanisms*: Mechanisms in place to keep an eye on, assess, and guarantee adherence to moral standards and legal requirements regarding the ethical performance of AI systems should be under vigilance. Supervising AI initiatives, handling ethical issues, and setting up impartial review boards or ethics committees should be done occasionally. Establish channels for reporting ethical transgressions or issues and respond appropriately to them.
- *Foster Collaboration and Transparency:* Encouragement of cooperation and information exchange between researchers, policymakers, developers of AI, and other interested parties to advance ethical best practices should be done by various methods, accountability, and transparency in the creation and application of AI. To promote the ethical application of AI, promote candid discussion and teamwork on moral dilemmas.

- *Regular Review and Updating:* Regular review and update of ethical policies and processes should be done to consider changing societal concerns, technology advancements, and growing ethical standards. To continuously develop ethical policies and processes and stay current on emerging ethical considerations and best practices in AI ethics.

AI systems have various ethical issues that should be resolved and used responsibly. The problems include fairness, transparency, bias accountability, and potential misuse of AI against individuals or society. Consequently, it is essential to refer to recognized ethical frameworks that give comprehensive guidelines for developing and using artificial intelligence technologies while dealing with these challenges. Among them is "Ethics Guidelines for Trustworthy AI" by the European Commission High-Level Expert Group on AI (2019), which suggests a model based on seven fundamental requirements: Human agency and oversight; Technical robustness and safety; Privacy and data governance; Transparency; At the same time, Human Agency and Oversight underscore the need for autonomy support by chatbots like ChatGPT. Technical robustness and safety, including their resilience to attacks and reliability in diverse conditions, are crucial for ethical AI (Land & Meier, 2012).

According to the Ethics Guidelines for Trustworthy AI and legislations like GDPR- General Data Protection Regulation, privacy is vital in ensuring trustworthy AI. Therefore, strict privacy measures should be implemented for AI systems dealing with sensitive personal data (European Commission, 2019). In ChatGPT systems, for instance, one could seek clarity through an explanation of response generation by the model during training; some datasets were utilized while acknowledging areas with potential prejudice or mistakes (Lipton, 2018). The Ethics Guidelines for trustworthy AI call upon developers to embrace diversity inclusion at all stages of development, thus avoiding discrimination against different demographic groups during the design process (Bender et al., 2021). AI systems must be developed and used to impact society and the planet positively. This principle requires developers to consider the broader effects of their technology, like environmental consequences linked with large-scale AI models and social implications associated with its deployment (Strubell et al., 2019). Finally, The Ethics Guidelines for Trustworthy AI demand accountability throughout all implementation levels of an artificial intelligence system. This can be achieved by setting up clear lines of responsibility when deploying any AI system. Failure to do so might lead to harm caused without possibly rectifying it later (Taddeo & Floridi, 2018). These instructions ensure that AI systems are technically robust and ethically acceptable by establishing a broad basis for trustworthiness, fairness, and responsible use. Since ChatGPT is an example of an AI application, it is necessary to ensure that established ethical concerns arising from the ethics of AI discourse are appropriately included. As artificial intelligence has become paramount across different sectors worldwide, following ethical guidelines like these will help us tackle the accompanying problems and maximize benefits without facing any problems.

4. Conclusion

An extensive examination of the complex field of ethics in artificial Intelligence (AI) has been given in this chapter. Through thorough investigation and discussion, several essential discoveries have been reached, highlighting how crucial it is to incorporate moral principles and responsible behavior into creating, applying, and using AI technologies.

The chapter emphasizes the importance of considering ethical issues when designing and implementing AI systems. It highlighted the moral obligations of AI researchers, developers, policymakers, and users to provide ethical standards, including accountability, justice, openness, privacy, and bias reduction, as top priorities. The chapter also discussed other important issues, such as the dynamic nature of AI technology, privacy problems, training data biases, and AI systems' opacity. It underlined the necessity of solid ethical frameworks, rules, and procedures to negotiate these difficulties successfully.

This chapter went into detail about how important it is to combat prejudice and advance fairness in AI systems. It emphasized identifying and reducing bias in algorithms, training data, and decision-making procedures to avoid biased results and guarantee fair treatment for all users. It promoted constant observation, assessment, and improvement of AI systems to recognize and reduce moral hazards, adjust to changing moral norms, and preserve moral values. The analysis highlights the need to consider the entire socio-technical AI ecosystem, not just particular problems, and offers insights into implications and interventions. To ensure that the benefits of AI, in particular large language models like those underpinning ChatGPT, are realized while harms are avoided, fully addressing the challenges will probably require multi-level societal engagement, from individual software engineers to international policies.

This chapter emphasized trust-building, societal acceptability, and realizing that AI technologies' full potential depends on ethical concerns and responsible AI practices. It is a collective commitment from AI developers, researchers, politicians, and users to prioritize ethical issues, encourage openness and accountability, and enforce ethical norms in all AI development and deployment phases. By embracing ethical principles and responsible practices, we can harness the transformative power of AI to benefit individuals, communities, and society while minimizing ethical risks and ensuring a more equitable and sustainable future.

References

Adadi, A., & Berrada, M. (2018). Peeking inside the black box: A survey on explainable artificial intelligence (XAI). *IEEE Access, 6*, 52138–52160.

Angwin, J., Larson, J., Mattu, S., & Kirchner, L. (2016). Machine bias: There is software used nationwide to predict future criminals. And it's biased against blacks. *ProPublica, 23*, 77–91.

Baker, R. S., & Hawn, A. (2022). Algorithmic bias in education. *International Journal of Artificial Intelligence in Education*, 1–41.

Bansal, M., & Garg, A. (2021). Do high-quality standards ensure higher accounting quality? A study in India. *Accounting Research Journal, 34*(6), 597–613.

Barocas, S., & Selbst, A. D. (2016). Big data's disparate impact. *California Law Review, 104,* 671.

Bender, E. M., Gebru, T., McMillan-Major, A., & Shmitchell, S. (2021). On the dangers of stochastic parrots: Can language models be too big? In *Proceedings of the 2021 ACM conference on fairness, accountability, and transparency* (pp. 610–623).

Birnbaum, L., & Kröner, S. (2022). A review on antecedents and consequences of leisure reading and writing in children. *SAGE Open, 12*(3). https://doi.org/10.1177/21582440221111

Boell, S. K., & Cecez-Kecmanovic, D. (2015). On being 'systematic' in literature reviews in IS. *Journal of Information Technology, 30*(2), 161–173.

Bolukbasi, T., Chang, K. W., Zou, J. Y., Saligrama, V., & Kalai, A. T. (2016). Man is a computer programmer, and woman is a homemaker. Debiasing word embeddings. *Advances in Neural Information Processing Systems, 29.*

Bostrom, N. (2016). The control problem. Excerpts from superintelligence: Paths, dangers, strategies. *Science Fiction and Philosophy: From Time Travel to Superintelligence,* 308–330.

Bostrom, N. (2019). The vulnerable world hypothesis. *Global Policy, 10*(4), 455–476.

Brown, T., Mann, B., Ryder, N., Subbiah, M., Kaplan, J., Dhariwal, P., & Amodei, D. (2020). Language models are few-shot learners. *Advances in Neural Information Processing Systems, 33,* 1877–1901. https://proceedings.neurips.cc/paper/2020/file/1457c0d6bfcb4967418bfb8ac142f64a-Paper.pdf

Buolamwini, J., & Gebru, T. (2018). Gender shades: Intersectional accuracy disparities in commercial gender classification. In *Proceedings of the conference on fairness, accountability, and transparency* (pp. 77–91). PMLR.

Caliskan, A., Bryson, J. J., & Narayanan, A. (2017). Semantics derived automatically from language corpora contain human-like biases. *Science, 356*(6334), 183–186.

Chinta, S. V., Wang, Z., Yin, Z., Hoang, N., Gonzalez, M., Quy, T. L., & Zhang, W. (2024). FairAIED: Navigating fairness, bias, and ethics in educational AI applications. arXiv preprint arXiv:2407.18745.

Coeckelbergh, M. (2020). Artificial intelligence, responsibility attribution, and a relational justification of explainability. *Science and Engineering Ethics, 26*(4), 2051–2068.

Crawford, K., Whittaker, M., Dobbe, R., Fried, G., Kaziunas, E., Mathur, V., & Schwartz, O. (2018). *AI now report 2018* (pp. 1–62). AI Now Institute at New York University.

Dastin, J. (2022). Amazon scraps secret AI recruiting tool that showed bias against women. In *Ethics of data and analytics* (pp. 296–299). Auerbach Publications.

European Commission. (2019). Ethics guidelines for trustworthy AI. In *High-level expert group on artificial intelligence.* https://www.aepd.es/sites/default/files/2019-12/ai-ethics-guidelines.pdf

Eynon, R. (2024). Algorithmic bias and discrimination through digitalization in education: A socio-technical view. In *World yearbook of education* (pp. 245–260). Routledge.

Floridi, L., Cowls, J., Beltrametti, M., Chatila, R., Chazerand, P., Dignum, V., & Vayena, E. (2018). AI4People—An ethical framework for a good AI society:

Opportunities, risks, principles, and recommendations. *Minds and Machines, 28,* 689–707.

Friedler, S. A., Scheidegger, C., & Venkatasubramanian, S. (2021). The (im)possibility of fairness: Different value systems require different mechanisms for fair decision making. *Communications of the ACM, 62*(7), 136–143. https://doi.org/10.1145/3433949

Goodfellow, I., Bengio, Y., & Courville, A. (2016). *Deep learning.* MIT Press.

Hendricks, L. A., Burns, K., Saenko, K., Darrell, T., & Rohrbach, A. (2018). Women also snowboard: Overcoming bias in captioning models. In *Proceedings of the European conference on computer vision* (pp. 771–787).

Hill, F., Cho, K., Korhonen, A., & Bengio, Y. (2016). Learning to understand phrases by embedding the dictionary. *Transactions of the Association for Computational Linguistics, 4,* 17–30.

Holstein, K., Wortman Vaughan, J., Daumé III, H., Dudik, M., & Wallach, H. (2019). Improving fairness in machine learning systems: What do industry practitioners need? In *Proceedings of the 2019 CHI conference on human factors in computing systems* (pp. 1–16). Association for Computing Machinery. https://doi.org/10.1145/3290605.3300830

Jobin, A., Ienca, M., & Vayena, E. (2019). The global landscape of AI ethics guidelines. *Nature Machine Intelligence, 1*(9), 389–399. https://doi.org/10.1038/s42256-019-0088-2

Kitchenham, B. (2004). *Procedures for performing systematic reviews* (Vol. 33, (2004), pp. 1–26). Keele University Technical Report.

Kizilcec, R. F., & Lee, H. (2022). Algorithmic fairness in education. In *The ethics of artificial intelligence in education* (pp. 174–202). Routledge.

Kosinski, M., Bachrach, Y., Kohli, P., Stillwell, D., & Graepel, T. (2014). Manifestations of user personality in website choice and behavior on online social networks. *Machine Learning, 95,* 357–380.

Kotek, H., Dockum, R., & Sun, D. (2023). Gender bias and stereotypes in large language models. In *Proceedings of the ACM collective intelligence conference* (pp. 12–24).

Land, M., & Meier, P. (2012). *ICT4HR: Information and communication technologies for human rights.* World Bank Publications.

LeCun, Y., Bengio, Y., & Hinton, G. (2015). Deep learning. *Nature, 521*(7553), 436–444.

Levy, Y., & Ellis, T. J. (2006). A systems approach to conduct an effective literature review in support of information systems research. *Informing Science, 9.*

Lipton, Z. C. (2018). The mythos of model interpretability: In machine learning, the concept of interpretability is both important and slippery. *ACM Queue, 16*(3), 31–57.

Madaio, M., Egede, L., Subramonyam, H., Wortman Vaughan, J., & Wallach, H. (2022). Assessing the fairness of AI systems: AI practitioners' processes, challenges, and needs for support. *Proceedings of the ACM on Human-Computer Interaction, 6*(CSCW1), 1–26.

Mashhadi, A., Zolyomi, A., & Quedado, J. (2022). A case study of integrating fairness visualization tools in machine learning education. In *CHI conference on human factors in computing systems* (pp. 1–7). Extended Abstracts.

Memarian, B., & Doleck, T. (2023). Fairness, accountability, transparency, and ethics (FATE) in artificial intelligence (AI), and higher education: A systematic review. *Computers and Education: Artificial Intelligence*, 100152.

Mitchell, M., Wu, S., Zaldivar, A., Barnes, P., Vasserman, L., Hutchinson, B., & Gebru, T. (2019, January). Model cards for model reporting. In *Proceedings of the conference on fairness, accountability, and transparency* (pp. 220–229).

Neff, G. (2016). Talking to bots: Symbiotic agency and the case of Tay. *International Journal of Communication*, *10*, 4915–4931.

O'Neil, C. (2017). *Weapons of math destruction: How big data increases inequality and threatens democracy*. Crown.

Rudin, C. (2019). Stop explaining black-box machine learning models for high-stakes decisions and use interpretable models instead. *Nature Machine Intelligence*, *1*(5), 206–215.

Sap, M., Card, D., Gabriel, S., Choi, Y., & Smith, N. A. (2019). The risk of racial bias in hate speech detection. In *Proceedings of the 57th annual meeting of the association for computational linguistics* (pp. 1668–1678).

Selwyn, N. (2019). What's the problem with learning analytics? *Journal of Learning Analytics*, *6*(3), 11–19.

Snyder, H. (2019). Literature review as a research methodology: An overview and guidelines. *Journal of Business Research*, *104*, 333–339.

Sonnad, N. (2017). Google Translate's gender bias pairs 'he' with 'hardworking' and 'she' with lazy, and other examples. *Quartz*, *2*, 2021.

Strubell, E., Ganesh, A., & McCallum, A. (2019). Energy and policy considerations for deep learning in NLP. In *Proceedings of the 57th annual meeting of the association for computational linguistics* (pp. 3645–3650).

Taddeo, M., & Floridi, L. (2018). How AI can be a force for good. *Science*, *361*(6404), 751–752.

Tranfield, D., Denyer, D., & Smart, P. (2003). Towards a methodology for developing evidence-informed management knowledge by means of systematic review. *British Journal of Management*, *14*(3), 207–222.

Vaswani, A., Shazeer, N., Parmar, N., Uszkoreit, J., Jones, L., Gomez, A. N., & Polosukhin, I. (2017). Attention is all you need. *Advances in Neural Information Processing Systems*, *30*.

Vincent, J. (2018). Google 'fixed' its racist algorithm by removing gorillas from its image-labeling tech. *Verge*, *12*.

Part IV

Transforming Industries With ChatGPT

Chapter 8

Transformative Pedagogy: ChatGPT as a Catalyst for Educational Innovation

Harjit Singh[a], Nidhi Shridhar Natrajan[a], Rinku Sanjeev[a] and Avneet Singh[b]

[a]Symbiosis Centre for Management Studies, Noida, Symbiosis International (Deemed University), Pune, India
[b]University of Toledo, USA

Abstract

The introduction of ChatGPT in teaching, learning, and research has resulted from information and communication technologies practicing for enlightening academia and students' knowledge. Machine intelligence and professional systems allow academicians to focus more on critical tasks, such as providing personalized attention to the learners. It has the potential to transform the modern education system by automating repetitive tasks and customized learning experiences. It is useful in various learning applications such as research and adaptive knowledge systems then changes the content difficulty depending on a student's performance. The study aims to measure the previous works on the informative implications of artificial intelligence (AI). It assesses the opportunities and challenges of Open AI, particularly ChatGPT competencies for instruction, education, and exploration. The study's findings showed that the ChatGPT delivers fast and quick responses for explorations and programmed test creation that look like conversational responses. The study also highlighted limitations experienced, such as a need for more citations and references. The authors suggested some references such as ensuring recognition and referencing the replies supplied by ChatGPT.

Keywords: ChatGPT; artificial intelligence; chatbot; OpenAI; natural language processing

The ChatGPT Revolution, 153–182

Copyright © 2025 Harjit Singh, Nidhi Shridhar Natrajan, Rinku Sanjeev and Avneet Singh
Published under exclusive licence by Emerald Publishing Limited
doi:10.1108/978-1-83549-852-120251008

1. Introduction

ChatGPT has recently become one of the most popular tools for conversational AI. It is an artificial intelligence natural language processing tool developed by OpenAI. The applications are still developing and varying from applying linguistic translation to user facility chatbots, and education is no exception. The term teaching is the communication of information or skill to another professionally. It is both an art and science. Teaching highlights the teacher's creativity and inventive quality while interacting with the students in the classroom makes this an art and as a science, it emphasizes rational, practical, or machine-driven procedures to ensure long-lasting learning (Azevedo, 2013).

Varied educationalists have diverse views on the conception of education. Education is the direct collaboration between an expert and a less matured one (Fang et al., 2018), which proposes to advance the latter's education (Rajagopalan, 2019). Education is knowledge, as marketing is to purchasing (Wallfisch & Wallfisch, 1979). Teaching is the organization and administration of a scenario in which the gaps between those who know and those who do not are overcome (DeAngelo et al., 2016). Teaching is a sequential act of producing learning. It is a kind of impact pointed at changing the behavior likely of a learner. Teaching as a system of actions involves an educator (agent), an end goal (learner), and a formal setting, including two sets of factors: uncontrollable (characteristics of learners, size of the class, physical facilities, etc.) and controllable (such as teaching methods and approaches) (Baglione et al., 2022).

Educationists define learning in quite a few ways and with varied meanings. Some researchers have defined education and learning as "quantitative growth" in knowledge, while some consider it in individuals "qualitative growth" (Darling-Hammond et al., 2019). However, one point is common: both lead to the enrichment and development of the skills, knowledge, and techniques that may be identified and applied as required (Englert et al., 1992).

Modern education followers highlight using information and technology for learning and knowledge. It comprises comprehensive, actual use of technological tools such as internet, mobile phones, computers, and other software packages (Georghiades, 2004). These technologies have offered infrastructural support for the students' diverse and personalized learning necessities (Rajagopalan, 2019).

AI tools are used extensively for personalized tutoring, interactive learning, homework assistance, language practice, and administrative support in various educational settings. Mogavi et al. (2024), Sandu et al. (2024); Singh et al. (2024) and Zhai (2021) opined that artificial intelligence (AI) can bring significant educational progress. AI utilization in education transforms the pattern of the current educational system (Knox, 2020). The study explains how AI transforms the future of education. The application of various generative natural language models, such as ChatGPT, will explore possible ways to impact the future of education by including industry-based cases or real examples.

It is, therefore, crucial to define the significant relationships used throughout the chapter to ensure that all readers consistently understand the concepts discussed (Table 8.1).

Table 8.1. Defining Key Relationships: Ensuring Consistency in Understanding Concepts.

Sl. No	Key Terms	Definition
1	Transformative pedagogy	An educational approach that seeks to foster deep, meaningful learning experiences by critically challenging students to examine their beliefs, values, and perspectives. It emphasizes not just acquiring knowledge but also transforming students' ways of thinking and understanding about themselves and the world around them.
2	Educational innovation	It refers to implementing new or significantly improved teaching methods, tools, or practices that enhance the learning experience and improve educational outcomes. It involves creative approaches to curriculum design, pedagogy, and technology integration to better meet learners' needs and adapt to evolving educational challenges.
3	Generative natural language model	Artificial Intelligences System produces relevant contextually clear text based on input prompt. Model such as ChatGPT learn from various informations of text data to create humanize responses, complete sentence or create content across various topics.
4	Natural language processing (NLP)	Artificial Intelligence enables computer to comprehend, understand, analyze, and generate humanize response. It bridges the gap between human communication and machine understanding by including language modification, speech recognition, and sentiment study.
5	Chatbot	Through Text or voice interaction an artificial intelligence planned to stimulate communication with users. It can answer questions, provide information, and perform tasks based on user inputs, often using natural language processing to understand and respond appropriately.

(Continued)

Table 8.1. *(Continued)*

Sl. No	Key Terms	Definition
6	Educational integrity	It refers to the adherence to ethical principles and standards in the academic environment, including honesty, fairness, and transparency. It encompasses practices such as avoiding plagiarism, upholding academic standards, and ensuring that assessments and evaluations are conducted fairly and accurately.
7	Personalized learning	It is an educational approach tailored to individual students' needs, interests, and learning styles. It involves customizing learning experiences and pathways to enhance each student's engagement and achievement, often using adaptive technologies and targeted instructional strategies.
8	Interactive learning	It is an educational approach that actively involves students in learning through engaging activities, discussions, and hands-on experiences. It emphasizes collaboration and real-time feedback, enabling learners to actively participate and apply knowledge in dynamic, participatory ways.

Source: Compiled by authors.

So, the study will discuss two significant queries. Primarily, how can ChatGPT improve the performance of educational sectors and the knowledge of the students? Then discuss the barriers of ChatGPT within educational institutions. This would focus on the various challenges or barriers arising to develop or implement ChatGPT in the educational institutions both in private and public.

2. Literature Review

ChatGPT can be a valued teaching, learning, and research tool. It offers students or learners a more individual and interactive learning experience in the education sector. By prompt replies, clearing doubts, preparing for competitive examinations, offering writing assistance, and contributing personalized tutoring, ChatGPT helps students learn and acquire more efficiently (Singh & Singh, 2023).

2.1 Role of ChatGPT in Education, Learning, and Research

Since ChatGPT is based on large language models, it responds similarly to those of a human being (Mogavi et al., 2024). There are many applications where this type of conversation could be assisted through this technology (D'Amico et al., 2023). Many customer care work can involve answering standard questions that can be automated without much loss of content and meaning (Atlas, 2023). Another strength of ChatGPT is its ability to learn and adapt to new contexts. As a human mind learns even when the output is incorrect, the tool also builds upon its learning by segregating the correct and incorrect outputs. Thus, even mistakes can lead to better learning. This supports ChatGPT in providing more personalized responses (Al Shloul et al., 2024).

The feature further supports these abilities to give responses similar to human responses by adding context to the information. So, the way the user asks a question, the responses are generated according to the same. Thus, the use of ChatGPT has become important in various aspects, including education, research, business, and training. The accuracy of the auto-generated response is what makes it useful for real-life applications. According to Azaria (2022) and Sandu et al. (2024) one of the beautiful examples of this is where the ChatGPT could generate the number a human thinks and does not reveal. In most cases, the tool could correctly guess the choice of number. They found a strong association between the frequency of numbers formed by ChatGPT and humans' desired numbers. The most common number created by ChatGPT matched respondent's most preferred number.

The application of ChatGPT in the education sector is highlighted by Singh and Singh (2023). According to them, ChatGPT can be used as a question–answer tool to support the learners. The learners, specifically those studying in distance learning mode, will have less assistance in terms of faculty availability. In such a scenario, many doubts can be clarified through these AI-based tools. Moreover, the algorithm's accuracy makes the answers reliable and have a specific context (Dilekçi & Karatay, 2023).

Apart from the classroom delivery of the content, the students are also required to do self-study to better understand the subject and perform better in the assessments. The ChatGPT assists the student with doubts during the self-study (van Dis et al., 2023). Not only is doubt clearance available but a proper explanation of various numerical and logic-based subjects is also possible. Along with the student's performance, the student's confidence was also enhanced with such assistance (García-Peñalvo, 2023).

In the research work, ChtGPT supports researchers in collecting and analyzing large and complex data. There is support in drafting an article and setting the flow of the report. Being trained on voluminous data, ChatGPT generates new research articles on a topic. The support is equally available for quantitative and qualitative data. This saves researchers enough time by automating the compilation of certain sections of a research paper, such as the Abstract, Introduction, or Research Methodology section. Language learning models can be used to review research studies, assisting researchers in comprehending the study's key findings (Kung et al., 2023). ChatGPT is also used to check for grammatical and language errors in research papers, making it suitable for international journals with increased chances of acceptance by journals. ChatGPT can also provide assistance to the researchers in identifying appropriate papers for systematic literature review, which otherwise becomes time-consuming for researchers if done manually (Sandu et al., 2024; Opara et al., 2023). It is to be noted that AI-based language models are not perfect and may generate faulty or objectionable text. So, it may lack human creativity, but when combined with proper editing and human oversight, ChatGPT can be an effective writing tool for research papers.

ChatGPT assists students in preparing for their academic or competitive examinations (Molenaar, 2022). It offers multiple-choice questions, sample questions, fill-in-the-blanks, and quizzes of varied dimensions (Times, 2023). It allows students to test their knowledge and identify weak areas where they need to concentrate more (Minh, 2024). This practice approach improves exam performance and higher scores (Rudolph et al., 2023). Further, the features also assist students in improving their writing skills and communicating their ideas more efficiently (Yang & Zhang, 2019).

Being an AI-enabled tool, ChatGPT understands the learning styles of students and responds accordingly. Moreover, ChatGPT allows students and scholars to learn independently (Tamara et al., 2023). This leads to ChatGPT as a "Personalized learning guide" and a more positive attitude toward advanced learning (Sandu et al., 2024). For students or coders who want to write code, ChatGPT assists them with being syntactically accurate and following best practices. However, it is imperative to note that it cannot restore or assess the code (Zou, 2017). It is also essential to assess the code, know the logic, and ensure it works as envisioned before using it in any production environment. Further, ChatGPT, a language model, generates text in several forms, including programming code (Tamara et al., 2023).

2.2 Artificial Intelligence in Education

In the current technology era, there is much support for making human life easy, and artificial intelligence applications further add to this benefit. A lot of manual work can be converted to AI-based automated tasks, thereby saving time and cost (Yu, 2020). AI has changed the way various sectors work, including education, teaching-learning processes, and research. The application benefits academia and the research fraternity greatly (Yilmaz, 2018). AI-based tools provide self-paced learning, thereby supporting learners of all ages and grasping abilities (Yang & Bai, 2020).

Thus, it can be stated that AI-based tools provide many benefits for both the learners and the educators. The educators must redefine their pedagogical approach using these tools (Dowling, 2023). It creates a better learning environment through ample engagement and flexibility. However, using these technology tools must be done while considering its pros and cons (Yufei et al., 2020).

Implementing artificial intelligence in educational institutions supports academicians to energies individualized learning (Dowling, 2023). It is still being determine to know that how much artificial intelligence is helpful in educational sector and to what extent it should be used for various pedagogical purposes (Yufei et al., 2020). Most researchers have studied the impact of artificial intelligence on educational sector along with its pros and cons. Gocen and Aydemir (2020) examined various possibilities and consequences with the implementation of artificial intelligence in educational sector.

Through the integration of AI and educational sector, teachers and institutes will have new mileages, benefits, and pitfalls (Bommarito & Katz, 2022). The findings offer recommendations for adopting AI and ways to mitigate possible glitches. Where most participants have positive attitudes about artificial intelligence, it appear to be some apprehensions about the future of educational sector, specifically among educators and academicians (Cowan et al., 2003). Jurists and lawyers are mainly concerned with the basics of legalities of artificial intelligence in educational sector and its possible challenges (Chatterjee & Dethlefs, 2023). At the same time, engineers see AI as a quality tool that benefits everybody in the education sector. Verma et al. (2021) presented AI's usefulness, various facets, the scope of artificial intelligence in allied domains, its conceptual dimensions, novelties and its searching policies, and the future.

Some researcher provided few primary answers both theoretically and practically in an analysis of the consequences of various investigational applications that have been documented in more detail elsewhere. He found that though artificial intelligence has much interference in the teaching domain, it cannot take the presence of a teacher in the formal set of automated computing techniques, as what AI accomplishes is fundamentally different from human intelligence (Cope, 2021). Despite observed constraints, AI has the likely to transform modern educational instruction in ways that may transform education more humanize rather than virtual assistants (Cotton et al., 2023).

While examining the role of educational artificial intelligence applications in personalized learning, Vorst and Nick (2019) found data mining, real-time analysis, learning analytics, are helpful in adaptive learning. Adaptive learning incorporates all aspects of teaching, learning, assessment, education, and training to facilitate students' long-term learning. Students who study one-on-one teaching perform better than those who learn via typical educational techniques by two standard deviations (Nsoh et al., 2023). Further, personalized learning is not realistic due to the inadequate number of teachers and associated expenses (Minh, 2024).

Recent machine learning advances support exciting individualized learning prospects (Delić et al., 2019). AI, therefore, may be very useful in unlocking the potential of personalized learning by letting apps offer tailored instruction to every learner (Cotton et al., 2023). From the socio-technical standpoint, they analyzed the likely influence of AI on one-on-one learning. Also, they explored the potential of AI in education vis-à-vis factors affecting AI adoption, such as social, ethical, and legal. Finally, they proposed legislative solutions for adopting AI-driven personalized learning applications. Similarly, Jain and Jain (2019) examined the notion of artificial intelligence while placing teaching and learning in higher education and the implications of adopting AI. The study concluded that (i). AI aids higher education services in becoming accessible at an unparalleled rate, in and outside the laboratory or classroom (ii). AI in higher education expressively improves students' learning outcomes, and AI has vast future potential in the higher education sector (Mogavi et al., 2024).

To summarize, artificial intelligence technology is not an exception for education sector as it has been extensively used in all facets of trade and commerce. It simulates individual listening (speech recognition, machine translation) (Walkington & Bernacki, 2020), speaking (human–computer dialog, speech synthesis) (Chiba et al., 2018), watching (text recognition, image recognition, and computer vision) (Cope, 2021), learning (machine learning, intelligent adaptive learning) (Colchester et al., 2017) thinking (Theorem Proving) (Sarma et al., 2017), and action (robot) (Khandelwal et al., 2017). To be precise, AI technologies such as intelligent adaptive learning, natural language processing, and computer vision have changed the traditional face of teaching (Yufei et al., 2020) and have provided teachers and universities with new philosophies for teaching reform. One of the significances of AI in education is its contribution to personalized learning and teaching. Today, AI has changed how educators teach in classrooms and how students learn.

3. Research Methodology

This study is primarily qualitative and is a blend of (a). literature review, (b). desk research, and (c). interviews. Case studies are needed to generate evidence for adopting ChatGPT in education and allied areas such as research and consultancy. With rapidly evolving AI-based technology such as ChatGPT, almost daily industry posts and announcements on specialist media, the usage of qualitative approaches signifies a rational approach in engaging with the subject at a time when research on the theme is at a nascent stage and industry use cases concerning the "role of ChatGPT in education" is exploratory (Table 8.2). To meet the desired objectives, our research approach involves a blend of three allied methods, as shown in Table 8.2 below.

4. ChatGPT in Education – Case-Based Application

Some of the universities, such as Imperial College London and the University of Cambridge, initially warned the students about the use of ChatGPT to prepare homework assignments, but later, they identified that it was an opportunity rather than a cheating tool. Academicians believe that it is not a ready machine for essay writing and preparing assignments. It could improve education also (Singh & Singh, 2023). Academicians realized that the advanced chatbot was used as a

Table 8.2. Methodology Layout.

Sl. No	Components of Methodology Layout	Objectives	Method Employed
1	Literature Review	• Adoption of ChatGPT in education. • Application of ChatGPT in teaching, learning, and research. • SWOT analysis of ChatGPT in education. • ChatGPT for educational records. • ChatGPT in education use cases.	• Jistor • Researchgate • Google Scholar • PubMed • Scopus • Web of Science
2	Desk Research	• Knowing technical specifications and requirements of ChatGPT in educational sector, mainly teaching, learning, and research. • Technical specifications of services offered by OpenAI to various industries, its governing structure, and operational and intellectual arrangements.	• Literature Review • Online Databases • Professional Journals
3	Interviews	To understand the various facets of ChatGPT and education, subject experts from academia and industry were interviewed.	• Semi-structured Interviews • Focus Group Interviews • Telephone Interviews • Face-to-face Interviews

Source: Compiled by authors.

powerful tool to make lessons more interactive and create customized lesson plans with less time and energy (Fig. 8.1).

ChatGPT can adjust itself to the student's learning pace and offer tailored explanations to guide him/her through problem-solving steps (Rajagopalan, 2019). It can engage in grammatical and vocabulary errors, offer contextual usage of phrases, and simulate real-life conversations to build learner's fluency and confidence (Rudolph et al., 2023). ChatGPT assists in brainstorming new

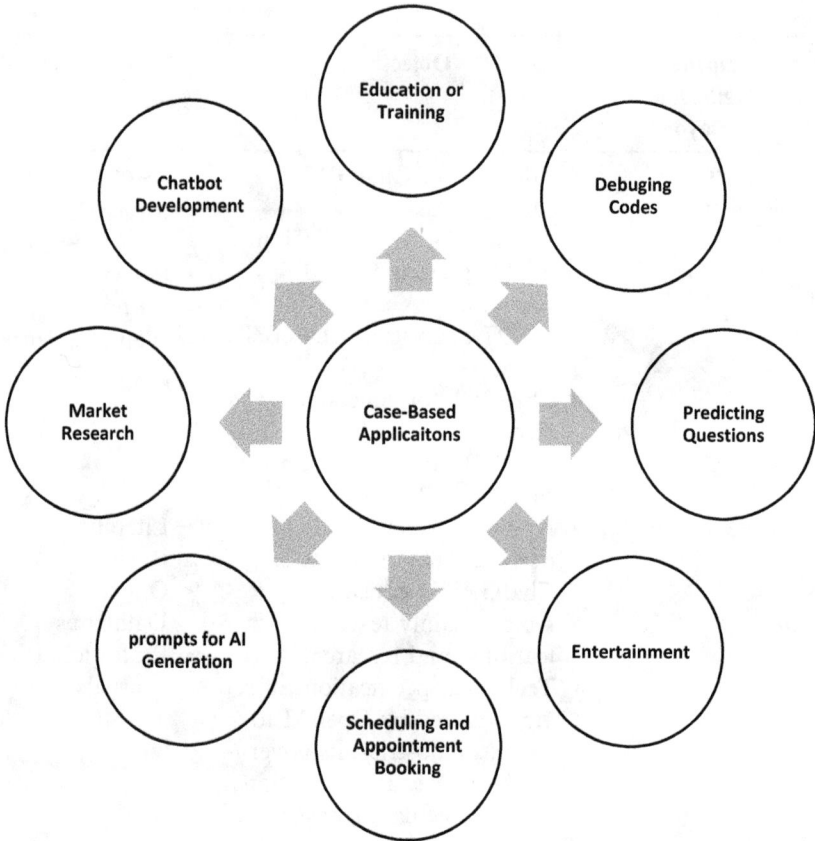

Fig. 8.1.   Case-Based Applications of ChatGPT. *Source:* Compiled by authors.

themes and ideas, offers grammar and style options, and even generates sample content. Proper prompts may help students understand how to organize their thoughts and improve their writing skills (Sarma et al., 2017).

4.1 Applications of ChatGPT for Teachers' Fraternity

4.1.1 Content Creation

ChatGPT is a very effective tool for teaching online learners and students. It helps teachers and trainers generate ideas for their classroom activities, lesson plans, and discussions (Tack & Piech, 2022) that align with student learning objectives (SLO) and program learning objectives (PLO). Academicians can use ChatGPT to curate and generate teaching materials, such as class tests, presentations, quizzes, worksheets (Singh & Singh, 2023), and other resources depending on the students' needs (Fig. 8.2).

Create Multiple Choice Questions for Financial Management Subject.

Answer

Multiple Choice Questions (Financial Management)

1. **What is the primary goal of financial management?**
   - a) Maximizing sales
   - b) Minimizing costs
   - c) Maximizing shareholder wealth
   - d) Maximizing market share
   Correct Answer: c) Maximizing shareholder wealth
2. **Which of the following represents the concept of liquidity?**
   - a) The ability to meet short-term obligations
   - b) The return on investment in the long term
   - c) The process of raising capital
   - d) The level of profit in a company
   Correct Answer: a) The ability to meet short-term obligations
3. **What does the term "capital structure" refer to?**
   - a) The division between operating costs and revenues
   - b) The mixture of debt and equity in financing
   - c) The dividend policy followed by the company
   - d) The method of valuation of assets
   Correct Answer: b) The mixture of debt and equity in financing
4. **The Net Present Value (NPV) method of project evaluation is based on:**
   - a) Only the future cash flows of a project
   - b) The difference between a project's cost and revenue
   - c) Discounting future cash flows to the present value
   - d) Estimating the equity value of a project
   Correct Answer: c) Discounting future cash flows to the present value.

Let me know if you'd like more information on any of the points!

Fig. 8.2. ChatGPT Creates a Quiz on Financial Management for University Students. *Source:* Created by ChatGPT (2024) in response to a prompt provided by the authors.

4.1.2 Designing Syllabus Outline

School teachers or university professors can use ChatGPT to create, shape, and structure course content comprehensibly and actively (Fig. 8.3) (Singh & Singh, 2023). AI capabilities of ChatGPT can be used in drafting course handouts compromising of:

🌀 **Provide Course curriculum for Corporate Finance Subject.**

Answer

1. Introduction to Corporate Finance
2. Financial Statements and Analysis
3. Time Value of Money (TVM)
4. Valuation of Bonds and Stocks
5. Capital Budgeting
6. Risk and Return
7. Cost of Capital
8. Capital Structure Decisions
9. Dividend Policy
10. Working Capital Management
11. Mergers and Acquisitions (M&A)
12. Corporate Governance and Ethics
13. Contemporary Topics in Corporate Finance
14. Case Studies and Applications

Let me know if you'd like more information on any of the points

Fig. 8.3.   ChatGPT Creating Course Curriculum on Corporate Finance. *Source:* Created by ChatGPT (2024) in response to a prompt provided by the authors.

- Course Background.
- Learning Objectives.
- Course Outcomes.
- Course Objectives-Program Objectives Mapping.
- Pedagogy.
- Prerequisites.
- Evaluation/Assessment.
- Course Outline.
- Readings (Text Books and References).

4.1.3 Grading

ChatGPT can be used to review and grade the students' assignments. Teachers can analyze the content, coherence, and structure of the writing. AI can offer feedback on spelling, grammar, syntax, and punctuation and evaluate the quality of the answer or analysis presented. As ChatGPT is under the testing and trial phase, it is not advisable to rely on ChatGPT while grading (Chatterjee & Dethlefs, 2023). Instead, instructors can use ChatGPT to define the rubric for grading (Fig. 8.4).

4.1.4 Grammar and Writing Check

Another valuable application of ChatGPT for instructors involves leveraging AI capabilities to assess and improve the quality of home assignments. This can be utilized as follows:

- Proofreading and editing: ChatGPT can quickly evaluate and correct punctuation, grammar, spelling, and syntax errors in notices, emails, circulars, memorandums, lesson plans, or course handouts prepared by instructors.
- Sharing feedback to students: ChatGPT can assist instructors in analyzing student projects, training reports, or home assignments. ChatGPT can be very helpful in describing the areas where students can improve themselves and highlighting precise feedback on syntax, word choice, and sentence structure (Singh & Singh, 2023).
- Educating writing skills: Academicians can use ChatGPT to create explanations and examples of grammar rules, writing conventions, word choice, and punctuation to improve students' writing skills (Chatterjee & Dethlefs, 2023).

4.1.4.1 ChatGPT Applications for Student Community

- Support provides in home assignments: Students looking for quick answers for their home assignments can use ChatGPT. Like the iPhone "Siri" feature, ChatGPT offers prompt and judicious answers to their queries (Fig. 8.3).
- Improved writing skills: Today, there are many writing tools, such as Grammarly and NoRedlnk, that help students improve their writing skills, similar to ChatGPT functions. A student can correct his written material like native citizens of that language. For this, he/she will have to type the sentence and ask ChatGPT to correct it for him/her (Fig. 8.5).
- Conducting research: ChatGPT, trained on voluminous data, is intelligent and a vast academic resource for research scholars to access national and international research studies. This implies that students can use ChatGPT as a Wikipedia and improve their general knowledge (Fig. 8.6).

Create a Rubric for Financial Accounting Subject.

Answer

Financial Accounting Rubric

Criteria	Excellent (4)	Good (3)	Satisfactory (2)	Needs Improvement (1)
Understanding of Concepts	Demonstrates a thorough understanding of financial accounting principles and concepts.	Shows good understanding with minor errors or misconceptions.	Displays basic understanding but lacks depth; some concepts are misunderstood.	Lacks understanding of fundamental concepts; major misconceptions present.
Application of Knowledge	Effectively applies accounting principles to solve complex problems accurately.	Applies principles correctly to most problems; minor errors may occur.	Some application of principles is evident, but errors are frequent.	Fails to apply accounting principles; solutions are incorrect or missing.
Analysis and Interpretation	Provides insightful analysis and interpretation of financial data; conclusions are well-supported.	Analyzes data correctly with reasonable interpretations; conclusions are mostly supported.	Basic analysis is present, but interpretations lack depth; conclusions may not be well-supported.	Analysis is superficial or incorrect; interpretations and conclusions are absent or flawed.
Clarity and Organization	Information is presented in a clear, logical, and organized manner; easy to follow.	Generally clear and organized presentation; minor issues with flow or clarity.	Some organization is evident, but the presentation lacks clarity in places.	Presentation is disorganized and unclear; difficult to follow the argument or data.
Use of Terminology	Uses appropriate financial accounting terminology accurately and confidently throughout the work.	Uses relevant terminology correctly most of the time, with occasional errors.	Limited use of terminology; some terms are misused or omitted.	Rarely uses appropriate terminology; significant misunderstandings evident.

Total Score:

16-20 points: Excellent

11-15 points: Good

6-10 points: Satisfactory

1-5 points: Needs Improvement

Instructions for Use:

Assign Scores: Evaluate each criterion based on the performance levels described.

Calculate Total Score: Sum the scores from all criteria to determine the overall performance level.

Provide Feedback: Offer specific feedback based on the scores to help students understand areas for improvement.

This rubric can be tailored further based on specific assignments or projects within your Financial Accounting course! If you need any modifications or additional criteria, feel free to ask!

Fig. 8.4.   ChatGPT Creates Rubrics for Financial Accounting Course.
Source: Created by ChatGPT (2024) in response to a prompt provided by the authors.

Here is the concept of **Millets** in tabular form:

Aspect	Details
What are Millets?	A group of small-seeded grasses, commonly grown as cereal crops, known for their high nutritional value.
Examples	Pearl millet, Finger millet, Foxtail millet, Sorghum, Proso millet, Barnyard millet, and Little millet.
Nutritional Benefits	High in protein, fiber, vitamins, and minerals such as iron, magnesium, and phosphorus. Gluten-free and good for digestive health.
Uses	Consumed as flour, porridge, or in savory dishes. Also used in beverages, animal feed, and for making fermented products.
Climate Suitability	Grown primarily in arid and semi-arid regions; drought-resistant, making them suitable for dry land farming.
Health Benefits	May help lower cholesterol, control blood sugar levels, promote digestion, and provide long-lasting energy.
Cultural Significance	Traditionally consumed in various cultures around the world, especially in Africa and Asia. Millets have been a staple food in ancient civilizations.

Let me know if you'd like more information on any of the points!

Fig. 8.5. ChatGPT Explaining the Concept and Types of Millets.
Source: Created by ChatGPT (2024) in response to a prompt provided by the authors.

4.1.5 Language Learning

The AI-based ChatGPT model valued as tool for linguistic knowledge, translations, vocabulary practice, grammar descriptions, and discussion simulations to aid students in training and improving their language skills (van Dis et al., 2023). Similarly, it supports learners schedule a database to improve their linguistic skills (Fig. 8.7).

> Provide Types of Research in the
> Management Domain. Just Share their
> Names.
>
> **Answer**
>   1. Descriptive Research
>   2. Exploratory Research
>   3. Explanatory Research
>   4. Causal Research
>   5. Empirical Research
>   6. Qualitative Research
>   7. Quantitative Research
>   8. Applied Research
>   9. Basic (Fundamental) Research
>   10. Action Research
>   11. Case Study Research
>   12. Longitudinal Research
>   13. Cross-sectional Research
>   14. Mixed-method Research
>   15. Experimental Research
>   16. Ethnographic Research
>   17. Phenomenological Research
>   18. Survey Research
>
> Let me know if you'd like more
> information on any of the points!

Fig. 8.6.   ChatGPT Explains Various Types of Research to a New
Scholar. *Source:* Created by ChatGPT (2024) in response to a prompt
provided by the authors.

5. SWOT Analysis of ChatGPT in Education

SWOT analysis is a widely recognized tool businesses and organizations use to evaluate their position or products based on four key aspects: strengths, weaknesses, opportunities, and threats. Understanding these factors is crucial for strategic growth rather than relying on trial and error. When introducing new technologies like ChatGPT into education, SWOT analysis becomes essential to assess both internal (strengths and weaknesses) and external (opportunities and threats) factors influencing strategy formulation (García-Peñalvo, 2023). This section explores how SWOT analysis aids in identifying areas for improvement and gaining competitive advantages, particularly within the education sector.

⑯ **I am a level-2 learner of the German language, and I want to improve my skills. Suggest a weekly schedule to practice and improve my German on alternate days.**

Answer: Alternate Day Schedule for Improving German (Level-2 Learner)
This schedule focuses on structured learning while allowing enough flexibility to accommodate your routine.

Day 1: Vocabulary and Grammar
- **30 mins**: Learn and practice 10-15 new words or phrases. Use flashcards (e.g., Quizlet or Anki).
- **30 mins**: Grammar focus (e.g., verb conjugations, word order). Practice with exercises from textbooks or online resources like Deutsche Welle.
- **15 mins**: Write 5-7 sentences using the vocabulary and grammar learned.

Day 3: Listening and Speaking
- **30 mins**: Listen to a slow-paced German podcast (e.g., *Slow German*, *Coffee Break German*). Focus on identifying key words and phrases.
- **30 mins**: Practice speaking by summarizing what you heard. Record yourself or use language exchange apps like Tandem or HelloTalk to converse with native speakers.

Day 5: Reading and Writing
- **30 mins**: Read a short text or article in German (e.g., children's stories, simplified news articles on DW's *Langsam gesprochene Nachrichten*).
- **30 mins**: Write a summary or reflection on the text, focusing on correct grammar and vocabulary usage.

Day 7: Mixed Practice and Review
- **30 mins**: Watch a German video (e.g., *Easy German* on YouTube) or a TV show/movie with subtitles.
- **30 mins**: Review vocabulary, grammar, and key phrases from the past sessions. Quiz yourself or create mock sentences to reinforce learning.
- **Optional**: Engage in a relaxed activity like singing along with a German song, playing language games, or trying to think aloud in German for daily tasks.

Additional Suggestions
1. **Apps for Consistency**: Spend 10–15 mins daily (even on off days) using apps like Duolingo, Memrise, or Babbel for bite-sized learning.
2. **Weekend Immersion**: Consider a weekend session combining casual conversation and cultural learning, like exploring German cuisine or traditions.
3. **Set Goals**: Aim to master a specific topic (e.g., shopping phrases, travel vocabulary) every two weeks.

This alternate-day schedule balances productivity and recovery while maintaining progress.

Let me know if you'd like more information on any of the points!

Fig. 8.7.   ChatGPT Suggesting Learning the German Language.
Source: Created by ChatGPT (2024) in response to a prompt provided by the authors.

5.1 Strengths

One significant strength of ChatGPT is its ability to understand and respond to human queries naturally and straightforwardly (Khalil & Er, 2023). This capability empowers customer service chatbots to handle multiple queries and issues effectively. Secondly, ChatGPT can easily be fine-tuned for definite tasks and businesses, letting it be trained on industry-specific language and accomplish further multifaceted tasks such as endorsing products, creating content for social media, providing information, writing articles or business reports, and handling complaints (Kung et al., 2023). Thirdly, ChatGPT can be trained on a large text dataset to handle unexpected inputs. This feature allows ChatGPT to reply to input that deviates from probable responses or has not been seen before (Tamara et al., 2023). This, in turn, increases the customer experience and lessens the number of customer care representatives otherwise required (Fig. 8.8). Another strength that makes ChatGPT different from other search engines is that the model is constantly being upgraded and restructured, making it practical and influential over time (Molenaar, 2022). Thus, ChatGPT offers the following benefits in the education domain:

5.2 Weaknesses

ChatGPT can generate human-like content identical to other AI-based models. Still, if the user tries to insert a long text and command GPT to summarize the information, it will show its inability to handle 4095 tokens (Singh & Singh, 2023). Secondly, the said model cannot access new information or browse the web, which means it can only generate replies based on the data it has been fed into.

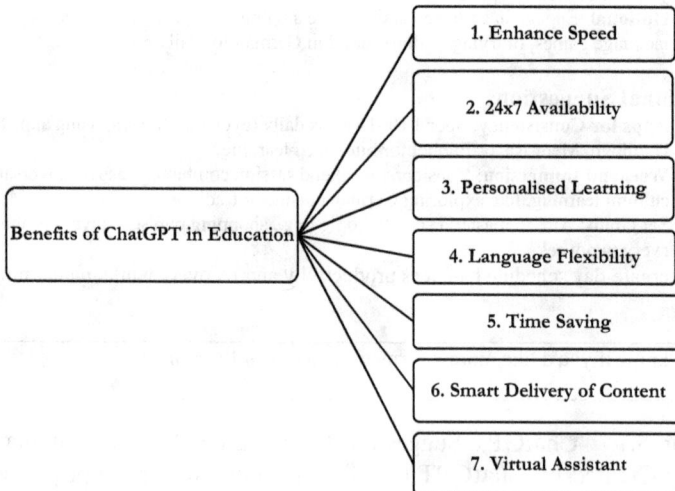

Fig. 8.8.   Strengths of ChatGPT. *Source:* Compiled by authors.

Thirdly, though it generates and interacts like humans, it is still a machine and can produce or make factually incorrect or inappropriate mistakes.

Relying solely on the data and information retrieved through ChatGPT may lead to incorrect and false outcomes as ChatGPT is not cloud-based, so information is neither updated nor complete (Times, 2023). ChatGPT does not own HOTS (higher-order thinking skills). Its responses and answers are based on patterns in data rather than comprehension, which can lead to superficial or incomplete explanations (Rahman & Watanobe, 2023). ChatGPT may find it challenging to understand the context of multi-step problems, complex queries, or lengthy prompts, leading to irrelevant or unworthy explanations (Chatterjee & Dethlefs, 2023). Unlike human teachers, ChatGPT lacks empathy and personal touch, so students are ignored (Opara et al., 2023). It also lacks timely mentorship and does not address students' needs, which can be crucial in understanding and addressing individual student needs (Nsoh et al., 2023). It is very much possible that students might use ChatGPT to do complex mathematical problems (Dilekçi & Karatay, 2023; van Dis et al., 2023), preparing home assignments, leading to undermining of learning and academic integrity (Chatterjee & Dethlefs, 2023). All such shortcomings are presented in Fig. 8.9.

5.3 Opportunities

Opportunities are favorable external factors that offer organizations a competitive advantage (García-Peñalvo, 2023). ChatGPT has the potential for OpenAI to be used for new industries and applications from customer care to education, learning, and research and to positively impact academicians' and pupils' lives (Kasneci et al., 2023). ChatGPT, an evolving technology, can be integrated with other emerging technologies, such as academic assistants and virtual chatbots, to make teaching influential (Khalil & Er, 2023). Further, as the inventors of

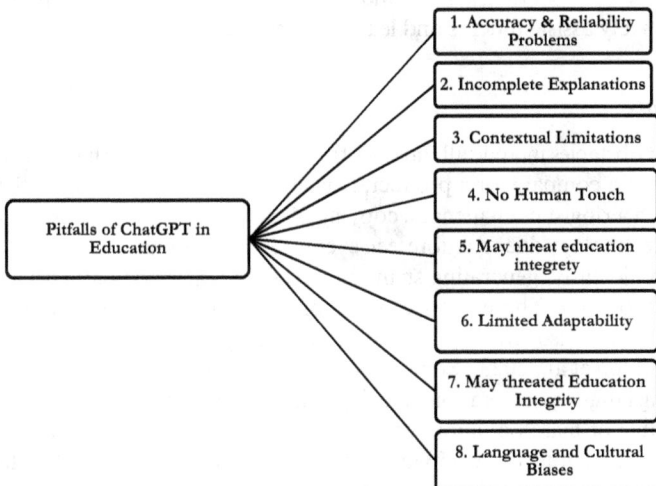

Fig. 8.9. Weaknesses of ChatGPT. *Source:* Compiled by authors.

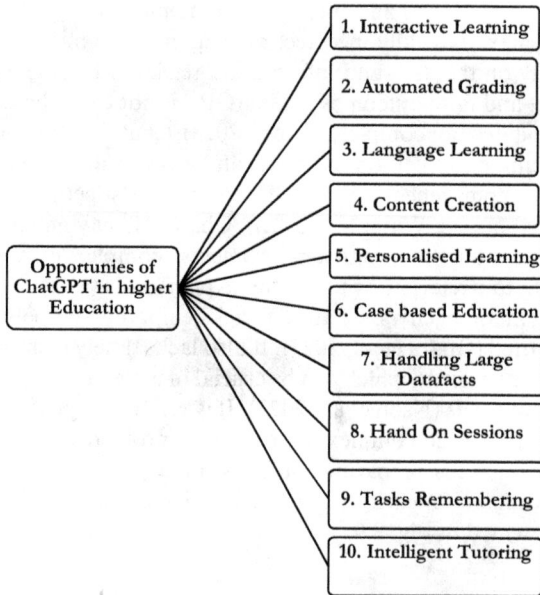

Fig. 8.10.   Opportunities of ChatGPT. *Source:* Compiled by authors.

ChatGPT have been working on improving its language models, there remain further breakthroughs and developments shortly.

The ChatGPT model can be used in various applications, from content creation to lecture preparation, PPT making, writing research papers, questionnaire drafting, and opinion polls (Kung et al., 2023). This offers opportunities for universities and academicians to use the model to improve the efficiency and productivity of modern teaching and learning (Mhlanga, 2023). The model can also effectively assist students and learners with language-related tasks (Fig. 8.10).

5.4 Threats

Threats or obstacles include all those worries and issues that may hamper the growth trajectory of a company or a product, reasons, or factors belonging to the external world, such as logistics challenges, copying of technology by competitors, or failure of recent technology due to unforeseen events (Singh & Singh, 2023). ChatGPT may be used maliciously, generating spam or spreading fabricated anti-social news like other technologies. The excessive usage of language generation models such as ChatGPT could also lead to the shifting of some jobs involving language-related tasks (Rudolph et al., 2023). Some concern exists regarding the ethical implications of applying language generation models, such as the possibility for the model to yield unacceptable or biased opinions or contents (Tamara et al., 2023). Therefore, it is significant for institutes and individuals using the model to be aware of such potential risks and take precautions to address them.

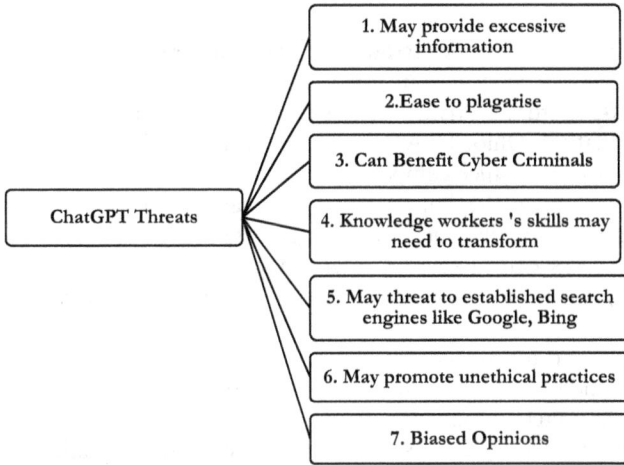

Fig. 8.11.   Threats of ChatGPT. *Source:* Compiled by authors.

Further, the black-box model nature makes it challenging to comprehend how it arrived at a particular response, making it difficult to improve or troubleshoot the performance of a chatbot employing ChatGPT (D'Amico et al., 2023). Moreover, ChatGPT requires much computational power, making it challenging to run on lower-end systems and less accessible to specific businesses (Fig. 8.11). ChatGPT also faces competition from other AI models created by renowned research organizations, such as Microsoft's Turing NLG and Google's BERT (Cowan et al., 2003). Besides this, despite its strengths, ChatGPT, like other AI models, is limited in its capabilities, and with testing time over, it may find tasks and cannot perform successfully (Dilekçi & Karatay, 2023). Lastly, the growth and usage of AI-enabled ChatGPT raise significant questions about general public trust and perception. It ensures that ChatGPT is used ethically and responsibly (García-Peñalvo, 2023).

6. The Market Adoption Challenge

This section discusses the market adoption challenges of ChatGPT in education by collecting the views of potential 'beneficiaries (such as private and public universities and start-up offering AI-based applications) toward usage of ChatGPT (e.g., Plag, fear, and privacy concerns) and the key players that may affect such adoption.

The perceptions presented are collected from existing research and interviews led by higher education institutions in management, law, dental, medical, and distance education, as well as AI-enabled education start-ups from India and the Midwestern United States (Exhibit 8.1). It was found that most educational institutes remain unwilling to use ChatGPT. The common reasons for this mistrust were the lack of required skills and expertise to manage students' data on such platforms, and no one wanted to initiate it as they were not sure about its success in the education field. In addition, most universities lack interest because of the lack of guidelines from educational regulating bodies. For instance, participant #3 is from a Private university in North India, and Participant #2, a public university in Ohio, USA, expressed that integrating AI, blockchain, and ChatGPT aims to enhance competitiveness and long-term IT proficiency among staff. This highlights the importance of educating school administrations on adopting and maintaining such technologies internally. The likelihood of adoption is crucial, as emphasized by interviewee #5, a startup founder providing AI-enabled services for democratizing higher education. The decision-makers for adopting these technologies are often university administrations rather than faculty, scholars, or researchers. Therefore, educating university leadership and raising awareness about new technologies is essential, particularly for gaining recognition in accreditation and rankings.

Moreover, regulatory bodies and governments play a significant role in the adoption of ChatGPT within the education sector. Interviewee #3, representing a leading private university in North India, noted that private or online universities are increasingly attracting students excluded from state-run colleges due to high demand. However, these institutions face challenges in securing formal recognition of their graduates' skills by corporations. ChatGPT could potentially enhance trust by validating credentials from non-traditional education paths, a point echoed by interviewees #4 and #1, who also highlighted governmental roles in promoting ChatGPT adoption. Collaboration among academia, government bodies, and corporations is crucial to overcoming challenges such as security issues, privacy concerns, funding shortages, and expertise gaps, ensuring the effective integration of ChatGPT in global education.

Interviewee #1, an Indian private university highlights another threat to the general adoption of ChatGPT in education applications: digital credentialing, a real demand coming from employers. For universities to be incentivized to adopt such AI-based platforms, actual demand must come from corporate. Graduates with expertise in emerging technologies like ChatGPT would be paid more than those in traditional languages such as Java, Python, and C++. As ChatGPT is an emerging technology, and its usefulness has yet to be tested and approved by academia, industry, and government, it is believed that it will do excellent and present win-win prepositions for all the stakeholders concerned. Thus, the issues highlighted above demonstrate that multiple parties (e.g., academia, governments, and the corporate) must cooperate and overcome implied concerns (e.g., issues of security, privacy, funding, lack of incentives, and expertise) to ensure an effective and sustainable integration of ChatGPT in the field of education globally.

7. Conclusion

This section addresses two primary research inquiries. Firstly, the study examines how ChatGPT could enhance the performance of educational institutions and

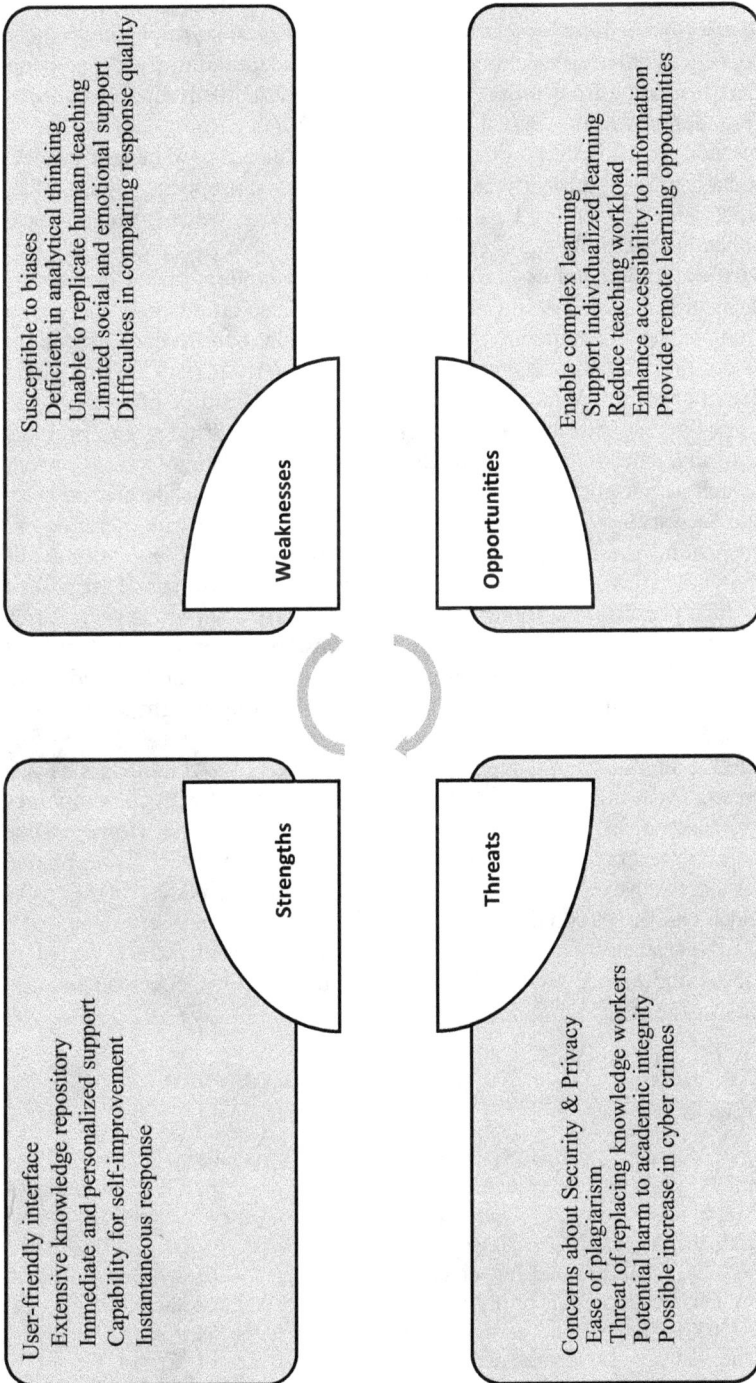

Strengths

User-friendly interface
Extensive knowledge repository
Immediate and personalized support
Capability for self-improvement
Instantaneous response

Weaknesses

Susceptible to biases
Deficient in analytical thinking
Unable to replicate human teaching
Limited social and emotional support
Difficulties in comparing response quality

Opportunities

Enable complex learning
Support individualized learning
Reduce teaching workload
Enhance accessibility to information
Provide remote learning opportunities

Threats

Concerns about Security & Privacy
Ease of plagiarism
Threat of replacing knowledge workers
Potential harm to academic integrity
Possible increase in cyber crimes

Fig. 8.12.   Resultant SWOT Analysis of ChatGPT in Education. *Source:* Compiled by authors.

improve student learning outcomes. It identifies three primary beneficiaries of ChatGPT solutions: educational institutions (e.g., colleges, startups, universities, NGOs) seeking to enhance teaching efficiency and student data privacy; students and learners benefiting from more engaging, consistent, and sustainable methods of acquiring, demonstrating, and sharing knowledge; and corporations in need of reliable methods to validate graduates' skills and certifications. The study delves into these stakeholders' motivations, concerns, and goals, proposing ChatGPT as a solution capable of creating both individual and shared value through educational applications (Exhibit 8.2).

Secondly, the study conducts a SWOT analysis and explores obstacles faced by ChatGPT in the education sector. Through expert consultations and analysis, it identifies challenges encountered by private and public educational institutions aiming to develop and implement ChatGPT solutions (Exhibit 8.3). Key issues discussed include identity management initiatives, certification processes (e.g., online or open-source university certificates, diplomas), and strategies to promote lifelong learning. The study also highlights threats and challenges across various domains, such as adoption, data privacy, scalability, legal considerations, innovation, and security.

In conclusion, the study identifies two critical stakeholders within the ChatGPT-in-education ecosystem: students, learners, and educators. It proposes a multidisciplinary research agenda comprising literature reviews, desk research involving online sources and academic publications, and interviews with subject matter experts. These approaches provide a comprehensive understanding of ChatGPT's potential in educational settings and effectively inform strategies to address its challenges.

One notable advantage of ChatGPT over other generative AI models is its vast scale, boasting more than 175 billion parameters that equip it with contemporary expertise to tackle diverse modern-day tasks (Singh & Singh, 2023). However, like other generative technologies, ChatGPT faces limitations, notably issues related to training on extensive datasets that may contain errors, biases, or offensive content. Such challenges could impact applications like customer service chatbots (Fig. 8.12). Nevertheless, ongoing technological advancements are expected to mitigate these limitations, ensuring ChatGPT's sustainability, effectiveness, and accessibility in the long run.

References

Al Shloul, T., Mazhar, T., Abbas, Q., Iqbal, M., Ghadi, Y., Shahzad, T., Malik, F., & Hamam, H. (2024). Role of activity-based learning and ChatGPT on students' performance in education. *Computers & Education: Artificial Intelligence, 6.* https://doi.org/10.1016/j.caeai.2024.100219

Atlas, S. (2023). ChatGPT for higher education and professional development: A guide to conversational AI. https://digitalcommons.uri.edu/cba_facpubs/548

Azaria, A. (2022). ChatGPT usage and limitations. *HAL Open Science, 1,* 1–9. https://hal.science/hal-03913837. Accessed on May 3, 2023.

Azevedo, F. S. (2013). The tailored practice of hobbies and its implication for the design of interest-driven learning environments. *The Journal of the Learning Sciences*, *22*(3), 462–510.

Baglione, S. L., Tucci, L. A., & Woock, P. (2022). Student perceptions of teaching excellence: A comparison of a public and private university. *Journal of Global Business Insights*, *7*(1), 78–93. https://doi.org/10.5038/2640-6489.7.1.1161

Bommarito, M., & Katz, D. M. (2022). GPT takes the bar exam. https://doi.org/10.48550/ARXIV.2212.14402

Chatterjee, J., & Dethlefs, N. (2023). This new conversational AI model can be your friend, philosopher, guide … and even your worst enemy. *Patterns*, *4*(1), 100676. ISSN 2666-3899. https://doi.org/10.1016/j.patter.2022.100676

Chiba, Y., Nose, T., Yamanaka, M., Kase, T., & Ito, A. (2018). An analysis of the effect of emotional speech synthesis on non-task-oriented dialogue system. In *SIGDIAL 2018 – 19th Annual meeting of the special interest group on discourse and dialogue – Proceedings of the conference* (pp. 371–375). Association for Computational Linguistics (ACL). https://doi.org/10.18653/v1/W18-5044

Colchester, K., Hagras, H., Alghazzawi, D., & Aldabbagh, G. (2017). A survey of artificial intelligence techniques employed for adaptive educational systems within e-learning platforms. *Journal of Artificial Intelligence and Soft Computing Research*, *7*(1), 47–64. https://doi.org/10.1515/jaiscr-2017-0004

Cope, B. (2021). Artificial intelligence for education: Knowledge and its assessment in AI-enabled learning ecologies. *Educational Philosophy and Theory*, *53*(12), 1229–1245. https://doi.org/10.1080/00131857.2020.1728732.

Cotton, D., Cotton, P. A., & Shipway, J. R. (2023, January 10). Chatting and cheating. Ensuring academic integrity in the era of ChatGPT. *Innovations in Education and Teaching International*. https://doi.org/10.1080/14703297.2023.2190148

Cowan, C., Arnold, S., Beattie, S., Wright, C., & Viega, J. (2003). Defcon Capture the Flag: Defend vulnerable code from intense attack. In *Proceedings DARPA information survivability conference and exposition*, Washington, DC, USA (Vol. 1, pp. 120–129). IEEE. https://doi.org/10.1109/DISCEX.2003.1194878

D'Amico, R. S., White, T. G., Shah, H. A., & Langer, D. J. (2023, April). I asked a ChatGPT to write an editorial about how we can incorporate chatbots into neurosurgical research and patient care…. *Neurosurgery*, *92*(4), 663–664. https://doi.org/10.1227/neu.0000000000002414

Darling-Hammond, L., Flook, L., Cook-Harvey, C., Barron, B., & Osher, D. (2019). Implications for educational practice of the science of learning and development. *Applied Developmental Science*, *24*(2), 97–140. https://doi.org/10.1080/10888691.2018.1537791

DeAngelo, L., Mason, J., & Winters, D. (2016). Faculty engagement in mentoring undergraduate students: How institutional environments regulate and promote extra-role behavior. *Innovative Higher Education*, *41*(4), 317–332. https://doi.org/10.1007/s10755-015-9350-7

Delić, V., Perić, Z., Sečujski, M., Jakovljević, N., Nikolić, J., Mišković, D., Simić, N., Suzić, S., Delić, T. (2019). Speech technology progress based on new machine learning paradigm. *Computational Intelligence and Neuroscience*, *2019*, 1–19. Article ID 4368036. https://doi.org/10.1155/2019/4368036

Dilekçi A., & Karatay, H. (2023). The effects of the 21st century skills curriculum on the development of students' creative thinking skills. *Thinking Skills and Creativity*, *47*, 101229. ISSN 1871-1871. https://doi.org/10.1016/j.tsc.2022.101229

Dowling, T. (2023). Fostering international student success in higher education, second edition. *Journal of International Students*, *13*(3), 389–392. https://doi.org/10.32674/jis.v13i3.6099

Englert, C. S., Raphael, T. E., & Anderson, L. M. (1992). Socially mediated instruction: Improving students' knowledge and talk about writing. *The Elementary School Journal*, *92*(4), 411–449. https://doi.org/10.1086/461700

Fang, Y., Ren, Z., Hu, X., & Graesser, A. C. (2018). A meta-analysis of the effectiveness of ALEKS on learning. *Educational Psychology*, *39*(10), 1278–1292. https://doi.org/10.1080/01443410.2018.1495829

García-Peñalvo, F. J. (2023). The perception of artificial intelligence in educational contexts after the launch of ChatGPT: Disruption or panic? *Education in the Knowledge Society*, *24*, e31279. https://doi.org/10.14201/eks.31279

Georghiades, P. (2004). From the general to the situated: Three decades of metacognition. *International Journal of Science Education*, *26*(3), 365–383.

Gocen, A., & Aydemir, F. (2020). Artificial intelligence in education and schools. *Research on Education and Media*, *12*(1), 13–21. https://doi.org/10.2478/rem-2020-0003.

Jain, S., & Jain, R. (2019). Role of artificial intelligence in higher education-an empirical investigation. *International Journal of Research and Analytical Reviews*, *6*(2), 144–150.

Kasneci, E., Sessler, K., Küchemann, S., Bannert, M., Dementieva, D., Fischer, F., Gasser, U., Groh, G., Günnemann, S., Hüllermeier, E., Krusche, S., Kutyniok, G., Michaeli, T., Nerdel, C., Pfeffer, J., Poquet, O., Sailer, M., Schmidt, A., Seidel, T., … Kasneci, G. (2023). ChatGPT for good? On opportunities and challenges of large language models for education. *Learning and Individual Differences*, *103*, 102274. ISSN 1041-6080. https://doi.org/10.1016/j.lindif.2023.102274

Khalil, M., & Er, E. (2023). Will ChatGPT get you caught? Rethinking of plagiarism detection. arXiv. https://doi.org/10.35542/osf.io/fnh48

Khandelwal, P., Zhang, S., Sinapov, J., Leonetti, M., Thomason, J., Yang, F., Gori, I., Svetlik, M., Khante, P., Lifschitz, V., Aggarwal, J. K., Mooney, R., & Stone, P. (2017). BWIBots: A platform for bridging the gap between AI and human–robot interaction research. *The International Journal of Robotics Research*, *36*(5–7), 635–659. https://doi.org/10.1177/0278364916688949

Knox, J. (2020). Artificial intelligence and education in China. *Learning, Media and Technology*, *45*(3), 298–311.

Kung, T. H., Cheatham M, Medenilla A, Sillos C, De Leon L, Elepaño C., Madriaga, M., Aggabao, R., Diaz-Candido, G., Maningo, J., & Tseng, V. (2023). Performance of ChatGPT on USMLE: Potential for AI-assisted medical education using large language models. *PLOS Digital Health*, *2*(2), e0000198. https://doi.org/10.1371/journal.pdig.0000198

Mhlanga, D. (2023). Open AI in education, the responsible and ethical use of ChatGPT towards lifelong learning. https://doi.org/10.2139/ssrn.4354422

Minh, A. N. (2024) Leveraging ChatGPT for enhancing English writing skills and critical thinking in university freshmen. *Journal of Knowledge Learning and Science Technology*, *3*(2), 51–62. https://doi.org/10.60087/jklst.vol3.n2.p62

Mogavi, R. H., Deng, C., Kim, J. J., Zhou, P., Kwon, Y. D., Metwally, A. H. S., Tlili, A., Bassanelli, S., Bucchiarone, A., Gujar, S., Nacke, L. E., & Hui, P. (2024). ChatGPT in education: A blessing or a curse? A qualitative study exploring early adopters' utilization and perceptions. *Computers in Human Behavior Artificial Humans*, *2*(1), 100027. ISSN 2949-8821. https://doi.org/10.1016/j.chbah.2023.100027

Molenaar, I. (2022). The concept of hybrid human-AI regulation: Exemplifying how to support young learners' self-regulated learning. *Computers & Education: Artificial Intelligence*, *3*, 100070. https://doi.org/10.1016/j.caeai.2022.100070

Nsoh, M. A. A., Joseph, T., & Adablanu, S. (2023). Artificial intelligence in education: Trends, opportunities, and pitfalls for institutes of higher education in Ghana. *International Journal of Computer Science and Mobile Computing*, *12*(2), 38–69.

Opara, E., Mfon-Ette Theresa, A. & Aduke, T. C. (2023, March 1). ChatGPT for teaching, learning, and research: Prospects and challenges. *Global Academic Journal of Humanities and Social Sciences*, *5*(1), 33–40. SSRN. https://ssrn.com/abstract=4375470

Rahman, M. M., & Watanobe, Y. (2023). ChatGPT for education and research: Opportunities, threats, and strategies. *Applied Sciences*, *13*, 5783. https://doi.org/10.3390/app13095783

Rajagopalan, I. (2019). Concept of teaching. *Shanlax International Journal of Education*, *7*(2), 5–8. https://doi.org/10.34293/education.v7i2.329

Rudolph, J., Tan, S., & Tan, S. (2023). ChatGPT: Bullshit spewer or the end of traditional assessments in higher education? *Journal of Applied Learning and Teaching*, *6*(1), 1–22. https://doi.org/10.37074/jalt.2023.6.1.9

Sandu, R., Gide, E., & Elkhodr, M. (2024). The role and impact of ChatGPT in educational practices: Insights from an Australian higher education case study. *Discovery Education*, *3*, 71. https://doi.org/10.1007/s44217-024-00126-6

Sarma, G., & Nick, H. (2017, August 8). Robust computer algebra, theorem proving, and oracle AI. *Informatica*, *41*(3). https://doi.org/10.2139/ssrn.3038545

Singh, H., & Singh, A. (2023). ChatGPT: Systematic review, applications, and agenda for multidisciplinary research. *Journal of Chinese Economics and Business Studies*. https://doi.org/10.1080/14765284.2023.2210482

Singh, H., Arora, M., & Singh, A. (2024). ChatGPT in marketing: innovative pathways, decision systems, and forward perspectives. *Journal of Decision Systems*, 1–28. https://doi.org/10.1080/12460125.2024.2438615

Tack, A., & Piech, C. (2022). The AI teacher test: Measuring the pedagogical ability of blender and GPT-3 in educational dialogues. https://doi.org/10.48550/ARXIV.2205.07540

Tamara, T., Doroudi, S., Ritchie, D., Xu, Y., & Warschauer, M. (2023). Educational research and AI-generated writing: Confronting the coming tsunami. https://doi.org/10.35542/osf.io/4mec3

Times. (2023). Dutch students are using ChatGPT to finish homework. Teachers aren't noticing. *NL Times*. https://nltimes.nl/2023/01/16/dutch-students-using-chatgpt-finish-homework-teachers-arent-noticing. Accessed on September 24, 2024.

Eim van Dis, E. A. M., Bollen J., Zuidema W., van Rooij, R., Bockting, C. L. (2023, February). ChatGPT: Five priorities for research. *Nature*, *614*(7947), 224–226. PMID: 36737653. https://doi.org/10.1038/d41586-023-00288-7

Verma, S., Sharma, R., Deb, S., & Maitra, D. (2021). *International Journal of Information Management Data Insights*, *1*(1), 100002. https://doi.org/10.1016/j.jjimei.2020.100002

Vorst, T., & Nick, J. (2019). Artificial intelligence in education: Can AI bring the full potential of personalized learning to education? In *30th European regional ITS conference, Helsinki 2019*. International Telecommunications Society (ITS). https://EconPapers.repec.org/RePEc:zbw:itse19:205222

Walkington, C., & Bernacki, M. L. (2020). Appraising research on personalized learning: Definitions, theoretical alignment, advancements, and future directions. *Journal of Research on Technology in Education*, *52*(3), 235–252.

Wallfisch, M. C., & Wallfisch, C. M. (1979). On the similarities between teaching and selling. *American Secondary Education*, *9*(3), 51–59.

Yang, S., & Bai, H. (2020). The integration design of artificial intelligence and normal students' education. *Journal of Physics: Conference Series*, *1453*(1), 012090.

Yang, J., & Zhang, B. (2019). Artificial intelligence in intelligent tutoring robots: A systematic review and design guidelines. *Applied Sciences*, *9*(10), 2078.

Yilmaz, B. (2018). *Effects of adaptive learning technologies on math achievement: A quantitative study of ALEKS math software*. Dissertation Abstracts International Section A: Humanities and Social Sciences.

Yu, P. K. (2020). Legal studies research paper series. The algorithmic divide and equality in the age of artificial intelligence. *Florida Law Review*, *72*(19), 331–389.

Yufei, L., Salehb, S., Jiahuic, H., & Syed Abdullahd, S. M. (2020). Review of the application of artificial intelligence in education. *International Journal of Innovation, Creativity, and Change*, *12*(8), 548–562.

Zhai, X. (2021). Practices and theories: How can machine learning assist in innovative assessment practices in science education. *Journal of Science Education and Technology*, *30*(2), 1–11.

Zou, S. (2017). Designing and practice of a college English teaching platform based on artificial intelligence. *Journal of Computational and Theoretical Nanoscience*, *14*, 104–108.

Weblinks

https://chat.openai.com/
https://www.mdpi.com/2076-3417/13/9/5783
https://www.niu.edu/citl/resources/guides/chatgpt-and-education.shtml
https://www.nature.com/articles/s41598-023-42227-6
https://www.frontiersin.org/articles/10.3389/feduc.2023.1206936/full

Appendix

Exhibit 8.1. Study Subjects (Interviews).

Participants	Institution Type	Area of Focus	Beneficiaries or Supplier
1	Private University	Management and Law Programs	Beneficiaries
2	Public University	Teaching and Research	Beneficiaries
3	Banking Professionals	Distance Education	Beneficiaries
4	IT Experts	Dental and Medical	Beneficiaries
5	Accounting and Finance Professionals	AI-based Applications	Supplier
6	Logistics/Systems	AI Adoption	Supplier cum beneficiaries

Source: Compiled by authors.

Exhibit 8.2. Interview Questions.

Beneficiaries	Academicians
1. What are some of the positives of ChatGPT?	What are some of the challenges that can hamper your teaching, learning, and research?
2. How can ChatGPT make your learning easy?	How can ChatGPT make your teaching and delivery easy?
3. In which ways can ChatGPT be used in learners' lives?	In which ways can ChatGPT be used in academicians' lives?
4. What are some latest trends learners envision for ChatGPT in education?	How can academicians make students use ChatGPT to learn in and outside of school or college?
5. What obstacles may educational institutes face when they explore implementing ChatGPT in education, research, and training?	What key challenges have you faced that discomfort you while thinking of ChatGPT for education?

Source: Compiled by authors.

Exhibit 8.3. Profile of Interview Participants.

Sl. No	Name	Designation	Company	Experience (Years)
1	Respondent 1	Professor	Christ University, Ghaziabad, India	24
2	Respondent 2	Associate Professor	Amity University India	17
3	Respondent 3	Associate Professor	Tribhuvan University, Nepal	20
4	Respondent 4	Senior Architect	Accenture Inc	24
5	Respondent 5	System Analyst	IBM India	22
6	Respondent 6	Manager (Systems)	Nokia	18
7	Respondent 7	General Manager	Sopra Steria India	20
8	Respondent 8	Senior Business Analysist	Equifax	20
9	Respondent 9	Business Analyst	Sopra Banking India	18
10	Respondent 10	Account Manager	Cognizant Technology Solution	20
11	Respondent 11	Professor	Delhi University	34
12	Respondent 12	Professor	Linkoping University, Sweden	20

Source: Compiled by authors.

Chapter 9

ChatGPT and Implications for the Banking and Financial Industry: New Horizons of Opportunities and Potential Perils

Suaad Jassem and Wisal Al Balushi

College of Banking and Financial Studies, Oman

Abstract

Technology is the greatest drivers of creative disruption in society that results from scientific discoveries and inventions. A recent breakthrough technology is the advent of ChatGPT, which has been absorbed into society at a speed that has never been witnessed with any other new technology in the past. ChatGPT is a generative artificial intelligence platform based on large language models. ChatGPT's capability is a game-changer for accessing, synthesizing, and acquiring knowledge. The impact of GenAI applications, such as ChatGPT, is not only influencing individuals but also transforming organizations' operations and business models. The influence of ChatGPT impacts organizations of all types and sizes, including those in the banking and financial services industry. This specific business sector is extremely sensitive to customer sentiments and social trust. Accordingly, the industry can either reap the benefits of ChatGPT by providing hyper-customization customer services or risk perilous consequences, such as data breaches and misinformation. Although scholarly interest in ChatGPT is extremely high nowadays, there appears to be a dearth of sufficient studies that focus on the potential impact of this technology on the banking and financial services industry. Therefore, this chapter primarily examines ChatGPT as a representative instance of GenAI. It attempts to explore the potential opportunities and possible perils for banking and financial services organizations that are affected by the deployment of ChatGPT. This chapter also delves into the individual-level outcomes with an emphasis on matters, such as customer experiences and organizational-level implications, considering the risks and potential benefits for the industry itself.

The ChatGPT Revolution, 183–202
Copyright © 2025 Suaad Jassem and Wisal Al Balushi
Published under exclusive licence by Emerald Publishing Limited
doi:10.1108/978-1-83549-852-120251009

Keywords: ChatGPT; generative AI; artificial intelligence; banking; financial services; industry; opportunities; benefits; risks; challenges

1. Introduction

The emergent technological capabilities created by GenAI are undeniable. One such advancement is the ChatGPT platform developed by OpenAI with investment from Microsoft. This platform is a game changer in the management paradigm for future organizations (Beckmann & Hark, 2024). In the context of the banking and financial industry, ChatGPT opens a vista of opportunities that are likely to transform the business models of these organizations in terms of how they create value for their customers. Presently, many banks around the world use AI in their digital banking services to enhance customer experience, reduce the risk of fraud, and collect and analyze big data to develop deeper insights into the needs and wants of their customers (Rahman et al., 2023). However, the emergent large language model-based platforms, such as ChatGPT, enabled a level of hyper-personalization in customer experiences previously deemed inconceivable (Paul et al., 2023). Such advanced capabilities of ChatGPT are not only poised to take digital banking services to new heights but they are also likely to transform how banks operate in each market starting from retail banking to corporate banking services (Skandali et al., 2023).

For the banking industry, customer experience is a critical success factor (Chauhan et al., 2022; Garg et al., 2012). A recent survey by Accenture indicates that 91% of retail customers and 87% of corporate executives decide to deal with banks that offer exceptional customer service through technology (Abbott, 2023). This finding has drawn substantial traction among strategic planners across the banking sector. Moreover, there is an anticipation of internal organizational processes adapting to accommodate the implications of this emerging technology. For instance, the benefits of ChatGPT usage for decision-making based on predictive accounting information are also likely to generate positive outcomes along with multitudes of difficult-to-predict negative fallouts (Singh, 2024). Therefore, the critical role of the leading ChatGPT platform for the banking and financial industry needs to be examined in further detail. It is crucial to understand not only the opportunities arising from these transformations but also to develop insights from the associated perils and risks. This comprehension is essential for key decision-makers in the industry to ensure the healthy adoption of this advanced capability in their organizations.

1.1 Introducing ChatGPT: Applications and Impact

Chat Generative Pre-Training Transformer, more widely known as ChatGPT, is an AI-driven chatbot that uses NLP (natural language processing) along with machine learning to mimic human communication. This phenomenal development in artificial intelligence can engage in conversations that include making errors and admitting mistakes. Most people using this chatbot type in their query may not be precisely structured; however, ChatGPT tries to make sense of the query and searches through the vast database provided to it by humans to present a coherent set of information presented in easy-to-understand human language. Therefore, this application's first use is to eliminate any need to search for information on the World Wide Web. Instead, ChatGPT goes through the entire database, so it has access to present a summary of the information sought. The more evolved versions of ChatGPT have even greater capabilities that include text-to-voice, voice-to-text, and text-to-video applications. These evolving versions of ChatGPT have given rise to multiple new applications that help people in different fields, including the banking and financial industry (Beckmann & Hark, 2024).

ChatGPT stands out as a unique entity that captures the essence of modern technology in the ever-evolving landscape of scientific discoveries. Developed as an extension of AI based on large language models, ChatGPT seamlessly integrates advanced natural language processing at blinding speeds and in real time, which offers users an engaging and personalized experience (Wu et al., 2023). At its core, ChatGPT embodies the fusion of cutting-edge technology with language that humans use to communicate, revolutionizing the way people interact with machines. Unlike traditional models that prioritize efficiency and accuracy, ChatGPT goes beyond mere functionality by giving the impression of a human-like persona that extends beyond mere linguistic fluency to encompass a deeper understanding of social dynamics. Through sophisticated algorithms and extensive training on vast datasets encompassing diverse cultural and linguistic contexts, ChatGPT analyses linguistic cues, tone, and context to tailor its responses accordingly. Whether the user seeks a friendly confidant, a witty companion, or a supportive mentor, ChatGPT effortlessly adjusts its feedback to establish rapport and foster meaningful interactions (Kocoń et al., 2023; Roumeliotis & Tselikas, 2023).

The new versions of ChatGPT (e.g., GPT 4.0) leverage state-of-the-art sentiment analysis and emotion recognition algorithms to discern the emotional states of users during conversations. By detecting shifts in mood, tone, and sentiment, GPT4.0 can adapt its responses in real time, offering comfort, encouragement, or humor as needed. This ability to empathize and provide information along with emotions distinguishes the new version from the earlier versions of ChatGPT as more than just a virtual assistant but rather a trusted confidant and companion (Bhattacharya & Nandi, 2023).

ChatGPT's capabilities serve practical purposes, such as enhancing user engagement, building brand loyalty, and driving customer satisfaction. By providing personalized, resonant interactions, the technology cultivates a sense of affinity and loyalty among users, fostering long-term relationships and driving repeat usage. Whether employed in customer service, management decision-making, or managerial processes such as accounting, ChatGPT's advanced capabilities enhance user experiences and create operational excellence in an increasingly competitive market. Therefore, this technological application represents a groundbreaking advancement in the field of AI, embodying the fusion of technology and human communication.

Such capabilities are likely to have major implications for the banking and financial services industry (Kocoń et al., 2023).

1.1.1 Historical Development of ChatGPT

The roots of ChatGPT can be traced back to the early days of AI research, where scientists and engineers grappled with the challenge of enabling machines with the ability to understand and generate human-like language. In the past, the relationship between humans and computers was that people were learning the language of machines, whereas now generative AI is about machines learning human language (Feuerriegel et al., 2024). Early endeavors in this field were characterized by rule-based systems that operated within constrained domains, unable to grasp the nuances and complexities of natural language. A significant breakthrough came with the advent of statistical neuro-linguistic programming (NLP) techniques, which leveraged vast amounts of text data to teach machines the probabilistic relationships inherent in language. This approach enabled the development of more flexible and context-aware systems, laying the groundwork for the evolution of modern AI models like ChatGPT (Al-Amin et al., 2024).

The journey toward ChatGPT gained momentum with the emergence of breakthrough research outputs in neural networks and deep learning in the late 20th and early 21st centuries. These computational models, inspired by the structure and function of the human brain, proved instrumental in revolutionizing various fields, including computer vision, speech recognition, and, crucially, NLP. The pivotal moment for ChatGPT arrived with the introduction of the Generative Pre-trained Transformer (GPT) architecture by OpenAI. First unveiled in June 2018, GPT marked a paradigm shift in the field of NLP, showcasing the potential of large-scale transformer models in understanding and generating human-like text (Cao et al., 2023). At its core, GPT employed a transformer architecture – a type of deep learning model renowned for its parallelization capabilities and attention mechanism. By pre-training vast volumes of text data, GPT learned to capture the intricate patterns and semantics of the language, enabling it to generate coherent and contextually relevant responses to user inputs (Al-Amin et al., 2024).

The initial iteration, GPT-1, laid the foundation for subsequent advancements, demonstrating impressive language generation capabilities albeit with some limitations in coherence and contextual understanding. However, with each successive iteration – GPT-2, GPT-3, GPT-3.5, GPT-4, and beyond – OpenAI continues to refine the model architecture, scale up computational resources, and enhance training methodologies. GPT-2, released in February 2019, garnered widespread attention for its remarkable ability to generate human-like text across diverse domains and topics. It showcased significant improvements in coherence, fluency, and context retention, setting new benchmarks for language generation models. The evolution culminated in the launch of GPT-3.5 in November 2022, which was announced as one of the most advanced and versatile language models to date. With 175 billion parameters – significantly surpassing its predecessors –

GPT-3.5 exhibited unprecedented levels of linguistic prowess, capable of engaging in nuanced conversations, composing creative narratives, and even performing tasks traditionally reserved for human experts (Feuerriegel et al., 2024).

The development of ChatGPT represents a collaborative effort involving researchers, engineers, and data scientists from around the globe. It reflects not only the advancements in AI and NLP but also the collective knowledge and expertise amassed over decades of interdisciplinary research and innovation (Cao et al., 2023). Looking forward, the trajectory of ChatGPT continues to evolve, driven by ongoing research efforts aimed at pushing the boundaries of AI and unlocking new frontiers in human–machine interaction. As it continues to learn and adapt from extensive datasets, ChatGPT holds the promise of reshaping how we communicate, create, and interact with intelligent systems in the years to come.

2. The Impact of ChatGPT on the Banking and Financial Industry

Conversational AI, such as ChatGPT, is having a significant impact on the banking and financial industry in several key areas. Although most of the impact of this new phenomenon is being examined through the lens of benefits for the industry in these key functions, many other areas are yet to be explored and discovered. Moreover, there are numerous challenges that the industry may encounter, some of which are anticipated while others are still unknown (Singh, 2024). The key areas where conversational AI is presently being deployed are customer service and support, fraud detection and prevention, financial advice and wealth management, loan processing and credit scoring, regulatory complaint, market engagement, data analysis and insights, and driving up operational efficiency. For instance, in terms of benefits from customer service and support functions, the system can provide round-the-clock customer support without human intervention. Furthermore, AI can easily analyze customer data to provide personalized solutions, thus enhancing customer experience. Bank of America has deployed ERICA (a next-generation AI-driven virtual assistant) that leverages advanced analytics and cognition messaging to provide exceptional customer experience to its account holders. In addition, Bank of America has reported an additional 42 million new clients after deploying this system (Bank of America, 2024).

In addition to the above positive applications of conversational AI, there are numerous challenges and considerations that the banking and financial industry must take cognizance. The first is data privacy and security of customer information. Unless oversight and governance of the AI-driven system are solid, there are possibilities of unwanted data breaches that may expose such organizations to major challenges. Second, AI models must be designed to avoid biases that may lead to unfair treatment of certain customers or customer segments. Finally, integrating AI-based systems into the existing infrastructure of financial institutions is likely to be complex and will require meticulous planning and execution.

The following presents a more nuanced discourse on the potential applications of ChatGPT in the banking and financial industry.

2.1 Personalized Financial Services

Personalized financial services refer to the ability to analyze vast amounts of customer data to offer personalized recommendations and insights that are tailored to individual financial needs and preferences. By leveraging historical transaction data, spending patterns, and account information, banks, and other financial services firms can deploy ChatGPT-powered assistants (e.g., chatbots) to provide proactive guidance on budgeting, saving goals, investment opportunities, and more, fostering a deeper sense of engagement and trust among customers (Skandali et al., 2023). Furthermore, ChatGPT can handle a wide range of customer inquiries, from basic account inquiries to complex financial planning strategies, freeing up human agents to focus on more high-value interactions. This not only reduces operational costs for banks but also ensures faster response times and round-the-clock availability for customers, enhancing overall satisfaction and loyalty (Rahman et al., 2023).

Adopting ChatGPT in personalized financial services is associated with issues regarding data privacy, security, and ethical use of AI. Therefore, the industry must prioritize robust cybersecurity measures to safeguard sensitive customer information and ensure compliance with regulatory standards related to General Data Protection Regulation (GDPR). Moreover, transparency and account-ability in AI decision-making processes are essential to maintain customer trust and mitigate the risk of algorithmic bias or discrimination. Despite these challenges, ChatGPT holds immense promise for transforming personalized financial services in the banking industry, offering unprecedented levels of convenience, customization, and efficiency (Rane, 2023). By harnessing the capabilities of AI-driven conversational agents, banks can elevate the customer experience, drive operational excellence, and unlock new opportunities for growth and innovation in the digital age.

2.2 Automated Customer Services

Automated customer service relies on technology to handle customer inquiries and tasks without direct human intervention. ChatGPT is also revolutionizing the landscape of automated customer service in banks, offering a plethora of benefits that streamline operations and enhance customer satisfaction. Through the application of ChatGPT, banks can deploy sophisticated virtual assistants capable of understanding and responding to customer inquiries with remarkable accuracy and efficiency.

One significant potential for the use of ChatGPT in automated customer service in banking is the improvement in customer experience. Traditional customer service channels often involve long wait times and repetitive interactions, leading to frustration among customers. ChatGPT-powered chatbots, however, provide instant responses to queries, offering a seamless and personalized experience round the clock. These virtual assistants can handle a wide range of inquiries, from account balances to transaction history and even complex financial advice, mimicking the capabilities of human agents. Moreover, ChatGPT will enable banks to scale their customer service operations effectively. As the volume of customer inquiries fluctuates throughout the day, AI-driven systems can dynamically allocate resources to meet demand without the need for additional human staff. This scalability ensures that customers receive prompt assistance regardless of the time or day, enhancing overall service reliability (Abbott, 2023).

ChatGPT also holds the promise of empowering banks and financial services organizations to analyze customer interactions and derive valuable insights. By leveraging machine learning algorithms, banks can identify patterns in customer behavior, preferences, and pain points, enabling them to optimize their services and tailor offerings to meet individual needs. For instance, by analyzing chat transcripts, banks can identify common issues faced by customers and proactively address them, thereby reducing the need for repetitive inquiries. Therefore, the influence of ChatGPT in automated customer service in banks is profound, revolutionizing the way customers interact with financial institutions. By enhancing customer experience, improving scalability, and facilitating data-driven insights, generative AI is poised to drive innovation and efficiency in the banking industry (Al-Amin et al., 2024).

2.3 Contextualized Personal Offers (Instead of Annoying Ads)

ChatGPT has the potential to transform the way banks engage with their customers by providing contextualized personal offers instead of intrusive advertisements. Through its NLP capabilities, ChatGPT can analyze customer interactions in real time, understanding their needs, preferences, and financial goals. By leveraging this insight, banks can deliver personalized offers tailored to each customer's unique circumstances, making the interactions more relevant and valuable.

For example, if the customer inquiry is about savings account options, ChatGPT can identify the customer's interest in saving money and recommend specific savings products or investment opportunities aligned with their goals. Similarly, if a customer discusses purchasing a home, ChatGPT can suggest mortgage options or home insurance plans tailored to their situation. By delivering contextualized personal offers, banks can enhance customer satisfaction and loyalty. Instead of bombarding customers with generic advertisements, ChatGPT enables banks to provide timely and targeted recommendations that address customers' immediate needs. This approach fosters stronger relationships between banks and their customers, ultimately driving long-term value for both parties (Beckmann & Hark, 2024).

2.4 Increased Workforce and Cost Efficiency

ChatGPT offers significant potential for increasing workforce and cost efficiency in banks and other financial services organizations through various applications, ranging from the frontline offices, such as customer service, to back-office operations optimization. In the realm of customer service, ChatGPT-powered virtual assistants can handle a substantial portion of routine inquiries, such as account balance checks, transaction history requests, and basic troubleshooting. By automating these tasks, banks can reduce the workload on human agents, allowing them to focus on more complex matters that require human expertise. This not only increases the efficiency of the customer service team but also improves response times and overall service quality.

Furthermore, ChatGPT can streamline back-office operations by automating repetitive tasks such as data entry, document processing, and compliance checks. Accordingly, banks can significantly reduce manual effort and minimize the risk of errors, leading to increased operational efficiency and cost savings. Additionally, ChatGPT can analyze vast amounts of data to identify suspicious patterns or anomalies, enabling banks to mitigate potential threats more effectively. Moreover, ChatGPT can facilitate knowledge sharing and training within the organization by providing instant access to information and resources. Employees can leverage ChatGPT to quickly find answers to their questions, access procedural guidelines, or undergo interactive training modules, thereby accelerating the onboarding process and improving overall workforce productivity. Overall, by harnessing the capabilities of ChatGPT, banks can optimize their workforce utilization, reduce operational costs, and enhance productivity across various departments (Cao et al., 2023).

2.5 Immersive Experience

ChatGPT has the potential to revolutionize the way banks and financial services organizations interact with their customers by enhancing immersive experiences through personalized interactions and innovative services. This can be achieved through powering virtual banking assistants capable of providing highly personalized guidance and support through interactive audio and video services. These assistants can engage customers in natural language conversations, understanding their needs and preferences to offer financial advice. Generative AI creates a more engaging and immersive experience by simulating human-like interactions, fostering stronger connections between customers and their banks (Al-Amin et al., 2024).

In general, ChatGPT tools enable the development of virtual reality (VR) and augmented reality (AR) applications that transform how customers interact with banking services. For example, VR simulations can immerse customers in virtual branch environments, allowing them to explore products, interact with virtual tellers, and conduct more intuitive and immersive transactions. Similarly, AR overlays can enhance the physical banking experience by providing real-time information and guidance through mobile devices, enhancing convenience and engagement. Overall, generative AI holds immense potential to elevate the banking experience by creating immersive environments that cater to the individual preferences and needs of customers, ultimately driving greater satisfaction, loyalty, and engagement in the digital era (Beckmann & Hark, 2024).

2.6 Predictive Analysis of Customer Behavior and Trends

ChatGPT is a game-changer in the predictive analysis of customer behavior and trends within the banking sector. ChatGPT can process vast amounts of data from various sources, including transaction history, customer interactions, market trends, and economic indicators, to forecast future behavior and trends with unprecedented accuracy. With the integration of analytical tools, ChatGPT can uncover hidden patterns and correlations within complex datasets. Traditional analytical methods often struggle to capture nonlinear relationships or identify subtle signals buried in noisy data. Recognizing patterns and generating synthetic data can reveal valuable insights into customer preferences, spending habits, and risk profiles. ChatGPT, in conjunction with advanced analytical tools, provides mechanisms to analyze customer interactions in real time and adapt to evolving circumstances, such as changes in market conditions or life events. This flexibility allows banks to anticipate customer needs more accurately and tailor their offerings accordingly.

Overall, ChatGPT is revolutionizing predictive analysis in the banking industry by enabling more accurate, adaptive, and efficient forecasting of customer behavior and trends. By harnessing the power of AI-driven predictive analytics, banks can gain a competitive edge, anticipate market shifts, and deliver personalized experiences that meet the evolving needs of their customers (Feuerriegel et al., 2024).

2.7 Real-Time Decision-Making Capabilities

ChatGPT transforms real-time decision-making in banking and finance by rapidly analyzing large datasets, offering insights, and enabling personalized customer interactions. ChatGPT can continuously monitor transactions, flagging suspicious activities in real time by comparing them against historical patterns and known cases. This proactive approach enables financial institutions to mitigate risks promptly, safeguarding both their assets and customers' funds.

Additionally, in trading and investment management, ChatGPT can analyze market trends, news, and social media sentiment in real time, providing traders and investors with actionable insights to make informed decisions swiftly. By leveraging NLP capabilities, it can process news articles, earnings reports, and analyst opinions at an unprecedented speed, helping financial professionals stay ahead of the curve. Overall, ChatGPT is a powerful tool for enhancing efficiency and accuracy in real-time decision-making within the banking and financial services sector (Rahman et al., 2023).

2.8 Risk Management and Fraud Detection

ChatGPT has the potential to play a critical role in fraud detection and risk mitigation within the banking and financial services industry by leveraging its NLP capabilities to analyze vast amounts of data and detect patterns indicative of fraudulent activities. Through real-time monitoring of transactions and continuously analyzing transactional data against established patterns and historical behaviors, ChatGPT can flag suspicious activities as they occur. This proactive approach allows financial institutions to intervene promptly, preventing fraudulent transactions and minimizing potential losses (Abbott, 2023). For example, sudden changes in spending habits or unusual login locations may indicate unauthorized access or compromised accounts.

ChatGPT can also assist in automating the review and verification process for identity authentication. By analyzing customer-provided information and comparing it against existing data sources, ChatGPT can help verify the legitimacy of individuals or entities, reducing the risk of identity theft or fraudulent account creation (Rahman et al., 2023). Besides, ChatGPT can aid in compliance efforts by interpreting and analyzing regulatory documents, policies, and guidelines.

3. Challenges of Unregulated ChatGPT in the Banking and Financial Industry

In a recent report released by the European Central Bank, the number of cyber security threats due to "phishing" incidences being encountered by banks has gone up substantially since the launch of conversational AI-based applications, such as ChatGPT (European Central Bank, 2024). This case illustrates that the unregulated use of platforms driven by the new generation of AI-driven software in the banking and financial industry poses multiple challenges. Firstly, without strong governance and regulatory oversight, there's a risk of privacy breaches as sensitive customer data may be mishandled or misused. Secondly, there's potential for misinformation or biased advice, leading to erroneous financial decisions. Thirdly, unchecked deployment of ChatGPT could exacerbate cybersecurity threats, with malicious actors exploiting vulnerabilities in AI systems. Lastly, without clear guidelines, there's uncertainty around liability and accountability in case of errors or misconduct (Singh, 2024). Addressing these challenges requires robust regulatory frameworks to ensure responsible and ethical deployment of ChatGPT within the financial sector. Some of the possible challenges that pose a clear and present danger are discussed next.

3.1 Perils for Customers

The key stakeholders of the banking and financial services industry are customers. The industry is highly dependent on the element of "trust." Considering the sensitive nature of customers in this industry, the sector must preserve customer confidence. Any mishaps or negative media reports can be disastrous for the industry. Some of the recent scholarly research reveals the following areas of concern as possible challenges for the industry in terms of their customers (Skandali et al., 2023).

3.2 Biased Credit Information and Analysis

ChatGPT's role in processing credit information about clients presents both advantages and risks, especially in relation to potential bias. While ChatGPT can streamline credit evaluation processes, its reliance on existing data may inadvertently perpetuate biases present in historical lending practices. One challenge lies in the data used to train ChatGPT models. If historical lending data reflects biases based on race, gender, or socioeconomic status, ChatGPT may inadvertently learn and perpetuate these biases when making credit decisions. For instance, if past lending practices favored certain demographics, ChatGPT may unfairly disadvantage others, perpetuating systemic inequalities (Singh, 2024).

Additionally, ChatGPT's decision-making process lacks transparency, making it difficult to identify and address biases. Without clear insights into how ChatGPT reaches its conclusions, it's challenging to ensure fair and unbiased credit assessments. This opacity exacerbates concerns about fairness and accountability in lending decisions. However, ChatGPT can mitigate biased credit information with proper oversight and safeguards. Financial institutions can minimize the risk of discriminatory outcomes by implementing fairness-aware training techniques and regularly auditing models for bias. It is also crucial to integrate a variety of data sources and regularly update training data to mitigate historical biases and foster fairer credit assessments. Furthermore, transparency measures, such as explainable AI techniques, can enhance accountability by providing insights into how ChatGPT arrives at its decisions, enabling stakeholders to identify and rectify biases (Skandali et al., 2023).

3.3 Inaccurate Information by Chatbots

Chatbots are widely deployed in the banking and finance industry. While they can streamline customer service and provide instant responses, total reliance on chatbots introduces a risk of misinformation. For instance, a chatbot operates by synthesizing responses based on patterns in data, but it lacks the comprehensive understanding and critical thinking abilities of humans. In banking services, inaccuracies can have severe consequences, such as financial loss or breach of privacy. These inaccuracies may stem from misinterpretation of customer queries, outdated data, or unforeseen scenarios beyond chatbots' training data. For instance, a chatbot might misinterpret a request to transfer funds as a query about account balance, leading to incorrect information being provided (Rahman et al., 2023).

Other aspects of misinformation by ChatGPT chatbots is that they may struggle with complex financial inquiries or nuanced situations requiring empathy and discretion. The chatbots might offer standard responses that fail to address unique customer concerns adequately. Additionally, they could inadvertently disclose sensitive information if not programmed to adhere to strict privacy protocols. Therefore, financial institutions need to prioritize means to mitigate such misinformation risks through robust training, monitoring, and oversight mechanisms for chatbots. Regular updates, human supervision, and fallback options to involve human agents in complex scenarios can help maintain accuracy and trustworthiness (Singh, 2024).

3.4 Privacy Breaches of Customer Information

Employing ChatGPT in banking and financial services without substantial oversight can inadvertently expose customers to significant privacy breaches. While ChatGPT is adept at generating human-like responses, its operation relies on vast amounts of data, including sensitive user information. This poses a substantial risk if not handled meticulously, especially since the ability of ChatGPT to comprehend and respond to user queries relies on previous customer interactions and transactions. In situations where personal customer details are available, there's a risk of this information being retained and disseminated by ChatGPT beyond the intended scope, violating privacy regulations (Wu et al., 2023).

Besides the above risks, the storage and processing of data by ChatGPT systems create vulnerabilities that malicious actors could exploit. If not properly secured, these systems could become targets for hackers seeking to access confidential customer information. Additionally, there's a risk of unintended disclosure of sensitive data during interactions with ChatGPT. Despite efforts to train the model to handle sensitive information appropriately, misunderstandings or errors could lead to inadvertent leaks of personal or financial data. To mitigate these risks, financial institutions must implement stringent data protection measures, including encryption, access controls, and regular audits of ChatGPT systems. Moreover, clear guidelines and training for employees and customers on data handling and privacy can help minimize the likelihood of breaches. Ultimately, while ChatGPT offers opportunities for enhanced customer service, safeguarding privacy must remain a top priority (Kocoń et al., 2023).

3.5 Menace of Deepfakes

Integrating ChatGPT into banking and financial services could potentially exacerbate the threat of "*deepfakes*," introducing significant risks to security and trust within the financial sector. Deepfakes are manipulated media, often using AI, to depict individuals saying or doing things they never actually did. When combined with ChatGPT, this technology could create convincing simulations of customer interactions, leading to a range of issues. The following are some potential concerns about the menace of deepfakes (Abbott, 2023).

Firstly, deepfakes generated using ChatGPT could be utilized for social engineering attacks, where fraudsters impersonate customers or bank representatives to extract sensitive information or initiate unauthorized transactions. These falsified interactions could mimic the tone, language, and mannerisms of genuine customer service interactions, making them difficult to detect. Deepfake technology could be employed to fabricate evidence of transactions or account activities, leading to disputes and legal challenges. By generating realistic-looking bank statements, transaction records, or audio recordings of conversations, malicious actors could manipulate financial records to deceive customers, regulators, or even internal auditors (Al-Amin et al., 2024).

The menace of deepfakes may erode trust in online banking services. Customers may become skeptical of the authenticity of digital interactions, leading to hesitancy in conducting transactions or sharing sensitive information online. This erosion of trust could have far-reaching consequences for the adoption and utilization of digital banking services. Banks must implement robust authentication and verification measures to address these risks to distinguish genuine interactions from deepfakes. This could include multi-factor authentication, biometric verification, and transaction monitoring systems capable of flagging suspicious activities. Additionally, raising awareness among customers and employees about the potential threat of deepfakes and providing guidance on identifying and reporting suspicious interactions is crucial in combating this emerging risk (Kocoń et al., 2023).

3.6 Data Poisoning

Data poisoning involves malicious manipulation of datasets to corrupt the ChatGPT model, leading to incorrect decisions or compromised security. Data poisoning could have severe consequences, including financial loss, regulatory violations, and damage to reputation. One way data poisoning can occur is through adversarial attacks, where attackers manipulate input data to deceive the ChatGPT model. For example, adversaries could feed false transaction records or manipulate customer profiles to trick AI systems into making incorrect decisions, such as approving fraudulent transactions (Cao et al., 2023).

Moreover, biased, or skewed training data can inadvertently lead to data poisoning. If the training data used to develop ChatGPT is not representative or balanced, it can perpetuate biases or inaccuracies, leading to erroneous predictions or recommendations in financial decision-making processes. Furthermore, malicious insiders or third-party attackers could intentionally inject poisoned data to undermine operations or exploit vulnerabilities. This could include inserting malicious code or manipulating datasets to compromise the integrity and security of the applications.

Financial institutions must prioritize data integrity and implement robust security measures to mitigate the risk of data poisoning. This includes thorough data validation and verification processes to detect and filter out malicious or erroneous inputs. Finally, promoting transparency and accountability in the development and deployment of ChatGPT tools is essential for building trust and resilience against data poisoning attacks.

3.7 Noncompliance Risks

Using ChatGPT in banking and financial services poses certain noncompliance risks, stemming from potential violations of regulatory requirements and industry standards that may be both local and global. These risks may arise from various aspects of using ChatGPT, such as in implementation, including data privacy, security, transparency, diversity, and equity.

In terms of data privacy concerns, due to the sensitive nature of personal financial information handled by banks, ChatGPT must adhere to strict data protection regulations to ensure the confidentiality and integrity of customer data. Failure to comply with these regulations can result in substantial penalties, punitive actions, criminal charges, and reputational damage. The next issue relates to security risks arising from the potential of cyberattacks targeting ChatGPT systems. Hackers may exploit AI algorithms or infrastructure vulnerabilities to gain unauthorized access to sensitive client data, leading to severe financial and legal consequences for banks and financial institutions (Abbott, 2023).

Furthermore, the opacity of ChatGPT's decision-making processes poses challenges to regulatory compliance and accountability. Regulators, such as central banks, may require banks to provide explanations for their algorithmic decisions, which can be difficult to detect and report due to the complexity of ChatGPT platforms. This lack of transparency can hinder compliance efforts and raise concerns about fairness and bias in automated decision-making without human oversight.

Financial institutions are strictly required to adhere to stringent regulations governing financial transactions. Such regulations came into effect due to various events over the past few decades, such as the 9–11 attacks, global financial crisis, changes to BASEL accords, Financial Action Task Force (FATF), etc. If ChatGPT fails to accurately identify and report suspicious activities, banks could face regulatory fines and legal penalties for non-compliance. Many globally recognized banks have already been sanctioned due to human malfeasance, and now with the uncontrolled use of generative AI, the potential for legal consequences is yet unfathomed (Wu et al., 2023).

A particularly sensitive area for banks in terms of compliance with regulatory frameworks connected to governing financial services is anti-money laundering (AML) concerns. AML requires banks and financial institutions to adhere to the principle of KYC (Know Your Customer) regulations so that banks can verify customer identities and detect suspicious activities. Hence, ChatGPT systems must accurately and reliably be able to perform these tasks to remain compliant, otherwise the bank or financial service company may face local and global sanctions from organizations such as FATF (Rane, 2023).

In addition, international data protection forums like GDPR impose strict requirements on the collection, storage, and processing of personal data. Generative AI systems interact with vast amounts of customer information, raising concerns about data privacy and security. Failure to adequately protect sensitive data could result in legal repercussions, including fines, lawsuits, and reputational damage. Moreover, liability issues may arise if ChatGPT produces erroneous outputs that lead to financial losses or harm to customers. Banks may be held accountable for the actions of AI systems under principles of vicarious liability or negligence, especially if they fail to implement adequate safeguards or provide proper oversight (Rahman et al., 2023).

Financial institutions must implement robust governance frameworks to address noncompliance risks, conduct audits of AI systems, and ensure ongoing monitoring and oversight by compliance professionals. Additionally, collaboration with regulators and industry stakeholders is crucial in ensuring that the banks can navigate the evolving regulatory landscape and mitigate noncompliance risks associated with using ChatGPT in financial services.

3.8 Institutional Risks

Integrating ChatGPT into banking and finance services is often associated with institutional risks. This digital transformation demands considerable time and resources for business process reengineering to ensure that processes are well-defined, efficient, and supportive of the desired outcomes. Additionally, seamless integration with existing technology infrastructure entails addressing compatibility issues. Most importantly, training employees to effectively utilize and oversee ChatGPT systems demands investment in skill development. Lastly, addressing concerns about job displacement and the human–AI collaboration dynamic necessitates clear communication and change management strategies. Overcoming these hurdles demands strategic planning, investment, and a commitment to fostering a culture of innovation and adaptability within the organization.

4. Conclusion

The integration of ChatGPT into finance and banking services presents both opportunities and risks that require careful consideration. ChatGPT offers significant potential to enhance customer service and streamline operations. ChatGPT enables banks to provide personalized, efficient, and round-the-clock customer support. Customers can engage with chatbots to benefit from various banking services without the need for human intervention. This not only improves the customer experience by offering convenience and accessibility but also frees up human agents to focus on more complex tasks, such as financial advising or risk management.

However, alongside the above opportunities come several risks that banks and financial services organizations must carefully consider when deploying ChatGPT in their operations. One of the primary risks is the potential for inaccuracies or misunderstandings that can erode trust in financial institutions and result in customer dissatisfaction or even financial losses. Furthermore, such institutions must implement robust security measures to safeguard against data security threats and ensure compliance with data protection regulations to protect customer privacy and maintain trust (Appendix-A).

In conclusion, while the adoption of ChatGPT in the banking and finance industry presents numerous opportunities for improved customer service, operational efficiency, and innovation, it also poses risks that require careful management. By addressing concerns related to accuracy, data privacy, security, and bias, banks can harness the benefits of ChatGPT while minimizing potential pitfalls, ultimately delivering better outcomes for both customers and the institution.

References

Abbott, M. (2023, May 26). *Breaking barriers: Exploring how banks scale generative AI for growth.* Accenture Banking Blog. https://bankingblog.accenture.com/how-banks-scale-generative-ai-for-growth

Al-Amin, M., Ali, M. S., Salam, A., Khan, A., Ali, A., Ullah, A., Alam, M. N., & Chowdhury, S. K. (2024). History of generative artificial intelligence (AI) chatbots: Past, present, and future development. https://doi.org/10.48550/ARXIV.2402.05122

Bank of America. (2024). *BofA's Erica surpasses 2 billion interactions, helping 42 million clients since launch.* Press Releases | Newsroom | Bank of America.

Beckmann, L., & Hark, P. F. (2024). ChatGPT and the banking business: Insights from the US stock market on potential implications for banks. *Finance Research Letters, 63*, 105237. https://doi.org/10.1016/j.frl.2024.105237

Bhattacharya, K., & Nandi, A. K. (2023). Goblin's challenge to ChatGPT: Exploring AI's dilemma resolution and mentalization through riddle tales. *SSRN Electronic Journal.* https://doi.org/10.2139/ssrn.4476837

Cao, Y., Li, S., Liu, Y., Yan, Z., Dai, Y., Yu, P. S., & Sun, L. (2023). A comprehensive survey of AI-generated content (AIGC): A history of generative AI from GAN to ChatGPT. https://doi.org/10.48550/ARXIV.2303.04226

Chauhan, S., Akhtar, A., & Gupta, A. (2022). Customer experience in digital banking: A review and future research directions. *International Journal of Quality and Service Sciences, 14*(2), 311–348. https://doi.org/10.1108/IJQSS-02-2021-0027

European Central Bank. (2024, May). Financial stability review. europa.eu

Feuerriegel, S., Hartmann, J., Janiesch, C., & Zschech, P. (2024). Generative AI. *Business & Information Systems Engineering, 66*(1), 111–126. https://doi.org/10.1007/s12599-023-00834-7

Garg, R., Rahman, Z., Qureshi, M. N., & Kumar, I. (2012). Identifying and ranking critical success factors of customer experience in banks: An analytic hierarchy process (AHP) approach. *Journal of Modelling in Management, 7*(2), 201–220. https://doi.org/10.1108/17465661211242813

Kocoń, J., Cichecki, I., Kaszyca, O., Kochanek, M., Szydło, D., Baran, J., Bielaniewicz, J., Gruza, M., Janz, A., Kanclerz, K., Kocoń, A., Koptyra, B., Mieleszczenko-Kowszewicz, W., Miłkowski, P., Oleksy, M., Piasecki, M., Radliński, Ł., Wojtasik, K., Woźniak, S., & Kazienko, P. (2023). ChatGPT: Jack of all trades, master of none. *Information Fusion*, *99*, 101861. https://doi.org/10.1016/j.inffus.2023.101861

Paul, J., Ueno, A., & Dennis, C. (2023). ChatGPT and consumers: Benefits, pitfalls and future research agenda. *International Journal of Consumer Studies*, *47*(4), 1213–1225. https://doi.org/10.1111/ijcs.12928

Rahman, M., Ming, T. H., Baigh, T. A., & Sarker, M. (2023). Adoption of artificial intelligence in banking services: An empirical analysis. *International Journal of Emerging Markets*, *18*(10), 4270–4300. https://doi.org/10.1108/IJOEM-06-2020-0724

Rane, N. (2023). Role and challenges of ChatGPT and similar generative artificial intelligence in finance and accounting. *SSRN Electronic Journal*. https://doi.org/10.2139/ssrn.4603206

Roumeliotis, K. I., & Tselikas, N. D. (2023). ChatGPT and Open-AI models: A preliminary review. *Future Internet*, *15*(6), 192. https://doi.org/10.3390/fi15060192

Singh, B. (2024). Generative artificial intelligence: Prospects for banking industry. https://doi.org/10.5281/ZENODO.10897014

Skandali, D., Magoutas, A., & Tsourvakas, G. (2023). Artificial intelligent applications in enabled banking services: The next frontier of customer engagement in the era of ChatGPT. *Theoretical Economics Letters*, *13*(05), 1203–1223. https://doi.org/10.4236/tel.2023.135066

Wu, T., He, S., Liu, J., Sun, S., Liu, K., Han, Q.-L., & Tang, Y. (2023). A brief overview of ChatGPT: The history, status quo and potential future development. *IEEE/CAA Journal of Automatica Sinica*, *10*(5), 1122–1136. https://doi.org/10.1109/JAS.2023.123618

Appendix A: Fictional Bank Case Study

Revolutionizing Customer Experience Through the Implementation of ChatGPT in the Banking Industry

This case study explores the integration of ChatGPT into the banking industry to enhance customer experience, streamline operations, and drive efficiency. Through a detailed examination of a fictional bank's journey, from initial implementation to ongoing improvements, this study demonstrates the transformative impact of ChatGPT on customer service, sales, and internal processes within the banking sector.

Case Background

In an era defined by rapid technological advancement and shifting consumer expectations, the banking industry faces the imperative to innovate and adapt to meet evolving customer needs. As digital transformation continues to reshape the landscape of financial services, forward-thinking banks are leveraging AI to revolutionize the way they interact with customers. Among these AI technologies, ChatGPT emerges as a powerful tool for enhancing customer engagement and operational efficiency through natural language processing and generation capabilities. Our fictional Bank operates in a highly competitive market characterized by increasing demand for personalized services, seamless digital experiences, and round-the-clock support. Recognizing the need to differentiate itself and stay ahead of the curve, Bank embarked on a strategic initiative to leverage ChatGPT to enhance customer interactions and streamline internal processes.

The implementation of ChatGPT within the bank's operations began with a comprehensive assessment of customer touchpoints and pain points. By analyzing data from customer service interactions, feedback surveys, and online inquiries, the bank identified key areas where ChatGPT could add value, including:

- *Customer Support*: Bank deployed ChatGPT as a virtual assistant on its website and mobile app, enabling customers to access information, resolve queries, and initiate transactions in real-time. Through NLP, ChatGPT effectively interprets user inquiries and provides accurate, personalized responses, reducing the need for human intervention in routine inquiries.
- *Product Recommendations*: Leveraging ChatGPT's ability to analyze customer data and preferences, Bank implemented personalized product recommendation systems to suggest relevant banking products and services based on individual customer needs and financial goals. By proactively engaging customers with tailored offerings, the bank increased cross-selling opportunities and revenue generation.
- *Process Automation*: Beyond customer-facing applications, Bank integrated ChatGPT into internal processes, such as loan processing, account management, and fraud detection. Through automation of routine tasks and decision support, ChatGPT accelerated workflows, minimized errors, and optimized resource allocation, enabling employees to focus on higher-value activities.

Results of Deploying ChatGPT

The adoption of ChatGPT yielded significant benefits for the Bank across various dimensions:

- Enhanced customer experience by providing instantaneous, personalized support round-the-clock. ChatGPT improved customer satisfaction and loyalty, leading to higher retention rates and positive word-of-mouth referrals. Customers appreciated the convenience and efficiency of interacting with ChatGPT for their banking needs, resulting in increased engagement and usage of digital channels.
- Improved operational efficiency through process automation and optimization, ChatGPT reduced the average handling time of customer inquiries, freeing up

human agents to address complex issues and strategic initiatives. The automation of routine tasks, such as account inquiries and balance transfers, minimized manual errors and operational costs, leading to greater efficiency and scalability.

- Revenue growth by leveraging ChatGPT's capabilities for personalized recommendations and targeted marketing, Bank experienced a notable uplift in sales of banking products and services. The ability to proactively engage customers with relevant offers and promotions increased cross-selling opportunities and revenue per customer, contributing to overall business growth and profitability.
- Insights into customer data were developed through ChatGPT's integration enabling the bank to capture valuable insights from customer interactions, including preferences, sentiment, and emerging trends. By analyzing these data points, the bank gained a deeper understanding of customer needs and behaviors, informing product development, marketing strategies, and decision-making processes.

Challenges and Future Directions

Despite the success of ChatGPT implementation, Bank encountered several challenges, including data privacy concerns, algorithm bias, and regulatory compliance. Addressing these challenges required ongoing investment in data governance, transparency, and ethical AI practices to ensure the responsible use of AI technologies in banking.

Looking ahead, Bank aims to further enhance the capabilities of ChatGPT by integrating advanced features such as voice recognition, sentiment analysis, and multilingual support to cater to diverse customer segments and preferences. Additionally, the bank plans to explore opportunities for ChatGPT's integration with emerging technologies such as blockchain, Internet of Things (IoT), and augmented reality to deliver innovative banking solutions and stay ahead of competitors.

In conclusion, the integration of ChatGPT has proven to be a game-changer for Bank, enabling the bank to deliver superior customer experiences, drive operational efficiencies, and foster growth in a competitive market. By harnessing the power of AI-driven conversational agents, the bank has positioned itself as a leader in digital banking innovation, setting the standard for customer-centricity and excellence in the industry. As technology continues to evolve, ChatGPT remains a valuable asset for banks seeking to redefine the future of banking and unlock new opportunities for success.

Questions for Critical Analysis

- How will the integration of ChatGPT impact the roles and responsibilities of employees at Bank, and what steps can the bank take to ensure a seamless transition and mitigate potential job displacement?

- What ethical considerations should Bank take into account when deploying ChatGPT, particularly regarding data privacy, algorithm bias, and customer consent?
- How can Bank measure the effectiveness of ChatGPT in enhancing customer experience and driving business outcomes, and what key performance indicators (KPIs) should the bank use to evaluate its success?
- What are the risks and constraints associated with relying on ChatGPT as the primary interface for customer interactions, and how can Bank mitigate these risks to uphold customer trust and satisfaction?
- How might the adoption of ChatGPT influence the competitive landscape of the banking industry, and what strategies can Bank employ to differentiate itself and maintain a competitive edge in the market?

Chapter 10

Leveraging ChatGPT to Provide Better Support and Learning Opportunities in Revolutionizing AI in Fintech and Customer Service

Anshul Srivastava[a], *Navita Mahajan*[a], *Anupam Sharma*[b],
Rita Mansukhlal Kotecha[c] *and Madhushree Guha*[a]

[a]Amity University, Noida, India
[b]Delhi Technical Campus, India
[c]H&M Hennes & Mauritz, Sweden

Abstract

The ChatGPT model, developed by OpenAI, is well known for its ability to understand context and generate relevant content. This system can effectively manage enormous amounts of data and produce text that is both coherent and instructive by utilizing the transformer architecture. It facilitates communication between patients and healthcare providers, helps overcome language barriers, and improves the patient experience by offering customized information and support. The use of this technology aims to maximize customer satisfaction by providing accurate and quick answers to their requests. Companies of all sizes are gradually adopting ChatGPT to provide 24/7 customer support without the need for human intervention. This article looks at how ChatGPT can improve services, with a particular emphasis on how to improve patient and customer support. It also examines the key components that enable ChatGPT to provide better support and highlights key areas of use, including the finance industry and customer and patient care. By giving quick, precise answers to financial questions, helping with transactional procedures, and providing individualized financial advice, ChatGPT is transforming consumer interactions in the fintech space. As technology develops, ChatGPT is positioned to become a vital tool for offering timely and customized support. But it's still challenging to retain information current and accurate.

The ChatGPT Revolution, 203–237

Copyright © 2025 Anshul Srivastava, Navita Mahajan, Anupam Sharma, Rita Mansukhlal
Kotecha and Madhushree Guha
Published under exclusive licence by Emerald Publishing Limited
doi:10.1108/978-1-83549-852-120251010

Keywords: ChatGPT; service; healthcare; communication; technology; OpenAI; fintech

1. Introduction

ChatGPT is an Artificial Intelligence tool that utilizes the Generative Pre-Transformer (GPT) algorithm. The main purpose of this technology is to imitate the development of language that is like that of humans, which makes it extremely beneficial in customer care services. ChatGPT leverages an extensive collection of solutions to offer customer care teams immediate access to pertinent information. This optimizes support procedures and results in notable reductions in time and expenses for organizations. ChatGPT excels in its capacity to accurately mimic the organic progression of human dialog. The inherent authenticity of this quality significantly enhances its ability to improve consumer satisfaction and cultivate brand devotion. The precise and personalized responses provided by the system guarantee that consumers receive correct and customized advice, resulting in elevated levels of satisfaction. In order to attain such a high degree of precision, ChatGPT necessitates training on specialized data and knowledge bases. This training guarantees that the responses given are not only pertinent but also uniform across different support channels. Consistency is essential in order to uphold a superior level of customer service, regardless of the communication channel employed. ChatGPT's efficiency is demonstrated by its capacity to respond to repetitive requests with contextual relevance. ChatGPT streamlines the handling of frequently asked questions by automating responses, hence alleviating the burden on support personnel. This enables them to dedicate their attention to more intricate or urgent assignments. This automation not only boosts efficiency but also elevates the overall quality of service. ChatGPT excels not just in resolving routine inquiries but also in effectively controlling negative feedback and seamlessly integrating with Customer Relationship Management (CRM) software. This connection facilitates customized engagements with clients, demonstrating the flexibility and applicability of ChatGPT in customer service environments.

In addition to customer assistance, ChatGPT is also utilized in the field of education. It serves to streamline intricate language, facilitate the formation of concepts, and support the proofreading of student assignments. Nevertheless, it is important to acknowledge that several educators enforce limitations on its utilization due to apprehensions regarding dependence on artificial intelligence in educational environments. ChatGPT's features also be advantageous for market research. Its Natural Language Processing (NLP) features enable effective identification of target markets, content generation, and survey conduction. The inclusion of multilingual support enhances its practicality by enabling organizations to provide worldwide customer service without requiring considerable training for customer care professionals.

ChatGPT is crucial in enhancing patient communication and increasing their overall experience in the healthcare industry. ChatGPT improves the overall quality of patient care by offering individualized support and effectively addressing linguistic obstacles. ChatGPT's capacity to mimic human conversation, automate replies, and seamlessly interact with other systems renders it a highly valuable resource in numerous sectors, notably customer service, education, market research, and healthcare.

On the other hand, the financial sector has, in the recent years, experienced a dramatic transformation facilitated by technological advancements (Tan et al., 2023). Recent technology developments are on technologies like artificial intelligence and Chat Generative Pre-trained Transformer, ChatGPT. The fintech industry has been rapidly changing, driven by the use of modern technology and by the need to carry out the entire process of financial services more effectively. Since the global financial crisis of 2008 (Suryono et al., 2020), fintech has grown at exponential levels to integrate technologies like AI and blockchain to innovate and streamline financial operations. Fintech can be defined as the new financial industry that applies technology to improve financial activities.

On the other hand, Fintech may also be referred to as "any innovative ideas that improve the financial service processes by proposing technological solutions according to different business situations." Advancements in e-finance and mobile technology for financial companies, driving the innovation of fintech, began after the global financial crisis of 2008. The development was characterized by the integration of innovation in e-finance, Internet technologies, social networking services, social media, artificial intelligence, and big analytics data. This challenges many traditional financial institutions, such as banks, to develop their business models more practically. Moreover, start-ups saw this opportunity to enter the financial service industry.

The primary research objectives of this chapters are:

- To provide an overview of ChatGPT and its role in enhancing services.
- To explore different perspectives on improving customer and patient services through ChatGPT.
- To identify critical factors enabling ChatGPT to refine customer and patient assistance.
- To examine application areas of customer and patient services management impacted by ChatGPT.
- To examine application areas of Fintech impacted by ChatGPT.

2. ChatGPT: OpenAI's Cutting-Edge Chatbot Redefining Conversational AI

ChatGPT, a cutting-edge chatbot created by OpenAI, use the Generative Pre-training Transformer language model to produce text that closely mimics human conversation. ChatGPT is specifically designed to facilitate dynamic conversations and provide timely responses to user queries. It guarantees the consistent and dependable delivery of information, regardless of how users interact with it. GPT, powered by machine learning (ML) techniques that imitate the human nervous system, has developed into a complex multi-layered network. It has gained a large user base globally in several fields, including professionals seeking help with resumes, as well as students and software specialists. ChatGPT has revolutionized the field of creative writing by providing writers with inspiration and effective strategies to overcome writer's block. It facilitates the process of generating ideas, practicing writing, creating articles or essays, developing story themes, and producing new material. Furthermore, ChatGPT allows writers to imitate distinct writing styles, rendering it a versatile instrument for authors and content providers (Park et al., 2024; Veluru, 2024). In addition to artistic pursuits, ChatGPT is capable of automating customer care interactions, demonstrating its versatility and usefulness in a wide range of applications.

ChatGPT utilizes a varied dataset sourced from books, web pages, and online articles. It employs sophisticated pattern recognition and language understanding to produce coherent, grammatically correct, and original responses. It is important to emphasize that ChatGPT needs to undergo specialized training for customer service interactions prior to being integrated with third-party tools to improve customer help. This is especially relevant for smaller businesses that may require additional technologies to fully utilize ChatGPT's capabilities. ChatGPT, developed by OpenAI for the Large Language Models class in natural language processing (NLP), demonstrates exceptional proficiency in generating engaging and authentic material on a wide range of subjects, including as biology, technology, sports, and fashion. The range of its capabilities includes summarization, spell-checking, paraphrasing, and even the generation of innovative slogans. ChatGPT is an invaluable tool for individuals looking to efficiently produce top-notch content because of its versatility and precision.

Furthermore, ChatGPT's expertise in sentiment analysis assists firms in swiftly discovering and resolving customer support concerns, hence improving overall customer happiness and engagement. The capacity to interpret emotional nuances in messages simplifies communication and enables prompt reactions to crucial talks, rendering it an essential tool for contemporary organizations navigating the digital realm as shown in Table 10.1.

3. Using ChatGPT to Improve Service Quality

It is crucial to train ChatGPT using a large dataset of service interactions in order to enhance customer and patient help. The efficacy of artificial intelligence relies on the caliber of its training data. Like other conversational AI automation solutions, ChatGPT necessitates this training in order to effectively comprehend typical service requests and provide responses that are natural and reminiscent of human interaction. Tasks such as managing repetitive operations, responding to commonly asked inquiries, offering advice on typical problems, and attending to small client requests can be effectively automated utilizing ChatGPT. ChatGPT enhances customer support by integrating with chatbots for customer care, allowing for continuous assistance outside of normal business hours and ensuring clients have access to help whenever needed. This level of accessibility enhances customer happiness and minimizes the probability of consumer aggravation or

Table 10.1. ChatGPT Navigating Different Digital Realms.

Customer support	Provides instant resolutions, personalized assistance, and efficient query handling.
Sales enablement	Guides users through product information, recommends relevant offerings, and facilitates purchases.
Task automation	Automates repetitive tasks, saving time and resources for organizations.
Multilingual support	Supports multiple languages, breaking language barriers for global engagements.
Contextual adaptability	Tailor's responses based on context, delivering personalized interactions.
Scalable performance	Handles multiple conversations simultaneously, ensuring prompt and uninterrupted service.

Source: Authors own creation.

discontent resulting from a lack of support. Furthermore, ChatGPT enhances support procedures by automating fundamental operations, aiding in prioritizing, and facilitating data gathering, so enabling organizations to allocate resources with greater efficiency. The difficulty of integrating ChatGPT into a system relies on various aspects, including the specific customer support system employed, the extent of customization needed, and the technical proficiency of the organization.

It is crucial to acknowledge that although ChatGPT is capable of producing responses that resemble human-like ones, users may still have to modify, customize, and verify the responses. This is because the program may display biases or inaccuracies that are inherent in its training data obtained from the internet. However, ChatGPT can assist in classifying and prioritizing enhancing Customer and Patient Services via ChatGPT. It plays a pivotal role in improving customer and patient care across multiple dimensions.

ChatGPT facilitates the development of virtual assistants capable of managing repetitive chores, addressing queries, and participating in significant dialogs with clients and individuals seeking medical assistance. This not only optimizes operations but also offers a customized experience to users, promoting improved communication and rapport. ChatGPT excels in offering multilingual support, showcasing its capability to aid in multiple languages. ChatGPT utilizes its language model skills to provide real-time translation services for clients and patients who speak different languages. This feature improves the accessibility and inclusivity of service delivery. Context-Aware Responses: ChatGPT utilizes advanced deep learning techniques to comprehend context and deliver pertinent responses that are sensitive to the given situation. This is especially beneficial in consumer and patient relations, where comprehending the subtleties of inquiries and delivering precise answers are of utmost importance. Sentiment Analysis: ChatGPT possesses the capability to assess the sentiment of customer and patient interactions, enabling organizations to measure emotions such as contentment, exasperation, or apprehension. This understanding assists in customizing solutions and rapidly resolving difficulties, resulting in enhanced customer/patient satisfaction and loyalty.

4. Growth and Impact of LLMs in FinTech

The integration of large language models like OpenAI's ChatGPT into FinTech operations is rapidly changing the outlook for FinTech companies. As forecasts predict considerable growth in the AI market related to FinTech, LLMs will radically change diverse areas of financial technology. This includes but is not limited to personalized customer interaction, fraud detection, risk assessment, and compliance. Forecasted growth from a market research firm suggests that the AI market in FinTech will grow at an impressive rate of 28.6% to hit $31.71 billion by 2027. This level of growth reflects the increasing reliance by FinTech firms on AI technologies and, most significantly, LLMs, to drive innovation and efficiency across their operations (Tan et al., 2023).

The integration of Large Language Models (LLMs) in FinTech has significantly improved various aspects of the industry. For instance, companies like Stripe are leveraging LLM technology to enhance documentation and streamline operations, as demonstrated by GPT-powered Stripe Docs. Similarly, collaborations between FinTech giants like Klarna and OpenAI have resulted in the integration of Klarna's services into ChatGPT, offering users a personalized shopping experience.

Innovations in AI training and implementation are also evident, with FinTech companies exploring novel approaches. For example, Chime collaborates with a third-party company to train AI using its code base within a private cloud, addressing concerns about intellectual property and security. Additionally, companies like SESAMm are integrating Generative AI solutions to assist financial firms in mitigating risks for environmental, social, and governance (ESG) issues, aiming to upgrade product functionality and streamline processes. Advancements in AI technology, such as the development of Perceptual MAE by Tractable, further innovate within the FinTech industry. This method efficiently learns domain-specific visual cues through self-supervision, enabling state-of-the-art performance on ImageNet while being more data and compute-efficient. Overall, the integration of LLMs is reshaping the FinTech industry, driving innovation, and efficiency. As FinTech continues to evolve, LLMs will play a central role in facilitating further innovation and transformation within the industry.

5. Exploring Diverse Approaches to Enhancing Customer and Patient Services With ChatGPT

ChatGPT has the capability to be taught in identifying and resolving frequently encountered complaints and grievances. ChatGPT utilizes client message analysis to deliver information, propose solutions, and provide help, thereby enhancing the overall service experience. ChatGPT can provide support not only for customer assistance but also for tasks like content development, search engine optimization (SEO), and language translation. It has the ability to generate content of superior quality, enhance search ranks, and guarantee precise translations, so improving the effectiveness of communication. ChatGPT's capacity to manage numerous conversations simultaneously allows for continuous assistance and automation, available 24/7. This minimizes the duration of waiting, guarantees timely support, and improves customer/patient contentment. The automation of monotonous operations also allows for the allocation of human resources to more intricate matters. Enhanced Communication and Engagement: ChatGPT's advanced natural language processing (NLP) abilities allow for discussions that closely resemble human interactions, resulting in improved communication and engagement with consumers and patients. This individualized approach enhances relationships and cultivates trust.

ChatGPT possesses the capability to scrutinize extensive volumes of data derived from customer/patient interactions, thereby yielding significant insights pertaining to patterns, preferences, and opportunities for enhancement. This data-centric approach informs decision-making and facilitates the formulation of strategies. ChatGPT fundamentally transforms customer and patient services by providing intelligent, streamlined, and customized interactions. The wide range of capabilities it offers, including support for several languages, sentiment analysis, and content development, makes it a highly valuable tool for organizations aiming to provide outstanding service experiences the issues that firms must solve, thereby reducing the process of manually categorizing each client interaction and facilitating the effective prioritization of crucial areas.

6. Primary Areas Where ChatGPT Enhances Customer Services

ChatGPT possesses the capability to precisely interpret human speech or text by employing NLP and advanced language models. ChatGPT facilitates prompt responses to inquiries and enables the collection of valuable information from clients regarding remarks. Additionally, it has the capability to read and write in an extensive range of programming languages. ChatGPT streamlines the process for businesses to segment and target their consumer base. Businesses have the ability to enhance engagement and conversion rates by delivering customized communications to specific audience segments through the use of advanced messaging capabilities. The straightforward interface of ChatGPT facilitates communication among team members. It can be used to establish team channels so that information can be accessed swiftly and without having to sift through a lengthy chat history. ChatGPT is capable of autonomously generating and interpreting natural language by leveraging ML and an extensive database. ChatGPT exhibits versatility across multiple disciplines, in contrast to conventional chatbot models that necessitate pre-programmed responses. It gains knowledge from human input, enabling it to discern the intricacies of real-world language and deliver relevant, tailored solutions. ChatGPT-powered chatbot applications have the potential to greatly benefit a company's customer service department by allowing them to respond to inquiries from customers as if they were conversing with a human employee. Companies seeking to capitalize on conversational AI technology would do well to consider ChatGPT due to its extraordinary feature set. By utilizing this efficacious instrument, enterprises can enhance their comprehension of the demands of their clientele and foster more intimate connections with them. When a user inputs text into ChatGPT, the software employs its trained algorithms to analyze the input and generate a response that is both contextually and semantically pertinent. ChatGPT demonstrates the capability to generate insightful responses that closely resemble human discourse due to its reliance on the patterns and correlations identified within the training data. Customers and enterprises hold divergent views regarding AI-powered chatbots. Already, these methods are applicable to sentiment analysis. These tools have the potential to identify discussions that require assessment and may also suggest opportunities or concerns that require attention in light of other participants' replies.

The key domains of customer service that benefit from the implementation of ChatGPT are detailed in ChatGPT and are an excellent choice for organizations that have a substantial customer base or a significant number of contacts with clients, as it possesses the capability to handle numerous customer interactions and inquiries. It has the capability to handle multiple interactions concurrently, relieving customer service representatives of their workload and allowing them to focus on more complex or time-sensitive issues. ChatGPT possesses the capability to deliver personalized responses to client inquiries and complaints through integration with customer service systems and training using unique customer information. A customized response has been modified to accommodate the specific conditions of the customer. ChatGPT could aid customers during the registration procedure by responding to frequent inquiries in the absence of a human representative (Gulshan et al., 2016; Park et al., 2024). By virtue of ChatGPT's proactive intervention capability, the onboarding process is significantly automated, which increases customer retention and guarantees product adoption. ChatGPT may present corporate offers to customers during support interactions, creating the illusion that they are receiving a better deal. ChatGPT may generate additional scenarios when a customer expresses interest in an upsell or cross-sell, for instance, when the limitations of their plan have been satisfied. ChatGPT chatbots can be utilized by businesses to automate internal communications, respond to employee inquiries, deliver corporate news, and even assist with HR-related tasks. ChatGPT will ultimately have the capability to modify client accounts and orders in conjunction with customer support systems. ChatGPT will possess the capability to not only provide responses to consumers but also execute actions on their behalf. When ChatGPT is uncertain as to the correct response, it tends to provide incorrect responses. When ChatGPT is unable to provide assistance to clients, the technology will progress to the stage where it will identify this and escalate the situation to a human agent (Topol, 2019). ChatGPT's transformative impact on customer support has the potential to provide businesses with a streamlined, efficient, and customer-focused methodology for managing inquiries and grievances. This, in turn, could result in heightened levels of customer contentment and sustained allegiance. ChatGPT-trained chatbots simplify the process of automating customer support interactions. The AI chatbot possesses the capability to autonomously respond to a wide range of client inquiries, delivering timely and accurate information and resolutions with minimal human intervention. Utilizing ChatGPT chatbots can potentially simplify the user experience, particularly for financial websites that require assistance with task estimation, loan calculation, investment return prediction, and tax estimation. By analyzing user preferences and behavior, ChatGPT has the capability to offer personalized product suggestions that enhance the overall purchasing experience. ChatGPT is incapable of becoming blocked and will invariably devise a resolution. Nevertheless, customer service representatives are cognizant of the fact that the most effective initial response frequently entails a subsequent inquiry designed to elucidate the client's need or solicit further specific details. ChatGPT enables organizations to efficiently construct engaging and natural dialogs with their clientele (Verghese et al., 2018) (Brown, 2020). ML is beneficial for generating accurate predictions and revealing latent data. Moreover, AI technology can be advantageous in a variety of materials science applications, including material as shown in Table 10.2.

7. Principal ChatGPT Application Domains for Patient Services

As it can generate human-like responses, ChatGPT is a valuable tool for healthcare professionals. Physicians and nurses can effectively engage in patient communication by utilizing ChatGPT to provide precise information and provide comprehensible responses to inquiries. Healthcare providers must prioritize this in order to enhance patient communication and the patient experience as a whole. As

Table 10.2. Impact of ChatGPT on Different Areas.

Application Area	Impact of ChatGPT
Customer support	Provides instant responses, reduces wait times for customers
Sales assistance	Offers personalized product recommendations, boosts sales
FAQ automation	Automates responses to common queries, saves time for agents
Lead generation	Engages potential customers, qualifies leads efficiently
Feedback collection	Gathers feedback through conversational interactions
Order tracking	Provides real-time updates on order status
Appointment scheduling	Assists in scheduling appointments, manages calendars
Complaint resolution	Resolves complaints through guided conversations
Upselling/Cross-selling	Suggests additional products/services based on customer needs

Source: Authors own creation.

telemedicine has expanded, individuals are increasingly utilizing virtual consultations to obtain medical care without leaving their residences. By using video conferencing equipment, physicians and caregivers can provide medical advice and treatment to patients remotely. ChatGPT has the potential to enhance communication between healthcare professionals and patients during virtual consultations. Personalized health plans are tailored to the specific requirements of each individual patient, taking into account their medical condition, way of life, and personal inclinations. The primary domains in which ChatGPT is implemented to provide patient services.

By integrating ChatGPT with a telemedicine platform, patients would be able to pose inquiries and promptly receive precise and comprehensible responses. Additionally, individualized educational materials, including pamphlets and films, may be provided to patients in accordance with their health concerns and available treatment options. By advising patients on the most effective course of action for their illness and reducing the likelihood that patients with significant problems will be neglected, ChatGPT can improve patient outcomes. This facilitates individualized health plans that are tailored to the needs and preferences of the patient, thereby enhancing outcomes and satisfaction (Radford et al., 2019; Strubell et al., 2020). Effectively managing a variety of complaints is the capability of ChatGPT. It can increase patient satisfaction by providing patients with transparent information regarding their health and treatment options – promotions to consumers, creating the perception that they are acquiring a more advantageous transaction. ChatGPT may generate additional scenarios when a customer expresses interest in an upsell or cross-sell, for instance, when the limitations of their plan have been satisfied. ChatGPT chatbots can be utilized by businesses to automate internal communications, respond to employee inquiries, deliver corporate news, and even assist with HR-related tasks.

Eventually, it will be possible for ChatGPT to communicate with customer support systems in order to modify client accounts and orders. ChatGPT will possess the capability to not only provide responses to consumers but also execute actions on their behalf. When ChatGPT is uncertain as to the correct response, it tends to provide incorrect responses. When ChatGPT is unable to provide assistance to clients, the technology will progress to the stage where it will identify this and escalate the situation to a human agent. ChatGPT's transformative impact on customer support has the potential to provide businesses with a streamlined, efficient, and customer-focused methodology for managing inquiries and grievances. This, in turn, could result in heightened levels of customer contentment and sustained allegiance. ChatGPT-trained chatbots simplify the process of automating customer support interactions. The AI chatbot possesses the capability to autonomously respond to a wide range of client inquiries, delivering timely and accurate information and resolutions with minimal human intervention. Utilizing ChatGPT chatbots can potentially simplify the user experience, particularly for financial websites that require assistance with task estimation, loan calculation, investment return prediction, and tax estimation. By analyzing user preferences and behavior, ChatGPT has the capability to offer personalized product suggestions that enhance the overall purchasing experience.

ChatGPT is incapable of becoming blocked and will invariably devise a resolution. Nevertheless, customer service representatives are cognizant of the fact that the most effective initial response frequently entails a subsequent inquiry designed to elucidate the client's need or solicit further specific details. ChatGPT enables organizations to efficiently construct engaging and natural dialogs with their clientele. ML is beneficial for uncovering latent data and generating accurate predictions (Amodei et al., 2016; Brown, 2020). Moreover, AI technology can be advantageous in a variety of materials science applications, including material as shown in Table 10.3.

Table 10.3. ChatGPT in Patient Care.

Application Area	Description
Patient queries	ChatGPT can handle patient inquiries regarding symptoms, medications, appointments, and general health information, providing accurate and prompt responses.
Appointment scheduling	ChatGPT can assist patients in scheduling appointments, checking availability, and sending reminders, streamlining the booking process and reducing administrative workload.
Telemedicine support	ChatGPT can support telemedicine services by guiding patients through virtual consultations, providing pre-consultation information, and facilitating follow-ups or prescription refills.
Health education	ChatGPT can offer educational content on various health topics, medication instructions, lifestyle recommendations, and preventive care, empowering patients with relevant and reliable information.
Medication management	ChatGPT can help patients with medication management, including dosage reminders, medication interactions, side effects, and adherence strategies, promoting medication safety and treatment compliance.
Mental health support	ChatGPT can provide mental health support by offering resources, coping strategies, relaxation techniques, and crisis intervention guidance, enhancing access to mental health services and support.
Disease management	ChatGPT can assist in chronic disease management by providing personalized care plans, monitoring progress, offering dietary and lifestyle advice, and connecting patients with relevant healthcare providers and resources.

(Continued)

Table 10.3. *(Continued)*

Application Area	Description
Remote monitoring	ChatGPT can facilitate remote patient monitoring by collecting and analyzing patient data, tracking vital signs, alerting healthcare providers to abnormalities, and supporting remote consultations for timely interventions.
Follow-up care	ChatGPT can streamline follow-up care by sending post-appointment instructions, conducting post-surgery checks, monitoring recovery progress, and ensuring continuity of care between healthcare visits.
Emergency assistance	ChatGPT can offer emergency assistance by guiding patients in urgent situations, providing first-aid information, connecting them with emergency services, and assisting in crisis management until professional help arrives.

Source: Authors own creation.

8. Applications of ChatGPT in Fintech

8.1 Customer Service

ChatGPT has become a potent tool for the enhancement of customer service within the Fintech sector. By employing natural language processing techniques, ChatGPT equips chatbots with the ability to communicate in real time with customers through personalized assistance and query resolution. According to a study by Juniper Research, AI-driven (Juniper Research, 2019) chatbots are estimated to save businesses more than $8 billion annually by 2022 through improved customer service and reduction in operational costs. Companies such as Bank of America have implemented virtual assistants powered by ChatGPT to provide 24/7 customer service support, leading to an increase in customer satisfaction levels and a decrease in response times.

8.2 Fraud Detection and Prevention

The role of ChatGPT in fraud detection and prevention in the Fintech industry cannot be underestimated. By analyzing textual data and communication logs, ChatGPT-powered systems can identify suspicious patterns and potential fraudulent activities in real time.

Research conducted by Accenture (Accenture, 2020) highlights how AI is effective in detecting fraud. The research finds that 77% of surveyed financial institutions reported a decrease in fraudulent transactions after implementing AI-driven solutions. Companies like PayPal use ChatGPT-based models to analyze transaction descriptions and customer communication, which allows them to detect and mitigate fraudulent behavior.

The surge in digital transactions and online financial services has brought a corresponding surge in cyber threats and fraudulent activities. AI is playing a huge role in bolstering cybersecurity and fraud detection efforts within the payments and FinTech sectors. Businesses will save over $10.4 billion in 2027 through the adoption of fraud detection and prevention solutions that are AI-powered. It analyzes huge amounts of data in real time and is able to monitor transactions continuously for patterns, anomalies, and potential security threats (Wadhwa & Kumar, 2023). Such sophisticated systems can be used to distinguish between genuine customer behavior and fraudulent activities and thus safeguard against unauthorized access and loss of money. By using AI-driven predictive analytics in fraud detection systems, financial services can significantly reduce false positives, or transactions misidentified as fraudulent.

Furthermore, AI is enhancing security procedures, safeguarding client data, and increasing customer trust. Financial service providers can have more control over their data because AI-driven systems can process sensitive information within their own infrastructure, reducing the need for third-party systems and increasing the general level of protection regarding privacy. Generally, AI-based technologies mean that fraud detection capabilities are not only improved but that sensitive financial data is also safeguarded, strengthening the resilience of the financial system to cyber threats.

8.3 Personalized Financial Advice

ChatGPT enables fintech companies to provide personalized financial advice that is tailored to meet all customer's preferences and goals. By analyzing user data and investment patterns, ChatGPT generates recommendations for various financial products, including stocks, bonds, and mutual funds. Multiple studies emphasize that personalized financial advice drives customer engagement and satisfaction. Platforms such as Wealth front are powered by ChatGPT in providing personalized investment advice and, subsequently, attract increased user engagement and loyalty (He et al., 2020; Willis, 2023).

Automated virtual personal assistants: AI technology in finance has revolutionized customer service through the introduction of automated virtual personal assistants. These AI-powered systems offer a myriad of benefits over traditional approaches, including 24/7 availability, instant responses, cost-effectiveness, consistency, multilingual support, personalization, and continuous learning. They handle tasks ranging from real-time financial updates to executing transactions, offering game-changing trading methods and tailored financial plans. By seamlessly integrating with various communication channels, these assistants enhance overall customer experiences, providing prompt and consistent support while optimizing efficiency and scalability.

AI-driven credit scoring: AI-based creditworthiness analysis is a long way from the traditional approaches used so far because it incorporates a host of other factors like social behavior, online presence, and transaction history. Such a wholesome approach makes the credit risk assessment much more accurate. As a result, financial institutions use AI to process consumer data in vast volumes to make very accurate evaluations of creditworthiness. Modern AI systems are capable of checking multiple financial accounts with the result that a complete picture of the financial health of clients is built and real-time account support is possible. In addition, AI determines one's eligibility for a product or service by comparing and analyzing data to make decisions regarding banks. Furthermore, FinTech companies use AI to tailor financial products to match client profiles and demands (Benjamin et al., 2024). All in all, AI has brought about sea change in the Fintech industry in terms of service delivery and consumption and has opened new vistas of opportunities and challenges.

9. Regulatory Compliance

For fintech companies, there lies the imperative task of ensuring regulatory compliance. In this respect, ChatGPT simplifies and automates compliance processes. ChatGPT-powered systems that analyze regulatory texts, compliance documents, and compliance officers' reports allow the latter to gain understanding from complex regulations and ensure adherence to the law.

According to Deloitte in 2022 (Deloitte, 2022), the number of AI technologies, including ChatGPT, for the automation of compliance-related tasks is gradually increasing; hence, there is increased efficiency and accuracy. By automating the process of documentation and reporting, ChatGPT will aid in the simplification of compliance efforts and the minimization of the risk of regulatory breaches.

From handling customer service issues to fraud detection and personalized financial advice, the applications of ChatGPT across the spectrum of the Fintech domain have only been a recent invention. By harnessing the power of natural language processing, financial institutions can improve customer experiences, risk mitigation, and compliance with regulatory requirements.

Regional and regulatory differences very strongly influence the adoption of AI in financial institutions and can, therefore, be a cause for totally different landscapes with respect to the integration of AI within financial services across the world as shown in Table 10.4. It provides an understanding of the differences that gives a nuanced view of the global AI fintech ecosystem. Here are the different factors which are shaping AI adoption in various regions (World Bank, 2024).

With vast resources at their command and a stable market in the US and Europe, financial institutions are well-placed to invest heavily in state-of-the-art AI technologies. The institutions enjoy a stable environment that allows them to integrate sophisticated AI systems without sweating easily. Through the enormous investments in research and development, these institutions are able to come up with unique AI solutions that match the highest standards. This also means that they face higher expectations of transparency and ethical use of AI. The enhanced focus on strict regulatory compliance and ethical practice is a feature of mature markets and a critical requirement for responsible AI deployment (Ochuba et al.,

Table 10.4. Regulatory Compliance of Different Regions.

Regions	Description
European Union (EU)	Regulation: The EU has enacted very strict regulations on AI, especially the EU Artificial Intelligence Act, that targets regulating high-risk AI applications. This Act enforces requirements on transparency, accountability, and data protection that will impact how AI technologies are developed and deployed for financial services (Siegmann & Anderljung, 2022). Impact: Artificial Intelligence systems that are imposed in financial institutions within the territory of the EU need to be in compliance with these regulations. This could imply more rigorous testing, higher costs of compliance, but greater confidence and protection for consumers as well.
United States	Regulation: The US regulatory framework for AI is less centralized and more diffused in nature, differing from state to state and sector to sector. However, this situation is slowly changing, with federal agencies like the SEC increasingly focusing on AI practices. Impact: This fragmented nature of regulation could bring about differences across states in the application of AI and its enforcement, hence most likely making the integration process more cumbersome for financial institutions operating cross-state or cross-country.
China	Regulation: China is more centrally driven toward the regulation of artificial intelligence, with policies like the New Generation Artificial Intelligence Development Plan focusing on fast-paced development and integration of AI (State Council of the People's Republic of China, 2017). However, data privacy and ethical considerations remain issues due to broader Chinese surveillance practices. Impact: This encouraging regulatory environment enables faster adoption of AI in China, raising questions related to data security and ethical concerns for financial institutions operating across borders.
India	Regulation: India is in the process of developing its regulations for AI; so far, most of the guidelines are focused on data protection under the Personal Data Protection Bill (Parliament of India, 2021).

(Continued)

Table 10.4. *(Continued)*

Regions	Description
	Hopefully, more attention will be paid to the ethical use of AI while taking care to ensure innovativeness. Impact: In India, there needs to be a balance between compliance due to emerging new regulations and competitively leveraging AI. The shifting regulatory landscape will drive uncertainty and, thereby, bring opportunities to the early movers.

Source: Author's own.

2024; Strusani & Houngbonon, 2019). On the other hand, markets in developing countries in Africa and parts of Asia are generally at a lower stage of development with respect to the financial system, with varying degrees of regulatory control. Such markets are very special opportunities for AI adoption, with reduced entry barriers because of an overall demand for technological innovation to fill gaps from existing infrastructure (World Bank, 2024). Banks in these regions, in particular, seem to embrace AI at an accelerated pace – providing the means for leapfrogging traditional banking infrastructure and speeding up growth. Indeed, such fast adoption may be hindered by underdeveloped regulatory frameworks or less robust standards in the protection of consumer data (Yang et al., 2020). These factors can create uncertainties and potential risks, so in this regard, it is very important for institutions in an emerging market to understand and navigate these challenges in a bid to harness the benefits associated with AI.

10. Impact of AI in Financial Industry

The recent survey conducted by the World Economic Forum and the Cambridge Center for Alternative Finance (CCAF) sheds light on the rapid adoption of AI within the financial services industry (World Economic Forum, 2023).

The findings from the WEF survey (see Fig. 10.1) illustrate varying perspectives on the impact of widespread AI adoption within the Fintech sector. Between 48% and 58% of respondents express concerns that mass AI adoption could exacerbate market-level risks, while a smaller proportion, ranging from 19% to 32%, believe it could mitigate such risks. Notably, respondents harbor particular apprehensions regarding the potential for AI applications to introduce pervasive bias and trigger systemic data breaches, both of which are cited as significant concerns in algorithmic decision-making processes. Additionally, 58% of organizations identify algorithmic decision-making as a domain where AI adoption may potentially yield adverse effects overall. These perceptions of risk associated with AI adoption are shaped by individual deployment experiences and industry

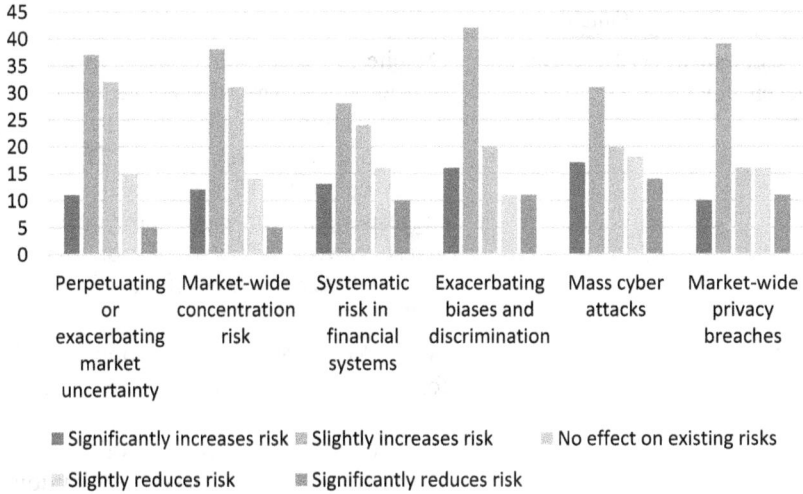

Fig. 10.1.   World Economic Forum Survey – Perceived Influence of AI Mass Adoption on Market-Wide Risks. *Source:* Authors own creation.

expectations, emphasizing the importance of considering the specific context and objectives of AI integration within Fintech businesses as shown in Fig. 10.1.

Key interpretations as shown in Table 10.5 from the survey include:

Overall, the survey underscores the transformative impact of AI on the financial services industry, with mass adoption expected to drive significant changes in business operations and customer experiences. However, addressing concerns related to bias and discrimination will be essential to ensuring the responsible and equitable deployment of AI technologies within the sector.

Table 10.5. Key Interpretations of AI.

Expected Mass Adoption of AI	Nearly two-thirds (64%) of financial services leaders anticipate becoming mass adopters of AI within the next two years, compared to only 16% currently doing so. These firms plan to leverage AI for various purposes, including revenue generation, process automation, risk management, customer service, and client acquisition (World Bank, 2024).

(Continued)

Table 10.5. *(Continued)*

Investment in AI Research and Development	Despite the potential for accelerating returns, the survey reveals that 60% of firms currently invest less than 10% of their research and development (R&D) resources on AI. However, evidence suggests significant payoffs for firms that invest between 10% and 30% or over 40% of their R&D resources in AI (Deloitte, 2022).
Concerns about Bias and Discrimination	While AI adoption presents opportunities for innovation and efficiency, executives express concerns about AI bias and market-wide risks. Over half of respondents fear that mass AI adoption could exacerbate bias and discrimination within the sector. However, 70% believe they are at least somewhat prepared to mitigate AI bias risks, particularly those firms utilizing Risk and Compliance teams in AI implementation (GPAI, 2023).
Differences Between FinTech's and Incumbent Firms	The survey highlights variations in how fintechs and traditional financial institutions approach AI adoption. Fintechs are more likely to develop AI-based products and services, employ autonomous decision-making systems, and rely on cloud-based offerings. In contrast, incumbent firms predominantly focus on using AI to enhance existing products and services (Tan et al., 2023).

Source: Authors own creation.

The way forward for AI in personal finance management will even get more sophisticated as it graduates from simple advisory roles to highly customized financial planning. Experts have predicted that soon, AI-based platforms will offer real-time and very customized investment strategy formulations in keeping with a person's changing financial behaviors and market conditions. This growth aligns with the vision of a Personalized Financial Ecosystem framework, in which AI systems will be deeply integrated into users' daily financial activities. This would sustain not only much more accurate financial consultation but also democratize access to more sophisticated financial tools and let larger numbers of the population afford resources to give way to sophisticated planning. With further technological development in AI, the likely shift shall be toward dynamic, adaptive regulatory frameworks. Further legislation, in the future, is likely to cater for real-time compliance monitoring and therefore will have dynamically changing rules that keep pace with technological changes. This places an Adaptive Regulatory Framework model in a better position, where the continuous assessment of AI systems for compliance is envisaged. In the current form, the framework is seeking to balance innovativeness with accountability so that AI systems remain ethical and transparent as they continue to change (Deloitte Insights, 2024).

On risk management, it is forecasted that AI will fundamentally alter the nature of capabilities by using advanced predictive analytics and real-time data to forecast and mitigate financial risks. According to the Global Risk Network framework, AI is increasingly going to be working in a connected global financial ecosystem, using cross-border data to offer comprehensive risk assessments – which could really affect the way risk management strategies are brought into play and thus bring forth more stability in the financial systems globally. Moreover, AI will help to further financial inclusion and make financial services available, accessible, and more affordable to underserved communities. Innovations in AI-driven microfinance and mobile banking bring services closer to distant or otherwise deprived areas that have remained out of reach for traditional financial institutions. According to the Inclusive Finance Model, AI technologies facilitate this inclusion by giving access to financial services and catering to the different needs of diverse communities (Zhang & Yang, 2019). Since financial transactions are increasingly becoming digital, AI is expected to play a very critical role in their detection and prevention. A future AI system, with the ultra-new machine learning technologies, could analyze patterns and anomalies in real-time to offer an advance fraud management approach. The proactive Fraud Prevention framework calls for AI, in conjunction with real-time transaction monitoring, to foretell and go ahead to prevent fraudulent activities, thus boosting security and trust in digital financial transactions (McKinsey, 2021).

11. Case Reviews

AI is deepening its influence on the fintech sector and driving a host of emerging trends looking to reshape this industry. The practical implications of those AI-driven trends bring along opportunities and challenges, underlining AI's transformative potential in financial services more generally. Some of the practical implications of these AI-driven trends already began changing the face of the fintech sector through increased personalization, fraud detection, credit scoring, customer service, risk management, financial inclusion, and market analysis. They will break more innovative solutions and further transform the financial industry as AI technologies continue to evolve.

AI technologies are making immense strides in the Fintech sector and show their practical implications through various successful case studies and real-world applications as shown in Table 10.6. Some specific examples where AI has been effectively implemented in the practical implications emerging trends:

Case: Sentient Investment AI Hedge Fund – The Sentient Investment Management AI hedge fund case is a pointer to the massive challenges and risks involved in the deployment of AI in FinTech. It is actually the real lesson for other FinTech firms: test thoroughly, be transparent, and make AI systems adaptable to plow through the complexities of financial markets. Sentient Investment Management launched an AI-powered hedge fund designed to trade stocks automatically using machine learning algorithms. This high-profile start-up hedge fund, which previously attracted USD 143 million in VC funding for evolutionary algorithms-based trading strategies, began losing money within two

Table 10.6. Real-World Applications.

Description	Applications
Fraud detection and prevention	1. Darktrace Cyber security firm Darktrace uses artificial intelligence and machine learning to identify cyber threats, including fraud, and automatically respond to them in real time. The Enterprise Immune System from Darktrace works through the continued monitoring of network activity, searching for anomalies that may indicate fraudulent behavior. This AI-driven approach empowers financial institutions to detect and mitigate the prospect of threats before they evolve into actual problems, hence offering a robust layer of protection against financial crimes (Heim et al., 2023). 2. Mastercard Mastercard has introduced AI into fraud detection through the Decision Intelligence platform. The AI analyzes transaction information in real-time, assessing any given transaction for its potential for fraud. In using machine learning algorithms that learn from the changing patterns of fraud, Mastercard can reduce occurrences of false declines, highly improving the accuracy of fraud detection and boosting general security and customer experience (Industry perspectives on AI and transaction fraud detection – retrieved from Mastercard).

Table 10.6. *(Continued)*

Description	Applications
Credit scoring and lending	1. ZestFinance ZestFinance deploys artificial intelligence in credit scoring models and across the lending continuum. ZestFinance AI models show more accurate assessments of credit in people and businesses because they can leverage a vast bank of information beyond what is used in traditional credit scores, like behavioral and transactional data. This allows making a better judgment about creditworthiness and giving loans to underserved or non-traditional borrowers (Forbes Article – ZestFinance Using AI To Bring Fairness To Mortgage Lending). 2. Upstart Offshoot utilizes artificial intelligence in enhancing its lending platform by assessing credit risk using non-traditional data points such as educational, employment history, and income. As indicated by its machine learning algorithms, the prediction of risk associated with loan default is more accurate compared to the traditional models of credit scoring. In that respect, Upstart is better positioned to offer improved loan terms alongside expanded credit accessibility across a larger section of borrowers compared to FICO's traditional credit scoring model because Upstart looks at more factors than a person's credit history (*Source:* NACFU).
Personalized financial advice	1. Betterment Betterment is the biggest robo-advisor; it applies AI in providing personalized investment advice and portfolio management. It sets users' financial goals, risk tolerance, and investment preferences against algorithms to provide tailor-made investment strategies and recommendations. This AI-driven personalization helps users to make educated decisions about their finances and create an optimized investment portfolio for their needs.

(Continued)

Table 10.6. *(Continued)*

Description	Applications
	2. Wealthfront Wealthfront is yet another leading robo-advisor that applies AI to deliver personalized financial planning services. It now powered its suite of financial planning tools – tax-loss harvesting and automated rebalancing – with complex algorithms that are further optimized for changing market conditions and specific user profiles. In using its AI technology, Wealthfront makes these sophisticated investment techniques available to users with minimal knowledge of the finances alone (*Source:* https://www.wealthfront.com/robo-advisor-investing).
Risk management and compliance	1. Ayasdi Ayasdi deploys AI in companies to achieve advanced risk management and compliance solutions. Through the use of machine learning techniques, the platform analyzes a huge amount of data to identify hidden risks and maintain compliance with requirements set by regulators. In discovering intricate patterns and anomalies, Ayasdi manages the risk factor for financial institutions and helps them comply more effectively with the set regulations (Morabito & Morabito, 2015). 2. Palantir Technologies Palantir Technologies uses artificial intelligence to power risk management and compliance for financial institutions. Its artificially intelligent analytic tools monitor transactions, trace suspicious activities, and assure conformance with regulatory standards. Their solutions help firms reduce the risks involved and remain compliant within the heavily regulated environment of financial markets (*Source:* www.palantir.com/offerings/financial-services).

Source: Author's own creation.

years, in 2018, representing a loss in finances and investor satisfaction. After firing thousands of computers around the world running millions of virtual traders, it became very hard for this system to adjust to the vicissitudes and complexities of real-world financial markets. This can be taken as an example of how only AI cannot make high-stake financial decisions (Buczynski et al., 2021).

The challenges and risks as shown in Table 10.7 that are associated to this case can be analyzed as follows:

Case: Bias in ZestFinance Algorithm

(Sourced from "Using AI To Bring Fairness To Mortgage Lending," Published in Forbes article, 2019)

In 2015, ZestFinance, which gained huge attention due to its bias in AI. It is an illustration of how AI, if left unmanaged, perpetuates and even exaggerates existing biases within society into a myriad of potential discriminatory outcomes. ZestFinance's AI-driven credit scoring system aimed at a finer-grained and more accurate measure of creditworthiness than traditional methods of credit scoring. It was found that algorithms for credit scoring by ZestFinance were biased against minorities. This bias naturally occurs due to the fact that training data used to develop AI models mirrored old biases and inequities – already present in conventional lending. It therefore favored applicants from demographic groups previously considered more creditworthy, hence discriminating against minorities and other underrepresented groups (Bajracharya et al., 2022). Bias in AI algorithms is often traceable to the data used in training models. If the historical data is biased – in terms of race, gender, or socioeconomic status – AI learns these and replicates them. The company's decisions made by the algorithm followed the

Table 10.7. Challenges and Risks.

Application Area	Description
Complexity and adaptability	The AI struggled to adapt to the dynamic nature of financial markets, leading to poor performance in real-world scenarios. It also failed to handle market anomalies effectively.
Over-reliance on historical data	The AI's dependence on historical data led to inadequate predictive power and poor decision-making. Biases in training data further impacted its accuracy.
Transparency and trust	The opaque decision-making process of the AI led to investor skepticism and dissatisfaction, highlighting the need for explainability in AI systems.
Operational risks	Technical failures and the resource-intensive nature of the AI system added to the operational challenges, including system glitches and high maintenance costs.

Source: Authors own creation.

same type of discriminatory patterns that were recorded in past lending practices that pitted minority applicants against their majority peers.

The challenges and risks that are associated to this case can be analyzed as shown in Table 10.8 are as follows:

The case studies of Sentient AI's hedge fund and ZestFinance's algorithmic bias underline important lessons for AI in Fintech. First, there is an obvious need to test and validate AI models rigorously for effectiveness within the high-stakes environments in which they are deployed. The extent to which they would work in such scenarios would require tests under different conditions and their updates with new data. Moreover, developing trust with investors and stakeholders requires transparency and explainability in models that provide clear reasons for their decisions (Buchanan, 2019). There are also ethical and regulatory considerations whereby AI applications have to be fair, not biasing, and compliant with regulations. In addition, there is an increasing requirement for transparency and accountability of AI decision-making processes, which calls for the development of interpretable models and detailed documentation within fintech companies. Fairness and effectiveness are ensured by the constant tracking and improvement of AI systems, including frequent updating of training data and adoption of

Table 10.8. Application Areas.

Application area	Description
Bias and discrimination	The case proved the possibility of bias and discrimination being a highly likely reality in AI-driven systems. Unless met with careful management and testing for fairness, models of AI can replicate and further amplify earlier inequalities. These may prove dangerous for the person or group concerned and seriously dent the very fundamentals of fairness and equality within the financial services sector.
Fair lending practices	The flak that ZestFinance took brought out the need to develop AI models for promoting fair lending practices. It was pretty clear that fintech companies have to ensure there is no bias in the AI systems and that they don't put any particular group at a disadvantage. Such continuous efforts are called for in scrutinizing and refining the data and algorithms of these systems.
Regulatory compliance	The case also made emphasis on compliance with anti-discrimination laws and regulations. Thus, financial institutions and FinTech companies are under obligation to comply with regulatory provisions that are laid down to prevent discriminatory practices.

Source: Author's own creation.

bias-reduction techniques. In the end, one also cannot forget the need for industry collaboration to bring about the acceptance of ethical AI standards and best practices. Organizations like Partnership on AI and AI Ethics Lab are taking a leading role in this regard (GPAI, 2023). In this respect, future research in AI robustness and debiasing will become instrumental in ensuring fairness and accuracy in decision-making. Better data privacy solutions to protect sensitive financial data from continuously evolving cyber threats, when combined with stringent data protection standards, will be very important. Ethical and fair AI frameworks are also urgently required to avoid biased output and ensure consistency in treating all customers equitably (IMF, 2023).

12. Emerging Trends in Fintech

AI and Fintech: An emerging trend is increased adoption of AI-driven personalization in financial services. With continued advances in AI technologies, for example, NLP capabilities embodied by ChatGPT, financial institutions will be able to offer highly individualized services responding to the needs and preferences of individual customers. This trend is projected to lead to higher customer engagement and satisfaction, driving growth and innovation in fintech.

Future Applications of ChatGPT: Going forward, ChatGPT has immense potential for a host of applications in fintech. Applications for the platform extend to advanced risk assessment, automated investment management, and regulatory compliance beyond customer service and fraud detection. Moreover, as AI research progresses, ChatGPT will evolve to possess not just text but also image and voice data to further enhance its utility in fintech applications, given its evolving multimodal capabilities (Deloitte, 2022).

The future of Open AI in fintech is marked by several emerging trends as shown in Table 10.9 includes:

It is important to increase the transparency and interpretability of AI-driven algorithms like ChatGPT in order to enhance trust with users and regulators in the financial space. Further, one may extend the research to trace the ethical implications of AI adoption in fintech, particularly in regard to issues that arise from bias, fairness, and accountability.

Table 10.9. Future of Open AI.

Explainable AI (XAI)	As AI algorithms become more complex, there is a growing need for transparency and interpretability in AI decision-making processes. Explainable AI (XAI) techniques aim to make AI systems more understandable and interpretable, enhancing trust and reliability in financial applications.

(Continued)

Table 10.9. *(Continued)*

AI-powered personalization	AI-driven personalization is expected to become increasingly sophisticated, enabling financial institutions to offer hyper-personalized services and recommendations tailored to individual customer needs and preferences. ChatGPT, combined with other AI technologies, will play a central role in delivering personalized financial advice and experiences.
AI governance and ethics	With the proliferation of AI in financial services, there is a heightened focus on AI governance, ethics, and responsible AI deployment. Future trends will involve developing frameworks and guidelines for ethical AI use, addressing issues such as bias, fairness, and algorithmic accountability.

Source: Authors own creation.

AI practices and data privacy lie at the heart of the ethical deployment of AI within a financial institution. This would foster responsible AI practices, building trust, compliance, and mitigation of risks associated with AI technologies. To this end, the following suggestions as shown in Table 10.10 can be considered:

Table 10.10. AI Practices Application Areas.

Application Area	**Description**
Presenting clear ethical guidelines	It is important that financial institutions develop comprehensive ethical guidelines on how AI should be deployed. These have to be principles-based statements that would guide fairness, transparency, accountability, and non-discrimination. Equipped with these standards, institutions will ensure that AI systems are designed and used in ways compatible with ethical values and regulatory requirements. This means putting in place the internal frameworks and committees governing the development and deployment of AI, and ensuring the funneling of ethical considerations throughout the lifecycle of the AI.

Table 10.10. *(Continued)*

Application Area	Description
Effective data protection	The protection of data privacy is one of the dimensions of practices of responsible AI. The financial institutions have to adopt robust processes for protecting data related to their customers. This involves introducing data encryption, secure access controls, and anonymization techniques to protect the data against any form of unauthorized leakage or access that may lead to misuse. Moreover, it should ensure compliance with the institution's policies on data protection, such as the General Data Protection Regulation and California Consumer Privacy Act. Audits of data security practices are conducted regularly in order to detect vulnerabilities and handle potential threats.
Conducting bias and fairness audits	In order to rid AI models of this bias, financial institutions have regular bias and fairness audits. This means detailed analysis of AI models and their output to establish any form of discrimination or unintended bias. This way, institutions can use fairness-aware algorithms or diverse datasets when training to ensure that AI systems equitably work across different demographic groups. Engaging external auditors or ethics boards in the review of the AI systems will add further oversight to the process of evaluation and maintain impartiality in the review process.
Inclusive data practices	Inclusive data practice can help lighten bias and improve the accuracy of AI systems. The training datasets for financial institutions should capture data from diverse populations, making sure that therein lies a wide scope of experiences and views. It considers the sourcing of data from different sources and demographics so that this base of information will not perpetuate any prevailing disparities. Through diversity in data collection and model development, institutions can enhance the reliability and fairness of AI systems.

(Continued)

Table 10.10. *(Continued)*

Application Area	Description
Promote ongoing monitoring and evaluation	AI systems must be continuously monitored and evaluated to ensure their responsible use. Financial institutions should incorporate real-time mechanisms to track performance indicators, evaluate model outcomes, and adjust algorithms as needed. Regular updates and improvements, utilizing new data and feedback, are crucial for maintaining the validity of AI systems. This includes tracking key performance indicators, evaluating model outcomes, and adapting algorithms to regulatory changes.
Education and training of the stakeholders	A culture of responsibility would need employee and stakeholder education and training on ethics in AI and data privacy. Such institutions should be offered constant training programs by financial institutions on ethical practices in AI, regulations around data protection, and how to reduce bias. Empowering the staff with knowledge and skills for the responsible implementation of AI means that institutions are assured of the fact that ethical dimensions are built into the day-to-day activities and decision-making processes.
Mechanisms for accountability	The responsible deployment of AI involves clearly spelling out mechanisms of accountability. Every financial institution should, besides setting out roles and responsibilities for the oversight of artificial intelligence systems, clearly set accountability for their outcomes. This stretches to the appointment of personnel or teams who will take charge in ethics within AI, data privacy, and compliance. A well-defined process detailing how the ethical issues will be managed and the way concerns will be raised keeps oversight on track in ensuring that AI systems are run responsibly.

Source: Author's own creation.

13. Prospective

The consumer and patient experience will be impacted by ChatGPT in the future as it evolves and becomes more sophisticated. ChatGPT become educated to identify circumstances to which it can react. Future brand interactions will be supported exclusively by ChatGPT, notwithstanding its status as a major disruptor in the AI industry. ChatGPT is an accomplished and humanoid character that has inspired those who were hesitant to adopt conversational AI solutions and reassured skeptics regarding the potential of chatbot technology. While several major brands have already integrated AI technology into their service offerings, a greater proliferation of chatbots and other similar features will expand the avenues through which customers can interact with a brand. This, in turn, will facilitate the resolution of a greater number of inquiries and ultimately lead to increased customer satisfaction. ChatGPT has the potential to aid organizations in collecting critical customer data, ChatGPT has the capability to collect data regarding the preferences, behaviors and needs of consumers and patients.

ChatGPT will evolve into a versatile language model that can be applied to a multiplicity of projects, such as support automation and content creation. ChatGPT will have a profound effect on forthcoming approaches to providing patient and client care. The progression of technology will engender a desire among customers and patients for expedited and tailored service. In order to address these requirements, ChatGPT offers a scalable solution that enables organizations to deliver individualized and effective customer service at any time. ChatGPT and AI will have a substantial impact on the future of customer service delivery.

These technologies offer accelerated response times, customized assistance, and financial benefits for enterprises. The advancement of technology will contribute to the improvement of customer service, and businesses that embrace these developments will maintain a competitive edge. ChatGPT expeditiously generates and summarizes text requests (Sutskever et al., 2014; Vaswani, 2017). The chatbots undergo ongoing training in response to user feedback. Subsequent iterations may therefore incorporate alterations. As a result, it is difficult to provide a definitive response to the issue at hand. Its capability to understand and respond to natural language input renders it a formidable instrument for organizations and software developers. In the future, patients will utilize ChatGPT to gain knowledge regarding the benefits, hazards, and outcomes of therapy. Additionally, it will be utilized to comprehend adverse effects of therapy and medication adherence. To aid the recovery process, ChatGPT will assist patients in locating local support networks and resources. This may entail providing patients with referrals to community programs, support groups, or therapists that specifically cater to their needs and concerns (McCulloch & Pitts, 1943; Hochreiter, 1997; Hinton & Salakhutdinov, 2006). It will furnish patients with encouragement, inspiration, and aid throughout their medical expeditions.

There is enormous potential for ChatGPT to revolutionize many aspects of the fintech industry. Its applications can make loan and mortgage processes more interactive by engaging users in conversational interactions, gathering requisite information, and filling in forms, thus eliminating errors and improving the user experience. ChatGPT can also be an intelligent investment analysis tool that aids an investor by giving them insight into the evaluation of market data and other information that may be useful in prudent decision-making. Another area of application may be in automated account management, whereby ChatGPT may replace routine tasks, such as balance inquiries and money transfers, to improve operating efficiencies and cut down on costs. Further, ChatGPT may enhance the credit score and loan eligibility assessment by processing the customer's data and giving accurate creditworthiness appraisal in real-time. Finally, providing compliance and regulatory support by delivering regulatory information with accuracy and guiding the compliance frameworks is critical for financial institutions. Describing existing gaps within current research and advancing the areas of study, including those to be proposed in the future, is vital for the better development of applications for ChatGPT within fintech. Future studies need to work in terms of robustness with regard to AI, addressing biases so that decisions are fair and accurate. The solutions to data privacy need to be further developed to secure the sensitive data in finance under the stringent standards of data protection (IMF, 2023). Frameworks for ethical and fair AI should be put in place to avoid biased outcomes and ensure equal treatment of all customers. New use cases, such as investment research and legal drafting, can expand the value of ChatGPT in the fintech sector. These aspects will ensure that the challenges are reduced as the full potential of ChatGPT is being realized in transforming financial services.

The future of AI in fintech is one of great potential, with ChatGPT likely to be at the very center of innovation and transformation in this industry. From the perspective of current trends, not to mention the research opportunities, financial institutions can use ChatGPT to deliver personalized experiences and enhance decision-making processes on their road toward sustainable growth in the digital age.

In consideration of future directions and identified gaps the areas that would contribute further to the understanding and development of AI applications in fintech. Some major areas of attention, such as data privacy and security. While most of the current AI models in fintech often overlooked advanced techniques of privacy-preserving like differential privacy and federated learning, there is an urgent call for robust frameworks that could account comprehensively for such concerns altogether. Future research can be oriented toward the strengthening of privacy-preserving technologies and inventing secure systems impervious to adversarial attacks. Another critical gap is in accountability and transparency. Most AI models in use within fintech remain very complex which is hindering trust and compliance. It, therefore, has to target research in creating models that are interpretable and transparent – in the sense that stakeholders and laymen can understand AI decision-making processes. This can also be further supported by the establishment of standardized frameworks about explainability, which would foster consistency and clarity across a range of applications. This means a deeper look into bias and fairness in AI systems is a scope of research. Most of the techniques for detection and mitigation of bias that are in place today are insufficient, while comprehensive fairness metrics are absent. The key focus of future research should provide advanced bias detection and mitigation techniques and develop standard fairness metrics to assess fairness across many demographic groups and a host of financial products. Another challenge is integration with traditional systems. Many fintech firms really find it difficult to merge AI solutions with pre-existing legacy systems, thereby inhibiting proper implementation (Strusani & Houngbonon, 2019). Researchers need to find ways for the integration of artificial intelligence with traditional financial infrastructure and models that use new AI technologies in combination with older, established systems for better performance.

Regulatory and ethical frameworks around AI in fintech are still evolving, leaving much uncertainty around how regulations affect AI deployment and innovation. Research focus should be directed toward analyzing the implications of the emerging regulations, resulting in practical ethics guidance to balance regulatory compliance against business objectives. This will help align ethical considerations with AI design and deployment processes. Finally, understanding of how AI will impact customer experience and adoption to consider how AI influences user satisfaction, acceptance, and trust in the context of financial technology services is a necessary approach. Especially in the design of strategies targeted at improving customer engagement and adoption, it would be critical to identify the barriers to AI adoption – particularly in emerging markets. By addressing these research gaps that stakeholders can really drive forward the responsible and effective development of AI in fintech, guaranteeing that technologies under design and development are at once innovative and ethical.

To conclude, ChatGPT, a modern language generation model developed by OpenAI, is widely recognized for its ability to discern context and produce appropriate content.

14. Conclusion

Development of ChatGPT and the AI technologies underlying it has been a landmark change for many industries – the broad-based impact on customer service, healthcare, and financial technology operations. As the system develops further, it will become much more nuanced at identifying and articulating what the user needs, making it an invaluable resource for the provision of highly customized, effective, and scalable engagements. In the sphere of customer service, the input ChatGPT is able to give instant answers, modify solutions, and provide ongoing support and make a new wave in the way enterprises are going to interact with their customers. By optimizing and automating standard queries, ChatGPT would allow organizations to handle more and more customer interactions with accuracy and satisfaction. This ultimately leads to higher brand loyalty and a better overall user experience.

ChatGPT's impact in healthcare would be much beyond answering basic questions. It is capable of developing into a very useful tool for patient education, enabling better understanding of complex medical procedures, relative risks, and benefits in a more accessible form. Furthermore, ChatGPT could act as a personal assistant during the healthcare journey of a patient; it can offer emotional support, connect patients to local health services, and enable them to adhere to prescribed treatment regimens. This comprehensive assistance could foster a more informed and engaged patient population, ultimately improving health outcomes and reducing strain on healthcare professionals.

Another field that will be affected in depth is the area of fintech. Organizationally, integration into financial operations would enhance processes like loan applications, investment analysis, and customer account management, thus providing seamless, error-free interactions. This ability of ChatGPT to analyze huge amounts of market data will be beneficial in making informed decisions for investors. The use in regulatory compliance will assure the financial entities in their ability to comply with the complex and evolving legal structures. In developing such technology, it not only enhances operational efficiency but also user experience, thus giving fintech companies the edge they need. However, the intensive integration of artificial intelligence and ChatGPT poses several barriers to be maximally exploited. Principally, areas of concern relate to data privacy and security, particularly in finance and healthcare where sensitive information is frequently involved. Despite the enormous promises that ChatGPT holds for data collection and analysis, significant work remains to be done on robust privacy-preserving frameworks, differential privacy, and federated learning in order to protect private information and comply strictly with regulations. Bias and fairness in AI systems present one of the most significant challenges. Contemporary machine learning models often exhibit biases due to the data sets with which they are trained, potentially leading to unfair outcomes in such fields as credit scoring and recruitment. It is a matter of significant importance to develop advanced bias detection and mitigation methods, in combination with comprehensive fairness metrics, to ensure fair treatment for demographic populations.

The principles of transparency and accountability in AI decision-making processes are crucial to create trust and to ensure that the outcomes brought forth by AI are explainable to all stakeholders and the general public. In many cases, the complexity of the explanation of these decision-making mechanisms creates skepticism and hinders the widespread adoption of any such algorithm. Further research should be conducted in building explainable AI models and standardization frameworks so that the decision process of the AI system may be open to understanding for non-experts. Another challenge lies in the hybridization of artificial intelligence technologies with existing legacy systems. Most financial and health organizations are relying on old infrastructures, which will not be responsive to modern AI solutions. Overcoming technical hurdles would require the development of hybrid systems that can preserve traditional frames within them without hampering the capacity to exploit AI advantages while preserving existing infrastructures.

In a nutshell, as chatbots like ChatGPT become increasingly prevalent, the regulatory and ethical structures that support them must evolve in tandem. The governance structures surrounding the implementation of AI are in their early stages, so firms need to navigate this complex tapestry of constantly evolving regulations and standards. To do this, high-stakes industries – including finance and healthcare – will need suitable research on the ethical implications of AI to be deployed. This means

AI systems that are innovative but also ethical: ones that are novel and protective of user data, fair, and reduce the probability of harm. Overall, it is an incredible tool that can revolutionize different sectors and transform customer service, healthcare delivery, and financial processes. However, to unlock all the strength, in-depth study is required for the tackling of basic questions regarding data privacy, biasness, transparency, and integration with the existing legacy systems. Developing robust solutions to these issues will enable organizations to ensure that AI technologies, including ChatGPT, are applied responsibly, ethically, and effectively into everyday operations. This shall make it a future whereby AI is the new norm in any organization, the approach shall drive innovation; encourage trust and sustainable growth in the digital age while changing how businesses and individuals interact with technology in the end.

References

Accenture. (2020). The future of fintech and banking: Digital innovation, AI, and security. https://www.accenture.com/us-en/insights/operations/future-ready-banking-operations

Amodei, D., Olah, C., Steinhardt, J., Christiano, P., Schulman, J., & Mané, D. (2016). Concrete problems in AI safety. arXiv preprint arXiv:1606.06565.

Bajracharya, A., Khakurel, U., Harvey, B., & Rawat, D. B. (2022, October). Recent advances in algorithmic biases and fairness in financial services: A survey. In *Proceedings of the future technologies conference* (pp. 809–822). Springer International Publishing.

Benjamin, L. B., Amajuoyi, P., & Adeusi, K. B. (2024). Marketing, communication, banking, and fintech: Personalization in fintech marketing, enhancing customer communication for financial inclusion. *International Journal of Management & Entrepreneurship Research*, 6(5), 1687–1701.

Betterment. https://www.betterment.com/how-it-works

Brown, T. B. (2020). Language models are few-shot learners. arXiv preprint arXiv: 2005.14165.

Buchanan, B. G. (2019). *Artificial intelligence in finance*. The Alan Turing Institute.

Buczynski, W., Cuzzolin, F., & Sahakian, B. (2021). A review of machine learning experiments in equity investment decision-making: Why most published research findings do not live up to their promise in real life. *International Journal of Data Science and Analytics*, 11, 221–242.

Deloitte. (2022). How AI is shaping the future of financial services. https://www.deloitte.com/nz/en/Industries/financial-services/blogs/ai-in-financial-services.html

Deloitte Insights. (2024). The implications of generative AI in finance - A new frontier in artificial intelligence and for finance. https://www.deloitte.com/global/en/services/consulting/perspectives/generative-ai-in-finance.html

Global Partnership on Artificial Intelligence. (2023). *Responsible AI*. https://gpai.ai/projects/

Gulshan, V., Peng, L., Coram, M., Stumpe, M. C., Wu, D., Narayanaswamy, A., Venugopalan, S., Widner, K., Madams, T., Cuadros, J., Kim, R., Raman, R., Nelson, P. C., Mega, J. L., & Webster, D. R. (2016). Development and validation of a deep learning algorithm for detection of diabetic retinopathy in retinal fundus photographs. *JAMA, 316*(22), 2402–2410.

He, M., Li, Z., Liu, C., Shi, D., & Tan, Z. (2020). Deployment of artificial intelligence in real-world practice: Opportunity and challenge. *Asia-Pacific Journal of Ophthalmology, 9*(4), 299–307.

Heim, M. P., Starckjohann, N., & Torgersen, M. (2023). *The convergence of AI and cybersecurity: An examination of ChatGPT's role in penetration testing and its ethical and legal implications.* Bachelor's thesis. NTNU.

Hinton, G. E., & Salakhutdinov, R. R. (2006). Reducing the dimensionality of data with neural networks. *Science, 313*(5786), 504–507.

Hochreiter, S. (1997). Long short-term memory. *Neural Computation, 9*(8). MIT-Press.

IMF. (2023). Generative artificial intelligence in finance. FinTech Notes Volume 2023 Issue 006.

Juniper Research. (2019). AI in fintech: Roboadvisors, lending, insurtech & regtech 2019–2023. https://www.juniperresearch.com/

Mastercard. *Industry perspectives on AI and transaction fraud detection.* Mastercard. https://b2b.mastercard.com/news-and-insights/blog/industry-perspectives-on-ai-and-transaction-fraud-detection/

McCulloch, W. S., & Pitts, W. (1943). A logical calculus of the ideas immanent in nervous activity. *Bulletin of Mathematical Biophysics, 5*(4), 115–133.

McKinsey. (2021). Managing the risks and returns of intelligent automation. *McKinsey Insights.* https://www.mckinsey.com/~/media/mckinsey/business%20functions/opera tions/our%20insights/managing%20the%20risks%20and%20returns%20of%20intel ligent%20automation/managing-the-risks-and-returns-of-intelligent-automation_final.pdf

Morabito, V., & Morabito, V. (2015). Big data and analytics innovation practices. In *Big data and analytics: Strategic and organizational impacts* (pp. 157–176).

Palantir. https://www.palantir.com/offerings/financial-services/

Park, Y., Kim, J., Jiang, Q., & Kim, K. H. (2024). Impact of artificial intelligence (AI) chatbot characteristics on customer experience and customer satisfaction. *Journal of Global Scholars of Marketing Science, 34*(3), 439–457.

Radford, A., Wu, J., Child, R., Luan, D., Amodei, D., & Sutskever, I. (2019). Language models are unsupervised multitask learners. *OpenAI Blog, 1*(8), 9.

Siegmann, C., & Anderljung, M. (2022). The Brussels effect and artificial intelligence: How EU regulation will impact the global AI market. arXiv preprint arXiv:2208.12645.

Strubell, E., Ganesh, A., & McCallum, A. (2020, April). Energy and policy considerations for modern deep learning research. *Proceedings of the AAAI Conference on Artificial Intelligence, 34*(09), 13693–13696.

Strusani, D., & Houngbonon, G. V. (2019). *The role of artificial intelligence in supporting development in emerging markets.* International Finance Corporation.

Suryono, R. R., Budi, I., & Purwandari, B. (2020). Challenges and trends of financial technology (fintech): A systematic literature review. *Information, 11.* https://doi.org/10.3390/info11120590.

Sutskever, I., Vinyals, O., & Le, Q. V. (2014). Sequence to sequence learning with neural networks. In *Advances in neural information processing systems* (pp. 3104–3112).

Tan, Z., Wang, H., & Hong, Y. (2023). Does bank FinTech improve corporate innovation? *Finance Research Letters*, 103830.

Topol, E. J. (2019). High-performance medicine: The convergence of human and artificial intelligence. *Nature Medicine, 25*(1), 44–56.

Upstart. AI lending platform. https://www.nafcu.org/upstart

Vaswani, A. (2017). Attention is all you need. In *Advances in neural information processing systems* (pp. 6000–6010).

Veluru, C. S. (2024). Investigating the impact of artificial intelligence and generative AI in E-commerce and supply chain: A comprehensive. *European Journal of Advances in Engineering and Technology, 11*(4), 131–143.

Verghese, A., Shah, N. H., & Harrington, R. A. (2018). What this computer needs is a physician: Humanism and artificial intelligence. *JAMA, 319*(1), 19–20.

Wadhwa, V., & Kumar, D. S. (2023). Role and impact of AI in fintech industry. *IJPREMS, 3*(11).

Wealthfront. https://www.wealthfront.com/robo-advisor-investing

Willis, M. S. (2023). *The impact of personalization in financial marketing on consumer sentiment and preference.* Wilmington University.

World Bank. (2024). Tipping the scales: AI's dual impact on developing nations. https://blogs.worldbank.org/en/digital-development/tipping-the-scales–ai-s-dual-impact-on-developing-nations

World Economic Forum. (2023). *Technology for a more resilient world, Davos 2023.* World Economic Forum. https://www.weforum.org/events/world-economic-forum-annual-meeting-2023/sessions/technology-for-a-more-resilient-world/

Yang, Z., Hyman, M. R., & Zhou, X. (2020). Impact of artificial intelligence on business in emerging markets. *Series: Earth and Environmental Science, 421*, 42020.

ZestFinance using AI to bring fairness to mortgage lending. *Forbes.* https://www.forbes.com/sites/donnafuscaldo/2019/03/19/zestfinance-using-ai-to-bring-fairness-to-mortgage-lending/#:~:text=ZestFinance%2C%20the%20artificial%20intelligence%20software,biases%20and%20discrimination%20in%20lending

Zhang, M., & Yang, J. (2019, January). Research on financial technology and inclusive finance development. In *2018 6th international education, economics, social science, arts, sports and management engineering conference (IEESASM 2018)* (pp. 66–71). Atlantis Press.

Chapter 11

Revolutionizing Financial Inclusion: ChatGPT's Role in Redefining Economic Growth and Poverty Alleviation

Richa Goel[a] *and Rupa Khanna Malhotra*[b]

[a]Graphic Era Deemed to be University, India and Symbiosis Centre for Management Studies, Noida, Symbiosis International (Deemed University), Pune, India
[b]Graphic Era Deemed to be University, India

Abstract

This chapter aims at exploring the opportunities posed by ChatGPT in matters concerning financial innovation for economic development with special reference to poverty reduction. The study's objective is to assess the abilities of ChatGPT for financial inclusion that enhances sustainable development in the underbanked communities. The method of analysis includes the compilation and examination of reviews found within the extant literature considering the themes of financial inclusion, artificial intelligence, and digital transformation. This chapter integrates evaluation of prior and current academic studies, industry and market reports, and case studies to account for the identification of ChatGPT as a solution to existing and emerging financial issues and as a potential means of creating value for underserved audiences. The analysis shows that ChatGPT has the potential to contribute greatly to the process of increasing the level of financial literacy, especially in the developing countries, as well as to assist in enhancing the banking experience by offering better and personalized recommendations, reducing paper burden and language barriers. The main benefits of AI chatbots include enhancing the access to banking services in the society thus contributing to the demographic financial inclusion, poverty alleviation. The study shows that ChatGPT has the prospect for the disruption of the financial services industry through affordable solutions that promote financial literacy. And it focuses on the need for AI adoption as a key driver of

The ChatGPT Revolution, 239–255
Copyright © 2025 Richa Goel and Rupa Khanna Malhotra
Published under exclusive licence by Emerald Publishing Limited
doi:10.1108/978-1-83549-852-120251011

financial change for unlocking economic development and eradicating poverty in emerging markets.

Keywords: Financial inclusion; ChatGPT; AI; economic growth; poverty alleviation; digital transformation; sustainability; financial literacy

1. Introduction

The relationship between financial inclusion and economic development has drawn much attention among the development organizations as the former holds a central role on the latter. Demirgüç-Kunt et al. (2018) hold the view that financial inclusion refers to the extent to which people and firms are able to use affordable and relevant financial services. It is necessary for eradicating poverty and enhancing the levels of inequality to transform the economy to one that will benefit all people. However, more than 1.7 billion people today do not have access to this product and most of them live in developing countries and this factor hinders the achievement of fair economic progress (World Bank, 2022). Financial inclusion is seen as one of the key preconditions for sustainable development of the economy. Further with the help of new technologies development including artificial intelligence – the aspect of financial inclusion becomes opened by new tools. Such innovation solutions as GPT allow for transforming financial inclusion for those who cannot apply for a traditional bank, since they are geographically isolated or they have no basic knowledge about finances. AI tools at work help underbanked population get better and efficient financial services which helps to increase the degree of economic development. In this chapter, the author aims to investigate how ChatGPT is helpful to the development of Financial Inclusion along with facilitating sustainable economic development in emerging regions.

1.1 Overview of Financial Inclusion and Economic Growth

The role of financial services in early economies and specifically, in the developing countries has been well acknowledged as a major factor for economic growth. A sample of these products includes savings, credit, and insurance services, enabling the needy communities to manage economically within the defined economy thus enhancing growth. The performance of financial inclusion with economic growth has been featured in analysis that proved that nations with higher index of financial inclusion provided better results on economy (Sahay et al., 2015). An efficient financial system which is in a position to serve the entire population is crucial in efficient provision of capital and to lower the costs of intermediation and encouraging more of entrepreneurial activities. Financial inclusion is considered useful in poverty decrease. When people have a form of financial services, then they are in a position to mitigate their risks in terms of their finance, learn, acquire health and innovate small businesses and hence in supporting economic growth as described by Cull et al. (2014). Furthermore, technological financial helps in wider economic stability in so far as it increases tax revenues base and a stronger economy whose financial system is not easily affected by shocks.

1.2 Role of Artificial Intelligence in Financial Services

Computerization is rapidly changing the face of financial services through mechanisms like automating processes and front facing services, enhanced consumers' services, and even on providing relevant data culled from databases to assist in correct decision making. Perhaps one of the largest benefits of AI applications in financial services is that it can improve financial access in remote areas. The ADC such AI enabled Chatbot like ChatGPT they can provide immediate and individualized response which can enable the banking and financial services to erase the physical need and make financial services more accessible. Arner et al. (2020) opine that AI technologies are currently in use by financial institutions in delivering advice as well as facilitating services to new and existing clients, including the inhibited regions with relatively low levels of banking. Singh et al. (2023) assert that, conversely, AI innovations such as the example of current solution. Chat GPT can assist in responding to the shortage of financial literacy. AI can enhance credit via big data analysis which can help lenders to make decisions for the customers, especially individuals and SMBs, who even have no credit history. Moreover, using AI-driven platforms customers' frauds are identified more efficiently, and the security of users, which is one of the significant components of developing trust in the financial system, will be enhanced.

The financial industry may be able to reduce costs and increase operational efficiency through the application of AI. They can maintain low costs of operations, hence realize low charges even to the low-income clients by embracing Artificial Intelligence where simple exercises like account maintenance, customer support, and transaction are automated. Thus, it could be noted that AI is one of the critical enablers of change driving the financial services industry with new possibilities of financial inclusion and economic opportunities.

1.3 Purpose of the Chapter: Exploring ChatGPT's Potential in Financial Inclusion and Poverty Alleviation

The goal of this chapter is to identify how an Artificial Intelligence Chat Bot, specifically ChatGPT can be utilized to solve problems related to financial inclusion and poverty. The constant acceleration of the digital transformation process has placed AI technologies at the center of the process of extending the access to financial services to the deprived and vulnerable groups. ChatGPT has the potential to cause a significant impact on the traditional banking sector by replacing branch-based services with more personalized and convenient options.

They can be used to deliver timely financial advice, increase financial literacy, and avoid the disadvantages that have excluded people from the financial sector for many years. The approach used in this chapter is the review approach that analyzes literature, case studies, and market reports on financial inclusion, AI, and digital transformation. In this way, the study assesses the feasibility of using ChatGPT to advance financial inclusion and establish whether the technology can facilitate appropriate financial service access in developing nations. The analysis also reveals that ChatGPT can help surmount barriers like low financial literacy and language as a barrier that have posed great difficulties in the past for promoting financial inclusion (Goldstein and McAfee, 2020). From an applications perspective, this chapter translates knowledge of financial inclusion issues into recommendations of how financial institutions and policymakers can utilize ChatGPT to advance a more participative form of financing. This chapter ends with the author stressing the importance of AI solutions in driving both economic growth and poverty reduction in new economies where conventional financial services have not been capable of filling the need.

2. Theoretical Foundation

The framework of financial inclusion, more so financial development and other theories in the advance technology links core theories that relate to these variables. The theories of economic development are discussed when considering financial inclusion, focusing on the financial services that should be available for sufficient development. More specifically, from the Capability Approach, it follows that access to financial services increases people's economic agency (Sen, 1999). Science delivers a key role in reshaping mature financial segments, including possibilities emerging from contemporary developments like artificial intellect (AI) offering novel channels to entry and novel approaches to productivity. Second, the Innovation Diffusion Theory (IDT), described by Rogers (2003), can provide an appreciation of the diffusion of new technologies in markets and how innovations may improve the level of financial literacy and catalyze economic growth. Taken as a whole, these theoretical approaches explain by AI-based solutions can enhance the provision of financial services to the poor and also the fight against poverty. These theories then point to the affirmative relationship between AI and the traditional financial services and technology to show how technology can transform the financial sector and support economic development.

2.1 Theories of Financial Inclusion and Economic Development

Concepts of financial services and economic development explain the basic understanding of why financial services matter to economic growth. According to Sen (1999), capability approach of financial inclusive shows that through financial services the individuals' standard in the economic realm is boosted gain freedom to make rational opportunities. This theoretical context closely postulates that stock raider commands power through financing thereby creating a sustainable economy. Also, the Financial Intermediation Theory explains the intermediation of savings and the efficient financial resource allocation (Zins & Weill, 2016). Hear when they get to those on the periphery, they erase poverty and promote business among the poor. Rojas-Suarez (2016) continues the documentation of the fact showing the diversification of financial access helps to stabilize the economy, which materially decreases the risks of the low-income households. Appropriate evidence shows that the more increase in financial access the higher economic performance is and the levels of poverty (World Bank, 2018). Providing healthcare and education for the long-term expansion of financial structures is another way that financial inclusion fosters the development of human capital. As a result, the incorporation of Fintech in economic development framework is imperative where the aim is to realize sustainable economic growth coupled with a favorable status in the formula: systematic approach to social justice.

2.2 Technological Disruption Theory in Financial Services

Technological Disruption Theory (TDT) looks at how advances can redefine the structure of industries in general and such field as financial services. Innovations targeting the financially underserved bring the disruptive technologies to a more streamlined and value-generating solution with a lower price and to markets that aren't reached by traditional financial institutions. In the financial services industry, the mobile banking industry is the primary area that has been affected with the delivery and consumption of services being revolutionized with the help of AI and artificial intelligence technologies inclusive of ChatGPT. The authors Arner et al. (2020) observe that such technologies assist in an elimination of barriers to financial information for such persons. Through financial advice and enhancement of customer experiences, AI thus enhances the level of financial inclusion. Access to financial services is made possible by technological disruption, which encourages those who are financially excluded to interact with the financial system. This shift is beneficial for the economy as a whole because it stimulates spending and the start of new businesses, in addition to the individual consumer. Understanding the consequences of technology disruption is the key factor for all parties interested in the application of AI in the finance to uplift financial inclusion and contribute to the evolution of the economy.

2.3 The Role of Innovation Diffusion Theory in AI Adoption

Innovation Diffusion Theory (IDT) helps to explain the process of using fresh technologies in various markets including AI. Nary developed by Rogers (2003), IDT also emphasizes on the aspects of communication networks, communication media, and perceived characteristics of innovations. In the case of AI in financial services, issues of ease of use, compatibility, adaptability, flexibility, divisibility, and visibility are considerations that apply to designing interfaces like ChatGPT. The relative advantage of AI in improving customer relationship and in increasing customer understanding of financial products is a basis for encouraging financial institutions (Goldstein & McAfee, 2020). Also, as organizations watch other financial services institutions implement AI, the noticeable positive results will prompt other companies to adopt the technology. The availability of internet and mobile technology have fast-tracked the diffusion of AI solutions to the unserved people to access the services. Through minimizing barriers like complexity and enhanced user interfaces, institutions in the financial sectors are capable of broadening the usage across different users (Venkatesh & Davis, 2000). Finally, IDT highlights how critical it is to use AI technologies to rethink financial services and implement the idea of financial inclusion for emerging nations with under-developed banking infrastructure.

3. ChatGPT and Financial Inclusion

ChatGPT an AI-based language model has the explicit ability to transform the financial sector especially in penetrating the hard-to reach individuals of financial services. Financial inclusion simply means offering of basic financial services including savings, credit, and insurance to people who are disadvantaged and cannot access formal financial institutions. Since one of ChatGPT's strong points is NLP, it can also help to popularize financial services among those who have limited access to relevant services due to limited literacy or language, or living in remote areas. Further sections discuss the general use of ChatGPT in the context of finance, coupled with the capability of the latter to increase users' financial literacy, as well as instances of AI integration into services provided to the underbanked people.

3.1 Overview of ChatGPT's Capabilities in Financial Services

ChatGPT has remarkable features through which it can help financial institutions and customers as well. Because of its capability to synthesize text that is as natural as that produced by human beings, it can effectively tackle the language barriers that exist when it comes to service delivery between diverse clients and providers from different parts of the world. This will reduce the cost of customer services as recommendations are made to the users, in general, cutting down overall costs. ChatGPT can be implemented into customer service as part of self-service to provide quick answers to frequently asked questions regarding products and services and also assist customers in the proper understanding of complex financial products and services (Ghatak & Lall, 2020). Through ChatGPT, financial institutions can be able to answer simple questions that customers might be asking frequently, offer prompt support to clients and help customers who are not very conversant with online banking platforms to create accounts. Moreover, with the help of AI such as ChatGPT systems fraud can be detected and prevented by analyzing patterns and making predictions which are highly desirable since they play essential role in building and maintaining trust regarding safety issues in the financial services (Dwivedi et al., 2021).

3.2 Potential of ChatGPT to Enhance Financial Literacy and Access for the Underbanked

Perhaps one of the most appealing and valuable features of ChatGPT is the ability to improve the utilization of financial services and products among the now lesser financially included population. The size, complexity, and current state of development of the formal financial sector influence the level of financial inclusion: people with better financial knowledge are more likely to use services of the existing organized financial institutions. Also, based on the type of query it can recommend books, describe an asset class, as well as share pointers and how-to-do-its related to a particular activity such as account opening or loan application (Rashid & Ratten, 2022). Because the model is designed to engage in conversations, it is possible for users to ask specific questions concerning their financial dilemmas and get appropriate responses to their questions making financial literacy possible. Moreover, we pointed out that, in addition to its ability to provide recommendations based on the requested information, ChatGPT can translate and simplify financial industry terms, thus increasing the prospects of financial services use by low literacy consumers. In multilingual settings and where illiteracy levels are high, deficiencies in language translation provide a clear opening for ChatGPT to extend the facility of banking services to the populace.

3.3 Case Examples of AI's Role in Improving Financial Services for Underserved Communities

AI has proved to be very effective in enhancing access to financial services for the marginalized groups across the world. Here are few detailed case examples illustrating its transformative role:

India: AI Chatbots for Digital Banking: In India many places especially in the villages geographical barriers are very common thus the use of the AI-powered chatbots has enabled many people in the rural areas to open and operate online banking accounts easily. HDFC Bank Limited and State Bank of India have made use of AI chatbots for enabling customers to open accounts, enabling them to transfer funds and availing loans. Such chatbots offer instant help meaning that users can accomplish functions that they would normally have to travel to the nearest branch to undertake this usually situated many miles away. The bots also support multiple regional languages, thus minimizing language barriers that limit the uptake of financial services by a non-English speaking rural population (Pal & Bandyopadhyay, 2022). This has greatly improved financial inclusion as it has extended digital banking services to those areas where it is practically difficult to access other financial services.

Sub-Saharan Africa: AI-Driven Mobile Banking In Sub-Saharan Africa: With more than 50% of the population being outside the formal banking system, mobile banking platforms based on artificial intelligence are now the most vital tools in the region (Mothobi & Kebotsamang, 2024). A perfect example of such an application is the M-Pesa launched by the Safaricom company combined with IBM's Watson AI. Through integration, AI has been able to check transactions carry out, point suspect activities and even recommend financial products depending on users' transactions profile. AI is also used to provide the financial education and share credit scores derived from the non-traditional sources so that users who have no credit history can get the loans (Dahlberg et al., 2015). AI in this context is definitely a tool that connects more individuals to the formally regulated financial system while also increasing their levels of financial education and incentives.

Kenya: The mobile money platform of Kenya is called M-Pesa and is a perfect example of how everyone in a society can have a basic account powered by technology. Together with AI systems, M-Pesa has gone to offer micro-financing service, savings, and loans products. Due to AI, M-Pesa has been in a position to track fraud as it occurs hence lowering the amount of money lost to fraud and thus increasing the amount of security in mobile cash services (Muthiora, 2015). As for the credit scores, AI also helps to create easy to understand financial products that are affordable for small business owners and low-income families with no credit history in most cases.

Brazil: In the Fintech Solutions: Fintech solutions like Nubank in Brazil explain how companies such as Nubank have disrupted the provision of financial services to communities that are often locked out by traditional banks using the incorporation of AI into their digital banking solutions. Nubank leverages artificial intelligence to deliver affordable and convenient financial services such as credit cards solutions, savings accounts, and personal loans to millions of customers who were locked out from the traditional financial system. One of the most compelling impacts and benefits for the consumer through the use of AI for Nubank is self-servicing of customer needs and servicing at a lesser cost compared to Nubank's cost of customer servicing. They also help to improve buyer experience by making recommendation on products from past transaction records and spending patterns (Kshetri, 2021).

Bangladesh: AI-Integrated Mobile Financial Services Through bKash: In the context of Bangladesh, the mobile financial services function through bKash has a step forward in the integration of AI-enabled financial services to the mass population. The platform's technical features include artificial intelligence that provides individualized financial recommendations, facilitates mobile payment, and optimizes customer support. AI chatbots facilitate customer relations through which people conduct banking transactions such as fund transfer and payment of bills using their mobile phones without having to visit a bank. AI offers flexible micro loan solutions to small business bearers' majority of whom operate in the rural areas and do not qualify for conventional banking services (Mukherjee & Chatterjee, 2023).

Indonesia: To fund small business owners – especially women in rural areas who lack official records of their financial history, companies such as Amartha use artificial intelligence to evaluate the creditworthiness of such borrowers. AI considers numerous data sources that are not specific to credit histories, including mobile phone usage and social media to build credit histories and allow these businesspeople to get credit facilities. This has helped under-privileged groups to care for themselves by engaging in business and ergo hence cutting the costs they need to meet (Mahmudi & Ramadhani, 2024). AI is also used to reduce risk by coming up with probability of loan default which enhances scalability of P2P lending.

Mexico: AI and Micro finance with Konfio which is a Fintech company of Mexico that provides micro-finance to SMEs which are restricted in accessing credits from conventional bank. Using machine learning, Konfio is also able to include other forms of credit data like sales, tax returns, and even social media activity to assess credit risk to extend loans to businesses that would be overlooked by traditional financial institutions. This has especially been a boost to SMEs in rural and semi urban areas where acquisition of capital is a major issue (Campuzano & Crisanto, 2020). Konfio through the use of automatons credit assessment of the borrower's ability to repay hence it was able to cut down on the time taken in the approval of loans hence making financial services more affordable to busi-ness that are consistence with the leadership's goal of developing the economy.

Understanding more about the real contexts in which ChatGPT-like AI technology operates, as revealed by the above actual case studies, is a step toward understanding how the use of AI to support and deepen financial inclusion is gaining increased influence. Today, Artificial Intelligence plays an essential role in coming to the edges of marginalized society because it reduces costs, enhances the flexibility of service delivery, and eliminates previously impenetrable boundaries such as language and geographical restrictions. AI holds the capacity to power financial services that, in turn, can alleviate poverty levels among the population especially in developing countries where the majorities of the citizens are locked out from other conventional banking systems.

4. Impact on Poverty Alleviation

The existence of ChatGPT is an exciting chance for financial organizations to move to the next level that targets the poverty-stricken population in the areas where financial services are still restricted. With such offered financial services, breaking linguistic barriers and complicated paperwork, peculiar focus on inclusion, and value, ChatGPT can bring major shifts to financially less fortunate societies. These contributions correspond with the main initiative that has been recognized as important in poverty minimization and economic growth commonly known as financial inclusion (Demirgüç-Kunt et al., 2022).

4.1 ChatGPT's Role in Providing Personalized Financial Solutions

Some of the advantages of using ChatGPT in financial services include the ability of ChatGPT to generate unique financial advice and solutions depending on the user. Consequently, using such data as user data, financial behavior, and preferences, ChatGPT is capable of recommending specific solutions including microloans, personal savings plans, and insurance products, which are rather significant for the population living in underprivileged districts (Awasthi, 2023). Personalized services can assist people in proper financial planning and avoid such mistakes as can lead to bad planning and spending or no planning at all and no savings for the financially unstable future. This is especially critical for Africa as they are among the under-banked population; AI systems can offer cheap and equally efficient services in areas where conventional banking services are either inaccessible or too expensive. The aforementioned can be achieved by a chatbot such as ChatGPT which can mimic financial advisors who are available to provide advise round the clock thereby being cost effective and introducing services to desk less areas. This democratization of financial advice is a significant force in poverty eradication because people have to make better decisions that would otherwise give them higher standards of living.

4.2 Reducing Barriers Like Language and Paperwork for Marginalized Populations

Among the key factors that hinder the growth of the financially excluded are language and bureaucracy, which go hand in hand in excluding the groups of people who mostly require such services. Most financial organizations demand formulation of complex documents and communication, a factor that may prove cumbersome to persons in areas of low literacy. Through natural understanding of text and speech, ChatGPT is able to communicate with users in different languages and thus enhance the provision of financial products and services since its target users' market encompass minority and illiterate population. Also, AI technologies as ChatGPT make repetitive and time-consuming tasks for preparing needed documentation for receiving loans or for accountancy easier. By automating these processes, ChatGPT saves time and energy thus extending the interaction with banking sector to those who cannot directly access financial services. This is especially useful in the developing world, where structural constraints such as bureaucratic red tape disbar people from the financial systems.

4.3 How ChatGPT Contributes to Inclusive Growth

ChatGPT's ability to render affordable, efficient, and promptly available financial services are of great importance in promoting Inclusive Growth. Financial sector is therefore inversely related with poverty because financial access enhances the capacity of individuals and firms to access loans and invest in products to reduce poverty levels in the economy (Demirgüç-Kunt et al., 2022). ChatGPT can help to mediate the provision of financial services thus helping to bring the cost of these services down and thus increase financial inclusion for the financially less well off in society. Furthermore, AI's applicability to promote financial illiteracy can help raise levels of consumer and investors awareness thus, serve as a tool to improve economy (Rane et al., 2024). Customers of ChatGPT can be given basic knowledge on how they can start preparing for their financial future through the various investment and savings' plans. However, the availability of basic financial services and the rise in financial literacy are crucial in helping the formerly marginalized populations of the population overcome poverty, advance economic development, and close the gap that separates them from the rest of society.

5. Challenges and Opportunities

There are many advantages and disadvantages of artificial intelligence (AI) in financial services, especially with regard to ChatGPT. Although there is great potential to increase financial inclusion, improve literacy, and decrease poverty, there are still significant obstacles to overcome, especially in emerging nations. These obstacles include inadequate infrastructure, unfavorable regulations, and technology limitations. As we examine these difficulties and possibilities, it becomes evident that, although artificial intelligence (AI) has a lot of promise, realizing these advantages and getting the most out of ChatGPT and other AI-driven solutions will be necessary for AI to be deployed effectively.

5.1 Barriers to AI Adoption in Emerging Markets

The often-compelling dynamics of emerging markets create issues which slow the pace of AI technology implementation. This is probably one of the biggest challenges, namely the absence of IT structures and restrictions with regard to internet connection and the use of artificial intelligence utilities. Many developing countries still face the problem of digital divide, and significant part of the population does not have the access to stable and affordable Internet connection (Zhao et al., 2024). Digital connectivity is already flawed, and such tool as ChatGPT cannot be utilized to reach such communities mentioned above. As such, the role of infrastructural issues and the ubiquity of regulatory and policy-related barriers contribute to the constrained use of AI technologies to the financial industry. Most of the emerging market governments have not yet established strong legal structures that can enable the application of AI while Aga (2017) mentions challenges like data privacy, cybersecurity, and corporate accountability for AI in decision-making. Lack of science around governed rules means that the integration of AI could unknown legal and reputational risks that may scare financial institutions away from applying AI in their various systems. In addition, cultural and societal dimension of AI adoption cannot also be completely ignored. Sides et al. (2024) pointed out that across most areas, people do not have confidence in technology, and the fear of losing jobs hinders the implementation of AI. Most consumer markets are situated in emerging markets that have low levels of financial literacy, and again, the idea that artificial intelligence could act as a substitute rather than an augmentation of human labor contributes to the there being so many concerns regarding AI-based solutions. These challenges imply that AI is amenable to development, but that circumstantial and cultural obstacles must be surmounted in emerging economies. A large number of the population in many emerging markets especially in the rural areas lacks the necessary skills for engaging with digital applications (Sarpong et al., 2023). This means that even with an increasing advancement in AI and financial service provision it might not reach everyone without an effective digital education programs in place.

5.2 Opportunities for Improving Access to Financial Services Through ChatGPT

The most significant and to some extent the exciting latitude of ChatGPT is that language barriers and bureaucracies, which have locked lowly and marginalized individuals out of the financial systems, can be majorly addressed here. As mentioned, with the help of natural language processing capabilities, ChatGPT is capable to speak different languages therefore, extend accessibility to the financial services to the non-English speakers and illiterates. Indeed, ChatGPT has vast potential in delivering tailor-made financial advice in real time to usage that has not been touched in the past, underbanked population. Based on the data provided by users, ChatGPT can provide financial services such as savings accounts, microloans, insurance products, and other types of financial products suitable for users in different districts, including districts with low income. The service provision can assist people in making sound decisions to manage their money properly without falling into the wrong hands due to financial absurdities; thus, it can decrease their economic risks (Sharma, 2023). Another advantage of AI is its modularity; people can gain access to this service at a large scale. These conventional services entail costly physical facilities, which limits the ability of the banks to scale their operations to the rural and other unserved markets. However, the applications of ChatGPT can be done online thus need a less set up and hence the cost of addressing the challenges affecting delivery of financial services (Holmes & Porayska-Pomsta, 2023). The last aspect is helpful since it enables financial institutions to expand their client base at a much lower cost when compared to traditional banking services. Of course, apart from quantitative solutions, ChatGPT can also serve as an educational tool by increasing people's financial literacy. A clear application of the technology in the finance sector is in the development of smart and stakeholder-useable financial literacy applications that actively teach learners about personal financial management, investment, and saving.

The other major benefit is that AI can help to reduce and robotic most of the bureaucratic procedures. It is common to find that many people in such areas experience challenges in their access to financial services because most transactions involve cumbersome paperwork and other bureaucracies. This way ChatGPT can handle these tasks and ease the burden on the users in order to open an account, apply for a loan or even access other financial services. This automation also eliminates chances of human errors but is also advantaging to the financial institutions and the respective customers. Last but not the least for AI-based fin-tech solution such as ChatGPT, there is most likely to affect traditional financial mechanisms by proposing cheaper and better solutions. For many areas, which have previously been locked out by high banking fees or more stringent eligibility requirements, ChatGPT offers an opportunity for those in the low-income bracket. Availing cheaper forms of financial platforms, AI solutions can thus help in the eradication of poverty and enhancing economic developmental approaches.

6. Conclusion

6.1 Summary of ChatGPT's Impact on Financial Inclusion and Economic Development

Chat GPT in the Financial Services Scenario can be seen as a revolutionary step that has moved to the new world of creating financial possibilities and ensuring financial accessibility. As a result of its state-of-the-art natural language processing functions, ChatGPT can overcome the challenges that previously less privileged groups encountered in engaging with the banking system. That's why the app provides users with an easy-to-understand interface for using various financial instruments and helps to eliminate barriers to financial illiteracy. Rather than entrepreneurial classes giving financial education to individuals and enabling them to manage their resources and contribute to the welfare of their economy. In addition, ChatGPT offers specific financial services and products that will directly target those underbanked populations. It can also make more relevant basic suggestions for saving, investing or spending money based on available input data and context. Such an approach not only guides the persons to manage their financial scenario but also contributes toward positive financial practices which are necessary for the overall economic development of any country. Also, it not only improves the financial literacy and provides recommendations based on the probabilities of success but also minimizes the operational constraints usually correlated to conventional financial services. It decreases the chance of having to go physically to offices thus helpful to those who live in the rural areas. Predictably, ChatGPT ushers' potential clients with logistical challenges into direct interaction with the financial system and well-developed financial services. This is much relevant in the developing world where traditional banking infrastructure such as checks and actually physical banking space and facilities are extremely lacking. When a number of people get financially included, they acquire the ability to engage themselves in the economy and hence increase on the levels of productivity and or output levels. Moreover, as more people accesses to financial resources, local businesses can be promoted, job opportunities shall be created and community capacity can be built and be strengthened.

6.2 Future Outlook for AI in Financial Services and Poverty Reduction

This chapter reveals that AI's future in the financial services sector and its implications on poverty reduction look optimistic, especially tools like ChatGPT. With technological advancement, the possibilities of artificial intelligence will still increase thus extending to the possibilities of more developments to cater for financial exclusion. One promising avenue is the potential to incorporate AI with other new trends like blockchain and mobile payments, which will improve the usability and safety of the financial operations to the target population, even without proper credits. On the same note, as algorithms advance, it will become easier to capture large data sets and therefore perform better risk profiling and credit rating. This will enable the financial institutions to extend credit facilities and financial products to more people, especially those who may be considered to be high risks thus increasing credit access for the minority groups will be made possible through the collaboration of governments, players in the private sector, and other non-profit making organizations. Efforts to promote effective adoption of AI tools in undeveloped communities will improve its effectiveness of these technologies. Policymaker will also have ensured that Apps, policies, and standards to endure responsible training and deployment of AI systems to Financial Services providers. While protecting the rights of the consumers and their data Further, the integration of ChatGPT into the financial services sector is a step toward increasing access to finance or achieving financial inclusion to reduce the level of poverty. With the continuous advancement of AI it is now possible and ideal to shape a fair financial environment to support sustainable economic growth. Sophisticating the understanding and management of global risk cannot only free up new potential for growth, it also ensures that any categorization of economic development does so equitably.

7. Practical Implications

7.1 Recommendations for Policymakers and Financial Institutions

With the help of such AI technologies as ChatGPT, financial services need to be integrated to foster the advancement of the financial inclusion and economic development. However, for it to be actualized to the optimal level, policy recommendations for policymakers and financial institutions require that, policymakers should encourage the formulation of policies with the goal of promoting FI as a strategic goal. Laying down policies that promote the uptake of AI in underprivileged regions is therefore critical to helping those most in need to access these technologies at a reasonable cost. Administrations and financial institutions thus need to fund efforts that enable underbanked individuals consume AI-based financial applications through training, e-learning, and awareness campaigns created in the form of workshops, films, or other forms of communal participation established with the objective of familiarizing individuals on how best to take advantage of advanced numerical applications. Additionally, such efforts can promote the formation of public–private partnerships that can develop the application of specialized solutions that can meet the needs of specifically meaningful models and collaboration between governments, non-profit organizations, and financial institutions will help support the development of the AI technologies that can satisfy the needs of the population and cultural standards. Which means that consumer protection has to be given due consideration as well. In the final place, policymakers should encourage innovation that brings more sensible and efficient use of AI systems while buying and investing. The final area policymakers should focus on is: Institutions that provide finance need to offer incentives such as tax deductions, grants, or other form of support to organizations that invest in AI technologies to offer products that will meet the needs of the societies that are usually neglected and also increase competition in the financial market.

7.2 Strategies for Encouraging AI Adoption for Inclusive Growth

Targeted initiatives that place an emphasis on inclusive growth are necessary to promote the adoption of AI technology in the financial services industry. Establishing pilot projects to evaluate AI-driven financial services across different locations and concentrating on how well they improve financial access and literacy is one sensible strategy. These pilot projects can offer insightful information and best practices that can be expanded to various communities. The significance of user-centric design in the development of AI apps is another important factor. It is imperative for financial institutions to involve prospective users from underserved groups in the design process to guarantee that the technology caters to their unique requirements and preferences. This interaction has the potential to increase trust and motivate more people to use AI-powered financial services.

Financial professionals must also receive training. Financial workers can become more proficient in serving underbanked populations by receiving training on the usage of AI tools. The main objective of this training program needs to be to use AI insights to enhance customer interactions and offer tailored financial advice. Increasing accessibility is a crucial additional factor. In order to expand their customer base, financial institutions need to make sure that their AI-powered services are available on several platforms, such as SMS services and mobile applications, to accommodate varying degrees of technological proficiency. Furthermore, knowing the particular financial difficulties that the local population has and how AI technology might help solve these problems depends heavily on community engagement. In addition to assisting in the development of customized solutions, this involvement builds community trust and motivates more people to take advantage of AI-powered financial services. Finally, understanding the effects of AI technologies on financial inclusion requires ongoing monitoring and assessment. In order to improve their services and increase their efficacy, financial institutions need gather data on user experiences and outcomes. Policymakers and financial institutions may leverage ChatGPT and other AI technologies to drive financial inclusion, reduce poverty, and foster sustainable economic growth by putting these suggestions and tactics into practice.

References

Aga, S. (2017). *Near data processing for efficient and trusted systems.* Doctoral dissertation.

Arner, D. W., Buckley, R. P., Zetzsche, D. A., & Veidt, R. (2020). Sustainability, FinTech and financial inclusion. *European Business Organization Law Review, 21,* 7–35.

Awasthi, S. (2023). The role of ChatGPT in enhancing financial literacy and education. *Journal of Applied Management-Jidnyasa,* 13–18.

Campuzano, M. G., & Crisanto, T. (2020). E-waste management: A case study of municipalities of Santa Elena province-Ecuador. In *Information and communication technologies: 8th Conference, TICEC 2020, Guayaquil, Ecuador, November 25–27, 2020, Proceedings 8* (pp. 587–598). Springer International Publishing.

Cull, R., Demirgüç-Kunt, A., & Morduch, J. (2014). Banks and microbanks. *Journal of Financial Services Research, 46,* 1–53.

Dahlberg, T., Guo, J., & Ondrus, J. (2015). A critical review of mobile payment research. *Electronic Commerce Research and Applications, 14*(5), 265–284. ISSN 1567-4223. https://doi.org/10.1016/j.elerap.2015.07.006

Demirgüç-Kunt, A., Klapper, L., & Singer, D. (2022). *Financial inclusion and inclusive growth: A review of global evidence.* World Bank Policy Research Working Paper, No. 9924.

Demirguc-Kunt, A., Klapper, L., Singer, D., & Ansar, S. (2018). *The Global Findex Database 2017: Measuring financial inclusion and the fintech revolution.* World Bank Publications.

Dwivedi, Y. K., Hughes, L., Ismagilova, E., Aarts, G., Coombs, C., Crick, T., Duan, Y., Dwivedi, R., Edwards, J., Eirug, A., Galanos, V., Vigneswara Ilavarasan, P., Janssen, M., Jones, P., Kar, A. K., Kizgin, H., Kronemann, B., Lal, B., Lucini, B., ... Williams, M. D. (2021). Artificial Intelligence (AI): Multidisciplinary perspectives on emerging challenges, opportunities, and agenda for research, practice and policy. *International Journal of Information Management, 57,* 101994. ISSN 0268-4012. https://doi.org/10.1016/j.ijinfomgt.2019.08.002

Ghatak, M., & Lall, S. (2020). Fintech revolution and financial inclusion: Chatbots and beyond. *FinTech Times.*

Goldstein, A., & McAfee, R. (2020). The role of AI in promoting financial inclusion. *MIT Sloan Review.*

Holmes, W., & Porayska-Pomsta, K. (2023). *The ethics of artificial intelligence in education.* Routledge Taylor.

Kshetri, N. (2021). The role of artificial intelligence in promoting financial inclusion in developing countries. *Journal of Global Information Technology Management, 24*(1), 1–6.

Mahmudi, A. A., & Ramadhani, I. (2024). Artificial intelligence (AI) and machine learning: The future of information technology and information systems. *Information Technology Studies Journal (ITECH), 1*(1), 01–21.

Mothobi, O., & Kebotsamang, K. (2024). The impact of network coverage on adoption of Fintech and financial inclusion in sub-Saharan Africa. *Economic Structures, 13,* 5. https://doi.org/10.1186/s40008-023-00326-7

Mukherjee, P., & Chatterjee, R. (2023). Financial sectors in Bengals: Towards development and inclusion. In *Two Bengals: A comparative development narrative of Bangladesh and West Bengal of India* (pp. 109–138). Springer Nature Singapore.

Muthiora, B. (2015). *Enabling mobile money policies in Kenya: Fostering a digital financial revolution* (p. 30). GSMA Mobile Money for the Unbanked.

Pal, S., & Bandyopadhyay, I. (2022). Impact of financial inclusion on economic growth, financial development, financial efficiency, financial stability, and profitability: An international evidence. *SN Business & Economics*, *2*(9), 139.

Rane, N., Choudhary, S., & Rane, J. (2024). Gemini versus ChatGPT: Applications, performance, architecture, capabilities, and implementation. https://papers.ssrn.com/sol3/papers.cfm?abstract_id=4723687. Accessed on February 13, 2024.

Rashid, S., & Ratten, V. (2022). Subsistence small business entrepreneurs in Pakistan. *Small Enterprise Research*, *29*(2), 109–137.

Rogers, E. M. (2003). *Diffusion of innovations*. Free Press.

Rojas-Suarez, L. (2016). *Financial inclusion in Latin America: Progress and challenges*. Inter-American Development Bank.

Sahay, R., Cihak, M., N'Diaye, P., Barajas, A., Pena, D. A., Bi, R., Gao, Y., Kyobe, A., Nguyen, L., Saborowski, C., Svirydzenka, K., & Yousefi, S. R. (2015, May 4). *Rethinking financial deepening: Stability and growth in emerging markets* (p. 41). International Monetary Fund. ISSN 2617-6750. Series: Staff Discussion Notes No. 2015/008.

Sarpong, F. A., Sappor, P., Nyantakyi, G., Ahakwa, I., Esther Agyeiwaa, O., & Blandful Cobbinah, B. (2023). From traditional roots to digital bytes: Can digitalizing ESG improves Ghanaian rural banks' brand equity through stakeholder engagement, and customer loyalty? *Cogent Business & Management*, *10*(2), 2232159.

Sen, A. (1999). *Development as freedom*. Oxford University Press.

Sharma, P. C. (2023). Influence of behavioural biases on market investment behaviour-mediating role of brand trust. *Interdisciplinary Journal of Management Studies (Formerly known as Iranian Journal of Management Studies)*, *17*(1), 1–19.

Sides, T., Kbaier, D., Farrell, T., & Third, A. (2024, September 19). Exploring trust in artificial intelligence among primary care stakeholders: A mixed-methods study. *Research Square*. PREPRINT (Version 1). https://doi.org/10.21203/rs.3.rs-4945818/v1

Singh, A., Schooley, B., & Patel, N. (2023). Effects of user-reported risk factors and follow-up care activities on satisfaction with a COVID-19 chatbot: Cross-sectional study. *JMIR mHealth and uHealth*, *11*(1), e43105.

Venkatesh, V., & Davis, F. D. (2000). A theoretical extension of the Technology Acceptance Model: Four longitudinal field studies. *Management Science*, *46*(2), 186–204.

World Bank. (2018). *The global findex database 2017: Measuring financial inclusion and the fintech revolution*. World Bank Publications.

World Bank. (2022). Financial inclusion. https://www.worldbank.org/en/topic/financialinclusion/overview

Zhao, D., Gao, G., Liu, T., & Zhao, Z. (2024). Population aging, digital divide, and household financial asset choices—An empirical study based on prefecture-level population census data. *Finance Research Letters*, 105691.

Zins, A., & Weill, L. (2016). The determinants of financial inclusion in Africa. *Review of Development Finance*, *6*(1), 46–57.